W9-COY-676

To Lead As Equals

UNIVERSITY OF PITTSBURGH LIBRARIES

TO LEAD AS EQUALS

Rural Protest and Political Consciousness in Chinandega, Nicaragua, 1912–1979

Jeffrey L. Gould

The University of North Carolina Press

Chapel Hill and London

©1990 The University of North Carolina Press
All rights reserved
Manufactured in the United States of America

The paper in this book meets the guidelines for permanence
and durability of the Committee on Production Guidelines for
Book Longevity of the Council on Library Resources.

94 93 92 91 90   5 4 3 2 1

Library of Congress Cataloging-in-Publication Data

Gould, Jeffrey L.
   To lead as equals : rural protest and political consciousness in
Chinandega, Nicaragua, 1912–1979 / by Jeffrey L. Gould.
      p.   cm.
   Includes bibliographical references.
   ISBN 0-8078-1904-2 (alk. paper).—ISBN 0-8078-4275-3 (pbk. :
alk. paper)
   1. Peasantry—Nicaragua—Chinandega—Political activity.
2. Peasantry—Nicaragua—Chinandega—History—20th century.
3. Agricultural laborers—Nicaragua—Chinandega—History—20th
century.   4. Chinandega (Nicaragua)—History.   5. Nicaragua—
Politics and government—20th century.   I. Title.
HD1531.N5G68   1990   89-29790
322.4′4′09728511—dc20   CIP

A los hijos de Juan Suazo,
los mismos de Sandino,
y a las mías,
Gabriela y Mónica

Contents

Contents

Part III. Campesinos and the Sandinista Revolution, 1964–1979

A section of photographs will be found beginning on page 147.

Acknowledgments

I am deeply indebted to the Fulbright-Hays Training Fellowship Program for funding the bulk of my research in Nicaragua. I am grateful for financial assistance from the Tinker Foundation, which provided a summer research grant. This study would not have been possible without the full cooperation of the workers and campesinos I interviewed. I am deeply indebted to all of the sixty-five informants who individually spent long hours trying to make a *gringo ignorante* understand their history. In particular, I am profoundly grateful for the extraordinary cooperation of Julio Argeñal, Ramón Cándia, Mariano Escorcia, Alejandro Malta, Toribio Muñoz, Oscar Osejo, Domíngo Ramírez, Éntimo Sánchez, Hermógenes Solis, Uriel Somarriba, Juan Suazo, Antonio Torres, Tomás Valle, and Engracia Zapata.

I would also like to thank the Nicaraguan Sugar Estates, Ltd. (the parent company of the Ingenio San Antonio), and its employees, especially Ing. Isaac Narvaez, for their cooperation with this project. Although the company may not like many of my perceptions about its history, I do have a great deal of gratitude and respect for their enterprise.

Despite the fact that Andrés Ruíz Escorcia has been seriously ill for some time and can only talk with great difficulty, he spent countless hours with me, often responding to my questions in writing. Moreover, he generously allowed me to freely study his personal records. I am deeply appreciative of his efforts on behalf of the project.

The Coordinadora Regional de Investigaciones Económicas Y Sociales (CRIES) sponsored my research. The director, Xavier Gorastiaga, fully backed my project and generously allowed me to work in the institute whenever I came to Managua from Chinandega. I am also extremely grateful to Alfonso DuBois, who went far out of his way to make my two years in Nicaragua as productive as possible. He was a constant source of wit, friendship, and constructive criticism, and I am deeply indebted to him.

In Costa Rica, I am very grateful for the cooperation and friendship of Oscar Rojas, the director of the Instituto de Estudios Latinoamericanos. I also appreciate the friendship and the scholarly assistance of José Antonio Fernandez and Mario Samper, my colleagues in the Escuela de Historia, Universidad Nacional. I would also like to thank Alexander Porras for coming through when it counted.

Professor Emilia Viotti da Costa (Yale University) took my work seriously from the beginning and encouraged me every step of the way. But she did more than that; her instruction deeply influenced my research. In Chinandega I often found myself wondering, "How would Emilia read this document or respond to this informant's testimony?" Moreover, she brilliantly and constructively challenged every line of this text. While Professor da Costa is not responsible for any of its errors, without my exposure to her teaching and criticism, this work would have been vastly inferior.

I am also deeply appreciative for the friendship and assistance of Professor Daniel James (Yale University), who introduced me to the study of Latin American populism. From the early stages of this project, he has been a tremendous source of encouragement and intellectual stimulation. When it looked very much like the United States was going to invade Nicaragua, James got a message to me in Chinandega that stated simply that my work was worthwhile. That message was exceedingly important to me. Back in the States, James read and criticized several chapters of my dissertation and after every reading reminded me that I had good reason to continue. Although James is not responsible for any errors of fact or interpretation, he is largely responsible for my capacity to finish the text.

Although Professor David Montgomery (Yale University) did not have a direct relation to my dissertation work, he did make important efforts on behalf of my research. Moreover, he opened up the world of labor history to me and encouraged me to enter it. I believe and hope that his intellectual imprint is very much engraved in this work.

Several friends helped me with criticisms and suggestions about this work. In particular, Eric Arnesen, Reeve Huston, Chris and Margarita Groeger, and Daniel Letwin far exceeded the call of duty, and I am most appreciative of their assistance. I am also deeply indebted to David Polonoff, who took time off from writing his own penetrating satire in order to read and criticize several chapters of this manuscript.

The two readers of the manuscript—Lowell Gudmundson and Florencia Mallon—wrote reports that were abundant with intelligence and creativity; their critiques were exceedingly useful to me.

I am also indebted to the following friends and colleagues who helped me at different points along the way: Casey Blake, John French, Romuoldo Gandolfo, Marianne Mahoney, Adriana Raga, Karen Shapiro, Richard Stahler-

Acknowledgments

Sholk, and the commentators and participants in the Third Annual Latin American Labor History Conference, New Haven, 1986.

At the University of North Carolina Press, I have very much enjoyed working with David Perry; I also wish to thank Anne Vilen for her excellent editorial suggestions.

My mother, Toni Stern Gould, provided constant encouragement and assistance for this project. Especially during the final stretch, she far exceeded the normal duties of a mother and a grandmother. During the past year, my daughters may have been somewhat deprived of a father, but they certainly gained a great grandmother and an excellent educator. We are all indebted to her.

David Gould, my father, and his wife, Margery Edson, gave us comfortable lodging and a warm environment on several occasions, so that I might do research in Washington.

My brother, Timothy Gould, first challenged me to do scholarly work. Moreover, he helped out in very concrete ways. He read part of the work, and we had long and fruitful discussions about it. I am deeply appreciative of his assistance and for his scholarly example. My sister, Kathy Gould, fortunately has been close by during the writing of this text. She has gone out of her way to help us out, and we are all thankful. I am very glad that we have all grown much closer.

Maria Elidieth Porras has borne the brunt of this work more than anyone else. I have unjustly thrown enormous burdens her way, and I can only state my appreciation for her heroic efforts and hope that now I can better assume my responsibilities as a father. But despite the constant piling on of adversity, she has kept us afloat, kept me working, and been a wonderful mother and *compañera*. Muchas gracias.

Gabriela, my eldest daughter, has been an inspiration to me throughout this process. I owe her a lot, as any father owes his child, but I also am indebted to her for the way she dealt with life in Nicaragua. She won the hearts, if not necessarily the minds, of a rustic and rugged barrio, and I suspect that I was treated so well because I was Gabriela's father. Mainly she just had fun, and that certainly gave meaning to my work.

Mónica was not along for the more interesting part of this ride. It is all too symptomatic of her relation to me that one of her first words was "Work?" Of course, a profound sense of guilt toward a two-year-old can be quite motivating. Hopefully, a better ride is coming.

To Lead As Equals

Introduction

Between the months of January and May, dusty winds blow across the cotton fields of Chinandega, Nicaragua. Three-foot dust drifts accumulate in the ruts along the road between the main highway and Campuzano, once the largest hacienda in the department. During those months called summer, tractors are the only vehicles that can make it down the four-kilometer road to the *casa hacienda* (manor house). With sheets and sombreros protecting their heads from the blazing hundred-degree sun and their faces wrapped in bandanas, several cotton pickers trudged along the road. Laughing children leaped ahead into the drifts as if they were sandy dunes. I walked along with a seventy-four-year-old man, Juan Suazo, who did not seem to notice the circumstances and who chose that moment to unleash a torrent of memories about his childhood on Campuzano.

During the 1950s and 1960s, Juan Suazo had become the leader of an agrarian protest movement that originated in the small village of San José del Obraje, situated on the western edge of Campuzano's former boundaries. After an initial period of probing, Suazo and his aged compañeros proposed that I write the history of that movement. At first, I was astounded by their eagerness to cooperate in such a venture. While not exactly a seasoned veteran, I had already been recording oral histories in other parts of Chinandega for nearly a year and had never encountered anything resembling this sense of mission in any of my informants, young or old.

Juan Suazo and Ramón Cándia, the two people with the most interest in "getting the facts down right" and who sacrificed the most time and effort to do so, did, I believe, have a particular mission—to make their history of struggle part of the cultural repertoire of their people. Although their movement had reshaped social and political relations in Chinandega, the *campesino* (peasant) militants felt that they had been misunderstood and maligned by non-campesinos since the beginning. That ignorance, a vestige of the past, remained active in the revolutionary present. Worse still, in the minds of the campesino youth, tales of their grandfathers' agrarian struggle were considered downright boring compared to the exploits of local Frente Sandinista fighters. To some extent then, Don Juan and Don Ramón hoped to correct decades of distortions about

Map 1. Department of Chinandega

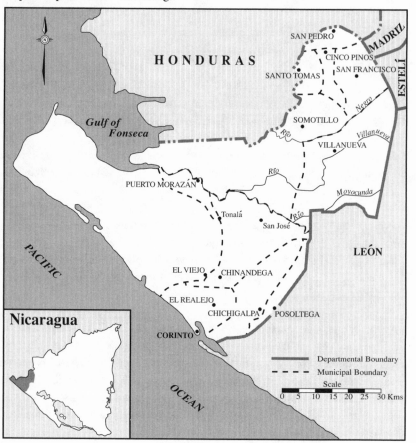

who they were and what they did. Without glamorizing their past, they desired some respect from the muchachos. They hoped that schoolchildren might learn the painful significance of their 1959 imprisonment, during which they signed away their right to protest, and of the events of 1961, when their village led hundreds of other campesinos into the battle for land. Similarly they hoped that their first leader, Regino Escobar, might be remembered along with other revolutionary martyrs. Nevertheless, giving credit where credit is due was only one part of Juan and Ramón's mission.

Introduction

Map 2. Hacienda Campuzano and Surrounding Communities

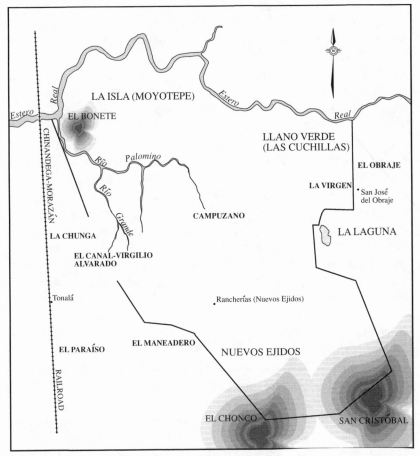

Source: Adapted from a map by Tesla de Alvarado and Virgilio Alvarado, in the possession of the San José community.

After what seemed like a long time, we arrived at the casa hacienda. Juan Suazo walked over to a group of men who were rounding up horses in a nearby field. A man who looked older than Juan turned and embraced him, then they walked over to me. Juan introduced us, and then, addressing his friend, he added, referring to me, "He's helping us write the history of our struggle."

Citing work commitments, Juan excused himself and started back up the dusty road.

Juan's friend gave me a brief tour of the casa hacienda. Other than its impressive size, very little of its former grandeur was still visible. The second floor had sagged down through the ceiling of the first floor. The government clearly had priorities other than restoring this old mansion, supposedly built at the turn of the century by the Liberal president, José Santos Zelaya. Juan's friend started walking up the creaking stairs to the back of the fallen mansion, where one part of the floor was still standing. A long hallway separated the remains of the second floor from its sunken half. He showed me a lopsided room that served as headquarters of the local reforestation project. Then the old man led me to an outside porch on the eastern side of the building. The air was fresher, mosquitoes stopped biting, and the floor seemed sturdy. The elderly employee gave me a short geography lesson on the region between Campuzano and San José. Graphically, he illustrated the march of cotton cultivation and its wake of uprooted trees and homeless, landless laborers. In the distance, he signaled where all the key *mojones* (boundary stones) were originally set and later moved by the landlords. But rather than discussing the conflict between the hacienda and the campesinos of San José del Obraje, he changed the subject and began talking about his life on Campuzano, where for many years he had worked as a cowboy. He had enjoyed the work, the camaraderie with the other cowboys and with the patron. He had especially fond memories of General Alvarado, a Liberal revolutionary from Honduras who had owned the hacienda from 1921 until his death in 1950. The "problems," as he put it, came with "cotton fever." I then asked him why he got involved in the land conflict. He replied in a pained tone, "I didn't really get involved, I just wanted to help out a little." He motioned for me to follow him. The old cowboy, who claimed to be ninety-five years old, began to talk about life at the turn of the century when Zelaya owned Campuzano. As we descended the broken steps, he recalled, "When Zelaya owned Campuzano people ate real well. You had to work hard, sure, but we all got free milk, free cheese and free soup bones." He stopped walking in front of a remarkably well preserved brick building and his voice suddenly waxed enthusiastic. "Look at this jail! This building was better built than the rest of the casa hacienda. Feel these bars, after all these years they're still solid, no? General Zelaya built this jail so that the Saturday night drunks wouldn't bother the people."

The peons' jail stood proudly, while the lavish manor house had succumbed to tropical rot. The veteran employee looked at this jail as something worthy and good compared to the decadence of the casa hacienda. And yet Zelaya had been a major proponent of forced labor and undoubtedly had had this jail built to keep his own rebellious peons in line. The old hand believed in his version of the jail's meaning, not because of a mystical attachment to a convenient symbol, but because the solid jail reinforced common beliefs about Zelaya among rural Chinandegans. The cowboy's version of Zelaya's jail underscored the influence on popular consciousness of myths about the Liberal revolutionary general and provided a valuable clue about the political development of the campesino movement. At the same time, his enthusiasm for Zelaya was connected to his ambivalent feelings about his own participation in the campesino struggle. As the old, toothless cowboy smiled at Zelaya's achievement as if it were his own, he seemed to recall his own dependency on the venerable patrón, a recollection that somehow atoned for his sense of guilt for participating in the rebellion.

In 1984 the old cowboy expressed the conflict experienced by all of the campesino activists twenty-five years earlier, between loyalty to the *hacendado* (landowner)—with all his grandeur, warmth, intelligence, and authority—and solidarity with the ragged, dark-skinned, illiterate campesinos who came to question the very ground on which the aristocrats stood so tall. Feelings of ignorance and dependence on their superiors did not disappear with the campesinos' first act of resistance. Only after years of working through different forms of dependency could the campesinos achieve their goals of land ownership and dignity. But even then their memories vividly reflected their old ambivalences.

My own task had to diverge somewhat from "helping to write about the struggle." For it was clear in the old employee's remarks that the problem of political, economic, and cultural dependency on the landowners reached farther back in Nicaraguan history than the dawn of the campesino struggle in the 1950s. The roots of rural consciousness were not planted just on the hacienda, for the campesinos had to think and express themselves in the only available political language—Liberalism—which had originated among urban and rural elites. Similarly, the campesinos had entered into relations of dependency and conflict with people and institutions far beyond the borders of Campuzano. Events in Managua had influenced the campesino movement, and that movement, in turn, had had a significant impact on the political system. Thus the campesinos' history could not be circumscribed to the arena of conflict around the latifundio Campuzano.

When Juan and Ramón see this history of their movement, they may be annoyed with some of its digressions, but I hope they will be pleased that it stays close to the raw facts of their struggle. For in the record of their lived experience—their daily labor, thoughts, decisions, failures, frailties, tortures, and acts of resistance—we may see something of how a people came to a qualitatively new collective understanding of their social world.

The campesinos' new social consciousness was not the result of a sudden, dramatic conversion. On the contrary, a class-rooted perception of the social world came about only after years of dealings and confrontations with politicians, businessmen, soldiers, and hacendados. At certain moments, these small, painfully slow, practical and mental steps, without changing their external form or pace, became qualitative leaps in the campesinos' perception of their own collectivity and its relation to the agrarian elite. If I have managed to convey those steps and leaps of consciousness, I will have accomplished the task entrusted to me by the people who merit not a romantic portrait but rather a chance to be heard.

Methodological Problems

The concepts of hegemony and counterhegemonic strategies suggested by Gerald Sider's anthropological study of Newfoundland fishermen were useful in my attempt to understand the relation of economic, political, and cultural transformation in the Chinandegan countryside. Sider's concepts particularly helped me to decipher the relations of the Chinandegan landed elite and the Somocista political elite to the villagers of San José and Tonalá. Sider defines culture as "the form and manner in which people perceive, define, articulate and express their mutual relations." "Hegemony," he writes, ". . . is that aspect of culture which, usually in the face of struggle, most directly seeks to unify production and appropriation, and to extend appropriation beyond the productive act itself into neighbourhood, family, forms of consumption—in sum into daily life."[1]

From this notion of hegemony, Sider goes on to discuss expressions of popular resistance that borrow from the symbols of elite cultural domination. Although such borrowings place limitations on the popular resistance, Sider argues that this weakness can be partially overcome by "the experience of opposition [and] by the fact that counter-hegemonic strategies can expose the contradictions within the existing hegemony. . . . Like other forms of culture, [they] do not just emerge out of people's thoughts and individual experiences, but out of their mutual understanding of their social relations."[2]

As we will see, the agrarian struggle of Juan Suazo and his fellow campesino militants was a lengthy apprenticeship in the use of elite language and symbols not only to make their claims but also to conceptualize their world in different and new ways. That these campesinos now so eagerly participate in the reconstruction of that history testifies to their creative role in constructing their own counterhegemonic culture.

In writing about these villagers, I faced a major problem in how to characterize them. The terms "rural proletarian" or "peasant" fail to capture the complexity of labor and tenancy relations in the Chinandegan countryside. Indeed, often the same person switched several times in one year from renting a parcel of land to working for wages on a cotton or sugar plantation. Some scholars have used the terms "semiproletarian" or "peasant laborers" to describe those people who possess inadequate amounts of land to meet family needs and thus must supplement their incomes with wages. While these terms do describe the situation of many Chinandegan rural residents before 1950, the export boom stripped away the laborers' access to hacienda land. By the end of the 1960s the majority of Chinandegan laborers had lost access to any land to cultivate during the cotton or sugar "dead season," thus making "peasant" or "semi" adjectives inappropriate.[3] On the other hand, "proletarian" did not prove to be an adequate category either, since a substantial minority of the villagers in two of the three hamlets I studied did preserve limited access to land.

Rejecting the above analytical categories, I resorted to the Spanish word "campesino" to describe the communities and organizations. Such a choice, to a certain extent, was a convenient way out of my dilemma. But "campesino" was also the word used by the subjects of this study to describe their own social condition and class. While informants used categories such as day laborer, permanent laborer, or tenant to describe particular forms of labor, they used the term campesino to describe their common condition of residence in small, poverty-stricken villages. More significantly, the informants used the term campesino movement to describe the agrarian protest organizations that struggled for land, higher wages, and improved working conditions on cotton and sugar plantations.

Craig Calhoun and others have pioneered an important theoretical approach to the study of popular movements, which posits community over class as the key variable in the process of political radicalization.[4] Although it operates within the contours of communal solidarity theory, this study nevertheless deviates from this analytical model of community in two respects. First, the

Chinandegan struggle, although clearly rooted in the community, does not fall within Calhoun's definition of traditional communities as "closely knit, largely autonomous collectivities that share a vital common culture."[5] On the contrary, the rise of agrarian capitalism uprooted and then thrust together the Chinandegan villagers. Anthropologist William Roseberry's analysis of such communities as "precipitates of capitalism," is thus quite relevant to the emergence of the Chinandegan villages and, moreover, to an adequate comprehension of their changing consciousness. Rather than focusing on the tension between capitalism and tradition, this book, following Roseberry's lead, attempts to understand how these peasant proprietors, tenants, and landless laborers from diverse geographic backgrounds, in less than a decade, forged, a class discourse.[6]

Our attempt to describe this process of community formation led to another divergence from Calhoun's approach, for the Chinandegan case suggests that community and class are not analytically separate concepts. As Carol Smith has argued, classes, rooted in communities, may emerge in "relational terms," in opposition to established classes or elites.[7] Both in rhetoric and in practice, the Chinandegan movement confirms Smith's findings in Guatemala. Regardless of their individual roles in the relations of production in the countryside, the participants came to view themselves as members of one social group in conflict against another, and eventually they began to speak of their *clase campesina* (peasant class) in opposition to the *clase terrateniente* (landlord class).

While staying close to the ground of local history, this study engages issues of relevance beyond Nicaragua's boundaries. Although there are probably few jails quite like Zelaya's, the descendants of his prisoners have surely shared experiences with other unwitting settlers on the frontiers of agrarian capitalism.

Sources

Earthquakes in 1898, 1931, and 1972 and revolutionary battles in 1927 and 1978–79, destroyed valuable archives in Chinandega and Managua that would have made this study more complete. Indeed, the paucity of documentary sources forced me to use oral sources as "documents," rather than as testimonial aids to understanding worker and campesino consciousness. Consequently I spent a great deal of time with informants attempting to locate unrecorded events in particular years or decades. Nevertheless, often with the aid of the campesinos, I did corroborate a substantial portion of the informants' testimonies by using written documents. A successful verification was often a joyful occasion for both the author and the informants, yet it invariably created new problems. For between the written statement of fact by a journalist or a politician and the personal memory of an illiterate peasant lay a gulf that the informants and I had to bridge in order to make sense of the event. Indeed, oral testimonies attained their greatest value when the informants could, as it were, enter into a dialogue with the previously unseen documents describing their own activities. As we shall see in chapter 7, this methodology resembles the campesinos' own experience of cultural transformation—for their real discovery and interaction with elite documents from an earlier era provided them with the intellectual weapons necessary to change their social world.

In my research, I was quite fortunate that the Nicaraguan revolution has made many written sources accessible for the first time in that country's history. Similarly, notwithstanding denunciations of Sandinista totalitarianism, anyone who has spent several weeks in Nicaragua will recognize that today everyone talks and argues about politics in loud voices. For decades such freedom was not only politically circumscribed by the regimes of Anastasio Somoza García (1937–56) and his sons Luís (1957–63) and Anastasio (1966–79), it was also a class privilege. Until the 1960s, only professionals, businessmen, and students argued for or against the Somozas publicly. The vast majority of the population simply had no public independent voice, or at least no voice that anyone else would listen to. Not only did workers and peasants operate within an authoritarian political system, they also had to survive in a social and economic world of arbitrary class power. Their conquest of a public and autonomous voice was thus the fundamental precondition for this study.

My reliance on oral testimony, even with documentary corroboration, nonetheless imposed a certain level of subjectivity. Specifically, did the informants' attempts to recreate a meaningful past involve the suppression or distortion of their thoughts and actions? If so, how could that be corrected? As other scholars have observed, one difficulty in using oral testimony is that present concerns and attitudes often influence the selection of and emphasis on past events, creating difficulties for the oral historian.[8] Indeed most of my sixty-five informants, not surprisingly, tended to compare and contrast the post-1979 present with the prerevolutionary past. I therefore had to treat testimonies concerning encounters with the Sandinista movement during the 1920s and 1930s with great caution. Indeed, I was probably overly cautious in this regard and, thus, may not have accorded due importance to Sandinismo or to the U.S. intervention in Chinandega during those years.[9] Similarly, few informants spontaneously revealed any positive thoughts about the regimes of Anastasio Somoza García and that of his son Luís. Rather, it took a fair amount of gentle prodding to free my informants' current, dark notions of the last years of the Somoza tyranny from their somewhat brighter perspective on the regime during its early years. Finally, these informants do not form a representative sample of the Chinandegan peasantry. Rather, most informants were participants in the campesino movement, often in leadership roles.

The informants all tended to mark off their individual and collective pasts by epochs, which served both as chronological reference points and as a means of contrasting and highlighting events. Although the revolutionary time marker tended to complicate my use of oral testimony, another marker in the informants' memory—the agro-export boom of the 1950s—proved to be an important counterbalance. The boom of the 1950s had a drastic impact on the lives of most of my informants, for during that decade they lost access to land and to stable employment. The campesinos thus reconstructed their past by using two distinct sets of oppositions: before and after the agro-export boom and before and after the revolution. The period before the agro-export boom (before 1945) was, to a certain degree, idealized by the informants' strong sense of loss associated particularly with the advent of cotton cultivation. Yet the idealization of that hacienda past brought the events of the period of this study into bold relief. Similarly, while the campesinos' current perspective undoubtedly distorted some elements of the past related to Somoza and Sandinismo, it also brought other events into greater focus. For many of the campesinos, their own historical role gave meaning to the revolutionary process. Thus, the informants' vantage point allowed them to look at the positive and negative elements in the revolutionary process in terms of their own struggles and expectations. Current reality, then, made the campesinos think harder about their own role in shaping that process. Thus, for most of the campesino informants, the pre-cotton period on one side and the revolution on the other marked off an era that stands out in their memories in bold relief as *el tiempo de los ricos* (the time of the rich).

Chinandegan Geography

Chinandega did not always present the image of dusty roads and endless, treeless cotton fields. In 1849, an American diplomat, E. G. Squier, traveling through the area saw a quite different Chinandega. While relaxing on a small sugar plantation near the town of Chinandega, he paused and reflected on the area's beauty and its potential for harmonious development. "From the corridor we enjoyed a magnificent view of field and forest, stretching away in billows of verdure to the base of the volcano of El Viejo, lifting its purple summit to mid-heaven, beyond and over-all. I ventured to imagine the intervening plain in the hands of an enterprising and vigorous people, dotted over with villages, and loaded down with the products of all-bountiful Nature, and queried if this generation might not witness the change."[10]

It took a century, rather than a generation, for Squier's vision to materialize through the mobilization of capital and labor. But material progress flawed Chinandega's beauty, for its economic development, "in the hands of an enterprising and vigorous people" destroyed its forests, tore up its famed orange groves and dried up its rivers and streams. During the early twentieth century, thanks to its high yields of corn, Chinandega earned the title, "the granary of Central America."[11] Since 1950, however, pesticides have desiccated Chinandega's once fertile soil. During the dry season now, from January until May, dust storms whip across the brown, barren cotton fields. During the rainy season, still the most copious in western Nicaragua, that ubiquitous dust turns to mud. Nevertheless, thanks to reforestation projects and the decline of the cotton industry, the region's ravaged soil, streams, and wildlife have received something of a new lease on life since 1979.

Located in the extreme northwest corner of Nicaragua, the department of Chinandega contains 4,600 square kilometers. It extends approximately 82 miles north to south and 105 miles east to west. More than two-thirds of Chinandega's 155,000 residents in 1971 lived along the narrow Pacific plain, which stretches from the six-thousand-foot-high Maribios volcano range to the Pacific Ocean, and this continues to be where most of the department's residents live. From the foothills of the Chonco, San Cristóbal, and Las Casitas volcanoes to the mangrove swamps along the Pacific coast, this strip, ten to twenty miles wide and some forty miles long, also contains Nicaragua's most important sugar, cotton, and banana plantations. David Radell, a geographer, described the exceptional fertility of the Chinandegan coastal plain thus: "Here, vast quantities of . . . volcanic deposits from the Maribios volcanoes have weathered into highly fertile soils. The combination of relatively flat topography and extremely rich volcanic soils makes this region the most suitable for mechanized commercial agriculture in Nicaragua."[12]

Since the 1890s, planters have profited greatly from Chinandega's fertile and (until recently) naturally irrigated soil. Especially during the 1920s and

1940s, large-scale growers enjoyed great success planting sugar, sesame, corn, and cotton along the Chinandegan plain. During the 1950s and 1960s, the owners of the same coastal plain swayed ecstatically in their own "dance of the millions" as cotton fever struck Chinandega. In 1965, cotton worth $71 million accounted for more than half of Nicaragua's total exports, and Chinandegan farms produced 46 percent of the country's cotton. Similarly, during the 1960s, as sugar began to rank as one of Nicaragua's important exports (5 to 6 percent of total exports), Chinandega accounted for well over 50 percent of the country's total production.[13]

While the rich plain and the imposing volcanoes dominate southern and central Chinandega, the basin of the Estero Real (Royal Estuary) geographically defines the north-central region of the department. From colonial times until 1960, the ports of Tempisque and Morazán on the estuary served as important entrepôts of Central American commerce. Although much of the delta soil is too saline and swampy for commercial agriculture, the Estero Real formed the northern boundary of all the principal haciendas in central Chinandega—Campuzano, El Paraíso, La Chunga, and El Obraje—which used the tributary for commerce. Until pollution and lumber operations mortally wounded it, the Estero Real supplied fish, crabs, and wood to hundreds of Chinandegan peasants, fishermen, and *mangleros* who extracted mangrove bark for use in tanneries.

The Cosigüina volcano was sliced in half, in 1835, in perhaps the most powerful eruption in the modern history of the hemisphere. Today the now three-thousand-foot stump of a volcano still casts a shadow over much of the peninsula that forms the northwest corner of Chinandega and of the nation. Like the Estero delta, the peninsula of Cosigüina is characterized by poor soils. Since colonial times, a few families divided up the dry, hilly peninsula into latifundios for extensive cattle-raising.

The northeastern region of the department, on the other side of the Estero Real, is dominated by a large, semi-arid valley lying between the Maribios and the central highlands. Like the Cosigüina peninsula, the northeast plain contains important cattle ranches but produces few crops. Los Pueblos del Norte, a mountainous region along the Honduran border, has neither good soils nor good grassland. Until the 1960s, the Pueblos region, dependent on subsistence agriculture, was cut off from the rest of Chinandega and was thus deprived of even the minimal services provided to the other regions. During the first half of this century, many people migrated from Los Pueblos to central Chinandega to work on cattle haciendas.

This book is not a social history of the department of Chinandega as a whole, for it does not include northeastern Chinandega or the Cosigüina peninsula. Along the plain, I focus on cities, towns, villages, and hamlets that lie within a twenty-five kilometer radius of the departmental capital of Chinandega. I have concentrated on these particular communities, not because they are representative of the whole region, but rather because they played central roles in the development of the labor and campesino movements from 1912 until 1979.

Since the turn of the century, the capital city of Chinandega, the center of regional commerce, has been the residence of at least 25 percent of the department's population and maintained the largest concentration of artisanal and manufacturing industries. Fifteen kilometers to the southeast of the departmental capital, stands the Ingenio San Antonio, the largest sugar mill in Central America, located in the municipality of Chichigalpa. Bordering on the northern edge of the San Antonio plantation, lies El Realejo, nestled inside the same mangrove swamps that, during the mid-nineteenth century, overran its famed port. After losing its port and nearly all of its inhabitants, the town came back to life in the 1950s, thanks to the growth of nearby sugar, banana, and cotton plantations. Corinto, Nicaragua's major port since the late nineteenth century, is located five kilometers to the south of El Realejo. By the 1950s and 1960s, some one thousand Corinto port workers formed one of Nicaragua's largest concentrations of urban wage laborers.

Fifteen kilometers due north of Chinandega, surrounded by cotton plantations, lies the village of Tonalá (the subject of chapter 7). Founded in 1946, Tonalá, by the 1950s, became a residence for roughly three hundred families of cotton pickers in addition to smallholders, merchants, and artisans. Ten kilometers east of Tonalá, across the now-shrunken latifundio, Campuzano (which formerly claimed 60,000 acres), lies the village of Rancherías, founded in 1962 by campesinos in struggle for *ejidal* (municipal) land (discussed in Part II). Five kilometers to the east of Rancherías, during the 1940s, peasants acquired land from a large cattle hacienda and founded the hamlet of San José del Obraje (the subject of chapter 4). In 1957, the villagers of San José would ignite an agrarian protest movement that, in the space of a few years, would spread to Rancherías, Tonalá, El Realejo, and the rural sections of Chichigalpa. In each hamlet the movement would develop with unique logic and strategies, but when those local organizations merged, they formed a powerful regional movement that would affect the lives of working people throughout Nicaragua.

Historiographical Themes

Nicaraguan historiography presents a coherent linear portrait of the period that begins with José Santos Zelaya's revolutionary assumption of power in 1893 and ends with Somoza's coup d'état in 1936. Its coherence derives, however, from a reductionist methodology: every political and ideological force is described as directly representing an economic class interest. At best, such an approach deals inadequately with details that do not fit the explanatory model. At worst, a model in which all cultural forms are reduced to mere epiphenomena of material reality leaves the Nicaraguan people with a history predetermined by objective forces. The richness of their lived experience and culture becomes trivialized by well-intentioned descriptions, ranging from "backward" to "heroic."[14]

The first part of this book challenges some of the assumptions that underlie the existing historiography. The Ingenio San Antonio (ISA) located in Chichigalpa, the largest manufacturing enterprise in Nicaragua, provides the vantage point to explore these assumptions. First, how did this mill, which after 1918 possessed an advanced productive apparatus and operated with capitalistic relations of production, function in the midst of economic backwardness? How did ISA recruit and control its labor force? How did the technical changes in the relations of production affect the workers' consciousness?

The answers to such questions should modify the historiographic portrait of the period between 1909 and 1940 as one of the "long-term stagnation" of a "rudimentary and strangled economy."[15] For ISA was certainly not an island in a semifeudal sea. Rather, if the company was isolated, it was the isolation of an entrepreneurial vanguard without a strong enough base of support to achieve its broader capitalist goals. At the most basic level, San Antonio could not function without at least a partially "free" labor market, which, indeed, it helped to create. Moreover, ISA was not an export enclave, for it sold more than half of its production on the domestic market. Since more than a handful of oligarchs consumed its sugar, ISA's capacity to produce and sell sugar domestically questions the two-dimensional portrait of pre-1940s society as essentially made up of oligarchs and "the masses."

San Antonio's great economic success was due in part to its political astuteness and its leadership role in the Conservative party. Under the Zelaya, Conservative, and Somoza regimes the company obtained government tax exemptions, tariff protections, and other concessions in order to modernize its mill. ISA's prominent political role also had important effects on both field and factory workers. Although the company's repressive apparatus intimidated the plantation laborers, the workers also reflected on the political sources of San Antonio's might. The consciousness of the sugar workers, as we shall see, was intensely politicized by the 1920s, for they came to view ISA as the embodiment of both exploitation and political oppression.[16]

Despite the radicalized political consciousness of the ISA workers, many became political supporters of Anastasio Somoza during the mid-1930s. Indeed, Somoza's consolidation of power can only be comprehended in the light of the support of broad sectors of the working classes. While the *Guardia* (National Guard) constituted one pillar of his regime, Somoza attempted with some success to erect another pillar out of the labor movement. A radical democratic movement of artisans, known as *obreristas*, played a vital role in transmitting labor support to Somoza. The Chinandegan obreristas, with the backing of ISA workers, had, by the mid-1920s, become the dominant political force in the department of Chinandega. Despite their earlier sympathy for the anti-imperialist Augusto César Sandino and their social democratic ideology, the obreristas threw their support to Somoza in 1936 in return for a promise of radical labor reform.

From the beginning of their dynasty in 1936, until the mid-1960s, the Somozas attempted to cultivate passive or active labor support not merely as a demagogic ploy (as most scholars have suggested) but as part of a populist-style strategy to establish hegemonic control over Nicaraguan society.[17] In Chinandega, Somoza García co-opted not only individual labor leaders but also the very language of obrerismo, the political idiom of the popular classes. Although Somoza García did repress the labor movement in the late 1940s when it escaped his control, he still attempted to portray himself as the *jefe obrero*, the guarantor of labor's aspirations in the face of Conservative opposition. Similarly, the weakness of the middle- and upper-class, anti-Somoza opposition resided in its inability to bridge the gulf in Nicaraguan political culture created by Somoza García and his son Luís's appropriation of obrerista ideology and their cultivation of labor support.

The second part of this book continues the analysis of Somocista populism, while shifting the area of study to the countryside. This section focuses on how a minor land dispute in the isolated hamlet of San José del Obraje turned into a mass movement that challenged both the agrarian elite and the regime. The radical change in the political consciousness of the Chinandegan campesinos was the result of a lengthy apprenticeship in the institutions of Somocismo, including the labor movement. Rather than an awakening brought about through proselytization by outside forces, the Chinandegan campesinos, to a significant degree, politicized themselves, for the barrier in Nicaraguan political culture, erected by Somoza García and the obreristas during the 1930s and 1940s, was still standing in the early 1960s.

Eric Wolf and James Scott have made major contributions toward our understanding of peasant radicalism.[18] Both authors have uncovered peasants' creative uses of their autonomous cultural past in order to defend themselves from the encroachments of agrarian capitalism. The Chinandegan case, however, is quite different. Despite formal similarities in styles of agrarian radicalism, the ideological transformation of the Chinandegan campesinos involved the use of symbols drawn from Liberal rhetoric and from a dependent hacienda past rather than from the depths of village tradition. The experience of the Chinandegan campesinos undoubtedly parallels that of many Latin American peasants who reside in the maelstrom of agrarian capitalism rather than in their ancestral villages.

The final part of this book shows how the campesino and the labor movements in Chinandega transcended the practical and rhetorical limits of Somocista populism, exacerbated divisions in the agro-export elite, and thereby pushed the regime to rely exclusively on its only remaining base of support, the National Guard. Rather than presenting another global interpretation of the Sandinista revolution, the latter section of the book focuses on the role of the Chinandegan campesinos and the San Antonio workers in the revolutionary process. In so doing, however, this study does discuss the limitations of the prevailing, urban-oriented interpretations of the Sandinista revolution.

Moreover, this book suggests an alternative methodological approach to the study of the Nicaraguan and other third world revolutions. Scholarly research usually focuses on the structural determinants of the breakdown of regimes, on the formation of the revolutionary vanguard and its ability (or lack thereof) to weld together alliances with dissident elite factions. From a variety of political perspectives, scholars have considered the revolutionary elite's capacity to politicize the subordinate classes as the key to the success or failure of the revolution. The Chinandegan case suggests the need to broaden the scope of such studies to include the construction of revolutionary alliances from the bottom up.[19] Decades before the Sandinistas welded together the revolutionary alliance that overthrew the Somoza regime, the campesinos had undertaken a "long march" through the institutions of Somocismo—the principle subject of this book. In the course of this march, with its small victories and bitter defeats, workers and campesinos chipped away and finally, together with the Sandinistas, knocked down those political barriers of isolation and silence that for decades had ensured the survival of Somocismo.

Part I
Labor and Politics, 1912–1949

1

We All Remember Joaquín: State, Capital, and Labor Relations in the Ingenio San Antonio, 1890–1936

Our company has always taken a great interest in the welfare of its workers, even before the introduction of the Labor code.
—El Ingenio San Antonio, 1953

Era un hombre muy fregado.
—Veteran worker recalling Constantino Lacayo, administrator of ISA, 1920–26

Since the 1920s, the San Antonio sugar mill in Chichigalpa, Nicaragua, has been that country's largest manufacturing establishment. The sugar mill/plantation complex employed close to two thousand workers in 1920 and has since consistently employed far more workers than any other single enterprise. The owners of San Antonio were—and continue to be—the most economically powerful group in the Nicaraguan elite (the revolutionary government expropriated the sugar mill in 1988).

Any consideration of the development of Nicaraguan capitalism must take into account the history of the Ingenio San Antonio (ISA). Politics and economics have always been inseparable for its workers. Particularly after the U.S. Marines occupied Nicaragua in 1912 and bolstered the Conservative regime, the political Liberalism of the San Antonio workers was something of a popular revolutionary ideology—an elastic body of ideas that identified the economic and political antagonist, ISA, as the Conservative, capitalist oligarchy.

San Antonio laborers forged a highly politicized consciousness, not because of an adverse labor market, but because of the Conservative-owned sugar mill's peculiarly tight relationship with the state. ISA depended on the state for antilabor repression, tariff protection, and high domestic prices. Politics and economics were inseparable for the San Antonio workers precisely because they also were inseparable for the company. Hence, sugar mill workers always seized opportunities presented by national political crises to gain support from elite sectors in undermining management's political and economic domination. Workers rebelled against the company during the Liberal revolutions of 1912 and 1926, and in 1936 workers greeted Anastasio Somoza García's rise to power by organizing a union and declaring a general strike.

But despite their adherence to Liberal revolutionary ideology and their periodic outbursts of fierce opposition to San Antonio, sugar workers remained unorganized and quiescent for long periods of time. While part of this passivity was clearly due to the fear of repression, management's paternalism also tended to promote quiescence. Thus San Antonio workers, who objectively had little chance of forging a successful union organization, developed what Juan Martínez-Alier has called a "double consciousness," at once revolutionary and conservative.[1]

"There's the Blackmail!": San Antonio Under Zelaya

The history of San Antonio is definitely not a rags-to-riches story. In 1890, two Italians, Alfredo Pellas and Luís Palazio, who had accumulated sizable fortunes in the steamboat, mining, and import-export businesses, joined with three oligarchic families from the city of Granada and founded Nicaragua Sugar Estates, Limited. The company purchased 8,500 acres of land in Chichigalpa, in northwestern Nicaragua. Pellas journeyed to Scotland to buy sugar manufacturing equipment capable of producing 5,000 tons of sugar a year. He also obtained credit from English investors in the enterprise. The company, in fact, incorporated itself as an English firm. English capital may have accounted for up to one-third of the stock, whose total value was approximately 120,000 pounds sterling, remarkably high by Nicaraguan standards.[2]

British interest in the Nicaraguan sugar industry was a small part of its heavy commercial involvement in the region. Between 1886 and 1890, Central America exported over six million pounds sterling worth of goods to the United Kingdom. During the same period, the Central American republics imported over four million pounds sterling worth of goods from the United Kingdom.[3] Sugar was a good investment in 1890, primarily because more than half of the sugar consumed in Nicaragua was imported from El Salvador. San Antonio planned to both supply the domestic market and export one-half of its production to neighboring countries.[4]

However, within two years of the first *zafra* (harvest) at San Antonio, the Liberal José Santos Zelaya came to power through a revolution. Zelaya ordered reprisals against his political enemies that ranged from public whippings to the confiscation of major haciendas. The Conservative stockholders of San Antonio were not spared this punishment.[5] In 1897, his government prohibited the company from manufacturing *aguardiente* (cheap rum), claiming that it had awarded monopoly rights to new distilleries in León and Masaya. In the words of Diego Manuel Chamorro, future Nicaraguan president and close friend of the San Antonio group, "Allí está el chantage!" (There's the black-mail!). "The situation was very serious for San Antonio since it meant losing large deposits of molasses. And then a saviour introduced himself to the Company's directors: a representative of a Managua-based syndicate offered to lift the restriction if San Antonio would sell one-quarter of its sugar production, ten thousand quintals [approximately five hundred tons], at four pesos less than the going price. . . . The stockholders accepted the deal after many discussions."[6]

San Antonio not only bowed to the demands, but also eventually joined the Zelaya-backed syndicate. It is possible that English investment in the company may have paved the way for San Antonio's harmonious relationship with the Zelaya regime. Although the U.S. consul did not directly implicate San Antonio, he underscored British influence in the Nicaraguan sugar industry in 1897 when he wrote, "Believing that the free import of sugar would break the sugar trust existing in Nicaragua in the hands of English capitalists and it would open a magnificent field for the export of the surplus of sugar manufactured, in the United States, I called on President Zelaya and interviewed him about the probability of his approval."[7]

President Zelaya refused the United States its request, arguing that he wished to protect "home industries." Whether or not the merger between San Antonio and the Zelaya-backed syndicate took place in 1897, it is clear that by 1903 San Antonio formed an integral part of an extremely profitable, state-sponsored aguardiente monopoly, backed by English and Italian investors.[8] Zelaya's stand in favor of protectionism must be understood in the context of policies designed to create production and/or distribution monopolies. Similarly, San Antonio's positive response to Zelayista extortion and trust-building must be seen as pragmatic business responses. By joining the local sugar-alcohol trust, Nicaragua Sugar Estates profitably swam with the dominant political tide.[9]

Zelaya believed that monopolies and tariff protection were essential aspects of an industrialization program. In the case of sugar, the domestic market amounted to only three thousand tons annually in the 1890s. Moreover, ISA faced stiff competition in the liquor trade. Nascent soap, cooking oil, shoe, beverage, and ice factories faced the same market restrictions, and, with the exception of the ice factory, all of these industries needed tariff protection.

Nonetheless, Zelaya's monopoly concessions to new industrialists were often corrupt. San Antonio reportedly had to pay off the president annually. In the case of rubber, banana, mining, and lumber export industries, the governmental concessions involved grants of tens of thousands of acres in eastern Nicaragua, usually to foreign companies.[10] The extent of Zelaya's corruption is perhaps less important, however, than the way he began stimulating industrial growth where only imports existed before. Given the size of the domestic market, Zelaya's monopolistic policy was quite rational and, at least with regard to nascent home industry, somewhat successful. For example, brick, soap, and oil factories, all employing over fifty workers, began operations under Zelaya.

San Antonio also expanded greatly during Zelaya's rule. Its territorial size doubled, while its sugar production increased from 2,486 to 3,698 tons between 1899 and 1909. During these years, San Antonio established a sales connection with canneries in San Francisco, California, supplying them with more than 300 tons of sugar in 1901.[11] The liquor monopoly was also extremely profitable. San Antonio and three smaller distilleries, partially owned by British and Italian investors, formed the liquor monopoly in 1904. The cartel rented the distribution rights from the government for $250,000. In 1903, once granted the monopoly, San Antonio and the other distilleries increased production and increased prices by an estimated 400 percent. The syndicate's profits were extraordinary. Despite the increased government revenue, the very profitability of the monopoly angered a variety of social groups. Some people morally opposed the increased consumption of liquor, while others resented the monopoly price increase.[12] The liquor cartel epitomized the political nature of the economy during the Zelaya era. When a United States-backed revolt drove out Zelaya in 1909, the new government's first decree was the abolition of the cartel.

During the Zelaya years, politics dominated the economy in two distinct ways. First, the state intervened in the economy. Such intervention ranged from forced labor recruitment for coffee and sugar plantations to tariff protection.[13] Second, since so much of the government's program involved the creation of monopolies, politicized economics became quite personalized and by definition a matter of government favoritism. This latter form of political economy alienated a large sector of the elite who felt discriminated against by the Zelaya regime.

Following Zelaya's fall, ISA managed to avoid political retaliation. San

Antonio's powerful connections in the Conservative party allowed it to avoid the economic reprisals that other Zelaya collaborators had to endure. On the contrary, ISA even received a $200,000 rebate on its liquor monopoly rent in 1911.[14] Moreover, the Conservative regime did not abolish sugar tariffs, and thus San Antonio continued to dominate the domestic market.

Despite political turmoil, between 1909 and 1912 San Antonio's sugar production increased by 26 percent.[15] Politically, the San Antonio group's reputation was damaged in some Conservative quarters, but their unparalleled economic power and their social prestige allowed them quickly to recover a dominant position in the party of the oligarchy. By 1912, when a Liberal revolution broke out, San Antonio was firmly identified with the Conservative government and its U. S. allies.

"For Their Skill and Strength"

On August 18, 1912, Liberal revolutionary forces occupied the town of Chichigalpa. Local residents, including San Antonio plantation workers, aided in the successful military operation against the governmental troops. The attack against Chichigalpa signaled the beginning of a revolutionary offensive against the United States-supported Conservative regime. During the next few days Liberal troops captured the nearby cities of León and Chinandega. Frightened by the revolutionary advance, and perhaps fearing for their lives, a group of foreigners connected to San Antonio sent an urgent message on September 3, 1912, to the U.S. Consul in Corinto, asking for military assistance. Within ten days, the U.S. government sent marines to occupy western Nicaragua.[16] The military occupation of Chichigalpa was not an easy operation since the large majority of its two thousand inhabitants sympathized with the Liberal revolutionaries. Two months later, Chichigalpa residents staged a protest against the U.S. occupation. An official report dated October 4 evaluated the events in the following terms. "Lieutenant Long, in attempting to seize arms and some dynamite bombs early this morning, was closed in on by a considerable mob of rebel soldiers and others armed with rifles and machetes. Several rebels, disregarding orders of their officers, fired upon our marines, which fire was promptly returned and a skirmish ensued during which 13 rebels were killed and quite a number wounded and five of our men were slightly wounded. . . . Lieutenant Long . . . obtained possession of four dynamite bombs, which it is reasonable to believe were intended for use either against the railroad or our forces."[17]

In 1983, eighty-two-year-old Alberto Cortés claimed to remember the events quite well. "The Chichigalpino rebels fought with machetes and one or two pistols," he stated assuredly, as if he were discussing last Saturday's barroom brawl. Don Alberto also remembered that when the battle ended, Lieutenant Long and his soldiers tied up thirteen insurgents and marched them to the steps of San Blás Cathedral, in the center of town. There, marines shot the rebels dead, including Don Alberto's father. Several Chichigalpino residents share Don Alberto's version of the events.[18] Whether or not the local or the marines' version is correct, the San Blás Massacre became part of local popular consciousness. This incident reinforced anti-oligarchic sentiments among Chichigalpinos who would begin to link their opposition to the Conservatives with their repudiation of U. S. activities in Nicaragua. These ideological developments, in turn, influenced the development of the social relations of production in San Antonio. For, following the U.S. defeat of the revolution, ISA had to face the political antagonism of its workers.

The territorial expansion of San Antonio from eighty-five hundred to seventeen thousand acres between 1890 and 1910 had forced local peasants off ejidal, indigenous, and individually owned land.[19] Few of the expropriated peasants, however, had become permanent wage laborers. On the contrary, more than five hundred seasonal sugar workers maintained access to a peasant economy through kinship ties.[20] Nevertheless, laborer resentment against ISA's land expropriations deepened their political opposition to the company.

Despite worker antagonism, ISA did not suffer any serious labor conflicts between 1912 and 1926. Through a combination of repressive and paternalistic measures, ISA was able to achieve substantial control over its work force. Indeed, ISA increased its sugar production during that same period from 4,400 to 12,750 tons, with a comparable rise in profit. In 1920 and 1925, with favorable export prices, ISA netted annual profits of more than $1 million, an unparalleled success in Nicaragua.[21]

Immediately following the San Blás episode, the company began to rent its cane fields to *colonos* (cane tenant farmers), as a buffer against laborer hostility. These local residents, often landowning farmers, employed and paid their laborers, who planted, cultivated, and cut cane on the rented San Antonio plots of 100–150 acres. In lieu of rent, ISA paid the colonos 20 percent less for the cane than the prevailing market price. Thus, the mainly Liberal field laborers did not face the Conservative managers at the point of production until the company ended the colono system in 1918.[22]

The sustained rise in world sugar prices from two cents a pound in 1913 to nearly twelve cents a pound in 1920 had an even more dramatic impact on ISA's development than the use of Liberal colonos.[23] The technological changes spurred by the price rise also contributed to maintaining labor harmony during a period of vastly increased production. In 1918, ISA installed state-of-the-art machinery in its sugar mill. An eleven-roller would grind the cane and extract the juice. Furnaces would heat the two quadruple effects— four interconnected steam evaporators used to separate the water from the juice. After making the molasses by passing the cane juice through two vacuum pan evaporators, six new centrifugal machines would separate the molasses from the final product, sugar. The new mill could process three times more cane than the old one.[24]

The new machinery required management to restructure the mill labor force. Between 1918 and 1926, ISA expanded its factory work force of semiskilled machine operators and skilled mechanics from about forty to more than two hundred men. The increased number and skills of the factory workers created the conditions for a social division between factory and field workers. Between 1918 and 1930, local residents worked almost exclusively in the cane fields, while ISA recruited its new industrial work force from the cities of León, Granada, and Managua. Local residents accounted for less than 10 percent of the mill workers but more than 50 percent of the field workers during that period.[25]

In 1925, during the height of the company's export boom, Gustavo Cantón, ISA plantation administrator, said, "The majority of field workers are Chichigalpas. When they do not like the work they just get up and leave the fields. But if today the wages go up, tomorrow dawn will find the colonias full of these workers, who for their skill and strength are the best in the country."[26] Cantón thus argued that the local field workers were excellent workers but were neither reliable nor loyal. Testimony by factory workers substantiates the idea that the managers and foremen were prejudiced against locals, and many of the mill workers shared that bias. Foremen often referred to the Chichigalpinos as *Indios* (Indians), idiots, or thieves.[27] The technical division of labor reinforced this racially based prejudice. For many years, the literate mill workers' feelings of superiority toward the illiterate field workers would weaken their collective defense.

Cantón's statement also points to the dependence of ISA on local workers. This dependence allowed the field hands to resist the company by means of a spontaneous march to the *parcela* (plot of land), a return to the subsistence sector. During the early 1920s, ISA field wages fluctuated between twenty-five and forty-five U.S. cents a day. During the same period, Managua coffee planters paid higher wages and Chinandegan cotton growers paid one dollar a day. The Chichigalpinos were aware of such pay differentials, and some sought seasonal work in these competitive sectors. But as Cantón indicated, the majority of the local field laborers, when dissatisfied, found refuge in the peasant economy, particularly in the region of Sirama. This temporary withdrawal of local laborers from the cane fields in turn pressured management to increase wages.[28]

The local peasant economy, however, had received a strong blow during San Antonio's initial territorial expansion (1890–1910), when peasants lost access to thousands of acres of communal and municipal lands. Furthermore, monopsonistic controls over the domestic market, as well as the lack of access to bank credit, forced peasants to sell their produce cheaply, often before the harvest (*al futuro*). The peasant economy also suffered from the prevalent form of inheritance, in which fathers distributed land equally among their sons and daughters, thereby creating a long-term trend toward minifundios. Nevertheless, extended household economic networks were elastic enough to incorporate most local seasonal laborers, at least for a few months of the year.[29]

The use of colonos to control the field labor force before 1918, the technical division of labor in the new factory, and the tolerance of laborers' passive resistance allowed ISA to gain substantial control over its workers and aided its struggle to increase production and profits. San Antonio also managed to pacify its labor force by rendering different services to the community. ISA acted, for example, as the area's only bank, providing some local farmers with credit. It also rented corn land cheaply to Chichigalpa's small- and middle-sized farmers. Since many of the small farmers worked seasonally on the plantation, such practices created paternalistic relations of dependency that also tended to improve labor relations. Similarly, the company sponsored two baseball teams, already an extremely popular activity throughout Nicaragua.[30]

Enchanted Burros and Devil Pacts

While banking, land rental, and recreational activities may have dulled resentment and often induced procompany attitudes among ISA workers, the company tended to foment a paternalistic ideology that depicted the owners as wise and beneficent father figures. ISA perhaps went as far as to manipulate the magical-religious elements of the workers' collective consciousness. Hermógenes Solís, a man who labored forty years for San Antonio, recalls, "They kept a burro in a special room out there in San Luís [the livestock section].

They bathed him and fed him milk. They treated him like a king. The people thought he was enchanted, a kind of god. The folks worshipped him. . . . The company used the burro to mount the mares [as a stud]. It was incredible to watch."[31]

Other informants confirm this tale about an "enchanted burro" whose sexual prowess helped produce work animals for the company. Perhaps to promote this myth, ISA lavished the burro with luxurious treatment. Although it is unclear how the burro became deified, the company seems to have appropriated the workers' belief in the enchanted burro and purposefully created the conditions for its worship. At the least ISA provided the burro with far better living quarters and food than it gave its workers. By symbolizing its own wealth and power in an object of worker veneration, the company encouraged identification with the owners.

Nevertheless, San Antonio field laborers also believed in a more powerful and terrifying myth: that the company had signed a pact with the devil in order to further accumulate wealth. According to those who worked at San Antonio during the 1920s, the devil pact specifically allowed the company to convert dead laborers and their families into cattle. ISA would then sell the "cattle" to the Conservative-owned Cosigüina hacienda, use the beasts as work animals, or sell the meat to the workers: "The meat was so yellow. Nobody wanted to eat it. They said it was 'people meat.' . . . One time they were slaughtering a cow and it shouted 'Ay, my son don't kill me!' "[32]

The workers' horrifying vision was nonetheless fairly common in the Nicaraguan countryside. Chinandegan peasants, for example, believed that the owners of the Campuzano hacienda had signed such a pact in order to increase the size of their landholdings. Nor was an elite-fostered belief in cannibalism unique to San Antonio: the indigenous inhabitants of the island of Ometepe claimed that a cattle rancher had converted an entire town into a hacienda and its inhabitants into livestock.[33] Many Nicaraguan tales are told of "steers" pleading for mercy as they were about to be slaughtered by family or friends. Despite their different origins in economically developed and relatively urban San Antonio versus undeveloped and rural Ometepe, these similar devil pact myths reveal a common facet of Nicaraguan rural mentalities in the early part of this century: a perception of the diabolic sources of the accumulation of wealth and the identification of rural wage labor with bestiality. Such myths attempted to make sense of the exploitative nature of wage labor and the loss of land, to a Nicaraguan audience that was undergoing the transition from a peasant-based to a wage labor economy.

The Nicaraguan devil myths, however, are but one variant within Latin American cosmology. Michael Taussig, for example, in a study of workers of the Cauca Valley in Colombia, analyzed their "proletarian devil contracts." Taussig's work shows how canecutters established pacts with the devil in order to increase their cane production. However, their increased piece-rate earnings were "barren," for they could not be invested in land or in other use-values. The earnings could only be spent on luxury goods. Through the pact the canecutter becomes "more productive of income and of barrenness."[34]

There are striking differences between the Colombian and the Nicaraguan devil pact myths. In San Antonio the pact was made by the elite owners against the sugar workers, whereas in Colombia individual workers made a pact with the devil but not directly against the owners. In Colombia, workers believed that their sorcery could not affect the mill owners because they were non-believers. The San Antonio workers considered management the sole possessor of such diabolic powers. These vastly different forms of devil pacts in the sugar fields may be the result of distinct ethnic origins of the workers (Afro-Latin in Colombia) or of ISA's comparatively more impressive concentration of power. Despite their dissimilar forms, however, both devil myths reveal similar feelings of worker impotence in the face of capitalist development. The Colombians offered an individual solution to the misery of wage labor, while the San Antonio myth offers nothing more than a collective portrait of a living hell. Thus, Taussig's analysis of Colombia is also valid for Nicaragua. "As the new form of society struggles to emerge from the old, as the ruling classes attempt to work the ruling principles into a new tradition, the preexisting cosmogony of the workers becomes a critical front of resistance, or mediation, or both."[35]

While the myths reveal degrees of impotence in the face of capitalist power, they also reminded their audiences of both the bestiality of wage labor and the immoral basis of capital accumulation. In this sense, perhaps the Nicaraguan myth was more damaging to capital's legitimacy than the Colombian version, in that it was a collective indictment of the company's complicity with the devil. One facet of the devil's presence in San Antonio was quite extraordinary even in the Nicaraguan context: the death of an ISA laborer did not mean the end of his service to the company. Rather, thanks to the company's pact with the devil, the worker continued to produce wealth for the company even after death, either as oxen or as food for the work force. This notion of postmortem worker exploitation, distinct from other Nicaraguan myths, may have reflected the lack of mobility for new generations of Chichigalpino workers before the

1930s. The mythical option for workers—cannibalism or eternal labor—was both a terrifying nightmare about the company's power and a scathing protest against its primitive labor practices.

Thus, the San Antonio workers held simultaneous beliefs about ISA's grotesque devil pact and about its marvelous, enchanted burro. The two visions illustrate double consciousness: the simultaneous acceptance and rejection of a system of domination. That little could be done to resist ISA's power conditioned resignation and the incorporation of symbols of domination. The abhorrence of the apparently immutable system led workers to portray ISA with such terrifying language that the burro-inspired apathy remained the only option. Yet the two forms of consciousness could only exist while ISA maintained the monopoly of force. Without the government's bayonets also arrayed against them, ISA workers might lose some of their fear of the devil.

The devil pact vision was rooted in the daily world of work. Labor in the cane fields was excruciatingly hard. Generation after generation of field laborers worked from sun-up to sundown for a pittance, only to suffer an early death from exhaustion and malaria. It is not surprising that laborers believed that the devil created such a world. During the rainy season (May–November) laborers dug holes to plant the cane. The holes had to meet specific dimensions and form perfect rows. Often plantation administrators like Sr. Cantón would force workers to remake an entire *surco* (a row roughly two hundred yards long) because of slight irregularities in size. During periods of expansion, many workers were sent to chop down junglelike woods after planting was completed, in preparation for future cane planting or cattle grazing. Thus, for example, from 1918 to 1921, ISA laborers cleared over five thousand acres of tropical land. Before the 1950s, poisonous snakes and malarial mosquitoes made this work particularly hazardous. Until the 1950s, workers had to cut crude cane rather than burnt cane. A canecutter expended more effort in cleaning nonburnt cane than in cutting it.[36] Management made the canecutter's life even more difficult by imposing strict quality control on cane production. Laborers, who earned twenty cents (the cost of daily food rations for two people) for cutting a ton of cane, would occasionally meet up with Don Constantino Lacayo, the general manager, while he was patrolling the fields on his white horse. Sometimes he would order the workers to go back to cut some cane stalks over again, this time "at ground level." Eighty-year-old men still scowl fiercely when they spit out the words, "Era un hombre muy fregado!" (he was a real bastard).

The infernal cane fields continued to breed malaria and rebellion alike, notwithstanding ISA's brilliant labor relations tactics. Beyond periodic refuge in the peasant sector, canecutters engaged in brief, apparently successful strikes at the start of the harvest to protest piece-rate cuts or food ration prices. Despite San Antonio's million-dollar-a-year profits, in the early 1920s the cane fields were, in the words of one former canecutter, one big "wasp's nest."[37] Faced with this elaborate wasp's nest, management engaged in the incentive and coercion methods described above. These measures, however, had only limited success. Management also had to rely on its own repressive power and its political clout. In 1907 a Conservative journalist approvingly wrote, "The company punishes the slightest infraction by sending the worker to jail."[38] In 1919, a less sympathetic journalist commented on the same disciplinary policy: "San Antonio throws anybody in jail it does not like."[39]

San Antonio in Times of Revolution and Crisis, 1926–1928

San Antonio's workers were aware that the company had decisive military backing. The dependence of ISA on the state became particularly clear during the Constitutionalist revolution (1926–27), when Liberals once again threatened the Conservative oligarchy.

Despite periodic Liberal insurrections, the Conservatives, supported by a symbolic detachment of the U.S. Marine Corps, ruled without serious threat to its power until 1923. In that year, Vice President Bartolomeo Martínez, a representative of a more progressive wing of the party, became president upon the death of Diego Chamorro. Martínez, with the support of a nascent labor movement, engineered a coalition between his Conservative group and the Liberal party. In 1924, Carlos Solórzano, a moderate Conservative, was elected president, and Juan Bautista Sacasa, a Liberal, became vice president. General Emiliano Chamorro, alarmed by the Liberal party's growing strength, staged a successful military coup against the new coalition government. Chamorro's coup set in motion the Constitutionalist revolution, which supported the exiled Sacasa's right to assume the presidency upon Solórzano's forced resignation. The United States intervened militarily to buttress the Conservative regime, while attempting to negotiate a peace treaty favorable to its interests. In May 1927, all Liberal officers except for Augusto César Sandino turned in their weapons. Sandino would lead a guerrilla war of resistance against the U.S. occupation until the marines departed in January 1933.[40]

Following the U.S. military occupation of 1912, artisans, especially in

Chinandega, León, and Managua, were the principal organizers of the anti-Conservative resistance. In Chinandega and Chichigalpa, the artisans organized around a clear anti-oligarchic program. In 1924, the Workers' Central of Chinandega, a federation of Liberal artisans, demanded agrarian reform, free elections, union rights, and the "overthrow of the government propped up by U.S. bayonets and the influence of Wall Street bankers."[41] These radical artisans, known as *obreristas*, formed an important faction within the Liberal party in the towns of Chinandega and Chichigalpa. For the average Chinandegan obrerista, San Antonio loomed as a giant symbol of oligarchic power. Allied with local sugar mill workers and peasants, by the mid-1920s they were ready to challenge this power.

On August 17, 1926, Santiago Callejas, owner of a small Chinandegan sugar mill, led a band of several hundred Liberals in an attack against government troops in Chichigalpa. The Liberals quickly defeated the small platoon of government troops. Callejas then ordered his troops to march on San Antonio, five kilometers to the south. Hundreds of Chichigalpinos, mostly ISA field laborers, eagerly joined Callejas's troops. The local recruits turned what began as a military expedition in search of provisions into a popular uprising. The workers burned the San Antonio distillery, sending "a million liters of spirits up in smoke."[42] The local rebels then marched on ISA where they sacked the commissary, burned several other buildings, and tried to kill the general manager, Constantino Lacayo. Several witnesses remember a fierce machete blow against the door of the casa hacienda. "They almost cut his head off. Lucky for him Nacho Paguagua got there in time. He told them, 'Well, boys, if you're going to kill Don Tino you're going to have to kill me too.' So, Don Constantino, along with Gustavo Cantón, escaped by rowboat to Corinto."[43]

Paguagua, a well-known Liberal, had been a San Antonio colono and contract wood supplier since 1912. Paguagua's opportune appearance at the manor house underscored the savvy of ISA's 1912 tactic of renting land to several Liberals. That Paguagua could easily save Lacayo's life and calm down the rebel troops also points to the dual character of the revolutionary movement in ISA. The action was paradoxically both organized and spontaneous. The Liberal army was both the organized framework for the popular uprising and the boot that kicked the wasp's nest. Many field workers who detested Lacayo seized upon the shift in power relations provided by the revolutionary assault, but the moral authority of Paguagua calmed the enraged workers. Nevertheless, the workers continued their rebellion by deserting the sugar plantation and joining the revolutionary army.

The massive incorporation of local workers into the revolutionary forces in 1926 provoked a more serious crisis for ISA than the company had faced in 1912. It was no accident that this political crisis, like that of 1912, had negative repercussions for San Antonio because of its dependence on state aid. In 1916, for example, the Conservative government had subsidized San Antonio's industrial expansion with a contract that included tax exemptions on sugar exports and machinery imports for fifteen years, military service exemption for ISA workers, and a tariff on imported sugar. The government's responsiveness to San Antonio's needs came largely in response to the national economic importance of the company and to the fact that members of the Benard family, its leading stockholders, were also key members of the Conservative government.[44]

The Liberal revolution hurt San Antonio. The mass desertion of its workers, not the international market price, was the main reason for a decline in sugar production from 12,750 tons in 1926 (before the outbreak of violence) to 8,300 tons in 1927.[45] The drastic drop in sugar prices in 1929 prompted another substantial decline in ISA's sugar production, but San Antonio's depression had already begun in 1926, when its field hands became revolutionary soldiers. Ignatius O'Reardon, the Irish-American who took over Lacayo's job, commented on this phenomenon. "During the days of revolution nearly all people able to work had gone off to the battle fields; when the zafra came, there were not enough workers."[46]

ISA responded to the labor shortage and to the fall in the price of sugar in 1929 with the introduction of new techniques for planting, irrigating, and cutting the sugar cane. In the depths of the crisis, ISA invested $100,000 in new mill machinery. The company also introduced a new system of góndolas for transporting the cane. Once the workers returned to the fields, management discovered that they could now produce more sugar with fewer workers, and accordingly they pared down the labor force and cut wages.

Once the civil war ended in May 1927, Adolfo Benard, ISA's president, became the Conservative presidential candidate pitted against the Liberal general, José María Moncada. Hedging its bets against a Conservative defeat, San Antonio incorporated itself as a U.S. enterprise. ISA then asked the State Department to push for an extension on the 1916 contract through the Nicaraguan Congress. Concerned about charges that they favored the Conservatives, State Department authorities turned down the petition.[47]

Despite Benard's electoral defeat and the State Department's rebuff of ISA's petition, ISA survived quite well. In 1929, the new Moncada government approved a new tariff on imported sugar and cut the export tax on sugar by 500 percent. This tax reduction was quite a boon to San Antonio, which continued to export sugar to the United States until a 1930 tariff closed off that market. The Moncada regime also authorized a large increase in the domestic price of sugar. Indeed, Moncada served the company even better than the Conservative regimes led by ISA stockholders.[48] Thanks to government support on prices and taxes, and to ISA's investments in labor-saving machinery, the company secured annual profits of $100,000 during the depression, while most of Central America's agro-export industries faced utter dissolution.[49]

Moncada and his U.S. advisers had one basic reason for supporting San Antonio during the crisis: the mill's importance to the Nicaraguan economy, for ISA was a major source of foreign exchange. In 1920, in a peak year, ISA's sugar accounted for nearly 20 percent of the country's export earnings. Moreover, ISA's distillery produced an average of 500,000 liters of aguardiente during the depression. Liquor taxes on the ISA product amounted to close to 10 percent of total governmental revenue. Finally, San Antonio provided jobs, contracts, and markets for more than three thousand families in the politically turbulent departments of Chinandega and León.[50]

Nevertheless, ISA's political role during the revolution had earned it the profound enmity of its workers. According to Liberal sources, ISA became the principal financial supporter of the Conservative regime from 1926 to 1927, even though the Benards had initially argued against Chamorro's coup.[51] The same sources claimed that Lacayo got his revenge by having troops "torture hundreds of Liberal workers. . . . Many died."[52] Finally, during the revolution, ISA had depended on the military protection of the United States, which reminded many Liberal workers of the San Blás Massacre.

"Just Like Slaves": Politics and Union Organizing

During the late 1920s, between 150 and 200 workers labored as machine operators, mechanics, or assistants in the San Antonio mill. Before technological advances were introduced in the mill during the 1940s, the majority of the mill workers performed exhausting physical labor, such as carrying large sacks of sugar from the warehouse to the train. Similarly, a company report described the work of filter operators as "very hard . . . done in such damp places that we always had to deal with complaints and strikes." Before the installation of large, automatic centrifugals, machine operators had to "wash," or empty, the sugar manually from the centrifugals.[53]

The overwhelming majority of workers resented management's excessively authoritarian control over the labor process. One worker complained, "If they get the idea to work us day and night straight, without good extra pay, they do it. . . . They treat us just like slaves."[54] In addition, many Liberals, particularly veterans of the civil war, had specifically political resentments. A San Antonio mill worker observed, "San Antonio thinks it is still back in the days of the Conservative regime, when it could do whatever it wanted to, to the detriment to the people of this area. . . . The working class only asks, in compensation for thousands of sacrifices in defense of justice, that the people be protected from this capitalist's abuse."[55]

Many workers believed that, as Liberals, they had won on the battlefield the right to defend themselves from the unrepentant San Antonio management. At the same time, though, the political discourse of Liberal obrerismo only vaguely resembled that of Moncada's Partido Liberal Nacionalista (PLN). There was a vast gulf between the official Liberalism of the regime and the revolutionary Liberalism that contributed to Moncada's rise to power. Obreristas, for example, opposed oligarchic capitalism and imperialism—hardly compatible ideals with the pro-U.S., Moncada government. A Liberal blacksmith summed up his sense of betrayal by referring to the ten dollar reward for turning in guns to the Guardia following the civil war: "We figured out that we had risked our necks fighting for a lousy ten dollars."[56]

Western Nicaraguan popular sympathy for Sandino grew out of this chasm between the revolutionary ideology of the Liberal workers and the Liberal practices of the elites. Although it is impossible to precisely measure Sandino's support, there is no doubt that many Chinandegan workers (including ISA workers) sympathized with the "Hero of the Segovias" without finding channels for organized participation in the Sandinista struggle. A State Department report on the January 1928 Corinto dockworkers' strike underscores the connection between Sandinismo and the Chinandegan working class: "Elements in Western Nicaragua, friendly to Sandino, are responsible for the strike. . . . The principal Nicaraguan labor organizations are controlled by persons who are at least under suspicion of sympathy with the rebels . . . and these organizations [could] prevent the recruiting of strike breakers in León and Chinandega. . . . There would also be strikes on the railroad and on the important sugar plantation at San Antonio, the largest agricultural enterprise in Western Nicaragua . . . if not for General Moncada's prompt intervention."[57]

Nevertheless, it must be stressed that workers' sympathy for Sandino did not translate into effective organizational solidarity or into the rebel recruitment of

Chinandegan workers. Indeed, Sandino's inability to mobilize his supporters in León and Chinandega into an organized political force became a fatal weakness. Thus, lacking a political alternative, the majority of Liberal workers and campesinos maintained their old loyalty to the PLN, despite the party's campaign against Sandino. In 1932, for example, the overwhelming majority of Chichigalpino workers cast their ballot for the Liberal Juan Bautista Sacasa, although a year earlier, in November 1931, many of those same workers had demonstrated their support for the Sandinista Juan Colindres when he briefly occupied Chichigalpa.[58] A journalist commented: "Many artisans joined the bandoleros."[59] Foreign Affairs Minister Leonardo Argüello showed great concern over the Chichigalpinos' response to the Sandinistas. The U.S. chargé d'affaires expressed Argüello's argument thus: "He referred to the kindly way in which the bandits talked to the masses with whom they came into contact in Chichigalpa and to the fact that they preached to them the theory that all goods were common property and that taking from the wealthy was not stealing. . . . [They were] encouraged by general dissatisfaction with the present administration."[60] This apparently contradictory loyalty to both the Liberal party and Sandino probably stimulated union organizational efforts. Sandinismo undoubtedly accentuated the anti-oligarchic elements in obrerismo and widened the gap between the Moncada regime and Liberal labor organizers.

ISA workers had organized a union in 1929, but it had suffered both from divisions in the Liberal party and bad luck. In March, the grinding mill broke, forcing ISA to end the zafra early. The company took advantage of the situation by firing a number of permanent workers, many of them Liberal union sympathizers. One Liberal worker commented: "The Liberal who is still here is gagged and humiliated."[61] A division in the union ranks also led to the rapid demise of the union. Carlos Alberto Zapata, the union president, sought to convert the San Antonio union into a base for his own political career, while other ISA labor activists opposed Zapata's pretensions. By September 1929, because of this internal division and the firing of union militants, the union had virtually ceased to function.

With no union or governmental opposition, San Antonio had a free hand to respond to the world depression of the 1930s. First, in 1931, management eliminated more than one hundred permanent jobs, while cutting the wages of the remaining mill workers by 10 percent. Second, management instituted a system of *media tareas* (half tasks) in the colonias in the early 1930s, a policy that amounted to cutting field workers' piece rates by 50 percent.[62]

During the early 1930s, many field workers retreated into the peasant economy as they had always done when faced with low wages at ISA. The company responded to the loss of experienced laborers by making a basic change in the previous sociogeographic division of labor: ISA began to employ Chichigalpinos in the factory during the harvest, on condition that they worked the fields during the planting season. The Chichigalpino presence in the mill began to narrow the social distance between factory and field workers. This change in the labor force—the transformation of some Chichigalpinos into mill hands—eventually made it possible for the factory workers to dismiss their prejudice against the field workers and even instilled a sense of community between the groups. This initial stage of field and factory worker social integration was an important precondition for the later development of the San Antonio labor movement, given mill workers' receptivity to union ideas and the overwhelming importance of the field labor force during the mid-1930s.

ISA employed a total of two thousand laborers during the zafra, 90 factory workers; 145 carpenters, bricklayers, and railroad workers; and 740 field workers—133 planting, 508 cultivating, and 99 on the cattle ranch.[63] The field laborers who planted, tended, and cut San Antonio's sugar cane represented 66 percent of the labor force (excluding 100 white collar employees). From the perspective of labor organization, the end of field worker isolation was indeed crucial. The 640 permanent field laborers, although fearful of company reprisals, bitterly resented their twenty-cent piece rate (most could complete only one or two tasks a day), and they objected to the obligatory expense of fifteen cents a day for food in the colono's kitchen. As they had during the prosperous postwar years, the angry cane fields of the early 1930s still resembled a wasp's nest waiting to be agitated.

The General Strike in San Antonio

The world depression had a severe impact on the labor movement. A sharp drop in the world price of coffee drove the value of Nicaraguan coffee exports down from $12.8 million in 1928 to $4.2 million in 1932. Since coffee represented more than 50 percent of all exports, the depression in that industry had repercussions throughout an economy already ravaged by war, revolution, and the devastating Managua earthquake of 1931. In response to the crisis, both the government and private industries cut wages significantly. In 1932, the British consul in Managua advised merchants that the Nicaraguan market for goods was very poor, given that "the population is mainly on the very margin of existence."[64] From 1933 to 1936, Nicaraguan laborers endured poverty with little overt resistance. But in early 1936, following a slight upswing in the economy, they began fighting to improve their circumstances.

The year 1936 stands out in contemporary Nicaraguan history because of two interrelated events: chief of the National Guard, Anastasio Somoza García, overthrew Sacasa; and the country endured its first strike wave. Sacasa, representing a moderate, oligarchic wing of the Liberal party, lacked a popular base of support; he had done nothing to encourage the labor movement. The rebirth of the Nicaraguan labor movement thus became intimately connected to Somoza García's rise to power. The general's political challenge weakened President Sacasa and created an opening for workers to voice their demands.

Inspired by the growing political crisis, taxi drivers, railroad workers, and dockworkers organized unions and engaged in strike actions during the first months of 1936. In early February, because of the national government's inability to pay a petroleum debt of over $200,000, the municipality of Managua rationed the drastically reduced amount of gasoline. Taxi drivers believed that the local government's rationing was not equitable and responded with a strike, halting all traffic in the capital. When the English consul and coffee grower Carlos Wheelock shot a striker, the work stoppage spread to other trades, involving between five and ten thousand workers out of a total city population of about eighty thousand. President Sacasa gave orders to General Somoza to shoot the strikers. Instead Somoza negotiated with the strike leaders and helped engineer a settlement that included their principal demand of removing Managua's mayor, an anti-Somocista who was responsible for the rationing. Somoza's response to Sacasa's widely known order to shoot the workers greatly boosted Somoza's prestige among workers and further deteriorated the legitimacy of the Sacasa regime.[65]

The same combination of economic demands and political motives underlay a brief, April strike by three thousand railroad employees. The anti-Somocista railroad manager, in a self-proclaimed effort to distribute available work, cut wages and instituted rotating shifts. The railroad workers struck, demanding the ouster of the manager and that the old wages and schedules be restored. Once again, the Guardia chief negotiated a victory for the workers. Through such actions, Somoza García projected himself as a friend of labor. Although many people, including some strikers, believed that Somoza García had cynically manipulated the strikes, the reality was more complex. In the case of the taxi drivers and the railroad workers, the immediate economic oppressors of the workers were identified with the Sacasa government. The unions' response to grievances accumulated over a decade was therefore strategically made at a moment of rupture between the executive branch and its repressive apparatus. Similarly, labor activists' support for Somoza was a response to his nonrepressive role during the strikes and to his prounion political promises, including a labor code.[66]

The labor movement that re-emerged in San Antonio in 1936 shared many of the characteristics of the wider Nicaraguan workers' movement. Like the national movement, the ISA union's leadership was predominantly Liberal, Somocista, and experienced. However, the San Antonio union organization was not merely a local example of a national phenomenon. ISA's large concentration of workers and its political-economic strategic value gave the sugar workers' union decisive national importance.

Although the pro-Somoza movement influenced the ISA union, workers felt such influence much more in the factory than in the fields. Joaquín Cordero, a non-Somocista, played a key role in organizing the field laborers. Cordero was "tall and dark," a canecutter, self-taught, and "bárbaro para hablar" (a great speaker). Some witnesses mentioned that he had quit a career with the National Guard. In 1931, Cordero demonstrated a rebellious streak when he escaped from a colonia reserved for workers with smallpox. Despite disagreements over details of Cordero's life, his former comrades all agree that "Joaquín wasn't afraid of either the hacienda or the Guardia."[67] Field workers saw in the courageous example of Cordero the chance to escape their infernal life in the cane fields. According to various witnesses, Cordero personally recruited close to five hundred field workers for the union. While that estimate may have been exaggerated, there is no doubt that Cordero, a rural *caudillo* (leader) with followers in the mill, represented a serious danger to both the company and Somocismo.

Unlike Cordero, at least five of the eight mill-worker union leaders, including the veteran obrerista leader, Carlos Zapata, identified themselves as Somocistas.[68] These leaders did not support Somoza out of unqualified enthusiasm, although they appreciated his obrerista rhetoric. Moreover, they perceived that the general's drive for power would directly or indirectly aid the union cause and that any opposition might have fatal consequences. Thus, they decided to use the unique political moment to wrest radical concessions from ISA's management.

In May 1936, the same month as Somoza García's military coup, the union demanded that the company fire general manager, O'Reardon, and replace him with Miguel Sandino, a mill cashier and union sympathizer; fire the company doctor and other high level employees; institute an across-the-board wage hike of 50 percent; reduce the work day from ten to eight hours; improve living quarters; and reduce rents. The fulfillment of the salary demands would have meant a $50,000 annual expense for the company, at a time when it was earning net profits of roughly $90,000.[69] The company, however, viewed the union demands as more serious than a simple financial problem. ISA considered demands for the replacement of company officials as an attack against ISA's hierarchical power relations, its "principle of authority." Adolfo Benard, company president and former Conservative presidential candidate, later commented, "In order to avoid disorder and possible violence the company agreed to grant a 10 percent wage hike and reduce the work day from ten to nine hours. . . . The majority of the laborers seemed more or less happy with having achieved that, but it appears that some of the leaders were not content and planned a strike for June 1, which did not come off because of the May 30 political movement [Somoza's coup]."[70]

Management thus attempted to provoke a split between the leadership and the rank and file. Beyond ideologically attacking the militants, the company launched an anti-union drive in June. One leader summed up the campaign as follows: "For some time now the mill mechanics have suffered all kinds of humiliations and insults coming from the General Manager. The only reason he does this is because we're members of the union movement. . . . We heard that O'Reardon was going to fire us for our union activities."[71] On July 6, 1936, San Antonio did fire twelve mill workers, Joaquín Cordero and an undetermined number of field hands, all union activists. The union immediately called a protest strike, demanding their reinstatement and the replacement of O'Reardon. At eight o'clock in the morning, a crowd of some four hundred mill and field workers, armed with machetes and sticks, shouting "Viva Somoza" and "Abajo O'Reardon" blocked the train from Chichigalpa. At nine o'clock, a National Guard patrol arrived and removed the strikers from the train without arrests or violence.[72] Meanwhile, Joaquín Cordero and his group of *jornalero* (field laborer) militants fanned out through the cane fields and colonias to spread the word. One field worker remembers that the rural organizers ordered rather than asked people to stop work. The San Antonio workers, like other contemporary strikers, needed military-like discipline to face any possible repression and an enforced unanimity to withstand any company attempts to sow divisions in their ranks. The next day, the Guardia occupied the mill section of ISA and the plantel, where those who did not work in the fields lived. Obliging a company request, the Guardia arrested Joaquín

Cordero and a dozen other fired workers. Shortly before his arrest, Cordero had led a march of hundreds of jornaleros to the plantel and, addressing a large crowd, denounced the company and the Guardia. Somoza García's troops hauled Cordero away, the last time the workers ever saw him.

In quite cynical, if revealing fashion, Benard commented to his stockholders about the military repression, "When they realized that the company had the support of the Guardia Nacional, everything calmed down and by July 9 the majority of the strikers returned to their jobs . . . but without doubt some of these people will bother us again as soon as they think that we do not have the support of the government. But we are very sure that General Somoza will not permit outbreaks of this nature . . . because he understands quite well that if he allows this sort of situation to develop, very soon he will directly have to suffer the consequences and the country will have serious problems."[73] Contrary to Benard's assertion, workers did continue the strike for three days despite the military occupation, and several militants attempted to prolong the strike even after the July 10 "agreement." Rather than expect that Somoza and the Guardia would win their battles, as Benard insinuated, many workers wished to show the company, in the words of one union militant, "the invincible force of the San Antonio worker."[74] At the same time, however, those union leaders who remained in the mill after the July 7 repression expected Somoza to intervene in their favor and were not ready to risk Guardia repression. Strike leaders did expect favorable treatment when they journeyed to Managua to negotiate. But the company prevailed. ISA ceded nothing but the jobs of those strikers who had not been arrested. Management did not even reinstate the workers it had fired on July 6. Faced with company intransigence, the union activists had to accept defeat in the first general strike in ISA's history.

Two weeks after the strike, the overwhelming majority of San Antonio workers joined management-level employees at a rally in honor of the visiting General Somoza. The Guardia chieftain and de facto ruler of Nicaragua arrived in San Antonio accompanied by Adolfo Benard and his son, the chief of protocol of the new government. Tomás Pantoja, the veteran leader of the mortally wounded union, made a welcoming speech full of praise for Somoza, but with no reference to the recent strike.[75] Somoza did not mention the strike either, but he did receive a warm ovation from the workers when he stated, "I assure you that the people's rights will not be mocked and that the workers and the proletariat will enjoy the privileges of full citizenship."[76]

The Guardia, under Somoza García's command, had most certainly mocked and scorned the workers' rights. Why then did these same workers applaud Somoza and join management in a demonstration of company harmony just two weeks after the strike? The testimony of San Antonio workers does a great deal to explain such apparently anomalous behavior. The strike's failure taught the remaining workers that they needed governmental support to win concessions from an economic giant like San Antonio. Unfortunately for the union, Somoza was attempting to consolidate his support in the Conservative party after his June coup d'état. The Benard family's support was thus crucial. Somoza had gathered the support of groups that ranged from fascists on the Conservative right to social democrats on the Liberal left. The ISA workers shouted *Viva Somoza* at the same time as they shouted *Abajo O'Reardon* because they hoped that their support for Somoza would translate into Guardia neutrality. They continued to support Somoza after the repression and the collapse of the union because the workers had no visible alternative except to await Somoza's fulfillment of his prolabor promises.

The appearance of labor-management harmony shortly after the strike is more difficult to explain. In fact, less than a year after the strike, the well-respected, progressive writer Gustavo Alemán Bolaños wrote about the workers' love for O'Reardon. While such a sudden change of heart for a man so universally despised seems quite unlikely, it is significant that a progressive like Bolaños would perceive such an aura of labor-management harmony a relatively short time after a very bitter conflict.[77]

Workers' testimonies about the 1936 strike offer an important clue to understanding the appearance of such harmony. None of the informants, with the exception of one strike leader, remembered the principal demands of the July strike: the rehiring of the union activists and the removal of O'Reardon. However, the informants did remember the demands advanced in May 1936. They recognized that they had won minor victories in May, but they unanimously viewed the July strike as not only a failure but also a mistake. Three informants sum up the July strike as follows. "We jumped the gun on the Labor Code, so we couldn't do anything. We were wrong." "The Guardia came and threatened us with their bayonets. They ordered: 'Whoever doesn't want to work, get out of the hacienda.'" "This strike was meant to support Somoza's movement. . . . Once he took the Fortín [the fort in León] he wasn't interested any more in strikes. That's why the Guardia broke up the strike."[78]

Although these three testimonies all touch on different aspects of the strike, they all, to a degree, adopt Benard's perspective. Benard's version emphasized the leaders' Somocismo, their expectation of Guardia neutrality, and the company's innocence. The company version, for obvious reasons, is also silent about the true causes of the strike. The strike participants quoted above, half a century later, seem to have accepted these aspects of the official discourse. Several factors influenced this partial acceptance of the company's interpretation of events. Clearly, the informant selection process suffered from an unavoidable bias. Many potential dissident witnesses either voluntarily left ISA or were forced out by the company. Thus, it is a temptation to argue that the less politically conscious workers who remained at ISA forgot key union demands and remembered only the ones they considered important: higher wages and the eight hour day. However, such an interpretation would overlook these workers' participation in a march of hundreds of machete-waving ISA workers shouting "down with O'Reardon." The memory of such a dramatic, frontal challenge to a decade of absolute, arbitrary, and arrogant company rule might well have been as important as the memory of bread-and-butter issues. Nevertheless, the workers do not remember the "down with O'Reardon" sentiment, nor do they remember that the firings of union militants were the cause of the strike.

The removal of Joaquín Cordero from San Antonio may have contributed to this retrospective myopia. Many workers spoke some variation of the phrase, "We all remember Joaquín, but nobody knows what happened to him after Captain Pereira took him away handcuffed."[79] To this day the mere mention of Cordero's name brings a glow to the face of the most hardened veterans of the mill and the cane fields; he is indelibly etched in their collective memory as a martyred savior of the ISA workers. Yet the workers sacrificed Cordero out of weakness. Called out on a solidarity strike, they could show Joaquín, a clearly beloved man, no solidarity when the Guardia teamed up with the company. Perhaps, then, the quick reconciliation with the company produced strong feelings of guilt about their comrades who had disappeared. The company's forgiveness of the workers' outrageous behavior, and its proffered paternalistic hand, may have deepened the workers' sense of guilt. To salve it, the workers forgot the strike, or at least those aspects which shed particularly unfavorable light on ISA or its loyal workers.

In any case, there is no doubt that the workers at least partially accepted management's version of the events of 1936. That discourse, in turn, became part of a fragmented consciousness that emerged forcefully after the strike. The devil pact/enchanted burro beliefs had become less important by that time, but their legacy of simultaneous sympathetic and antagonistic images of the company continued to dominate worker consciousness.

The resolution of the 1936 strike stimulated worker acceptance of a strain of obrerista ideology that tended to legitimize the Somoza García regime. ISA workers had long experienced the company's economic exploitation and understood its political place in the oligarchy. Given the profundity of the workers' analysis and its emotional pitch, it is perhaps surprising that ISA workers actively resisted the company only during times of national political crisis. But ISA's close relationship with the Nicaraguan state also encouraged labor passivity. ISA, because of its relatively remote geographical setting, its economic importance, and its company-paid police force, resembled a national enclave. Workers correctly considered such an enclave as a separate republic. The fear of jail or the loss of a relatively well paid (especially since the 1940s) industrial job conditioned the workers' acceptance of this paternalistic discourse. The workers' awareness of the essential falsity of San Antonio's claims to represent the best interests of its workers could only come during political crises that revealed the basic interests of the company as a political and economic actor. The workers' understanding of ISA's role in the Conservative oligarchy led them to join other obreristas in alliance with Liberal elite groups. Obrerismo, during the 1920s and 1930s did not, however, critically question such alliances with the Liberal elites. Thus, in 1936, San Antonio workers expected that Somoza García would support their strike. Lacking political alternatives, militants could do little but accept the Guardia repression. Indeed, over the next decade any questioning of the company would be done from a decidedly Somocista variant of obrerismo. Although ISA workers would continue to learn from their past and their present conditions, for decades that learning process would be cluttered with detours, dead ends, and a contradictory acceptance and simultaneous rejection of the dominant exploitative system.

2

The Auspicious Fields: The Labor Movement in the Ingenio San Antonio, 1944–1949

This sugar mill is an auspicious field for the development and growth of a social labor movement.
—Lieutenant Granera to President Somoza, 1947

Although Anastasio Somoza García came to power in 1936 with ample labor support, he only recalled his commitments to the workers of San Antonio and to the nation eight years later. In 1944, prompted by an elite-supported opposition movement, Somoza García legalized unions in order to obtain the active political support of the urban working class, thereby unleashing a wave of class conflict. But his relation to the unions was plagued with contradictions, for Somoza García had to balance his need for labor support against his own economic interests and those of his elite supporters.

Both Somocista and leftist union militants faced their own sets of contradictions. They had to weigh their need for regime support against their commitment to the needs of the rank-and-file membership. In other words, the union leadership had to grapple with the problem of forging autonomy from a regime to which it was beholden. Throughout Nicaragua, Somoza García's sponsorship of union organization helped create a significant labor movement, but the regime could not always control this movement. The leftist Partido Socialista Nicaragüense (PSN), or Socialist party, by 1946 dominated the large majority of the country's unions, including San Antonio's labor organization. But even the PSN owed much of its cultural formation to the same radical-democratic obrerista currents that Somoza García had appropriated. Socialists too spoke in a political language that the jefe obrero helped to create.

Somoza and the Birth of the Nicaraguan Labor Movement

In 1936, Somoza García had crushed the San Antonio workers' strike, in part, because he needed the support of the Conservatives to consolidate his newly won power. Between 1937 and 1944, however, the general began to lose that support and search for new allies. Inflation and import restrictions gnawed away at Somoza García's support from all social classes, and especially from the elite.[1] In response to his declining popularity and the development of an elite-led opposition movement, Somoza García ceased to repress the labor movement in an effort to regain popularity through his sponsorship of labor unions.

International considerations also influenced Somoza García's actions. Nicaragua was allied to the United States and thus, during the Second World War, to the Soviet Union. After the triumph of Stalingrad, the prestige of the Soviets grew significantly, even beyond the Left. The Somocista labor paper *Tribuna Obrera* exclaimed in late 1943 that the USSR "was going to lead humanity's way." Somoza García's subsequent tolerance of the labor movement reflected apprehension about the growth of an opposition movement constituted by students, professionals, businessmen, and Conservative oligarchs, as well as about students' efforts to attract PSN support.[2] The pro-Soviet PSN, in 1944, thus could emerge out of secrecy to agitate for a long promised labor code and to organize unions, notably in the new cigarette and textile factories.[3]

Since the 1920s obreristas had struggled for labor laws that would guarantee basic rights in the workplace, including the right to organize. In April 1944, spurred by the need for new allies against the elite and middle-class opposition movement, Somoza García proposed a labor code that incorporated many of the labor movement's long-standing demands: the legalization of unions and strikes, compensation for on-the-job accidents, one month's paid vacation, and minimum wage guarantees.

Somoza García also strove to unify the labor movement, so that its support could be more effectively used against the opposition. In April 1944, he urged the creation of a "unified union confederation" to terminate the "sterile rivalry" between the PSN and the Somocistas. The following month, he offered to preside over a workers' and peasants' congress that would bring together the two factions of the labor movement. Somoza García inaugurated the congress on May 26, 1944, with an expression of unequivocal support for the labor movement. Indeed, he made new promises of sweeping social security legislation and of agrarian reform. His speech concluded, "I have desired to inspire hope and faith in the weather-tanned farmers who work from sun-up to sundown in the fecund task of sowing the earth, and in the workers in the shops and factories, as in the mines, who with their sweat and blood add to the national wealth in nights without stars. Let us have hope and faith in a future which will have bread, laughter and song."[4]

Through his rhetoric and actions, Somoza García expected labor endorsement for his reelection plans. The PSN-dominated congress, however, denied Somoza García an endorsement of his candidacy, even as it gave the dictator "a qualified vote of confidence."[5] This statement from the Left can only be understood in the context of a young, potentially expansive labor movement, weakened by internal division, constantly harassed by management, and seriously threatened by the possibility of a rightist takeover. PSN militants saw that while Somoza García "offered rights to the workers," the powerful Conservative-led opposition seemed to offer only a return to the Dark Ages. Moreover, as the above excerpt reveals, Somoza García, unlike the opposition, could speak the language of obrerismo.[6]

The rapid development and expansion of labor unions and the first industrial conflicts were a direct consequence of the tactical alliance with the Somoza regime. The government was in no position to repress a movement that, in effect, was a key base of support. Labor organizers took advantage of this peculiar situation and participated in the greatest period of union expansion in prerevolutionary Nicaraguan history, from 1944 to 1946. By June 1945, predominantly leftist labor militants had organized more than seventeen thousand workers into more than one hundred unions. Unions represented more than 50 percent of all mine, transport, and factory workers, and roughly 25 percent of the nonagricultural, economically active population.[7]

Labor organization was an integral component of Somoza García's strategy to politically debilitate the landed oligarchy, neutralize the opposition, and establish hegemonic control over the Nicaraguan polity. Somoza García confronted two fundamental constraints in his efforts to use the labor movement to further his project. First, an increasingly independent Left continued to maintain a leadership position in the movement. Second, the Somocista wing, in response, attempted to organize in the nascent industrial sector, dominated by Somocista economic interests. During the mid-1940s, Somoza García had acquired interests in the sugar, match, lumber, cement, textiles, milk, and liquor industries. Although the regime tended to favor Somocista labor militants in those industries, these leaders nonetheless confronted serious organizational difficulties. The exigencies of maintaining worker support, often in the face of PSN competition, impelled Somocista union leaders to act with some degree of autonomy from the state, which responded by imposing limits on union activity. During the mid-1940s, for example, it was not unusual for the regime to arrest local Somocista labor leaders while attempting to maintain the political loyalty of the rank and file.[8] Regardless of the general's intentions, the regime could not impose a hierarchical relation in which Somocista unions simply responded to state orders.

"The Obreristas of Chichigalpa and San Antonio Salute the Greatest Protector of the Nicaraguan Proletariat"

From 1945 to 1948 Somocistas and Socialists battled each other for control of the union organization in San Antonio. The sugar mill's strategic value to the labor movement hinged on ISA's importance in the national economy, its large work force, and its Conservative ownership, long a target of obrerista rhetoric.

Throughout the late 1930s and early 1940s San Antonio continued to dominate the production, distribution, and export of Nicaraguan sugar. In 1944, some 2,450 San Antonio workers produced approximately 80 percent of the country's sugar supply. ISA's accumulation of capital on the domestic market allowed it to modernize and expand sufficiently to respond to rising international prices. In 1944, ISA exported 40 percent of its production and earned an annual profit of C$1.5 million (about $300,000).[9] In the late 1940s, ISA built one of the most advanced factories in Central America.

This economic preeminence was, in part, due to the company's continued support from the Somocista regime. In 1937, ISA obtained a concession from the government exempting the company from all import taxes. Moreover, it benefited from state-controlled domestic sugar prices, which were six to ten times more than the international market price. In 1939, however, Somoza García showed that the government's support had its price. He attempted to buy out the company. Although ISA successfully resisted the takeover, Somoza García did manage to extort "contributions" from the owners over the next three years.[10] Nonetheless, by 1944 ISA enjoyed harmonious relations with the regime and economic success unparalleled by other domestic industries.

San Antonio's government-aided success did, however, provoke hostility. Various newspapers attacked San Antonio's monopolistic practices, arguing that they had created a severe shortage of sugar. In 1945, during the peak of these attacks on San Antonio, referred to in the press as the "Octopus," Somoza García introduced legislation in Congress that would extend its government contract. In an unprecedented action, the Congress rejected Somoza García's proposed contract. After months of intense lobbying by ISA however, the Congress approved the contract by two votes.[11]

Somoza García's aid to ISA did not mean, however, that the new regime was merely the puppet of capital. He still needed popular backing and cultivated labor support by giving aid to the San Antonio workers. Thus, after eight years of enforced silence in the mill and in the fields, the factory workers established contact with the pro-Somoza Comite Organizador de la Confederación de Trabajadores Nicaragüenses (COCTN) and began a clandestine union drive.[12]

The principal leaders of the union, which soon claimed five hundred members, were almost all survivors of the 1936 strike. They were all well-respected craftsmen, and most were Somocistas. To cite one example, the secretary general, Toribio Ortiz, a foundry mechanic, had supported Somoza in his 1936 drive for power. Moreover, by 1944, all of the union leaders agreed that their success depended upon good relations with Somoza and the COCTN. On December 31, 1944, the unions published a manifesto that clearly articulated their perspective. "The Obreristas of Chichigalpa and the Ingenio San Antonio salute the greatest protector of the Nicaraguan proletariat . . . the only government in our history that has wanted to give us what justly belongs to us."[13]

The organizers acted consciously within the political tradition of obrerismo. Their declaration drew on the language of that tradition, which blended paternalistic and class-oriented appeals. As we will see in more detail in the following chapter, obrerismo in the 1920s was an artisan-based, reform movement that stressed class pride and anti-imperialism. During the mid-1930s Somoza appropriated the obrerista tradition and language. Although the Somocista transformation of obrerismo did not affect the movement's appeal to worker/artisan pride, it accentuated paternalistic dependence on the jefe obrero.

Like the obreristas who backed Somoza García in 1936, the new San Antonio unionists, steeped in the same tradition, offered conditional support, dependent on Somoza García's prolabor actions. Congressional approval of the labor code in November 1944 seemed to vindicate that support. The code called for the right to organize, the right to strike, paid thirty-day vacations, and overtime pay. Moreover, the code obligated large establishments to construct schools and hospitals.

The imminent enactment of the labor code, as well as the early end of the harvest in March, spurred the company to action against the growing union movement. On March 31, two days before the labor code went into effect, ISA fired three hundred union members, including the entire Somocista union leadership. The management argued that the action was merely the annual lay-off at the end of harvest, which had ended earlier than usual because of a drought. This argument was not very convincing since many of the fired union members were skilled permanent workers with more than ten years of experience. In addition, many activists did not accept the drought argument and suggested that the company had engineered the early end of the harvest.[14] The labor and Somocista press protested vehemently against the firings and called for the rehiring of the militants. Some workers attempted a strike, but the massive firings and the end of the harvest, which sent seasonal workers home, precluded this form of resistance.

Meanwhile, the focus of the struggle shifted to Managua, where the principal Somocista labor leaders—Absalón González and Alejandro del Palacio—negotiated with ISA at the Ministry of Agriculture and Labor. Despite accusations that ISA was trying to set up a "vertical" or company, union, the Somocista labor leaders withdrew their demand that the union workers be rehired. In exchange, ISA promised to tolerate future union organizing and to comply with the labor code, which required the company, at great expense, to build schools, decent housing, and a hospital.[15]

ISA made its concessions from a position of strength, for the very process of industrialization had deepened the social and economic divisions in the union ranks by favoring factory workers over field hands. Moreover, a new form of social distance emerged between the two groups as a result of the increasing proportion of canecutters that were migrants. In 1936 some 30 percent of the canecutters came from outside the department of Chinandega, replacing a growing number of local field hands who were leaving in response to wage cuts. And in 1945 that figure jumped to 50 percent. Due to the canecutters' isolation in the colonias, miles from the mill area and without transportation, organizers had a difficult time making contact with the migrant workers.

Although the wage differential between industrial workers and field hands did not change significantly between the 1930s and 1940s, mechanization reduced the size of the mill's industrial labor force, and workers who remained were freed from heavy manual labor to operate automatic machinery. This mechanization increased the demands on workers in the fields, which were reduced only in 1945, when ISA began introducing tractors for land preparation. Although there were no improvements in the planting, harvesting, or transportation of cane, production tripled between 1945 and 1952. Since there was no corresponding increase in the permanent work force, one may assume that there was a corresponding increase in the exploitation of field workers.[16] Such an increase may well have widened the gulf between factory and field workers and further complicated union organization by lubricating the points of friction between management and the machine operators. In a 1946 report to the shareholders, the company president underscored the importance of new technology in diminishing the impact of labor militancy. "The sugar will be packed in only one shift; instead of men carrying the sacks to the warehouse or to the train, the sugar will go on the conveyor belt, thus eliminating the work stoppages that this department has suffered in the past."[17]

In addition to the transformation of its physical plant, ISA was able to take advantage of an essentially exogenous factor in its attempt to weaken the union: the division within the national labor movement between Somocistas and Socialists. Between 1945 and 1948, as we shall see, the factional struggle helped ISA to keep the union from threatening either its industrial expansion or its managerial principle of authority.

A Gentlemen's Agreement is Broken

In January 1946, leftist participation in an anti-Somoza demonstration attended by seventy thousand people signaled a new round of labor activity.[18] Somoza, forced on the defensive and looking for ways to prevent a labor-opposition alliance, granted the Socialists a degree of political and union freedom. Thus he allowed PSN exiled leaders to return, and in February he permitted the founding convention of the Confederación de Trabajadores Nicaragüenses (CTN). Dominated by leftists, the convention was attended by sixty-seven unions and seven departmental federations with a combined membership of more than fifteen thousand.[19] Two weeks after the founding convention, the leftist ISA union leadership (possibly without consulting the rank and file) added its five hundred members to the CTN rolls.[20]

Somoza's response to this impressive consolidation of the independent union movement was contradictory: despite allowing the convention, he denied legal status to the CTN while simultaneously seeking an alliance with the PSN for the February 1947 general elections. To this end, he offered to support the election of four Socialist members of congress and promised to endorse several PSN-supported measures in the next legislature in return for leftist backing for the Somocista presidential candidate, Leonardo Argüello. Although a minority of PSN leaders were willing to enter this alliance, the party eventually broke off negotiations.[21] Faced with a growing opposition movement that seemed capable of establishing an alliance with the PSN, Somoza had to look for labor support through the nearly moribund COCTN. Given the extreme weakness of the COCTN in the labor movement, the struggle for control of the sugar workers' union became a crucial part of Somoza's overall political strategy. Indeed, Somocista labor leaders wasted no time in starting a smear campaign against the ISA leftists.[22] Yet ultimately they would need company support in order to gain control of the union.

During the first week of May 1946, ISA took advantage of the end of the harvest to fire "various unionized workers." To protect the company legally, O'Reardon proclaimed a lockout: "Consequently this administration notifies all permanent workers that they are hereby terminated as of June 15th."[23] The union responded to the lockout with protests, work stoppages, and demonstrations that had a national impact. In the course of these actions, the organization turned a campaign of self-defense into a struggle to force ISA to implement the labor code. They appointed as their representative Manuel Monterrey, a well-known, independent leftist lawyer who then entered into negotiations with management. On May 27, Adolfo Benard and Monterrey signed a "gentlemen's pact." In addition to rescinding the dismissal of unionized workers, ISA made important concessions, including agreeing to time-and-a-half payment for overtime and paid vacations, and to continue to bargain in good faith on the matter of wages.[24]

Although the company's about-face was quite dramatic, with the exception of the union hall and the wage issue, all of the points in the agreement were already mandated by the labor code. However, no other large private or state enterprise had complied with the code. Thus the ISA workers seemed to be creating a historic precedent for the Nicaraguan labor movement. It was, nevertheless, a pyrrhic victory. Three days after the signing of the agreement, the Ministry of Labor "destroyed the pact."[25] The minister of labor nullified the agreement using arbitrary power; he vetoed vacation payment for certain low-level categories of workers and prohibited overtime pay for all sugar mill workers. The government sent a squad of Guardia to the mill to enforce these decrees. Reminiscent of their role in the strike a decade earlier, the Guardia adopted a "threatening attitude" toward the workers.[26]

Management's role in the labor ministry's intervention is unclear, although ISA obviously benefited from the nullification of the contract. The regime's move was more obvious; the Ministry of Labor skirted the labor code, arguing, "We cannot demand either overtime pay or the eight-hour day, otherwise the industry is finished."[27] Somoza was undoubtedly conscious of the danger of setting a precedent of overtime pay in the sugar industry, in part because he owned Montelimar, an expanding plantation-mill complex.

Stunned by the labor ministry's intervention, the militants denounced the governmental abrogation of the "gentlemen's agreement" as a betrayal, arguing in particular that governmental actions fomented social injustice by hurting the weakest sector of the ISA working class, the temporary laborers. "The seasonal worker receives a wage of C\$4.35 (córdobas) for 12 hours of labor . . . when food and laundry costs C\$4.56 a day. They cannot demand vacation and pay increases because in Managua . . . there are 5,000 unemployed."[28] Unfortunately for the union leaders, the majority of the field workers had gone home after the harvest. The union probably reached more receptive ears with its criticism of ISA's treatment of mill workers. "ISA's workingmen's compensation is to fire the worker. . . . Desiderio Salgado, the foreman, still uses a whip on his workers. . . . The Chichigalpinos pay high fares for the ISA train."[29]

The union did not, however, criticize or clarify the role of the state in disrupting labor-management negotiations, perhaps because of their own confusion about the state's role in the labor movement. The union leaders asked Armando Amador, the secretary general of the leftist CTN, for help. On June 13, 1946, Amador took the train to the mill. Two hundred and fifty union members assembled to listen to the leftist leader, but the Chinandegan labor inspector, Tomás Céspedes, had already denounced Amador as a "revolutionary enemy of the government."[30] As the leftist entered the mill area, Lieutenant Gabuardi of the National Guard arrested him.

Manuel Aguilar's Silence: Sugar Mill Workers and the Image of Somoza

The unarmed union members could do nothing to prevent Amador's arrest; instead, they sought help from the Guardia commander-in-chief. More than fifty members, mostly permanent field workers, signed a letter to Somoza asking him to meet with three union militants who would "explain to your excellency the arbitrary actions which have been committed against the union movement."[31] Evidently the letter referred specifically to the arrest of Amador, but when the ISA militants arrived at Corinto to meet with Somoza, the

CTN leader was already free. Two of the union members remembered the following conversation from the meeting with Somoza:

M. Aguilar: General, we have some problems over there in San Antonio.
Somoza: Tell me about them, boys.
M. Aguilar: Well . . . they don't have a night school, they don't have a hospital.
Somoza: They don't have a night school? Well I'll talk to them. Now what else can I do for you?
M. Aguilar: Well no not really, there's nothing else my General, thank you.[32]

The silences in this conversation were as important as the spoken words. Rather than complaining about the actions of the Ministry of Labor and the Somocista union leaders, Aguilar focussed on seemingly peripheral and less controversial issues. Aguilar's silence reflected the organizational weakness of the union. At least thirty-five of the fifty signatures on the letter belonged to field workers. This signified, on the one hand, a degree of organizational success among permanent field workers. But only fifteen factory workers' signatures—out of some two hundred members—indicates, on the other hand, an atmosphere of passivity, apathy, and fear in the factory, the former bastion of union strength. Aguilar's silence thus revealed his appreciation of the union's weak position.

Yet the meeting—a caricature of the humble petitioner before the powerful authority—also says something about the ideological relations between Somoza and the labor movement. Somoza had come to power ten years earlier with the support of significant sections of the Nicaraguan working class. The political expression of these sectors, obrerismo, during the 1930s assumed a political relation with the government and with Somoza that still permeated the labor movement during the mid-1940s. Both factions of the labor movement, nurtured in obrerista political culture, depended on the benevolence of the regime symbolized by Somoza's ceremonial title, jefe obrero.

Somoza maintained the aura of the jefe obrero by personally guaranteeing that the workers' least expensive and least threatening demands (like that for a night school) would be met. When workers made unacceptable demands (like that for a hospital or overtime pay), he simply ignored them. Of course, the general could maintain his status as the workers' benefactor only so long as workers did not see the blood on his hands. During the mid-1940s, the National Guard's repression of the unions was neither constant nor excessively violent. Hence the attacks on the ISA union could be interpreted by workers as

isolated actions of regime subordinates like Céspedes or Lieutenant Gabuardi.
The conversation between Aguilar and Somoza reveals a game in which both projected the images of themselves they felt necessary to continue their leadership. Somoza could not project the image of a benevolent authority without a receptive audience. Aguilar was not silent in front of Somoza out of stupidity or fear; he was known for his intelligence and bravery. For years he had fought against the most powerful company in Nicaragua but not against Somoza. That experience conditioned him to accept the image of a man with seemingly absolute military power, yet with compassion for *el pueblo* (the people). Faced with the fragmentation of his union, which had been created at least indirectly by Somoza, Aguilar was ready to believe in the friendly general. Conversely, to Somoza, Aguilar seemed like a very respectful, humble and reasonable man—all qualities that made him a good union leader. For Aguilar, such an image was important because the local Somocistas considered him to be a dangerous Communist. Somoza, on the other hand, needed to project the jefe obrero image to Aguilar because he needed the workers' support to help protect him from a growing wave of oppositional activity.[33]

Somoza's role in the attacks on the ISA union is unclear, for the general maintained a certain distance from the internal labor strife, as evidenced by his friendly manner with Aguilar. Somoza's followers in the union, however, continued to lash out against Aguilar and the other leaders. One week after the meeting with Somoza, Rafael Mayorga, a leftist union leader, sent the jefe obrero a telegram. "Juan Silva called an illegal union meeting yesterday—ousting me—I await orders."[34] We do not know Somoza's response to Mayorga's request to restrain Juan Silva, a well-known Somocista militant since 1936. Nevertheless, we do know that within a week, Mayorga regained his union presidency. Immediately, he accused the Somocista COCTN of meddling in ISA affairs and announced that the union would break all ties with the "politicians" of the Somocista union group, the COCTN.[35] Thus, Mayorga made a clear differentiation between Somoza and Somocista labor groups. The recourse to military language—"I await your orders"—is, like the Aguilar conversation, symptomatic of the relations between Somoza and the union leaders. In order to defend himself from the Somocista unionist, Mayorga legitimized Somoza as his general. Then Mayorga portrayed himself as a captain of the labor movement battling the corrupting influence of politicians. Nevertheless, it was a dangerous situation for leftist leaders like Mayorga and Aguilar: if Somoza helped them, then the leftist militants would be obliged to carry out his orders.

Mayorga and Aguilar assumed that they were exempt from military discipline precisely because Somoza did not have the legal right "to engage in politics" inside the unions. According to Article 204 of the labor code, the legal status of the union "could be forfeited as a consequence of joining political parties or associations . . . or because of any involvement in political activities."[36] The pro-Socialist unions, being extremely careful not to violate this article, used it to condemn the Somocista unionists. Thus, when leftist militants addressed Somoza as "jefe obrero" or "general" they appealed to him as a neutral executor of laws but not as a partisan politician. The survival of the ISA union depended on the faithful enforcement of existing labor laws. Unfortunately for the militants, Somoza was not exactly famous for his respect for legality.

Within the ISA union, the two factions fought directly over the issue of union "apoliticism." Somocistas like Juan Silva were not concerned about the accusation that they had introduced politics into the union. They argued that only "the Man" (Somoza) could help the workers. Moreover, the Somocistas alleged that Aguilar and Mayorga had angered Somoza by their "involvement with Communists." The Somocista discourse was simple and direct and reflected the common sense of that period: "Whoever is not with the Man is fighting a lost cause."[37]

The leftist counterattack included an appeal to the "apolitical unionism" of the labor code, thus demarcating its independence from regime-sponsored unions. Yet to the rank and file it was obvious that the ISA union would always need powerful allies. The fact that Mayorga and Aguilar had turned to "the Man" ironically gave Silva's position more credibility. After all, the Somocistas had better relations with Somoza than Aguilar or Mayorga. But the union's criticism of the COCTN was not limited to charges of involvement in politics. The militants also attacked the COCTN for organizing their new Federation of Sugar Workers through sweetheart deals.[38] The leftists also denounced the corruption of many Somocista unionists. With these criticisms, the Left attempted to draw a line between independent and officialist unionism without attacking Somoza directly.

In spite of their ideological weakness, the leftist militants survived the COCTN attacks because of Somoza's decision not to intervene in the union conflict. Somoza probably did not aid the ISA officialists because such an action might have alienated national working-class electoral support. At least until December 1946, U.S. pressure for uncorrupted presidential elections in February 1947 restrained the general's field of action in the unions, for labor movement members represented perhaps 15–20 percent of the electorate.[39] Similarly, ISA management soon discovered that it would be politically inexpedient to continue to provoke the rapidly consolidating leftist union. In July 1946, the company announced that it would honor some of the promises of the May 28 agreement: the construction of housing, a hospital, and a union hall. This announcement further augmented the credibility of the independent labor leaders who had won those concessions. Thus the leadership of the ISA Left depended on the delicate balance of forces between Somoza, ISA, and the PSN.

In 1947, this balance was upset. Somoza's handpicked candidate for president, Leonardo Argüello, won the February elections through massive and transparent fraud. In a fair election, the Liberal Independent Enoc Aguado, the opposition candidate, would have won by a margin of three to one.[40] The elections showed that Somoza's strategy of basing his power on the Liberal party and the labor movement had clearly failed. To stay in power Somoza now had to depend more on the National Guard, the economic elite (including ISA), and the U.S. government.

Although the election results forced Somoza away from his populistic politics, San Antonio enjoyed a stronger economic position than it had in the two previous decades. While other sugar companies suffered a drought in 1946, ISA's irrigation system helped it avoid production losses. Thanks to its technical advantage, San Antonio gained a larger share of the domestic market. ISA had also obtained a five-thousand-ton quota on the U.S. market. Finally, the company benefited from an oversupply of harvest labor, the result of increasing urban unemployment. In 1946, ISA could thus achieve a profit of more than $1 million.[41]

San Antonio's Solution to the Social Question

On March 2, 1947, San Antonio held an impressive ceremony to celebrate its economic success, in which it rendered tribute to its veteran workers and inaugurated the irrigation system for another one thousand manzanas (seventeen hundred acres) of cane. The company invited more than two hundred members of the oligarchy to help award medals to 279 veteran workers. Whether to symbolize the life cycle in San Antonio or as a tribute to paternalistic tradition, the management brought in a priest to baptize fifty children. Later, ISA bestowed its first pension on Aparicio Castro, who had worked loyally for fifty years. For a change of pace, the oligarchs were entertained with a canecutting contest.[42] The exhausted winner received an ovation and two hundred córdobas, almost a month's salary. *La Prensa* reported effusively on the party and its social content: "The Ingenio San Antonio has found the solution to the social question."[43]

By an apparent coincidence the union leaders chose that same Sunday to invite CTN leaders Armando Amador and Ricardo Zeledón to a union meeting concerning the labor code. Although the meeting was scheduled for nine o'clock in the morning, two hours before the party which some union members wished to attend, Mr. O'Reardon could not stand any blot on the company's special day. He accused the union militants of "sabotage and subversion" and ordered the National Guard to arrest them.[44]

The union members resisted ISA's repression, preparing themselves for a strike in defense of their right to assembly. Although the labor code prohibited the harvest worker strikes, the ISA union clandestinely mobilized the canecutters to fight for a raise.[45] On March 20, field and factory workers attempted to initiate a strike, but management was forewarned and well prepared. First the company fired and expelled various union leaders. Then it ordered the Guardia to arrest once again the CTN leader, Zeledón. In addition, the Guardia arrested a CTN lawyer and Dr. Rubén Leytón, a labor sympathizer and official of the Ministry of Labor.[46] The Somocista union militants seized the moment, engineering a coup of the union leadership. The new leaders immediately issued a statement justifying their action. "It was an illegal strike instigated by . . . socialist leaders . . . [who are] traitors to the union movement."[47] Finally, ISA ended the work stoppage by promising a piece-rate increase to the harvest workers who then returned to their labors.[48]

The March events highlighted the relations between the company and the National Guard. Since 1912, ISA employed a security force that also belonged to the national army or to the police. This arrangement continued following the U.S.-sponsored organization of the National Guard during the late 1920s. However, the precise limits of the company's authority over its Guardia were not well defined. On company orders, the Guardia would jail a worker for infringements such as drinking on the job or tardiness. But the Guardia's jailing of a government functionary was a new event, pointing to a potentially important realignment in ISA-state-union relationships.

San Antonio could repress the strike precisely because of the company's relatively autonomous sphere of authority, enlarged by a crisis of transition in the government. Somoza's postelection strategic interests were now tied more closely to ISA and the rest of the Conservative oligarchy. Nevertheless,

Somoza had no interest in destroying the labor movement, for he still nurtured an ambition to win ideological control over the masses.

The March repression severely weakened the Left at San Antonio, but it did not destroy it. When Dr. Leytón was released from jail, he attended a meeting where the deposed leftist union leaders confronted the Somocistas. Three hundred union members were to decide between the Somocista COCTN or the Left. Leytón reported, "All answered in favor of this last option [the Left]. In those days there had been changes in the union's executive committee; there had been a fight for control between the Federation [the Left] and the Organizing Committee [Somocista COCTN]. Nonetheless, out of political expediency, the Ministry of Labor authorized the leadership of the Organizing Committee since the [others] are allied with the Socialists."[49]

Leytón's report reveals the high degree of support that the Left maintained after the March events. Clearly the unanimous support of the rank and file showed the limits of ISA's anti-union assault. But despite this support, the union could not resist the combined attacks of the company and the regime. For when the Ministry of Labor directly intervened in the internal affairs of the union, the Left and the rank and file could only protest passively. In the words of Leytón, "This union did not meet again for more than five months."[50]

When the regime directly backed ISA, the union, despite its internal strength, was simply too physically isolated to resist actively. Effective solidarity with the Managua-based CTN was hard to imagine and harder to organize. For San Antonio, on the contrary, the company's isolation aided labor-management relations. Aside from its semiprivate repressive apparatus, physical isolation perpetuated and reinforced traditional forms of paternalistic dependence, including practices like loaning money or giving jobs to workers' children. That union members wished to attend ISA's celebration, thereby actively endorsing the paternalistic image, testifies to the company's influence over the minds of even its most independent workers.

The union leadership had difficulty combating the company's paternalism, in part because they operated within the political culture of obrerismo, forged in the paternalism of the small workshop. Obrerismo in the 1940s, even among its more radical exponents, continued to draw moral distinctions rooted in the artisanal world: between those capitalists and politicians who treated workers decently and those who did not. Even though Manuel Aguilar or Rafael Mayorga spoke of class struggle, the workers accepted the dependent relations not only with *el Hombre* but also with the company. O'Reardon and Aguilar were good friends.

The Decline of the Left, 1947–1949

The Somoza regime and San Antonio had dealt a serious blow to the leftist CTN by demobilizing one of its largest and most strategic unions. Yet the CTN in Managua followed a different rhythm of advance and retreat. Thus, on the day of the abortive strike in the sugar mill, the CTN organized an impressive demonstration against unemployment.[51] In April 1947, some two hundred brewery workers went on strike. Simultaneously, other CTN unions threatened to strike against the PAYCO textile factory and against the largest firms in the construction industry.[52] But beyond the heightened activity of the labor movement in Managua, the CTN looked on the national political scene with increased interest. Leonardo Argüello, inaugurated as president on May 1, began to set a moderately prolabor course that was independent of Somoza. A Liberal party leader for thirty-five years, Argüello claimed devotion to the principles of political democracy since 1912, when he fought against the U.S. intervention.

On May Day, after his inauguration, Argüello met with a group of Socialist party leaders and promised them that he was going to "quickly push Somoza out of power and then work towards a democratic government of reconstruction."[53] According to CTN leader Amador, Argüello immediately began "to develop policies favorable to workers and their class organizations through the Ministry of Labor."[54] Specifically, in exchange for political support from the PSN and the Partido Liberal Independiente (PLI), Argüello had promised to enforce the labor code, especially in the "sugar mills and the mines." Argüello showed his good faith on May 16, 1947, when he sent Dr. Leytón back to San Antonio.[55] However, the National Guard immediately expelled Leytón from the mill, thereby serving notice that neither Somoza nor ISA were going to accept Argüello's program for political and economic change. On May 27, Somoza, with the active support of General Carlos Pasos, a rightist leader of the PLI (and owner of PAYCO), and the complicity of the Conservative caudillo, Emiliano Chamorro, staged a coup that forced Argüello to leave the country. Somoza, still the National Guard chief, justified his action by charging the elderly but lucid Argüello with "mental incompetence."[56]

The PSN and Sandinista students linked to the PLI rank and file organized massive street demonstrations in protest against the coup. The PSN-PLI alliance forced Somoza to resort to an unusually systematic and brutal repression of urban popular sectors, particularly against the Socialists and the Sandinista students.[57] The ISA management took advantage of the right-wing shift of national politics to fire four "vagabonds and agrarian revolutionaries," including Rafael Mayorga, despite his seventeen years of service to the company as a maintenance mechanic.[58]

The Somoza regime engaged in intense military repression for two months and succeeded in smashing the popular resistance to the coup. Nonetheless, by ousting Argüello, Somoza had seriously alienated the U.S. State Department, which refused to recognize the post-Argüello government. Somoza therefore had to ease up on his repressive measures and schedule elections in order to receive diplomatic recognition, a precondition for obtaining foreign loans.[59]

At San Antonio, Manuel Aguilar and other activists were sensitive to the subtle change on the national political front. In October 1947, they offered to join forces with the fourteen-member Somocista union. Despite the Left's willingness to collaborate with the local Somocistas, the COCTN pressured its local allies to break with Aguilar and form a new, exclusively Somocista leadership group. The maneuver provoked the ire of many among the rank and file. Internal union strife soon disrupted the calm that had followed management's March victory. Dr. Leytón described the atmosphere as *de machetazos* (on the verge of machete blows).[60]

Lieutenant Granera, stationed in the sugar mill, sought an interview with Somoza in order to deal with the threat of civil disorder. Granera recommended that Somoza try to negotiate a compromise between the rival groups. Somoza, confident that the National Guard had already crushed the Left and that the ISA group posed no ideological threat to his regime, endorsed Granera's proposal. Upon returning to the mill, Lieutenant Granera called a meeting of both factions, in which they agreed to form a new leadership coalition. Granera wrote about the meeting in a letter to Somoza. "After the agreement was signed, Javier Pérez and Manuel Aguilar came up to me to offer their services by organizing a National Guard auxiliary unit—a special civic group which cooperates in carrying out its policies. . . . This sugar mill is an auspicious field for the development and growth of a social labor movement; I fervently desire to steer [the workers] on this road that our supreme government has laid out."[61]

Granera's report illustrates both the defeat of independent unionism in San Antonio and the survival of Somocista obrerismo. The leftist Aguilar's real motives for wishing to organize a National Guard auxiliary were not clear. But in any case, his action demonstrated the bankruptcy of independent unionism and certainly gave new meaning to the Somocista message: he who is not with El Hombre is fighting a lost cause. Ironically, Aguilar already had lost. Two months later, in early January 1948, the National Guard in a nationwide sweep would jail him along with more than one hundred PSN leaders and other opponents of the regime.[62] Yet as Granera's report shows, at least some Somocistas were still eager to lead a social labor movement.

Granera and Somoza intervened in the ISA dispute to strengthen the union. Similarly, the political repression of June 1947 and January 1948 was directed against the PSN and the opposition but not directly against the labor movement; the paralysis of the union movement was only a secondary effect. Although Somoza no longer wished to play ball with the Left, he had no desire to extirpate unionism from Nicaraguan soil—much less so from that Conservative-run sugar mill, that "state within a state" in Chichigalpa. With the exception of the events of March 1947, the regime and the management did not coordinate their labor policies. Their contradictory political and economic interests therefore created a space in which unionism could survive.

In December 1948, the ISA was in the last stage of the construction of its new mill, by far the largest one in Central America. However, much to the chagrin of the American and European technicians, the new evaporator did not function properly. The management thus had to delay the beginning of the zafra. In a tactic both economically sound and designed to eliminate union militants, the management gave a one-month termination notice to five hundred workers, nearly one-half of the permanent work force.[63] Manuel Aguilar, recently released from prison, denounced the company with fiery oratory and called the field and mill workers out on a strike to protest management's arbitrary tactics. Virtually the entire labor force supported the strike, while the National Guard stood by impassively. Three days later, management gave in, canceling the termination notice and beginning negotiations with the revitalized union.[64]

During the course of the strike and negotiations, management apparently realized that they would always have to deal with some labor organization and that some union types were better than others. During the negotiations, ISA fired seven union leaders (including Aguilar and several Somocistas) who would not accept management's final offer. Management then allegedly "bribed" the other union leaders.[65] Bribed or not, the remaining union leaders did sign a formal agreement with the company without consulting the rank and file, in violation of customary union practice. ISA agreed to pay time-and-a-half for overtime for mill workers but reduced the piece rate for canecutters by 20 percent.[66] Although some workers objected to the undemocratic practices of the new union leaders, the majority were very pleased with winning overtime pay. Yet the victory was San Antonio's, for at last it had indeed found a solution to its "social question."

For three decades, San Antonio had pursued a strategy based on the technical and social division of its labor force. Briefly in 1936 and more consistently between 1944 and 1948, ISA workers were able to break those barriers by forging unions that were open to field and factory workers alike. By 1949, the conditions that allowed for field and factory solidarity began to erode. Somoza had crushed the leftist CTN, a labor movement committed to rural organizing. Moreover, ISA possessed a new mill, capable of producing some two and a half times as much sugar as the previous one. The decline of leftist unionism and new relations of production in the mill and fields conditioned management's acceptance of a union.

But the union that functioned in the mill after January 1949 was qualitatively different from the union led by Manuel Aguilar: it cemented rather than eroded the structural inequalities between field and factory workers. Rather than striving toward an independent political culture, this union would march to the beat sounded by "the supreme government." It was a union of mill workers whose rank and file was made up primarily of skilled workers and automatic machine operators, with higher salaries and better working conditions than most other Nicaraguan workers. Yet their victories, the result of long years of collective struggle, were not shared by their brothers in the field. The virtual exclusion of field workers from the post-1948 union made it easier for mill workers to endorse management's paternalistic claims and accept a certain identity of interests with the company. But the field workers were in no such position to forget their struggle. Indeed, the workers in the cane fields would eventually become management's Achilles' heel.

3

But We Were Hardly Beginning: The Chinandegan Workers' Movement, 1920–1948

For an organized Nicaragua.
For complete social justice.
—Strike declaration of tannery workers, 1945

In the city of Chinandega, as in San Antonio, the Somoza García regime would exert a powerful influence on the development of the labor movement. Somoza's need for broad political support to fight the opposition spurred the creation and development of the labor movement in Chinandega also. Here, the jefe obrero started out with an important advantage in comparison with other areas of Nicaragua: the continuity and strength of the obrerista tradition among Chinandegan artisans and workers. Since 1936, Somoza had both appropriated the language of obrerismo and built a solid alliance with its principal exponents in the town.

However, unlike in San Antonio—where the sugar mill's economic might, and thus the union's effectiveness, depended on cooperation with the regime— in Chinandega—since there were no major manufacturing employers—the unions could chart a much more independent course. Socialist party (PSN) leaders, who emerged from the same obrerista tradition, did not need regime support beyond the promulgation of the labor code. This greater autonomy from the regime allowed the militants to recast the language of obrerismo, stressing the independence of the labor movement and thus transforming the most paternalistic elements of the artisan-rooted discourse.

Chinandega lies fifteen kilometers northwest of the San Antonio sugar mill. Since the nineteenth century, town life has been closely tied to agriculture. In 1920, 688 farmers and 1,352 farm laborers were counted among Chinandega's economically active population (EAP) of 3,200.[1] The remaining Chinandegan adults worked as merchants (most of whom were women) or as artisans in tanneries, shoe, or butcher shops. In addition, small businesses employed about 240 carpenters who built transport carts and furniture, and some 50 mechanics repaired what little agricultural machinery existed in the area, especially that installed in Chinandega's small sugar mills.

The First World War stimulated the development of the sugar industry in Chinandega. Although the ten sugar mills together only produced about 20 percent of ISA's output, the sugar industry had a profound impact on Chinandega's social and economic life. About six hundred city dwellers worked at industrial tasks in local sugar mills (not including ISA) during the two and a half to three months of the sugar harvest.[2] Apart from creating new sources of employment, the sugar industry helped to consolidate the economic power of the predominantly Conservative provincial elite. Between the years 1920 and 1926, the owner of an average mill with a sugar production of 150 tons made an annual profit of ten to fifteen thousand dollars. Although such profits were but a fraction of ISA's profits, given that the annual income of a mechanic rarely surpassed two hundred dollars, the sugar industry significantly enlarged the social and economic gap between the Chinandegan elite and laboring classes.

The development of the sugar industry also affected the artisanal household economy. On the one hand, seasonal work at the mill permitted the artisans to supplement their craft incomes and often to save enough to survive as independent proprietors. On the other hand, the sugar economy fostered an increase in monetary circulation and a corresponding demand for consumer goods on the part of both the elite and the working population. During the early 1920s, because of the increase in demand for their crafts and the seasonal nature of the sugar harvest, some artisans were able to employ nonfamily workers during the off-season. Taking advantage of the favorable market for their products before the revolution of 1926–27, some artisan employers were able to acquire machinery that permitted an accumulation of capital. For example, a young shoemaker, although using manual machines, succeeded in building up a shoe factory employing more than twenty workers. In the same manner, a carpenter established a furniture factory with about fifteen permanent workers.[3]

The growing economic differentiation among Chinandegan artisans, however, did not produce significant ideological divisions within the working population during the 1920s. On the contrary, this structural change coincided with the rise of a homogenizing ideology—obrerismo. The Central de Obreros, founded in 1917, was the principal exponent of obrerismo. In 1924 the Central united more than one hundred members (of whom approximately twenty were artisan employers or self-employed workers, fifty were wage workers, and thirty were without a listed occupation) around a radical democratic program. The program criticized "corrupt" parties and the government controlled by "the bankers of Wall Street" and demanded an agrarian reform that would distribute the land "monopolized by capitalists," a social security system, and union rights.[4]

The radical content of the workers' program had much to do with the political role of the artisanal workers during the previous decade. These people formed the heart of the resistance against the Conservatives and the United States intervention. Their central role in this resistance informed the class pride which underlay obrerismo. The fundamental element of this ideology was the notion of the "worker," which meant an artisan with a trade whether or not he owned the means of production. This ideological vision, shared by artisan employers and their workers, stressed the identity of interests between employers and employees in the crafts, as well as in unskilled annual labor. As the carpenter/journalist Domingo Ramírez affirmed, "There was no social distance between the small entrepreneur and the worker. In those years the small entrepreneur was himself a worker, who made economic sacrifices to start his little workshop. Therefore he was considered a comrade in the struggle and this showed itself in their joy and sorrow."[5] "Worker" also referred to anyone of humble origins. This meaning can be noted in the phrase, "Victorino Sáenz, distinguished worker and successful merchant."[6] Sáenz was raised in a poor home, and the fact that in the 1920s he was already rich did not change his status as a "worker." Indeed artisan success stories came to form an essential element of obrerismo. Finally, workers were referred to as "90 percent of the Nicaraguan population." The connotation of worker as the majority of the population was generally used only in electoral campaigns to refer to the nonelite.[7] The first meaning of worker possessed the greatest political importance because of its ideological capacity to unite the nascent manufacturing bourgeoisie, self-employed artisans, and wage workers into one bloc opposed to the Conservative oligarchy. By the mid-1920s, obrerismo had become a dominant force in local politics.

Nevertheless, the Constitutionalist revolution that broke out in 1926 weakened radical obrerismo. The ravages of war and, above all, the disastrous fire of February 1927 (probably caused by American bombs) caused great human and material losses to all Chinandegans, including the obreristas. Moreover, the May 1927 peace treaty engineered by Henry Stimson, which guaranteed Conservative rule until U.S.-sponsored elections in 1928, deeply divided the workers' organization. One important group, led by Domingo Ramírez and Horacio Sequeira, fought politically against the U.S.-supported Moncada administration that won the elections. This obrerista faction openly backed the Sandinista struggle against the United States Marines.[8] In 1929, President

Moncada, the former head of the Liberal revolutionary army, suppressed the obrerista newspaper.

Nevertheless, following the withdrawal of the marines in 1933, many of the obreristas reunified despite their antagonistic positions on Sandino's struggle and managed to achieve an important degree of local political power. In an electoral battle with another faction of the workers' movement—which was allied with the Liberal, oligarchic Callejas family—the more radical obreristas won the municipal and departmental elections in Chinandega in 1934–35.[9] From January to May of 1936, the majority of the obrerista leaders pressed for the creation of a labor party that would be completely independent of the Partido Liberal Nacionalista (PLN), or Liberal Nationalist party. In May, they founded the Labor party and ran candidates for national office on a social-democratic, antifascist platform.[10] But the Labor party's campaign was cut short by Somoza's overthrow of the Sacasa government one week after their convention.

The response of the obreristas was not uniform. Those who still maintained strong ties to the Liberal party offered their unconditional support to Somoza. Colonel Ernesto Pereira, a famed veteran of the Constitutionalist revolution and earlier Liberal insurrections, was the leader of this group. Domingo Ramírez led another faction, which offered Somoza support contingent on the implementation of a prolabor program including a labor code.[11] Finally, some artisans, among whom the names of Francisco Miranda and Manuel Santamaría stand out, denounced Somoza's regime and continued their work of building up a workers' party.

Because of the prestige of their local leaders, the support of the obreristas was crucial to the consolidation of the Somocista regime in Chinandega. Somoza promoted several obrerista leaders to prominent posts and repeatedly promised labor reforms in order to win over the others. Thus, the general won the collaboration of the obreristas, connecting himself to key representatives of the area's principal political tradition.

The first eight years of the Somocista regime transformed the obrerista faction of the PLN. Members of what had been a party faction now occupied important posts in the local and national governments and dominated the regional party. At the same time, the obreristas continued to press for their historic demands, particularly for a labor code. In April 1944, Domingo Ramírez, the obrerista owner of a carpentry shop, announced that he had organized 180 carpenters into a union. As part of the same drive, Colonel Pereira (jefe político, or departmental governor) helped to organize the mechanics' union. Above all he acted as the legitimator of the workers' movement, by virtue of both his official position and his prestige as an obrerista.[12]

Unlike workers at ISA and in the mines during the mid-1940s, the early Chinandegan unions did not face significant opposition from most employers.[13] The artisan employers stimulated rather than suppressed trade unionism in Chinandega for two reasons. First, because the worker ideology of obrerismo included both owners and nonowners of craft shops, the fundamental opposition was between workers and the elite, including large, "unscrupulous and foreign" merchants, monopolists, and the rural elite. Because of their own membership in the class of wage earners, the lack of previous class conflicts in the crafts, and the objective need to standardize prices and wages among workshops, the obreristas demanded rights for the workers as a whole, including their own employees. Second, the ideological congruence of trade unionism with the artisans' obrerismo was also closely related to the artisan employers' political interests as leaders of a faction (now informal) of the Liberal party. The obreristas hoped to use their power as both union leaders and grassroots Somocista political brokers to gain greater positions of power at the departmental and national levels.

In spite of their role as leaders of the workers' movement, toward the end of 1944 the obreristas faced several important obstacles. According to the labor code the shop owners were excluded from the workers' unions, and the issue of the eight-hour day highlighted the fact that to some extent the interests of the artisanal shop owners were antagonistic to those of the wage earners they wanted to lead. Before very long the PSN began to take advantage of these obstacles to obrerista leadership of the unions.

From Obreristas to Socialistas

The Socialists had deep roots in the radical current of obrerismo. Francisco Miranda, owner of the most modern tannery in the city, and Manuel Santamaría, owner of a shoe workshop and a barber's shop, had been obreristas since the 1920s. They were promoters of the Labor party in 1936, but, unlike most obreristas, they did not support Somoza after the coup. Their conversion to the Marxism of the PSN derived from their perception that the Liberal party was bankrupt.[14]

During the 1944–48 period in Chinandega, as in ISA, the militants were careful not to discuss political matters within the union. But in Chinandega, in contrast to ISA, the PSN recruited the most combative union members, most of whom shared peasant backgrounds and sugar mill experience.[15] Thus, given that the initial organizing efforts were Socialist, the development of trade unionism tended to favor the PSN. The simultaneous development of the PSN and the labor movement fostered a competing definition of obrero. The PSN and the labor code transformed the definition of obrero to mean a wage laborer exploited by an employer. Although the PSN did not personally attack the obrerista employers, they stressed the separate economic interests of the workers and their employers. The code reinforced this separation by prohibiting employers from participating in unions.

By 1946, members of the PSN, despite intense opposition from obrerista leaders, occupied key posts in nine of the twelve urban unions in Chinandega. However, the unions developed independently of the PSN. The case of the tanners' union illustrates the relationship of the party to the unions. In January 1945, some fifty unionized tannery workers asked for a raise of 25 percent. Miranda, the PSN leader, immediately agreed to the raise, but the four other tannery owners rejected the demand, arguing that the raise would bankrupt the businesses; that the workers were irresponsible, drunkards, and did not work well; and that the wage demands were a plot by Miranda to gain political and economic advantage.

After owners, alleging worker theft, placed guards in their tanneries, some rank-and-file tanners called for a strike. The union leaders (four out of five of whom were Socialists) did not think the time was ripe for a strike. The unions had successfully organized in only three of the five tanneries. Furthermore, the position of the employers was strong enough to resist a strike. As producers of over 40 percent of the leather in Nicaragua, the Chinandegan tannery owners represented a relatively powerful opponent to the trade unionists.[16] On the other hand, it was precisely the wealth and profits of the entrepreneurs that encouraged many tannery workers to fight for wage increases. Also, the workers recognized that the period preceding Holy Week was the best time for a fight, given the extraordinary demand for leather shoes, but the Socialist leaders preferred to wait until the labor code went into effect before going on strike, so as to ensure Guardia neutrality.[17] Nevertheless, when a worker was injured by the grinding machine in a tannery, the rank and file demanded action.

On the first of February, the tanners' union, in an extraordinary session, voted unanimously to begin the first strike in Chinandega since 1936. That same night they wrote a manifesto that was distributed throughout the city. The workers denounced the "inflexible attitude" of the employers and guaranteed that they would respect the employers' persons and property. Then they expounded the basic reasons for the strike. "Naturally we must economically defend our homes against hunger, against sickness, against the lack of clothing, and against humiliations. This is the reason for our STRIKE. In this crusade of redemption of one small part of the Great Working and Peasant Class we are counting on the material and spiritual support of the unions which coexist in the emancipatory shadow of the Casa Obrera and in the Workers' Federations of Corinto and Managua. For an Organized Nicaragua. For Complete Social Justice."[18]

The union leaders' justifications were thus constituted by popular notions of material necessity, Somocista/obrerista rhetoric, and a vague appeal to spiritual unity. Both as an analytical statement and as an appeal for support, the declaration made the lack of basic necessities the fundamental reason for the strike. The rise of an agrarian protest movement in the late 1950s, as we shall see, would add a new dimension to the popular notion of "necessity."

The strikers identified their particular struggle with the movement of the "Great Working and Peasant Class. . . . For an organized Nicaragua, for complete social justice." Here they used a class language shared with both the PSN and Somocista militants. In fact, the phrase "for an organized Nicaragua" was a slogan of Somoza García. PSN militants quoted Somoza not opportunistically but rather because their tactical strategy was to put into practice the official prolabor rhetoric. If the Somocistas reneged on the goal of union organization, the Socialists could benefit politically from the gap between official ideology and official practice.

The union's call for "spiritual solidarity" is indicative of the mood of the tanners, who felt a responsibility to stimulate the incipient workers' movement. It also reflects a religious consciousness on the part of many of the tanners, including some Marxist militants. The unionists' appeal thus reflects both a recognition of the religiosity of Catholic Chinandegans and their own belief (and I am referring specifically to Alberto Orozco and Eduardo Briceño) that the workers' struggle was fueled by religious convictions. The rigid opposition of the church in Chinandega to trade unionism and to the PSN made this appeal even more imperative.[19]

Although the rest of the Chinandegan labor movement helped the tanners materially, it did not have the resources to support the strikers for more than two weeks, and the strike soon began to come apart. Just as the Socialist leaders had foreseen, the majority of workers in two tanneries broke the strike and kept their tanneries operating.[20] Faced with bleak prospects, the trade unionists went to the local Guardia comandante to ask him to intervene as a mediator. Although the comandante was prepared to mediate, the response of the employers was that there was nothing to negotiate since "there was no strike."[21] Nonetheless, the tannery owners did eventually give in to the workers, but not to their union. They offered a raise of 15 percent to all workers but fired the main leaders of the union. As in the rest of Nicaragua, however, management repression of unions by itself could not destroy the labor movement. The tanners' union continued to function until 1948.

The tanners' strike underscores the complexity of the PSN's relationship to the labor movement. The PSN leaders had been opposed to the strike, but when pressure from the rank and file became irresistible, they assumed leadership of the walkout. Moreover, as we saw in the strike declaration, the PSN helped link the popular democratic expressions of obrerismo to a new working-class militancy. Indeed, the Socialists strove to shape the trade union movement into a popular force that would create a democratic political and social opening in the country. The PSN was relatively successful in Chinandega. The party spearheaded the organization of some five hundred workers, representing more than one-third of the city's work force. Moreover, between 1944 and 1946, the PSN controlled nine of the city's twelve unions, including the largest four—the carpenters (eighty members), shoemakers (fifty), bricklayers (sixty), and mechanics (sixty).[22]

However, union or Socialist militancy cannot be inferred from the level of development of the capitalist relations of production. In the case of the carpenters, mechanics, and shoemakers, capitalist relations of production had barely progressed beyond the basic division between employers and wage earners. With the exception of one furniture factory and one shoe factory, the other workshops employed an average of about three or four workers. In many of these small workshops, especially those of the old obreristas (who had in many cases played a part in union organization), harmony reigned between employers and workers. That harmony allowed union organization to continue unopposed by employers, but quite logically it did not encourage trade union combativeness.

Although this analysis of the relations of production helps explain some aspects of Chinandegan trade unionism, it does not explain why—in contrast to workers' movements in other areas—the peak of trade unionism in Chinandega did not coincide with an intensification of class conflict over salary or working conditions. What, for instance, attracted the bricklayer or the mechanic to the union? Part of the explanation rests in the union's function of monitoring compliance with the labor code. But that does not explain the high turnout at ordinary union meetings, since only the leaders were responsible for such monitoring. In order to understand the low level of class conflict during the rise of the labor movement, we must look at the cultural dimension of the unions.

Working-Class Culture and Chinandegan Unions

Chinandegan workers flocked to the labor movement, above all else, because it offered them a new identity, one that both freed them from the culture of deference and expressed their new independence from their employers. While both employers and workers in the artisan shops were good obreristas and proudly identified themselves as obreros, the pride of being a skilled worker was felt differently by owners and employees. The owners and self-employed artisans were already forming a social class, not only because they owned the means of production, but above all because their prestige and political power freed them from the obligation of showing deference to the oligarchs. By contrast, the workers had not achieved any improvement in their social, political, or economic situations. Workers—most of whom had strong roots in the countryside—continued to suffer under the cultural domination of the oligarchy. Before 1950, when a field laborer, for example, encountered a landlord in the street, he often stepped into the street, joined his hands together as if praying, and said "Santito patron," asking for the patron's blessing.

Chinandegan trade unionism dealt a strong blow to such humiliating cultural practices, first in the city and later in the countryside. Trade unionism's undeclared war against the cultural domination of the oligarchy was part of a larger task of creating an autonomous culture, one that partially contradicted the obreristas' emphasis on the harmony of interests between workshop employers and wage earners. Although there was a great deal of camaraderie between working owners and their employees, outside of work the artisan employers had their own social club whose exclusive membership served as a sharp class barrier. The union workers even referred to the artisans of the social club as "the aristocrats" and made fun of their elegant style of dress. And the militants felt the need to educate themselves in order to achieve social equality with these aristocrats of labor.

The Casa del Obrero, established by Somoza in 1945 as a concession to his union sympathizers, was converted by the PSN leaders into a cultural center for the working class. Every week trade unionists and sympathizers from

Managua gave lectures on a variety of topics of more cultural and scientific than political interest. Workers still remember with great fondness the dances the Casa held every Sunday. For two years there was a contest for female workers called "the Flower of Labor." In contrast to the elite-sponsored beauty contests, the contestants were judged only on their work-related qualities and camaraderie (*compañerismo*). Even more than the lectures, these contests allowed the workers to articulate and celebrate their own values.[23]

Anti-Communism and the Labor Movement

Although Socialist leaders exerted a powerful influence over both the trade unions and the Casa del Obrero, they did not enjoy unilateral control of either institution, and by the mid-1940s, they found themselves under attack from Somocistas. While the old obrerista leaders were excluded from the labor organizations, the Somocistas had cadres and sympathizers in almost all the unions. While the union struggle from 1945 to 1946 was centered on monitoring compliance with the labor code, and since the Socialists took care not to introduce questions of politics into the unions, the Somocistas opted for collaboration with the leftists. But in May 1946 that collaboration gave way to factional competition. During that month the labor inspector, Tomás Céspedes, began to harass Socialists by visiting their homes at all hours of the day in order to check union books. In addition, he undertook a campaign to liberate the Chinandegan Workers' and Peasants' Federation (FOCCH) from the Communists.[24]

For the Somocista labor leaders, anti-Communism represented a convenient and potent ideological weapon against their factional enemies. Although many Somocistas were sincere anti-Communists, they were also quite aware that such a rhetoric echoed the dominant elite religious and political discourses. Moreover, they knew that the Somocista regime had to respond to charges of Communist infiltration of the labor movement, not only because of the regime's need to control the movement, but also because of international and domestic political pressures.

Somocista attacks on the Chinandegan union leaders coincided with those in San Antonio. Just as at ISA, the growth of a political campaign against the regime, potentially supported by the PSN, required the Somocistas to bid for direct control of the labor movement. The political question was even more important to the Somocistas in Chinandega than at ISA because the PSN and the Liberal Independents had begun to overturn the bipolar political culture, which had traditionally pitted the Liberal majority against the Conservatives—a tradition that had benefited Somoza.

At the beginning of June 1946, the principal Somocista unionists went to Managua to talk to Somoza. They stressed the need to remove the Socialists from the FOCCH, citing the violation of both Article 204 of the labor code (which prohibited political participation in the unions) and the constitutional exclusion of "exotic ideologies" (a euphemism for Marxism). Apparently Somoza and his local allies resolved that the first step toward weakening the Socialists would be to remove them from the Casa del Obrero.

When the FOCCH leaders became aware of the maneuver, they wrote to Somoza denying the charge of politicizing the unions and arguing, "They [the Somocistas] are directly injuring the autonomy of the unions." Later the leftists asked to meet with Somoza and were granted a meeting for June 22.[25] Although the events were strikingly similar in the union movements of ISA and Chinandega, the constellations of political forces in the two places were quite different. In San Antonio the pro-Socialist militants were defeated by a combined attack of the Somoza regime and the most powerful company in Nicaragua. But in Chinandega, employers were too weak to seriously harm the leftist-dominated labor movement. As a result, the Somocista trade unionists found themselves fighting the Socialists without allies. Moreover, the success of leftist labor militants in enforcing compliance with the labor code and its reputation as an effective and honest organization won the FOCCH enough worker support to defeat the Somocistas' attack in Chinandega.

A few days before the encounter with Somoza, the leftist-controlled FOCCH organized a demonstration against the regime's attempt to repeal parts of the labor code. The union leaders also condemned the black market and demanded a social security act and a "democratic and anti-feudal land reform." The enthusiastic reaction of the demonstrators—representing perhaps 25 percent of the adult laboring population of the city—revealed the Left's strength.[26] The Left's power conditioned the union's relations with the state. When Antonio Torres, secretary general of the FOCCH and leader of the PSN, came face to face with President Somoza, he eschewed the silence and deference exhibited by the ISA union leader Manuel Aguilar a few days earlier. Torres demanded that Somoza fire Céspedes, guarantee the autonomy of the Casa del Obrero, enact price controls, eliminate the black market, and close down rural cantinas because of their harmful effect on the peasants' lives and finances.[27]

Somoza accepted the last three demands, but as to the firing of Tomás

Céspedes he said only, "I don't know. I have to see."[28] In fact, Somoza soon relocated Céspedes to Managua, but he failed to fulfill his other promises. And, in August 1946, the regime handed over the Casa del Obrero to the Somocista trade unionists.[29] Although the Socialists dominated the union movement, their power was functional only within Somoza's game rules. Without a strong organizational base in the countryside, the numerically weak urban unions were in no position to resist arbitrary acts by the government. Thus they had to accept their loss of the Casa del Obrero. Stripped of their central organizational headquarters and cultural center, the FOCCH entered a period of relative decline in the city; but in the countryside the pace of development was different.

Talking Peasant Union

Union organization in the Chinandegan countryside responded to the development of agrarian capitalism in the 1940s. Following the Second World War, capitalist agriculture spread rapidly but remained within the boundaries of the latifundios—less than two percent of the property holders owned 65 percent of Chinandegan cultivable land. Although neither land tenancy nor the percentage of rural workers in the population changed significantly between 1920 and 1950, there were dramatic qualitative changes in the social relations of the countryside.[30]

The great majority of field laborers in 1920 had access to enough land to satisfy the consumption needs of their families. The owners—especially those with cattle ranches, but also, to a lesser extent, those with sugar plantations— usually supplied one or two manzanas of land, work tools, and food. However, in the 1940s, this paternalistic system began to unravel, especially in the areas adjoining the towns of Chinandega and El Viejo. This social change had its roots in the development of the cotton and sesame industries and in the continued growth of the sugar industry. In order to expand production for export, the cotton, sesame, and sugar growers denied their workers the paternalistic benefits that were still the norm in cattle raising areas—access to subsistence plots, food allotments, work animals, and housing.[31]

Spurred by high prices in neighboring countries, several latifundistas switched from livestock production to corn during the 1940s. Thus, production of corn in Chinandega jumped from 30,000 fanegas (1 fanega equals 312 pounds) in 1938 to more than 100,000 fanegas in 1946. Although about two thousand peasants produced corn, much of the production and marketing was controlled by the Palazio-Horvilleur family, which exported nearly $300,000 worth of the grain in 1948. Their plantation, El Paraíso, the largest corn and sesame seed producer in Nicaragua, was operated with only wage labor.[32] The sesame boom also stimulated capitalist relations of production. In 1938, about seven hundred peasants produced approximately 25,000 quintals of sesame seed. By 1946, sesame production had doubled despite a drought that year. Moreover, wage laborers on capitalist farms had replaced independent peasants as the predominant cultivators of sesame.

The Chinandegan trade unionists, out of both ideological conviction and the need to enlarge their bases of support, began to organize those field laborers in early 1946. Their organizing was made easier by the fact that many of the trade unionists were of peasant origin. More importantly, organizing was greatly facilitated by the fact that many union activists lived in the same neighborhoods as the field laborers. In the 1950s, for example, 816 of the 2,825 field laborers in the municipality of Chinandega lived in the working-class neighborhoods of Chinandega, where the union militants also resided. Similarly, 530 of the 2,787 field laborers in the municipality of El Viejo lived in the area's main town.[33] Daily contact and friendship in the towns between trade unionists and field laborers and the opportunity to organize outside the repressive walls of the haciendas aided the union drive. The significance of the agricultural laborers' town residence for union organizing is underscored by the fact that the three haciendas that were organized first—El Carmen, La Concepción, and Toro Blanco—were only a few kilometers from Chinandega and El Viejo, and many laborers from these haciendas lived in those urban centers.[34]

In 1946, the only year in which they operated with relative freedom, the rural unions grew quite rapidly. In December of 1946, one hundred permanent workers on the La Concepción sugar plantation threatened to strike. In response, the owners granted a wage increase of 25 percent and pledged compliance with the labor code. Similarly, about one hundred unionized laborers on the hacienda Toro Blanco persuaded the Conservative owners to raise piece rates on clearing land and to comply with the labor code. In Aguacatillo, an area inhabited by minifundistas who worked at the Monterrosa sugar mill during the zafra, field laborers from El Viejo organized a union that demanded land, credit, tools, and the closing of sixteen local cantinas.[35]

Thus the peasant unions succeeded in organizing both small landowners and field laborers and struggled successfully for moderate goals. Above all, their success began to crack the oligarchical order in its most vulnerable spot—the

Chinandegan countryside. The FOCCH in Chinandega could strike the hacienda walls because, in the words of an urban militant of rural origin, "We talked the peasants' language."[36]

Within ten months, aided by family, neighborhood, and cultural affinities, the trade unionists organized about seven hundred peasants and rural workers into six rural unions. The number of members represented a tiny percentage of the total rural population of the department, but in the area to the west of Chinandega and El Viejo, which contained the most fertile farm land outside of ISA and held much of the region's sugar cane, sesame, cotton, and corn land, union membership represented over 20 percent of the adult population.[37]

There is no doubt that the rural unions preoccupied the rural elite: not only did they upset the elite's paternalistic vision, but also labor's demands for costly wage increases threatened to obstruct the elite's agro-export development project, predicated as it was on cheap harvest labor. More ominously, the FOCCH began to voice demands for land reform. By 1947, the elite had resolved to crush the movement, and it succeeded in getting Somoza's help.

On the eighth of January 1947, 150 rural workers attended a meeting with the leaders of the FOCCH in Punta de Plancha, an area four miles south of Chinandega. Minutes after a peasant leader had begun to speak, a squad of Guardia arrived. The lieutenant announced that union meetings were prohibited in the countryside, delivering the first serious blow against the rural union movement in Chinandega. The rural trade unionists decided to march to town to continue the meeting. Nevertheless, like the repression at ISA in March 1947, the Guardia's prohibition was a warning of what the unions could expect.[38]

The pace of repression after January was the same in Chinandega as in the rest of the country. From June until August 1947 unionists were subject to intense pressures by the Guardia. After August they enjoyed a brief respite from jailings and prohibitions, only to be dealt a fatal blow in January 1948. After 1948, however, the Chinandegan unionists would earn an exceptional status grounded primarily on their impressive gains in the countryside. For the FOCCH's success threatened Somoza's new alliance with the oligarchy and the joint project of fomenting large-scale agro-export industries, particularly on the fertile plains of Chinandega. Thus, although in 1949 and 1950 the regime let unions function in other departments, the Chinandegan unions remained outlawed until 1958.[39]

When Somoza singled out Chinandega as the only department in which union organizing was prohibited, he inadvertently paid tribute to the labor militants' efforts to challenge the oligarchic order. A rural trade unionist recalls the prohibition with bitterness: "Pero estábamos principiando" (but we were hardly beginning).[40]

The Demise of Somocista Populism

This analysis of ISA and Chinandega has examined the development of the workers' movement in two geographically close but socially and economically very distinct environments. In both areas, Somoza pursued labor policies, with uneven results. In San Antonio a Somocista union survived and prospered, while in Chinandega the labor movement ceased to exist from 1948–1958. In the city of Chinandega, Somoza's strategy with respect to the workers' movement failed despite his ability to connect himself ideologically and politically to the local political tradition of obrerismo. The obreristas' loss of control over the Chinandegan labor movement was a direct result of the labor code, which excluded proprietors from the unions. Most of the artisan obreristas had only recently become owners. Thus, although politically and emotionally tied to the egalitarian world of the workshop, the very labor code that they had struggled to obtain isolated them from their former compañeros who were now their employees. The Left thus stepped in to fill the vacuum of labor leadership.

Between 1944 and 1948, union struggles threw ISA workers into a complex set of political, economic and ideological relations between the state, the company, and competing trade union factions. This web of relations was complicated by the company's preeminent economic and political posture, which necessitated its alliance with the Somoza regime. In the growing economic crisis during and after World War II, Somoza could not risk alienating or endangering San Antonio because of its value to the national economy as a source of foreign exchange, jobs, and domestic consumption. In addition, Somoza's consequent support of ISA mollified, to some extent, the Conservative opposition.

Somoza also wanted a functioning union at ISA, however, as a source, potentially, of political support, as a check against the company's stance on political and economic issues, and as a necessary ingredient in his recipe "for an organized Nicaragua." When Somoza had to resort to blatant fraud in order to win the February 1947 election against a centrist-led democratic opposition, however, he also had to admit his failure to attain political and ideological hegemony over the Nicaraguan popular classes. With his populistic project crumbling before his eyes, Somoza veered sharply to the right and cracked down on the Left in Chinandega and San Antonio. Although the desertion of the leftist union forces aided the defeat of his populist project, Somoza's desire to control a labor movement did not change. Indeed his anti-Communism corresponded to the political and ideological needs of the Somocista labor activists, both in Chinandega and Managua. Somoza also saw the opportunity to divide the opposition movement by crushing the Left and allying with the Conservative Right. The political imperative of the Cold War to defend Western interests from Communism at all costs coincided with Somoza's need to split the leftist and rightist wings of the opposition. It was thus surely no coincidence that the regime's mass jailing of PSN leaders in January 1948 came shortly before the Pan American Conference in Bogotá, which was designed to proclaim the anti-Communist solidarity of all the American republics under the hegemony of the U.S. Indeed, a State Department report cited Somoza's need to gain "international capital in anti-Communism" as a key motive for the jailings of 1948.[41]

Somoza was able to eliminate the Left in San Antonio without destroying the labor movement. Mill workers formed the nucleus of a pro-Somoza union until the 1970s. His success derived, in part, from a steadfast commitment to unionism in San Antonio, inspired by economic competitiveness and political enmity toward the company. More importantly, Somoza's success hinged on the Left's organizational weakness. The ISA labor activists needed external allies in their daily confrontation with a national economic and political giant. The PSN had great difficulty in breaking through the enclave-like barriers of ISA. Thus leftist sugar workers sought the direct assistance of Somoza. However, the Left's uneasy friendship with Somoza blurred the distinction between the "independents" and the "Somocistas" in the labor movement. The Somocista union discourse, itself rooted in the obrerista political tradition, evolved out of a direct relation with "the Man." The Left's dependence on the state reinforced this rightist variant of obrerismo and communicated an unintended message to the rank and file: "By our own forces we cannot win social justice in the sugar mill. The union needs Somoza or the company on its side."

Such powerful logic was firmly rooted in the history of San Antonio: since 1891, sugar workers had resisted the company only in moments of national political crisis. Yet, the company emerged intact after each local and national challenge to its power, recast its paternalistic discourse, and continued to buck the challenge of Somoza's labor policy as well as the challenge of the regionally dominant obrerista ideology. Despite leftist efforts during the 1940s, workers' consciousness continued to oscillate between resistance and resignation—between an enchanted burro and the devil.

The Chinandegan PSN, also rooted in the *obrerista* tradition, forged a semiclandestine political force between 1945 and 1947 mainly because of its predominance in the trade union movement—a fertile field for party recruitment. At the same time, the Chinandegan trade unionists could organize in the workshops without repression from powerful employers. Moreover, the Chinandegans, like leftists throughout much of Latin America, initiated a drive to organize rural workers.[42] These rural unions potentially threatened the power of the oligarchy much more than did the urban unions. Already during the 1940s, national policy makers regarded Chinandega as a vital growth sector. Trade unionism challenged this agro-export project mainly because labor's demands threatened to put capital needed for expansion and new machinery into the workers' pockets. Somoza, also an important landowner, saw the rise of rural unionism in Chinandega as politically and economically dangerous. State repression of the peasant unions in Chinandega thus delineated the rigid limits of Somocista populism.

The U.S. government played an important role in defining the limits of Somoza's populism. From 1944 until early 1947, U.S. policy indirectly stimulated his populistic tendencies. By prodding Somoza toward allowing free elections, the United States forced him to consolidate an electoral base of support. Consistent with a policy of nonintervention (the Good Neighbor Policy) the U.S. did not pressure the regime to repress the Left or the labor movement, thus allowing Somoza to court those forces politically.

But soon U.S. policy had the opposite effect, contributing to Somoza's abandonment of populist politics. The regime's blatant robbery in 1947 revealed the weakness of Somoza's political support among the working classes. When the United States failed to recognize his new puppet government (following the coup d'etat against Argüello), Somoza had already begun to search for elite allies. At the same time, the Cold War against Communism (represented in Nicaragua by the PSN) was beginning to undermine U.S. democratic goals in Latin America. Somoza astutely read those changes, and in that sense U.S. policy in 1947 further pushed him away from any rapprochement with the labor movement or the Left. Indeed, the imprisonment in 1948 of more than one hundred PSN militants helped pave the way for U.S. diplomatic recognition of the Somoza regime and for a firm alliance with the Conservative Right.[43]

In abandoning its populist project, the regime also bolstered the power of the Chinandegan oligarchy. During the 1950s cotton boom, landowners consequently faced no organized opposition even as they revolutionized labor relations in Chinandega. But this liberty of entrepreneurial action, sustained by the resolute support of the Guardia, would not last long. The cycle of violent repression that began in 1947 would give rise to new forms of rural resistance. The enforced silence of the endless cotton and sugar fields of rural Chinandega would soon erupt into cries of rage for land and dignity.

Part II
The Campesino Movement and Somocismo, 1950–1964

4

So We Have Nothing to Discuss Doña Tesla: The Origins of the Campesino Movement in Chinandega, 1957–1959

Ustedes son unos abusivos!
—Doña Tesla de Alvarado to campesinos as the National Guard arrested them, May 1958

Anastasio Somoza García's repression of the urban and rural labor organizations in 1947 and 1948 ended the formative phase of that movement in Chinandega. During the mid-1950s, in response to structural economic changes, another movement set its roots in the Chinandegan hamlet of San José del Obraje and later spread throughout the region. This movement was a departure from past labor mobilizations; for although the rural insurgents would receive important support from a revitalized labor movement in the early 1960s, its leaders had no previous union experience.

The rural movements of the 1940s and the 1950s used different forms of struggle to attain distinct goals. The San José campesinos organized in their community rather than in the workplace. Although nearly all of the campesinos worked seasonally in the cotton fields, their initial fight was for land and fishing rights rather than for trade union demands. The different focus of the San José campesinos was indirectly a result of the failure of the rural unions of the 1940s. For the elimination of all dissent in the countryside had allowed the agrarian bourgeoisie to remake the Chinandegan landscape in its own image. With no rural unions to restrain them, hacendados evicted thousands of laborers from their subsistence plots and converted municipal ejidos that had been used for hunting, wood gathering, and subsistence farming into cotton plantations. Without any unions, the campesinos were powerless to resist the agrarian bourgeoisie's massive attack on their standard of living and way of life.

The San José campesinos also faced a different antagonist than did the labor movement of the 1940s. The agrarian bourgeoisie that transformed the region during the 1950s into the center of an agro-export revolution was a divided class in a formative stage of development. Landed oligarchs on different stages of the "Junker road" to capitalism (the transformation of a latifundio into a capitalist farm) shared few economic or political interests with urban professionals who sought to become capitalists by investing in cotton. Somocista politicians and Guardia officers provoked further animosities in their efforts to attain instant status as members of the agrarian bourgeoisie. The San José campesinos, unlike the ISA workers, took advantage of these divisions and eventually learned to play one elite faction off against another. Like the Chinandegan labor militants of the 1940s, however, the campesinos in San José sought allies within the Somocista state, an increasingly complicated task after 1956.

In September 1956, a young poet, Rigoberto López Perez, assassinated Anastasio Somoza García in the Casa del Obrero in León. Somoza's elder son, Luís, immediately assumed the reins of power, winning a formal (and fraudulent) presidential election in 1957. The principal political effect of the assassination was a wave of state repression directed against the anti-Somoza opposition. The Guardia jailings and tortures drove many dissidents to armed insurrection, particularly after the triumph of the Cuban Revolution in January 1959.

Notwithstanding the increase of political violence following the assassination of Somoza García, the renewal of the opposition in 1958 and 1959 produced a somewhat similar political situation to that of the mid-1940s. Luís Somoza, like his father before him, sought to maintain elite support while at the same time co-opting the popular movements. As during the labor upsurge of the 1940s, the Somoza regime, juggling several tactical alliances between different factions of the emerging agrarian bourgeoisie, alternated between supporting, ignoring, and repressing the campesino movement.

All factions of the agrarian bourgeoisie tried to perpetuate the "fragmented consciousness" of the campesinos, but the lords of the land were ultimately much less successful in San José than they had been in San Antonio. Beginning in 1957, campesino militants constantly chipped away at the rank-and-file tendency to accept paternalism and rationalize their own oppression. Over the next six years of struggle, the campesinos began to develop their own discourse, one that radically transformed the meaning of Somocismo.

The People's Land: Las Cuchillas

In early 1955, as the first cotton harvest on the Obraje hacienda, in eastern Chinandega, came to a close, a small group of laborers gathered together in the recently formed hamlet of San José del Obraje. For years many had worked as permanent laborers, with access to land for cultivation and livestock grazing, as well as food supplies and living space. Now unemployment threatened their existence. Several campesinos present at the informal meeting had worked for many years as tenant farmers (*arrendatarios*) on middle-sized farms. In the past five years, however, their world had changed dramatically as haciendas and farms switched from cattle raising and basic grains to cotton cultivation. In 1949 Chinandegan growers cultivated less than 1,700 acres of cotton, but in 1955 they grew over 5,100 acres of the fiber.[1] For the hacienda laborers and tenants, the transformation of land use signified a loss of access to hacienda land and a change from permanent to seasonal labor. The growth of the cotton industry often meant the loss of one's home and consequently the necessity to squat on land of neighbors or kin.

As the laborers discussed their unfortunate lot, Ramón Cándia, a foreman on the hacienda, declared that he was fed up with working on the haciendas "because the rich don't have any heart anymore."[2] He suggested that they look for land to cultivate. Regino Escobar gestured toward the jungle underbrush and spoke. "Look over there . . . that's people's land. We've always gotten kindling, lumber, palm leaves and oil from over there. Let's go clear the land and plant."[3]

Within two weeks, thirty campesinos began to clear and fence off three hundred manzanas (510 acres) of "the people's land," dividing it into lots of ten manzanas (seventeen acres) each. They planted and harvested corn for two years, supplementing their farm income by working the cotton harvests. By the second harvest, the campesinos were harvesting corn from the full ten manzana plots of virgin land, producing up to 10 fanegas (3,300 pounds) per manzana, an unusually high yield by local standards.[4] In late October 1957, however, Guardia captain Napoleón Ubilla Baca, police chief of Chinandega, appeared at the cornfields. With him was Doña Tesla de Alvarado, owner of the 50,000-acre latifundia Campuzano, which flanked the campesinos' land to the west. Ten Guardia followed closely behind them. Captain Ubilla ordered the campesinos to leave the fields or face arrest as trespassers, for the land belonged to Campuzano. Then Doña Tesla spoke. She told her silent audience that for years Campuzano had tolerated campesinos gathering palm and firewood, but putting up barbed wire was *demasiado atrevido* (too uppity). The campesinos gathered up their ears of corn and walked back to their village.[5]

Several weeks later the Guardia arrested Captain Ubilla on charges of leading a conspiracy to overthrow President Luís Somoza.[6] Ubilla's last mission in San José del Obraje had not been fortuitous; it had, moreover, underscored the complexity of the anti-Somocista opposition. The Guardia captain and two urban associates had rented the people's land from Campuzano for the sum of C$100,000 ($14,285) for five years.[7] Ubilla planned to plant cotton on the people's land, also known as Las Cuchillas. The terms of the deal, of course, were sweetened by the fact that the campesinos had already cleared and prepared three hundred manzanas of good, fertile land. Ubilla's combination of financial dealings with the landed oligarchy and armed defense of that oligarchy's prerogatives against the campesinos' customary rights was typical of one segment of Guardia officials. His hostility toward the campesinos, however, was typical also of many of his allies in the anti-Somoza movement. The San José campesinos would have to make sense of this maze of roles and interests.

Regino Escobar vowed to the rest of the campesinos that he would find help to get the land back. The help offered by lawyers, politicians, and union leaders over the next several years, however, never amounted to much. But the San José group's refusal to accept the legitimacy of Campuzano's action marked the beginning of a campesino movement that in the late 1950s and early 1960s would contest fundamental political, social, and economic relations in the region and the nation, for the San José group sparked a far broader agrarian movement. However, when Regino Escobar first decided to lead the fight for the land, he neither had a clear notion as to the rights of the campesinos, nor did he guide a unified or homogeneous group.

The San José campesinos came from two very distinct social and geographic worlds. Many had migrated during the 1930s and 1940s from the economically depressed, mountainous region of Chinandega that bordered Honduras, known as *los Pueblos del Norte*. The other San José campesinos had come from the hamlet of La Grecia, about ten kilometers east of San José. Most of the Grecianos had moved because their family farms, through generations of division through inheritance, had become too small to maintain families. Although most of the Pueblos group had worked previously on haciendas, many Grecianos had labored primarily as tenant farmers. Of the 30 campesinos evicted by Doña Tesla from Las Cuchillas in 1958, 13 were from the Grecia region, 11 (including 3 Hondurans) were from Pueblos del Norte, and 6 were from other places. At the time of the eviction 3 of these owned small plots of land, 6 rented land, 12 were wage laborers, and 9 engaged in some combination of wage labor and tenant farming.[8]

The social and economic differences of the two groups were compounded by cultural differences. The Grecianos perceived the Pueblos group as "backward" and "Indian." Such attitudes were a source of friction and a potential organizational problem. In addition to their disunity, the San José group simply had no experience in resisting elite claims. Most campesinos were used to thinking of hacienda labor as a part of reciprocal aid. The campesino "helped" the landlord with labor, and the landlord "helped" the campesino with a few acres of land, food, and some cash. Before the advent of the cotton industry, campesinos viewed many of the *ricos* (rich folk) as kind-hearted. Although after several years of cotton harvesting, many local residents began to think that many ricos had changed for the worse, during the 1950s, Chinandegan campesinos did not question the legitimacy of elite land ownership.[9]

Most peasants and laborers continued to accept elite domination primarily because the cotton industry developed without expropriating small peasant landowners. In 1950, before the expansion of capitalism in the Chinandegan countryside, less than 2.6 percent of the landowners owned 65.1 percent of the land.[10] The cotton boom did not significantly alter land ownership patterns. Thus, in 1971, 2.1 percent of the landowners possessed 61.3 percent of Chinandegan soil.[11] Nor did the development of the cotton industry create a proletariat. Rather, it reshaped a preexisting rural working class, for before 1950 wage laborers had worked in sharply different situations on the cattle haciendas. Thus, between 1920 and 1963, despite changing relations of production, the percentage of wage laborers in the economically active Chinandegan rural population remained between 60 percent and 70 percent.[12]

For the majority of Chinandegan rural laborers what changed with the influx of cotton growing was the quality and stability of work and their access to hacienda land. Few of the San José campesinos had ever owned land. But before the cotton boom, nearly all of them had planted their own corn and grazed their own cattle on hacienda land. After 1950, however, elite cotton growers needed all available land for their export crop and denied the campesinos their traditional claim to the land. This change in land use provoked campesino resentment, but it generally did not lead to the questioning of elite legitimacy. When Campuzano expropriated Las Cuchillas, the campesinos felt hostile toward the owners of the latifundio but not toward their social class in general.

The campesinos' immediate justification for their claim to the Las Cuchillas land derived from a notion of traditional rights. Although the village of San José was only eight years old at the time, Grecianos and local hacienda laborers had used Las Cuchillas for generations. Moreover, local tradition held that the founder of the hacienda El Obraje, Manuel Antonio Baca, had donated the land to the campesinos in the 1890s because he found it distasteful to border directly on Campuzano, owned by President Zelaya.[13] Although the story is politically and chronologically plausible, the campesinos would discover two years later that Baca, in 1891, had actually attempted to expropriate rather than donate the land, which, in fact, then belonged to the Chinandegan Indians.[14] The gift story might well have been suggested by someone connected to the Baca family. As we shall see, gifts, real or fictitious, would play an important role in shaping relations between the elite and the campesinos.

Regino Escobar, the campesino who took the initiative to plant on Las Cuchillas and to defend the land in the face of powerful enemies, was not typical of the group he led. A few years earlier, he had owned and worked a twenty-acre farm in La Grecia. Regino lost his farm during the mid-1950s. The banks dispossessed many campesinos who borrowed money to finance cotton in the early 1950s. When cotton prices declined during the mid-1950s, many campesinos defaulted on their loans, and the banks repossessed their farms.[15] Regino probably suffered this fate as well, but his case differed from other Grecianos in that he originally possessed more land than most of them and was able to acquire nearly one acre of land in San José. Not only had Regino once been relatively wealthy, he now enjoyed both land ownership and a higher social status than other campesinos because of his marriage to Cándida Pastrán, a schoolteacher and the daughter of a former Liberal general.[16]

During his years as a small farmer, Regino had made influential friends in the Grecia area; he was a famous cockfighter, and because cockfighting was an activity that crossed class lines, his skill allowed him to befriend powerful people in the region. When Regino spoke to his compañeros about getting help in their fight against the expropriation of Las Cuchillas, he was thinking of Major Salomón Lagos, departmental commander of the Guardia. Lagos, like Regino, was an avid cockfighter. The San José leader went to the Guardia headquarters in Chinandega, bringing him a special gift, a prize fighting cock.[17] Undoubtedly, the Comandante was thrilled with the gift, coming as it was from such a skilled fighter. However, he was less than enthusiastic about helping Regino fight Captain Ubilla Baca, for conflicts with other Guardia officers were dangerous to a military career. He suggested that Regino visit a common friend, Marcelino Reyes, the *jefe político* (roughly equivalent to state governor) and chief physician of the Guardia in Chinandega.

Regino's visit to Dr. Reyes marked the beginning of what would be a long and arduous march through the institutions of Somocista rule, a journey that would permanently alter the consciousness of the campesinos. The march would eventually require the campesinos to expand their network of social contacts and to reflect on how power and ideology operated in Nicaraguan society. Their new understanding would come especially hard because they were illiterate in an institutional world dominated by the written word.

Dr. Reyes's initial response to the campesinos was sympathetic. He told Regino that he knew about the lands and that they were indeed *tierras nacionales* (national lands). He advised Regino to form a *directiva* (a directorate) and then return to initiate the legal and political actions necessary to take back the land. Reyes worked both to steer the movement into manageable and legitimate channels and to take the first step toward developing a political clientele, for Dr. Reyes had his own agenda against Campuzano. Reyes had discovered the titles to the municipal lands known as the Nuevos Ejidos, destined by the 1916 Nicaraguan Congress for "the poor campesinos of Chinandega."[18] He had skillfully appropriated nearly two thousand acres of the land on the southern boundary of Campuzano for himself, his friends, and his family. Since 1921, the Alvarado family, owners of Campuzano, had considered the ejidal land to be part of their hacienda.[19] Dr. Reyes's favorable reception of Regino must thus be understood in the light of what was rapidly becoming an important fissure in the Chinandegan elite.

When he returned from his mission to Reyes, Regino began thinking about the problem of forming a directiva. Since the San José del Obraje group was neither homogeneous nor deeply rooted in local soil the tenants and laborers had slightly different stakes in the struggle for land, and the two groups certainly ran different risks. The tenants generally rented several acres of land from kin or farmers, who were not involved in the conflict and not easily subject to elite pressures. Thus, for the tenants, the risk of involvement, outside of possible state reprisals, was not great. For the *jornaleros* (landless laborers), however, the principal risk was the loss of their seasonal jobs. Involvement in the campesino movement might mark them as potential agitators even on a hacienda not involved in the land conflict.

Different tenure relations, however, were not necessarily a cause of social differentiation; the social boundaries between smallholders, tenants, and landless laborers were quite fluid. San José smallholders often let landless community members live on their land and cultivate some of it without expecting any form of payment (a relationship known as *arrimado*). Tenants also often worked as laborers. While different degrees of militancy or commitment could not be predicted from geographical origins or occupational status, such differences might provoke divisive reactions to concrete stresses. Regino seems to have taken such factors into account when he decided on his directiva.

He chose six of the original thirty campesinos to form part of the directorate. Three of the appointed leaders belonged to the Pueblos group and three to the Grecia group; three were laborers, two were tenants, and one was a smallholder.[20] Regino's choice of leaders from outside the original thirty showed an even more impressive organizational shrewdness. First, he recruited Celina Meza, the only literate person in the community (aside from Regino's wife, Cándida) as secretary of the directiva. Not only was Celina literate, she was also the daughter of the hamlet's largest landowner. Her father, Gerardo Meza, owned eighty acres and was one of the few middle peasants in the area who showed any sympathy for the campesino organization.

Regino also recruited another landowning peasant, Juan Suazo Martínez. Suazo's involvement signified the incorporation of a large, extended family.[21] Juan Suazo, although only forty-five years old at the time of the conflict, was the head of a kinship group that included sixteen adults in the village. Don Juan was born near Somotillo, in the Pueblos area. When he was a young child, his father migrated to Campuzano, where Juan began his working life as a *vaquero*, helping tend and milk cows. During those early years of labor, he often thought bitterly of how the owners slept so peacefully while at three in the morning he was "hasta el cuello en mierda" (up to his neck in cow dung). His life changed for the better when the owner of a smaller hacienda persuaded his father to change jobs, offering him the free use of pasture and one manzana of land to raise corn and grow plantains. Don Juan remembers the next fifteen years as a time without hunger, in which "el rico tenía buen corazón" (the wealthy man had a good heart), for he supplied the hacienda laborers with land, cheese, and soup bones. Although the laborers received miserable wages, they recognized the land and cheese as payments in return for helping the patrón. Indeed, laborers often harvested four times more corn than their families consumed. They sold their surplus corn and cheese in the town of Chinandega.[22]

Juan Suazo was tired of hacienda life by the early 1940s and began his struggle to become independent. Saving cash by selling his surplus corn and cheese, Suazo bought a team of oxen, which he used to transport other campesinos' goods to the Chinandega market. After two years, he began to rent five manzanas of land and raise corn. By 1948, he had saved enough money to put a down payment on a twenty-five-acre farm and to help his sister do the same. The Suazos purchased the land from Manuel Antonio Baca at C$170 an acre. Juan Suazo thus became a founding member of the hamlet of San José del Obraje.[23]

When Regino Escobar walked up the hill to Juan Suazo's hut, which overlooked Las Cuchillas, he did so to recruit (*conquistar*) a man who had struggled all his life to rise above the laborer's lot and who, "through his own sweat," had acquired enough land to support his family. Escobar had chosen Juan because of the Suazo family's relative size and economic strength. Four Suazos in San José owned a total of forty-one manzanas of land, and eleven other adult family members rented land and worked on haciendas.[24] There was no immediate material reason for Juan Suazo to join a fight against the largest hacienda in Chinandega. Escobar did, however, appeal to Juan's most basic sense of family solidarity—typical of the campesinos in the area—by appointing two landless Suazos to the directiva, despite their lack of involvement in the original occupation and cultivation of Las Cuchillas. He also appealed to Juan's sense of community loyalty, his pragmatism, and his pride. Three decades later, Juan Suazo recounted his meeting with Regino. " 'Look,' Regino said to me, 'it's the people's land, the land belongs to the *comarca*. Dr. Reyes, and he's *Jefe Político*, says so.' So I said to Regino that I'd help out. He made me president of the directiva."[25]

Curiously, Escobar did not appoint himself to the directiva. He made this decision not out of democratic modesty or fear of repression, but out of the realization that he was already a well-esteemed leader. He viewed his directiva as an organizational tool to maintain community solidarity and expected that effective decision making would remain in his hands alone. Regino's choice to stay outside of the formal organizational leadership probably reflected his own sense of informal but absolute power.

If hierarchy was implicit in the organizing process, the level of commitment demanded of the directiva placed certain limits on Escobar's authority. Ramón Cándia, for example, quit his year-round, relatively well paid job as foreman on the Obraje hacienda in order to devote more time to the cause. Clearly he expected some voice in the affairs of the organization in return. Similarly, Juan Suazo, a proud and independent man, would not submit blindly to the leader's authority.

When Escobar sought his help, Dr. Reyes was engaged in negotiations with Dr. Timoteo Baca concerning the sale of eighty acres of land on the eastern boundary of El Obraje. Several hacienda laborers had previously approached

Reyes to intercede against efforts by El Obraje to evict them from the hacienda. Part of El Obraje's transition to cotton cultivation from cattle raising involved the use of all available acreage for the fiber. The campesinos were in the way of that transition. In the words of one witness to the process, "Ya estorbaban" (they had become a nuisance).[26] Nevertheless, the hacienda still needed the laborers to harvest the crop. Motivated by his need to win the good wishes of both El Obraje and the campesinos, Reyes proposed a solution that was advantageous to both parties. The doctor suggested that a new *comarca* (hamlet), similar to San José, be created on the western flank of the hacienda. This would be a cotton pickers' town, providing labor to the neighboring haciendas.[27]

As soon as Regino had formed the directorate, he returned to Chinandega to visit Reyes. The jefe político suggested that they both visit Timoteo Baca, who might be helpful to his San José neighbors. The next day, the two physicians and the campesinos met in the Obraje hacienda. Dr. Baca was indeed cooperative with his San José neighbors. During the meeting, Baca repeated the story about his father's donating the land to the campesinos. Baca stated that he possessed two original maps, in which the *mojones* (boundary stones) showed without a doubt that Las Cuchillas was national land.[28] Baca invited the directiva to see the maps in his Chinandegan office the following week.

The San José campesinos initially profited from Reyes's and Baca's grievances against Campuzano. Yet the split in the agrarian elite, manifested by Reyes's and Baca's animosities, had not reached a point in 1958 where one hacendado would openly mobilize campesinos against another. Thus neither Baca's nor Reyes's offer to help the campesinos to resist Campuzano's claims stood up under pressure from the powerful Alvarado family. The Monday after the meeting, Baca received an unexpected visit from Virgilio Alvarado, the son of Doña Tesla. He stated simply, "If you want to live some more days, you better stop getting mixed up with the campesinos."[29] The threat worked effectively. Baca recounted the story to Reyes, the jefe político. He then apologized for withdrawing his offer to show the maps of Las Cuchillas to the San José group, saying that he wished to live out his days peacefully. The elderly Dr. Baca had inherited an antagonism for Campuzano and had kind intentions toward the campesinos. However, Baca was not about to risk his life on their behalf or even in defense of his family's honor.

Alvarado's threat and Baca's refusal to show the campesinos the crucial maps shocked the San José group. They asked Dr. Reyes for advice. The jefe político was in a difficult position, for his appointment was only temporary.

Moreover, his Guardia position certainly was no guarantee of success in a battle against Campuzano. To provoke the Alvarados' wrath would not be prudent before he had consolidated his position in the Nuevos Ejidos. Rather than risking public involvement with the campesinos, Dr. Reyes stalled Regino, advising him to consult an attorney.

The San José organization was discouraged but agreed to follow Reyes's advice, especially when the jefe político agreed to introduce them to a lawyer. The attorney, Alcídes Acosta, agreed to take the campesinos' case against Campuzano in return for C$6,000 ($857). The San José campesinos' joy at the prospect of imminent victory, however, did not last long. Shortly after initiating court proceedings, Dr. Acosta sent a message to the San José directiva requesting their appearance in his office at eight o'clock the following morning. Dr. Acosta informed them that he was too busy to continue the case. Once more, depression set in as they returned to Reyes's office. The doctor, however, was cheerful. He sent them to Osman Buitrago, a lawyer in León. The campesinos once again took Reyes's advice and delegated Escobar, Juan Suazo, and Ramón Cándia to travel, by horse and train, the seventy kilometers from San José to León.[30]

After contacting Buitrago, the campesinos' fortunes seemed to improve. Buitrago visited the disputed land and studied the legal situation. Only then did the León lawyer agree to take the case in return for ten thousand córdobas, which he would collect only upon actually winning the litigation. After several months of filing land claims in the Chinandegan court with no response from Campuzano, both Buitrago and Escobar became confident of victory. In May 1958, at the beginning of a new planting season, Escobar ordered the members of the directiva to re-mark the boundary lines that separated Las Cuchillas from Campuzano. This was a preliminary step in the reappropriation of the "people's land." According to a newspaper account of the action, the San José campesinos actually divided the land into parcels saying "Aquí voy a sembrar yo, allá vos" (I'll plant here, you plant there).[31] The campesinos acted in accord with what they perceived to be legitimate claims. Doña Tesla and the cotton growers of Campuzano, nevertheless, viewed the action as a provocation. Immediately, Juárez Callejas, a cotton grower, and Doña Tesla called on the Guardia to evict and arrest the campesinos. A patrol soon arrived with tear gas to remove the land invaders; they beat the campesinos with truncheons, and "committed atrocities," in the words of one of their victims. As the Guardia dragged off thirty campesinos, Doña Tesla shouted, "Ustedes son unos abusivos!" (you people are abusive).[32]

Although Major Lagos complied with Campuzano's request for repressive action, he released the campesinos within a day. He then called in Escobar and told him that the campesinos should stay away from the three hundred manzanas of Cuchillas land that were occupied by the cotton company formed by Juárez Callejas and the jailed Ubilla Baca. However, he also informed Escobar that they could legally battle for the remaining five hundred manzanas.[33] Perhaps friendship with Escobar or a conviction about campesino rights influenced Lagos's decision not merely to serve the elite. Yet an economic and political crisis would soon influence the tactics of both the comandante and the campesinos.

An Opening for Popular Struggle, 1958–1959

Since 1954, the ten-thousand-member Sutiava Indian community, located to the immediate west of the city of León, had been battling neighboring *terratenientes* over land claims. The Sutiavas faced the pillars of both oligarchic factions: the Liberal Sacasa family and the Conservative Ingenio San Antonio. San Antonio's industrial expansion required new sources of sugar cane. By the mid-1950s, San Antonio had acquired possession of El Polvón, a sugar plantation that stood on 10,200 acres of largely uncultivated land between ISA and Sutiavan territory.[34] The Indians customarily had used the land claimed by San Antonio for hunting, wood gathering, and subsistence farming.

By the mid-1950s the majority of Sutiavas had become minifundistas or landless seasonal laborers with an urgent need for access to land to increase their incomes to a minimum level of subsistence. In March 1958, bands of several hundred Indians set out nightly to destroy the fences of the Sacasa and Polvón haciendas.[35] The Guardia responded by arresting community leaders. Yet night after night the tightly organized Sutiavas cut barbed wire, an action baptized as the *pique de alambre* (wire fence cutting), which soon came to symbolize campesino resistance to the agrarian elite. The Somoza regime attempted to defuse the movement, which was rapidly gaining the admiration of many Nicaraguans. The government's first move backfired when Argüello Vidaurre, the vice minister of *Gobernación* (in charge of municipal government and Indian affairs), went to Sutiava to negotiate. The community knew that Argüello, a local hacendado, was an actor in the dispute and thus could not be an impartial arbiter. The Sutiavas responded by driving Argüello out of the neighborhood with stones.[36]

The Sutiava rebellion became a national issue, revealing new fissures in an elite whose political divisions were already serious enough to adversely affect the climate for investments.[37] Conservative opposition leader Pedro Joaquín Chamorro, for example, despite his political ties to ISA, offered his solidarity to Sutiava. Chamorro, promoting more progressive politics within the Conservative party, wrote in *La Prensa*, "Sutiava is not a conspiracy, nor is it a plot: it is an explosion which should show Nicaraguans the road to justice."[38] More predictably, students and labor leftists also supported the Sutiavas. Faced with both an Indian rebellion and with major political gains by the opposition, President Luís Somoza acted decisively. He removed the prolandlord mayor of León, who was despised by the Sutiavas, and ordered that the roads and trails the Sutiavas needed for subsistence be opened. In addition, the Guardia released all Sutiava prisoners.[39]

The Somocista state had begun to recognize that the massive agro-export expansion in western Nicaragua (León and Chinandega), spurred in large part by government tax exemptions, credits, and public works projects, had unleashed new social forces. The regime also realized the value of neutralizing those forces and perhaps even using them against the resurgent elite and middle-class opposition movements.

Comandante Salomón Lagos had to reconcile this new political strategy with a complex local situation. Only weeks before he had intervened in the San José conflict he had been forced to cope with by the General Workers' Confederation (CGT) convention in Chinandega. The CGT, Nicaragua's leading labor organization since 1949, had held its convention, attended by Socialist and Somocista delegates from twenty-seven unions, to denounce and defy the regime's unique prohibition against unions in Chinandega.[40] The convention delegates vowed to organize Chinandegan agricultural laborers and passed resolutions calling for the expropriation of latifundios and for the release of Tomás Borge, a student leader recently jailed for his antiregime activities.[41] The unity of leftist and progovernment unionists around such a radical program indicated that the Somocista union activists were moving to the left of the regime. Both factions of the labor movement wished to rebound from the catastrophic decline in membership since 1947. Several weeks later, the labor convention would bear its first fruit; in protest over a wage cut, the workers at the INA cotton processing plant launched the first strike in Chinandega since the 1940s.[42] The strike was preceded by a new conflict in the countryside.

In early April 1958, more than fifty peasants marched together from La Grecia to the Chinandegan office of Colonel Pereira, who had recently returned to his post as jefe político. The peasants came to protest the fencing of the roads they used to travel from their farms to ejidal lands on the slopes of the Chonco volcano, where they planted additional crops and gathered wood. A group of local landlords and businessmen had blocked the roads, which cut through their recently acquired properties, with the apparent intention of forcing the campesinos off the ejidal land. These landowners were linked to the ex-jefe político, Dr. Marcelino Reyes. In league with the Guardia doctor, they were attempting to convert the ejidal land into valuable real estate. But the peasants responded to the threat by organizing a group of three hundred to support their petition. Despite pressure from Reyes, Comandante Lagos refused to act, and Colonel Pereira, rather than jailing the agrarian protesters, consulted directly with Somoza. As in the Sutiavan case two weeks earlier, the president ordered that the campesino roads be reopened.[43]

The development, expansion, and crisis of the agro-export economy in Chinandega and León conditioned this new upsurge of popular movements. In the 1940s the expansion of the sugar industry (primarily ISA) and the development of sesame cultivation for export had triggered the growth of capitalist social relations and the inflation of land values in the region. From 1950 until 1954, spurred by a tremendous jump in world prices induced by the Korean War, cotton production increased by over 500 percent. By 1955, cotton replaced coffee as Nicaragua's leading export, representing 39 percent of total exports.[44] In Chinandega and León, the center of cotton expansion, growers and investors accelerated the transformation of productive relations and the increase in property values. Cotton growers, often in family-based companies, converted land previously used for cattle and basic grains. Finally, cotton producers—one half were tenants and one half owned their land—struggled to expand the agricultural frontier.[45] During the 1950s hired laborers chopped down over five thousand manzanas of jungle and forest land and converted it into cotton fields.[46] Much of that land had previously been in the public domain, and peasants had used it to supplement their livings by wood gathering, hunting, cattle grazing, and corn growing. Conflicting claims to such municipal or communal land were at the root of the agrarian struggles in Chinandega and Sutiava.

The cotton boom came to an end in 1956, with a decline in world prices from $33.40 per quintal (100 lbs.) to $26.81 in 1957 and $21.88 in 1958–1959.[47] Most large cotton growers responded to the drop in prices by pressuring the government for protectionist measures, including generous deferrals on loan payments and more favorable exchange rates for exporters. Such state and private initiatives prevented the price decline from ruining the industry and allowed the elite to maintain its control over land and labor.[48] In fact, although production dropped from 43.9 million kilos in 1955 to 36 million kilos in 1957, and then climbed back to 42 million in 1958, the value of cotton exports declined from $30 million in 1955 to $24.9 million in 1958. The crisis pruned the ranks of cotton growers, eliminating some peasants who had switched to the fiber from basic grains. However, its effects fell disproportionately on laborers, who suffered not only from wage cuts and unemployment but also from the decrease in grain production and the consequent price increase in basic food commodities.[49]

In San José, Comandante Lagos confronted still other symptoms of unrest in the Chinandegan countryside—demands for protection from a prominent cotton grower, Juárez Callejas, and the anger of the threatened landed oligarchy personified by Doña Tesla de Alvarado. Lagos astutely tried to divert the target of the campesino struggle from the cotton grower to the landed oligarch. For although Campuzano had fenced off much of Las Cuchillas, Juárez Callejas was cultivating only 325 manzanas of cotton. The rest of the land remained untilled—a more reasonable campesino objective from Lagos's perspective.

The campesinos, however, did not follow Lagos's friendly orders to leave the cultivated land alone. Influenced by news of the Sutiava struggle and impressed by the quick success of the Grecia campesinos the San José group hoped that their pressure would also force the government to favorably resolve their problem. They also observed the outstanding productivity of Las Cuchillas. Juárez's land produced almost one ton of ginned cotton per manzana, more than double the national average. Finally, nothing had shaken their belief that Las Cuchillas was the people's land.[50]

Despite the upsurge of nearby protest movements and faith in the justice of their cause, the San José group found itself quite alone. When fifty San José campesinos visited Colonel Pereira's office, they met a chilly reception. Juárez Callejas was already in the office, making a convincing case to the jefe político. The cotton grower informed Pereira, in front of the campesinos, that the San José group had no documentary evidence to substantiate their claim and that he possessed a notarized rental agreement. Regino Escobar's reply, restating the story of the Baca gift, sounded weak by contrast. Fredi Callejas, a local journalist, made their story sound fabricated.[51] The campesinos still believed that Timoteo Baca could corroborate the story, but he would not do so out of fear of Campuzano's wrath. For the moment, therefore, the group realized that the authorities respected the rental agreement and not their own undocumented claim.

In May 1958, following their disappointing meeting with Colonel Pereira,

Regino Escobar and the directiva decided to continue pressing their claims through litigation. Survivors of the movement now insist that during the next five months they pursued no extra-legal action. Juárez Callejas, who managed the occupied people's land, claimed, however, that the campesinos constantly harassed him and actually threatened his life.[52] This last allegation may well have been fabricated, but more subtle forms of harassment are not unlikely, for the campesinos were becoming aware of the weaknesses of their adversaries and may have been inclined to take advantage of the conflict between Juárez Callejas and the owners of Campuzano.

Indeed, the usurpers of the people's land presented a significantly less formidable front in May 1958 than they had in the previous year. First, Captain Ubilla Baca, who had led the police force in defense of the landowners' and cotton growers' interests, was in jail on conspiracy charges. Second, the actions of the campesinos had provoked conflict between the latifundistas and the cotton producers, like Juárez, who rented their land. Third, Doña Tesla was well aware that her claim to Las Cuchillas rested on very weak evidence. This evidence consisted of two documents: a 1921 land title with what appeared to be purposefully vague boundaries and a map with the date 1906 clearly penned in at a later time, which showed Las Cuchillas as part of Campuzano.[53] Finally, broad political debate was becoming increasingly supportive of peasant rights and antagonistic toward latifundistas. In response to the Sutiavan protest, Somocista and Conservative deputies introduced land reform bills.[54] Doña Tesla began to think of ways of ridding herself of the San José problem.

Alfonso Juárez was also disappointed with the rental agreement with Campuzano, and, given the decline in cotton prices, he may have become a little disillusioned with the business itself. Although his claim that he feared for his life may have been unfounded, he did consider the San José campesinos to be a nuisance, and he held the owners of Campuzano responsible. Juárez Callejas initiated legal proceedings against them, arguing that his cotton company had not been forewarned of the campesino claims to Las Cuchillas and charging that Campuzano was unwilling to protect its tenants by settling the dispute.[55]

Colonel Rodríguez Somoza and the Fiestas

The San José del Obraje organization was aware of its role in provoking tensions within the enemy camp. Moreover, through their tactics of legal and indirect action, the campesino leaders gained a growing understanding of the world of urban politics. Regino Escobar made nearly biweekly trips to check on Dr. Buitrago's progress toward legalizing the community's claim to Las Cuchillas. After every trip to León, he would give a detailed report of the status of the court case and what he had learned.

Although Escobar may have not contacted the Sutiavas directly, he was certainly aware of the course of their struggle.[56] In 1958, the Sutiavas' struggle was also being carried out in the courts and in the fields. While Alfonso Valle, a former revolutionary general, acted as their lawyer, the elite Guardia force, the Cascos de Acero (the Steel Helmets), occupied the principal haciendas in the region. General Valle, who claimed Sutiavan roots, had constructed an effective case against ISA by showing that the legal boundaries of the recently absorbed El Polvón sugar plantation encompassed only one thousand of the six thousand manzanas claimed by the new owners. On the basis of their legal case, President Somoza granted the Indians an audience.[57] Although Escobar was unsure of the result of the conference, he was impressed that the Sutiavas had successfully taken their case to such a high level.

Regino also became aware of changes within the state power structure and worked out ways to use these changes to his group's advantage. In September 1958, Anastasio Somoza Debayle, Luís's brother and commander in chief of the National Guard, announced important changes in the military. The hard-line Major Aurelio Somarriba replaced Lagos as Guardia comandante in Chinandega. At the same time, Luís Somoza named Colonel Juan José Rodríguez Somoza, his first cousin, as the new comandante of León. Rodríguez Somoza had a well-deserved national reputation as a moderate element within the Guardia. For example, a few weeks earlier, Rodríguez Somoza, while still chief of the Managua transit police, had ordered his police force to cease carrying arms "to avoid any possible tragic abuses of authority."[58] Regino demonstrated his understanding of the significance of the appointments by visiting the new comandante of León in order to present the case of the San José campesinos.

In keeping with his moderate approach, Rodríguez Somoza was extremely polite and solicitous to Regino. After inquiring as specifically as possible into the nature of the dispute, he ordered a meeting of Doña Tesla, the Campuzano lawyer, and Buitrago. Significantly, he stipulated that the meeting take place at Regino's *ranchito* (hut) in San José.[59] The San José campesinos were optimistic about the meeting. They thought it quite important that the Colonel had chosen Regino's ranchito, which bordered Las Cuchillas, as the location for the meeting. The families prepared food and purchased rum and fireworks and the directiva, with the ostensible purpose of providing a more festive atmosphere, but probably also as a symbolic act of provocation, cleared an additional portion of Las Cuchillas land that bordered Regino's hut.

Two weeks later, in October 1958, Rodríguez, Buitrago, Doña Tesla, her lawyer Meza Salorío, and two uninvited guests arrived in San José, where one hundred campesinos greeted them. Doña Tesla had brought along Edmundo Deshon, a Chinandegan landlord and cotton grower and a member of a powerful Liberal family, along with his lawyer, Hugo Astacio Cabrera. The young lawyer had an outstanding reputation both as an attorney and as a leader of the anti-Somocista Partido Liberal Independiente, and he had done some prison time following the assassination of Somoza García in 1956. Juan Suazo knew Astacio as a man who would defend poor campesinos and lend them money without interest.[60] He was therefore surprised to learn that Astacio was helping Doña Tesla sell the unrented portion of Las Cuchillas to Deshon.

Before the negotiations began, the campesinos offered their guests ample food and liquor. Since Colonel Rodríguez and Dr. Buitrago had imbibed a good deal of liquor, Escobar decided to take the initiative. He directly addressed the owner of Campuzano. "Look, Doña Tesla, we don't want to take away any of your land. Why don't you just tell us the mojones [boundary markers] of Campuzano, on this side." Doña Tesla responded immediately, citing the boundary markers as "La Barquita," "Tololo," and "Laguna Seca." Regino Escobar jumped to his feet and looked straight at the latifundista, but addressed all those present. "So there's nothing to discuss, Doña Tesla. We're not touching one inch of your property. These lands belong to us. You, yourself, are saying so!"[61]

The campesinos shouted their approval, for Doña Tesla had described the very mojones that separated the latifundia from the people's land. Doña Tesla's lawyer pleaded for calm. Then, while leaning towards Comandante Rodríguez Somoza, he stated, "Look, you can't take what the señora said seriously, she's very nervous."[62] Unfortunately for the campesinos, their two allies were too drunk to take advantage of Regino's verbal victory over Doña Tesla. With a profound sense of disillusionment and remorse, they still lament today, "If only the colonel had said something, we would have taken over the land, right then and there."[63] Meza y Salorío motioned to his contingent that it was time to depart. As Edmundo Deshon started to follow the others, the intoxicated colonel tugged at his arm. "Why do you get involved in this business, when you know the land belongs to the campesinos?" Deshon replied to the colonel only with "a diabolic grin."[64]

The meeting was a crucial turning point in the way San José campesinos thought about their struggle, their allies, and their oligarchic antagonists. Although heavy drinking is almost invariably condoned by male residents of the area, drunkenness at such a crucial moment at the very least demystified the comandante and the lawyer. However, a far more important demystification process took place in front of Regino's Escobar's thatched hut. Escobar had, once again, demonstrated to his people why he was their leader. He had outwitted the oligarch, who until that moment had appeared in their lives always surrounded by armed Guardias. Escobar had caught her off guard, forcing her to admit the truth about Las Cuchillas, a truth that reinforced their convictions. Not only was the oligarch a land robber, but also she had been outwitted by a campesino. If their intoxicated allies had shown that they were only human, Doña Tesla had revealed to the campesinos that what they had to fear from their antagonists was not superior "breeding" or education but rather their privileged access to power.

The meeting in San José del Obraje unnerved Doña Tesla and her lawyer. Tesla Alvarado's admission and the colonel's sympathies forced them into a precarious position. They sent word for Escobar to come to Chinandega to negotiate. Doña Tesla offered to sell Las Cuchillas for the low price of one hundred córdobas per manzana (roughly ten dollars an acre), perhaps one-quarter of its market value. Escobar and Justo Vega, another campesino leader, briefly discussed the proposal. Vega argued that Buitrago's legal fees alone could buy one hundred manzanas and suggested that they demand reasonable installment payments for the rest. Escobar disagreed sharply. He then informed Tesla and Meza that they did not have any right to sell the land, as it belonged to the community of San José del Obraje.

When the two campesino leaders arrived back in San José, Escobar was not interested in discussing the offer with the rest of the directiva. The others made it clear that they thought the deal was worth considering. Escobar insisted that it was absurd for the campesinos to buy back their own land and that they must fight to win it back. Escobar's recently enhanced prestige and his appeal to the dignity of the campesinos finally convinced the directiva to accept his decision. This decision, indeed, seems to have been a moment of qualitative change in the consciousness of Regino Escobar and the San José campesinos. Until then, the campesinos had justified their struggle in terms of their need for land to cultivate in order to survive the cotton dead season. The campesinos would continue to describe their struggle strictly in terms of *necesidad*. But when the organization accepted Escobar's decision to reject the practical alternative to buy the land, the campesinos added to the category of necessity, not only the struggle for subsistence, but also the notion of social justice.

Regino Escobar acted as a catalyst in the creation of this new meaning of necessity. Although even he probably only came to his new understanding as a result of his confrontation with Doña Tesla—in which a member of the landed elite revealed the real source of her wealth and power and Escobar, in turn, revealed the worth of the community—that experience, shared by the other campesinos, convinced him that their fight must be for land *and* dignity. The other campesinos accepted this vision, in part because Escobar shamed them. But their recent collective experiences helped them to reach a plateau of understanding that allowed them to see that Escobar was indeed right.[65]

Campuzano was outraged by Escobar's rejection of the deal and prepared a counterattack. Two days later, Astacio, newly appointed as lawyer and opposition leader, arrived in San José del Obraje with a platoon of Guardia and marched directly to Regino Escobar's hut. Immediately, a crowd followed the soldiers to Escobar's hut to inquire what they wanted. Upon learning that Escobar was visiting Colonel Rodríguez, Astacio ordered the Guardia to arrest the entire community on trespassing charges for their participation in clearing the two acres of Campuzano land bordering Escobar's hut. The Guardia bound all of them together and marched them for several kilometers to the Deshon family's hacienda, La Laguna. There they left the women, children, and elderly people and took the twenty adult males off to jail in Chinandega.[66] Once the rest of the community got word to Colonel Rodríguez, he contacted the Chinandegan comandante, Somarriba, and informed him that the cleared acres of land were in litigation and that nobody could be arrested for trespassing. Somarriba released the prisoners, but within a week Astacio returned to San José with a dozen Guardia and arrested Regino Escobar and three others. Once again, Rodríguez obtained their release after a short prison stay.[67]

Astacio's strategy apparently aimed at heightening the tension between moderates and hardliners within the Guardia. By forcing Rodríguez to repeatedly intervene against the orders of the Chinandegan comandante and by drawing the enmity of Guardia hardliners, Astacio perhaps hoped to isolate and weaken Rodríguez as a powerful ally of the campesinos.[68]

As part of this aggressive strategy, Deshon, the new de facto owner of Las Cuchillas, put up barbed wire fences in the hope of keeping out the San José del Obraje residents.[69] The San José organization considered the fences to be an affront, a provocation, and a direct assault on their livelihood. The fences denied them access to the Palomino and Royal estuaries, where, especially during the cotton dead season, the campesinos fished and extracted mangrove. These activities were vital to fulfill the minimal dietary and monetary needs of the seasonal laborers. In their eyes, Deshon had committed an act of violence against the San José community.

The campesinos retaliated by knocking down the fence posts during the night. In response, Deshon persuaded the Chinandegan Guardia to establish a command post on the occupied land.[70] Escobar and the directiva realized that further action against Deshon's fences would involve an attack on the Guardia. Although their situation was desperate, their reasoning was not. Just as Astacio Cabrera and Campuzano had tried to manipulate the state and the Guardia, the campesinos tried to use the divisions among the elite to further their own ends. Although attacking the Guardia would not elicit sympathy from the regime, they expected a degree of tolerance because of the political pressures from the opposition. Finally, their broadened understanding of necesidad and their need to defend their rights impelled the San José campesinos to direct action.

The first Saturday that the soldiers left Deshon's land to collect their pay in Chinandega, a group of one hundred San José campesinos broke through the barbed wire fence and marched to the command post.[71] They ordered a frightened Deshon employee to remove the soldiers' belongings, then they burned the command post. The campesinos thus symbolically reenacted the expropriation of the land and created a powerful image of retribution for the scorched campesino huts left by the capitalists' expansion in the countryside.

The Chinandegan elite, along with its Guardia allies, reacted to the retributive image with horror and anger. The next day, they sent the soldiers back to San José to arrest the campesino leadership and teach them a lesson in retribution. The Guardia tied Regino, Suazo, Vega, and Cándia to horses and dragged them for fifteen kilometers through Campuzano, stopping in the town of Tonalá. There the prisoners spent the night in jail. One wonders why the Guardia took them through Tonalá instead of straight to Chinandega. Perhaps it was to serve as a warning to the residents of that misery-ridden, cotton pickers' town. The spectacle of the bound, tortured campesinos, personal acquaintances of the Tonaleños, did make a lasting impression—not of fear, but of anger. That night many Tonaleños brought food to the jailed campesinos, beginning a long relationship of solidarity.[72]

Colonel Rodríguez was furious when he learned of the attack on the Guardia post. Nevertheless, the León comandante once again exerted his authority to obtain the campesinos' release from prison. When they were freed, he ordered them to report to León, where he reprimanded them but also promised them an audience with President Luís Somoza.

Regino then began to see the colonel's family ties as a strong motive for turning their legal case over to Rodríguez and dropping Buitrago.[73] Fredi Callejas (the journalist who had written negatively about the May 1958 incident) strongly influenced Regino's reasoning. Callejas insisted that Buitrago was stealing the organization's money and failing to perform his legal work on their behalf. It is difficult to ascertain why Regino let himself be manipulated by the journalist. Callejas seems to have been one of a peculiar breed who inhabited the landscape of Somocista Nicaragua: a man who appeared to back the campesinos but with intimate ties to the elite; both a member of the opposition and a Somocista. He protested so vehemently in favor of workers when acting as labor inspector in 1956 that he was thrown in jail.[74] Now he worked with the elite. Finally, he was so corrupt and opportunistic that he could not distinguish between his scheming fantasies and reality. Such was the man, who, in league with Deshon, won the confidence of the leader of the San José campesinos.

Juan Suazo and Ramón Cándia were shocked by Regino's decision to fire Dr. Buitrago, who had just assured them that the case was nearly won. Furthermore, neither Callejas nor Escobar could produce any evidence to substantiate the claim of dishonesty. When Suazo and Cándia insisted on presenting their point of view to the community assembly, Escobar expelled them from the directiva, producing the first significant division in the campesino ranks. The entire Suazo clan; José González, an original member of the directiva and owner of two and one-half manzanas; Ramón Cándia's family; and Juan Suazo's neighbors all withdrew from the organization.[75] They formed an informal parallel organization of about twenty-five adults—slightly less than one-half the size of Escobar's group.

Both factions were led by smallholders, minifundistas, and laborers. Thus, sociological differences had less to do with the division than the authoritarian structure of Escobar's organization. From its birth, Escobar courageously defended the campesinos' rights and played a key role in developing their consciousness. However, his very success at resisting and dealing with the power structure served to reinforce his own authoritarianism. Escobar's undisputed power over the organization thus allowed Fredi Callejas to subvert the entire organization by conquering its leader.

Suazo and Cándia attempted to defend the integrity of the organization against outside usurpation. While it went against their moral code to call Buitrago a thief and to hire the colonel in his place, Suazo and Cándia also felt it was wrong that after more than a year of collective sacrifices Escobar should continue as dictator of the organization. Nevertheless, the majority of the San José campesinos continued to support Escobar.

Unfortunately, Regino was guilty not only of authoritarianism but also of misreading a complex political situation. In early April, the anti-Somocista opposition began to make its presence felt in Chinandega. Leftist students painted black crosses on prominent Somocista houses and left "Viva Sandino" slashed across the Somocista Liberal party headquarters. While ideologically divided, all branches of the opposition were inspired by the Cuban revolution and many planned to initiate guerrilla warfare against the regime.[76]

As the regime prepared for battle with the opposition, the Sutiavas rebelled again. San Antonio continued to fence off land, and the prominent Somocista owners of the hacienda Nagualapa had women arrested for picking from the plantation a plant used only for wrapping tamales. On the night of May 5, 1959, at the start of the rainy season, the Indians initiated their offensive. First, they invaded the land occupied by San Antonio. They rounded up thirty ISA workers and ordered them to cut two kilometers of barbed wire fences.[77] Groups of 50 to 250 armed Sutiavas simultaneously cut fences on Nagualapa and other haciendas that encroached on the community's territory.

President Somoza immediately called his cousin Colonel Rodríguez to Managua, while Captain Juan Angel López acted as Rodríguez's substitute in León. Declaring that the Sutiava movement was Communist, López crushed the Indian organization with an unprecedented viciousness. Arresting and torturing Sutiavan leaders, he threatened that he would "leave Indians hanging by the same barbed wire that they cut."[78] But before López had a chance to fulfill his threat, Guardia superiors ordered him to release the Indian prisoners.

Several days later, however, Captain López boldly arrested his superior, Rodríguez Somoza, thus removing the most valued ally of the Sutiavas and the San José campesinos.[79] Anastasio Somoza Debayle, the President's brother and chief of the Guardia, responded to López's coup by arresting both López and Rodríguez Somoza.[80] However, Anastasio Somoza's hardline sympathies became clear within two weeks. In response to a revitalized student movement, to campesino agitation in León and Chinandega, and to the organization of an anti-Somocista guerrilla group in neighboring Costa Rica, Somoza declared a state of emergency, suspending all constitutional guarantees. Symbolic of the regime's hard turn to the right, the Guardia promoted Juan Angel López to the rank of major.[81] López would go on to become the single most infamous man in the memory of Chinandegan campesinos.

From Campesinos to Indians

Although it is doubtful that Regino admitted his error in turning the campesinos' case over to Colonel Rodríguez, an error highlighted now by the dramatic changes in León, he did make some friendly overtures to Suazo and Cándia. The campesinos held an assembly, attended by the entire community, in order to evaluate the newly unfavorable situation. Despite the loss of their ally, the assembly voted unanimously to resume direct action against Campuzano. The militant example of the Sutiavas clearly influenced their decision, but even more importantly they were reminded by the May rains that only the elite would benefit from nature's bounty: the campesinos had neither jobs (the cotton harvest had ended) nor land to cultivate.

On the night of May 18, 1959, two days after López deposed Rodríguez Somoza, some eighty campesinos knocked down all the barbed wire fences that blocked the paths to the estuaries.[82] Several hours later, the campesinos, described in *La Prensa* as "shouting, drunken mobs," knocked down over two thousand meters of fences.[83] The raid through Las Cuchillas represented an important step in the campesinos' organizational development, for it was based on a democratically made decision that reunited the two factions. Moreover, the decision did not depend on the support of elite allies. The landed elite did not, however, think so highly of the action. The next morning, the Guardia combed the comarca, rounding up all the leaders they could find and providing them with their now-customary lessons in brutality. But the Guardia found no evidence that would place the leaders at the scene of the crime. Aristides Acosta, now a Chinandegan judge and an opposition leader, ordered the release of the prisoners less than a week after their arrest. Fredi Callejas, the man who turned Regino away from their attorney, Buitrago, played a curious role in the incident. Callejas apparently had nothing to do with planning the action, but he wrote two favorable articles about the San José case after the campesinos were jailed. He also put the organization in contact with the Confederación General de Trabajadores (CGT).[84]

In his articles, Callejas emphasized the campesinos' dependence on the estuaries for food and mangrove bark. He also retold the story of the Baca land donation to the campesinos, which he had previously scorned. Most significantly, Callejas referred to the San José organization as a "Comunidad Indígena" (Indian community) and to Escobar and Juan Suazo as "Indios." Callejas's definition of the San José campesinos as Indians was later accepted and reiterated by Escobar and by the CGT in their public declarations about the San José struggle. Escobar's acceptance of the Indian definition was indeed surprising, given that no San José campesino had ever defined him or herself as an Indian. Escobar probably reasoned that the Sutiavas' relative success derived from their claim to be Indians with historic rights to the land. Moreover, in January 1959, the Somocista-dominated CGT had initiated a national campaign in defense of the Comunidades Indígenas in the northern zones of Nicaragua.[85] The fictitious creation of the Comunidad Indígena del Obraje thus allowed the labor federation to aid the San José campesinos without antagonizing the regime, for, in Somocista discourse, Indians embodied the soul of the Nicaraguan people and were thus worthy of protection and esteem. Finally, in the eyes of the landed elite, the San José del Obraje campesinos were, in fact, "Indios." The "white" elite both inside and outside the regime looked with scorn at the campesinos around them and voiced that scorn in the word "Indio"—a word that combined an accurate description of the rural lower classes' ethnic extraction with racial and class hostility. Whether or not Callejas really believed that the campesinos were Indios, Escobar and the CGT surely recognized the political usefulness of playing on the elite's racist perception of the Obraje community. As Hobsbawm and Martínez-Alier have observed in other contexts, the transformation of campesinos into Indians was part of Escobar's "search for common ground" with the authorities.[86]

In fact, during the 1950s there were few visible differences between the Sutiava Indians and the San José del Obraje campesinos. They were both monolingual speakers of roughly the same Spanish dialect. They dressed in similar fashion. The women of the two communities carried *pailas* on their heads to transport food. The men farmed, hunted, and fished using similar techniques. Finally, both groups carried the physical features of both Indians and Europeans.[87] Nevertheless, the class structures and experiences of the communities conditioned distinct evolutions of the two agrarian movements. Although smallholding peasants played an important role in the San José leadership, its rank and file was landless. On the contrary, some 40 percent of the Sutiavas still farmed their own land in the 1950s. It was the Sutiavas' multiclass alliance, welded together by an ethnic community, that distinguished it from the Chinandegan movement. One Sutiavan activist expressed this difference explicitly. "All of us had the right to Sutiava's land. We never asked who had and who didn't have land. Maybe they did in Chinandega, but here in Sutiava it was a question of the *derechos* (rights) of the whole people."[88]

These derechos, deeply ingrained in the Sutiavan view of history and sustained by carefully guarded colonial documents, unified different Sutiavan classes in opposition to the *ladino* (non-Indian) elite. Such an alliance enriched the movement ideologically, strengthened it organizationally, and made it extremely difficult for the regime to contain the Sutiavas. In San José del Obraje, a similar, if less tradition-bound, notion of common rights united the community—in particular, their right to "the people's land"—but it failed to glue them together into a broad-based alliance. Despite smallholder leaders and common antagonists, the San José campesinos never effectively united with the smallholders in area villages such as La Grecia. Such an alliance perhaps required an explicit ethnic dimension such as existed in Sutiava—a collective historical vision of the elite's usurpation of their communal lands. In Sutiava, for example, an understanding of ethnic unity predated the agrarian movement. The Indians recreated their ethnic unity by struggling to overcome their internal class differences in combat against the elite who defined them all as Indios.

Two or three generations earlier the San José campesinos would have considered themselves Indians, but the breakup of their original communities—La Grecia and Los Pueblos—during the Zelaya epoch had effectively buried their sense of indigenous identity.[89] Inspired by the Sutiavas' remarkably cohesive organization and eager to gain CGT support, Escobar attempted to recreate this lost sense of indigenous identity by labeling himself and his colleagues Indios. However, Escobar apparently never spoke to the community about its new, public indigenous identity. The leader was probably afraid that the campesinos would interpret the new denomination as an insult. Nevertheless, within a year the San José campesinos would come to understand and value the fact that they were indeed descendants of Indians who had been dispossessed by the agrarian elite during the 1890s.

Regino Escobar's unilateral decision to redefine his people as Indios also reveals the campesinos' vulnerability to manipulation by leaders and outsiders. In addition to the weakness of the authoritarian organizational structure of the San José movement, the campesinos' need for urban allies made them vulnerable to outside control. Finally, nothing made the campesinos more vulnerable to manipulation than their illiteracy. The near total illiteracy of the San José del Obraje community reflected a scandalous level of social neglect throughout the Nicaraguan countryside. In the 1950s over 80 percent of the rural adult population was illiterate. In 1959, Ramiro Gurdian, a leading cotton exporter, called for legislation, which would remedy the illiteracy problem. His proposed legislation, quite expressive of the elite's social vision, authorized landlords to pay only one-half of a minimum wage (which was to be established) to those campesinos who failed to learn to read![90]

In its battle against San José, campesino illiteracy became Campuzano's key weapon. In July 1959, after Suazo, Escobar, and Vega's latest period of incarceration, Hugo Astacio and Deshon filed new charges of criminal trespass and destruction of property against the campesino leadership and served a written summons for the campesinos to appear in court. Following Callejas's misleading advice, Escobar, Suazo, and Vega ignored the summons, which, after all, they could not read. Several weeks later, the Guardia arrested the three leaders for refusing to appear in court. Once in jail, Astacio offered to drop the charges in return for a signed statement promising to respect Deshon's property. Callejas paid daily visits to the prison cell. He continually urged the trusting Regino Escobar to sign as the only way to avoid a lengthy prison term. Juan Suazo remembers the experience bitterly. He argued constantly with Callejas and Escobar, blamed them for the jailing, and argued that they would sell out the campesino struggle by signing the paper. "This is your harvest," he told the San José leader.[91] Fredi Callejas' deception and the campesinos' illiteracy contributed to the animosity between the two leaders, but their signing a paper, the text of which had to be read to them, created far more serious problems for the movement. Juan Suazo preferred to risk a long jail term rather than oblige the organization to recognize the expropriation of Las Cuchillas. But once Regino gave in to Callejas's prodding, Juan Suazo and Justo Vega considered it pointless to hold out.[92] After eighteen days, the three left jail, believing themselves severely constrained in their struggle.

It is important to understand the meaning of the signed document for the campesino leaders. Escobar and Suazo's high esteem for documents and agreements created an inordinate respect for their own coerced signatures. At the time, they did not realize that Astacio Cabrera had blackmailed them. To the campesino activists, their signatures symbolized crippling defeat, a defeat already suffered on the battlefield outside the prison walls. Nonetheless, through that defeat the San José campesinos would come to understand the likes of Dr. Reyes, Doña Tesla, Fredi Callejas, Hugo Astacio, and Mundo Deshon. As they learned about the inner workings of the agrarian elite and the Somocista power structure, they also learned the futility of alliances with *las autoridades*. They then grew to recognize the necessity of forsaking their immediate goal—Las Cuchillas—in order to organize a broader campesino movement capable of remaking the social fabric of rural Chinandega.

5

Elite Divisions and Campesino Unity: Toward a Community-Rooted Class Perspective, 1959–1961

Class hatred is arising.
—*La Prensa*, February 15, 1961

Between 1959 and 1961, the Somocista regime continued to maintain contradictory relations with the campesinos. As before, the government alternated between repressive and co-optive policies toward the agrarian protest movement. During the same period, the continual growth of the campesino movement, however, exacerbated intra-elite fissures. These divisions, in turn, contributed to the development among the campesinos of a community-rooted class perspective. Although many campesinos still considered patron-client relations to be viable, the San José militants began to move away from dependency on elite patrons and toward more autonomous modes of consciousness and struggle. Regino Escobar and Juan Suazo, although still restrained from occupying Las Cuchillas by their own coerced signatures, began to see how they could effectively carry on a wider campesino struggle. The San José militants began to view themselves as part of a class in conflict with another class, the agrarian elite. Thus they helped to organize a broader agrarian protest movement. Nonetheless, not everyone in that broader movement shared the "same learning curve of experience," so they exhibited markedly different forms of consciousness. As the elite divided still further and the movement expanded, the San José militants sought the aid of the revitalized Confederación General de Trabajadores (CGT). Although the San José leaders had to sacrifice some of their autonomy, this horizontal alliance further broadened the campesino movement as a whole, as well as its class perspective.

In September 1959, Andrés Ruíz Escorcia, secretary of conflicts of the CGT, made his first trip to San José del Obraje.[1] Escorcia was accompanied by CGT chief Roberto González and by their guide, Fredi Callejas. The CGT leaders were ignorant of Fredi's role in the July arrests of the San José campesinos; they knew of him only as a progressive former labor inspector in Chinandega. They also did not understand the campesinos' division and demoralization. Unbeknownst to them as they sat down for lunch with Fredi

Callejas and Regino Escobar, Juan Suazo and Ramón Cándia were walking through the cotton fields of Deshon's Llano Verde. In an attempt to reconstruct a mental map of the precotton landscape, Suazo and Cándia searched the fields for remains of the old mojones, the boundary stones torn down by Deshon's laborers.[2] Escorcia and González obtained only a partial version of the San José struggle from Escobar and Callejas. Nonetheless they were impressed with their story and repeated Escobar's version of Baca's gift in their official report. Moreover, the CGT promised its full support to the "indigenous struggle" for land and fishing rights on the Estero Real.[3] Notwithstanding its pledge, however, the Somocista-controlled union confederation maintained only superficial contact with the San José campesinos until February 1961.

A week after the CGT visit and declaration of solidarity, Dr. Hugo Astacio Cabrera sent a letter to the newspapers presenting evidence that Baca had not given Las Cuchillas to the campesinos but had attempted to steal the land from the indigenous Cofradía (lay brotherhood) de Santa Ana. Less convincingly, Astacio argued that Manuel Balladares, jefe político in Chinandega from 1893 to 1895, legally purchased the land from the same Cofradía. The rest of the lawyer's case consisted of showing how the land passed through a series of legitimate sales from Balladares into the hands of Doña Tesla and Deshon. The lawyer added that no Indian community currently existed in San José del Obraje.[4]

Astacio's legal counterattack was only one aspect of a strategy to defeat the San José movement. Simultaneously, Fredi Callejas publicly announced his support for his secret patron, Deshon, against his erstwhile allies, the San José campesinos. Of even greater significance, Callejas approvingly quoted Astacio to the effect that the "real struggle of the campesinos" was to take back the ejidal land occupied by Marcelino Reyes and his associates. Dr. Astacio added that "the Municipal government has the obligation to file suit for one thousand manzanas of its land that Dr. Reyes claimed while he was jefe político one year ago."[5] By endorsing the campesinos' right to the ejidos, the Campuzano group (the Alvarados, the Deshons, and Astacio, who thanks to Doña Tesla, was now a landowner) were giving up any hope for the land which the hacienda first claimed in 1918. The Campuzano owners were willing to make this sacrifice and attack another elite group in order to eliminate the campesino threat from San José del Obraje. By transforming the image of Campuzano from oligarchic oppressors into defenders of the campesinos, they hoped to weaken San José's case, and by creating another target for the movement, they hoped to deflect the campesinos' attempt to reclaim Las Cuchillas. Moreover, the great fertility of Las Cuchillas demanded the sacrifice of the less fertile, poorly irrigated, and hilly land under dispute with Reyes. Finally, it appeared that Campuzano would lose the court case against Reyes, precisely because the Guardia physician presented documents showing that the land did not belong to the hacienda but had been awarded to the poor peasants of Chinandega by Congress in 1916, to be distributed in fifty-manzana plots. Dr. Reyes, of course, was neither poor nor a peasant, and he had appropriated one thousand manzanas. Thus, Campuzano made the best of an unfortunate situation, even if its personal interest conflicted with the general interests of the Chinandegan elite and compromised its unity in the face of the agrarian protest movement.

This intra-elite conflict had some of the aura of class conflict between a nascent agrarian bourgeoisie (the Reyes group) and a semifeudal, landed oligarchy (Campuzano). But the protagonists only superficially fit such a structural mold. By 1959, Campuzano was on a rapid Prussian-style march to agro-export capitalism.[6] The middle-peasant and professional group headed by Reyes (see Table 1) actually received its major source of income from land rent paid by campesinos, often considered a feudal form of surplus appropria-

Table 1. The Ejidatarios: Antagonists of the Rancherías Campesinos

Name	Manzanas of Ejidos	Other Properties
T. Aguilar	150	85 mz.
R. Alvarado	100	200 mz.
E. Cáceres	100	250 mz.
M. Cáceres	200	200 mz., 2 urban properties
A. Castillo	75	2 urban properties
A. Delgado	200	reportedly "a millionaire"
D. Escobar	100	75 mz.
A. Méndez	100	several rural properties
T. Pérez	200	40 mz.
M. Reyes and 5 family members	1,000	farm and various urban properties
M. Tercero	200	400 mz.

Source: Study by CGT official Leonídas Morales, 1961, in CGT archives, and *La Prensa*, October 31, 1961.
Note: 1 manzana = 1.7 acres.

tion.[7] Still, the socioeconomic gulf between the two groups did fuel the conflict.

The Reyes group's political base was made up of local smallholders and Chinandegan political bosses. Their support among local peasants came in part out of Reyes' manipulation of anti-oligarchic sentiments. Yet, eight of the sixteen *ejidatarios* were local peasants with middle-sized farms who had good relations with their poorer neighbors and could count on limited support against the attacks from Campuzano. Over forty local peasant proprietors, for example, signed a letter in support of Reyes in February 1960.[8]

The Guardia doctor's chief political allies in Chinandega also provided a measure of popular support. Irma Guerrero and Ernesto Pereira represented the remnants of the obrerista wing of the Partido Liberal Nacionalista (PLN), or the Liberal party.[9] By the 1950s, several such obreristas, formerly social-democratic antagonists of the oligarchy, had enriched themselves while in governmental office. Yet they continued to use anti-oligarchic rhetoric and thus had to make minimal concessions to the working class and to peasant demands in order to maintain a degree of credibility. Like the peasants allied with Reyes, the obreristas also brought a measure of genuine popular support to the fight against Campuzano.

The Deshons and the Alvarados were also prominent members of the Liberal party.[10] The Campuzano group was concerned primarily with using its influence in the Somocista regime to obtain economic favors and political protection. The family members, well placed in the local and national bureaucracy, constituted a formidable political group. Campuzano's attack on the Reyes group thus set off a factional battle with the obrerista leaders of the Chinandegan Liberal party.

The Campuzano group cared little for their petty bourgeois allies in the development of agro-export capitalism. Despite their modern capitalist methods of production, the Alvarados and Deshons maintained a class consciousness that blended harmoniously with the Conservative oligarchy and excluded petty bourgeois Somocista politicians. Virgilio Alvarado, Doña Tesla's only son, expressed this sense of elite class solidarity when he wrote to Pedro Joaquín Chamorro, a member of the Conservative oligarchy who was nonetheless sympathetic to the campesino cause, "It is perhaps understandable that Sr. González [of the CGT], who knows nothing of our family, makes such inconsiderate statements about a lady [Doña Tesla], but it is quite strange indeed that you, who are my friend and belong to my same *sociedad*, could publish such calumnies."[11]

Alvarado's talk of *nuestra sociedad* (our society) surely angered nouveau riche Liberals who were excluded from such elite status and thus contributed to the split in the Chinandegan agrarian bourgeoisie. The Reyes group strove to form a part of that agrarian elite, and they shared fundamental interests with the oligarchy: to maintain low wages and demobilize the campesino movement. In this sense, Campuzano's call for the campesinos to struggle against the Reyes group was a betrayal of the collective interest of the agrarian bourgeoisie. The split in the agrarian elite did not derive from the antagonisms of separate classes, but rather it represented a conflict between two factions of the same emergent class. The active legacy of oligarchic and obrerista ideology dangerously exacerbated that fissure.

While the elite split up before their eyes, Regino Escobar and Juan Suazo reunited the two factions of the San José organization. The San José campesinos observed the new Campuzano strategy with great interest and understanding. They did not believe for a moment that Doña Tesla and Deshon had become benevolent overnight. They recognized that the call for redistributing the ejidos was a diversionary tactic. Recalling Reyes's early support of their efforts against Campuzano, they sympathized with his new convictions, but they no longer trusted him. Reyes had lost their trust by failing to follow through on their case against the oligarchs and by fencing off the ejidal roads. Thus the San José campesinos adopted a cautious neutrality in the face of Campuzano's efforts to stir up an agrarian insurgency against Reyes.

Although Dr. Astacio's destruction of the story of Baca's donation made the campesinos feel somewhat foolish, it also forced them to reconsider their political justification for their claim to Las Cuchillas. The Baca story had never been a significant part of their legal case, nor had it been the foundation of their renewed belief in their rights. Juan Suazo, to cite one example, felt that the story would help their struggle but never believed in its veracity. At the same time, Astacio's documentary disproof of the gift also recounted something of the history of the Cofradía de Santa Ana. In Nicaragua, cofradías were primarily indigenous lay fraternities, politically and economically powerful during the colonial era. Until the 1890s, the Cofradía de Santa Ana had owned large sections of central Chinandega (including Campuzano). The cofradía ownership of what became Campuzano's property thus provided an historical underpinning to Escobar's previous efforts to identify the San José campesinos as Indians.

The indigenous background of the disputed land intrigued the CGT leader, Escorcia, who urged the campesinos to forge a cofradía identity to use against

Campuzano. Escorcia's close reading of Astacio's document suggested that Manuel Balladares, the legitimate buyer according to the lawyer's interpretation, had actually usurped Las Cuchillas. When Balladares had purchased the cofradía's property, known as La Virgen, he had also expropriated the eight hundred manzanas of land to the east, which would eventually become the focus of the campesino rebellion.[12] At the time, Escorcia and the San José campesinos were unaware that Balladares's fraudulent purchase of La Virgen had provoked an unsuccessful rebellion by the last of the Chinandegan Indians in the late 1880s.

Thus, in 1959 the descendants of Chinandegan Indians, who still lived and worked in miserable circumstances, decided to adopt the mantle of the cofradía to justify their fight for that same strip of land. Throughout 1960, the San José leadership, reconstituted as the Cofradía de Santa Ana, continued to work through legal and government channels. Thanks to some assistance from the CGT, the campesinos obtained a verbal commitment of support from the ministers of development and agriculture. The governmental ministries even ordered surveyors to measure the land. Although the surveyors lost their way on the long bureaucratic highway from Managua to San José del Obraje, the campesinos had not yet exhausted their options.[13]

The campesinos based their identity as members of an indigenous cofradía on the very 1895 court case that Astacio had used against them. While not actually practicing cofradía rites, they began to consider themselves legitimate heirs of their indigenous forebears. Moreover, a form of folk Catholicism played an increasingly important role in their community life. Regino Escobar had convinced his fellow campesinos to adopt San Martín de Porras, known in Central America as *el negro* as the patron saint of the community. This was not a frivolous adoption, for the Obraje campesinos soon converted this nonwhite figure into "the defender of the community." They built a small chapel for San Martín and appointed Juan Suazo's sister as its *mayordoma* (caretaker). In March of each year the village celebrated their patron saint's day. Not only did San Martín help maintain communal bonds, his image also lent an aura of sacredness to their struggle. Their devoutness to San Martín, however, did not open any of the right holy doors. Regino and Juan Suazo quite sincerely asked for and expected aid from the Catholic church.[14] They specifically asked Padre Andrade of the Santa Ana Church in Chinandega to recognize their cofradía and to help them recover their land. After a visit from Dr. Astacio, Padre Andrade, in a gesture typical of the Nicaraguan clergy of the epoch, wrote a public letter to Deshon that concluded, "Consequently, as the new possessor of that land [Las Cuchillas] you are its absolute owner."[15] The Padre's letter diminished the ardor of the cofradía, but the campesinos continued to base their appeals to the authorities on the legacy of the aggrieved Cofradía de Santa Ana.

Toward a Community-Rooted Class Perspective

From 1957 to 1961 the inhabitants of San José del Obraje developed a consciousness of themselves as campesinos in struggle with the agrarian elite. Their understanding of the world of agrarian capitalism and their commitment to change placed the San José community in the vanguard of a broader protest movement. By 1961, the San José organization began to see the identity of interests among all of the rich, and they came to suspect all of the institutions *los ricos* had created.

Population growth also influenced the community's changing consciousness. From 1957 to 1960 the community nearly doubled in size—from approximately 60 to more than 110 adults and more than 400 children. The geographical origin and occupational structure of the new residents remained remarkably similar to that of the original community; indeed, many of the recent migrants had kinship ties to older community members. Of the 35 adults who moved to the community during these years, 16 were from Pueblos, 10 from Grecia, and 9 from Chinandega or León. Twenty-four were field hands and 11 were tenant farmers. The similar geographical origin of the new residents of San José challenges the standard view of Nicaraguan cotton pickers as rootless migrants.[16] Although some of the rural workers of San José may have moved around during the cotton dead season, they had roots in a cohesive community. The absolute growth of the wage laborer sector of San José reflected the general pattern of absorption of all cultivable land into cotton production, thus eliminating tenant corn farming.

The increase in the number of landless proletarians in San José added urgency to the struggle for land. The pressure on the privately owned small farms in the community encouraged the few small- and medium-scale peasants in the community to redefine private property as an object of social utility. Consequently, in 1960, several of the small-scale farmers from the original community rented land to fellow community members at far lower rates than in the surrounding area. Similarly, ten smallholders allowed the rest of the community to live free on their land, as *arrimados* (free squatters). While arrimado relations existed between campesinos before the movement began, they usually had involved kin. During the late 1950s in San José, such relations began to extend beyond kinship groups, thus deepening a specifically campesino notion of property.[17]

The same sense of solidarity with less fortunate members of the community carried over into the area of production decisions. Juan Suazo, to cite one important example, started planting cotton on fifteen acres of his land when the export prices began to rise, in 1961. He hired ten family and community members to plant, thin, and harvest the cotton. Suazo grossed over five hundred dollars, a decent income compared to a full-time laborer's annual income of only two hundred dollars. Despite the profitable harvest, Suazo did not plant cotton again because one of his workers nearly died as a result of aerial fumigation.[18] Such a production decision, as well as the *arrimado* relation, distinguished Juan Suazo and his fellow peasants from the agrarian elite. The San José peasants valued the well-being of their community over their own profits. That unique set of values allowed the peasant proprietors to participate actively in all aspects of community affairs, including the struggles of increasing number of laborers. The daily work experience of the large and growing number of *jornaleros* (day laborers) in San José also contributed to the forging of a distinct consciousness in the community at large. Whereas before the advent of cotton, wages had represented a small portion of a hacienda laborer's income, by 1960 the jornaleros had become almost totally dependent on the seasonal income from planting and harvesting hacienda cotton. During the three-month harvest, most laborers earned six córdobas a day, and in the one-month planting season, workers earned four or five córdobas daily. These wages compared quite unfavorably with the urban unskilled worker who earned eleven córdobas daily. During the cotton harvest season, the jornalero could barely feed a family since in 1960 the basic elements in the rural diet—a liter of milk, a pound of cheese, rice and beans—cost more than a day's wage of five córdobas.[19] During the dead season, these workers' families could depend only on limited community resources to fend off starvation.

The difference in worker-employer relations after the onset of the cotton boom could not have been more striking. Campesinos, as we saw earlier, used the concept of "mutual aid" to describe pre-1950 laborer-patrón relations. By 1960, as a way of making sense of the radical change in elite behavior, the same workers, like the San Antonio workers of the 1920s, believed that the hacendados had made "pacts with the devil."[20] The laborers' changing perception reflected the transformation of more or less paternalistic oligarchs into agrarian capitalists. Rather than worrying about a sick colt or the sick child of a resident laborer, the new agrarian capitalist mainly worried about profit margins; the anonymous laborer who no longer lived on the hacienda became a cost of production. Those hacendado businessmen who were enterprising enough to journey to the fields sometimes did so only to pretend to pay their workers. The hacendado would arrive, call the laborers together, thank them for their efforts, and then ask the *mandador* (general foreman) for the pay envelope. The embarrassed employee would make some excuse for not having the pay and then would receive verbal abuse from the outraged patrón. Through this brazen form of postponing the payment of workers' wages, the hacendados gained in cash liquidity but forfeited the possibility of maintaining any legitimacy save that attained through naked power.[21]

February 1961: The Victims of the Storm Fight Back

In October 1960, just as San José's religious and legal roads to justice seemed hopelessly blocked, nature intervened in the struggle. A powerful rainstorm caused floods and mud slides, killing twenty-five Chinandegans and leaving more than six hundred families homeless. The mud slides devastated the crops and ruined the land of many campesinos from La Grecia.[22] Many families sought aid from their friends or kinfolk in San José. The Obraje campesino organization took in several families temporarily, but it was obvious to all that the community's already scant resources could not sustain the storm's victims. On the recommendation of the San José leaders, many of the displaced families moved onto unoccupied ejidal land; others joined tenant farmers on the nearby hacienda, La Laguna.

In early February 1961, Eduardo Deshon, Edmundo's brother and owner of La Laguna, evicted sixty-six families for failure to pay their rent. The October storm had rotted the corn of the tenant farmers, they had neither corn nor cash to pay the rent or to hire a lawyer, and they lacked any legal recourse with which to fight Deshon's eviction notice.[23] After consulting the San José leaders, the evicted tenants joined other storm victims in the Nuevos Ejidos. In the space of three months, then, several hundred landless campesinos from the immediate area settled on the land claimed by the Reyes group.

Because of their prestige among the area campesinos, Regino Escobar and Juan Suazo assumed leadership roles in the occupation.[24] Neither Escobar nor Suazo had any intention of abandoning the San José struggle against Deshon and Campuzano, but they recognized that the solution to their conflict would depend on the development of a broader campesino movement. After they had spent three days constructing ranchitos and clearing land, police chief Enrique Castillo arrived with the Guardia and ordered the campesinos off the Nuevos Ejidos land. Some campesinos obeyed the police chief's orders, but the majority followed the counsel of Escobar and Suazo to stay and fight, especially since they had nowhere else to go. Two days later the Guardia arrested Escobar and other leaders and reiterated the eviction order. The campesinos responded with a slow exodus from the lands, but they did not go far. Apparently by design, many opted to build ranchitos along the Chinandega-Puente Real highway (under construction) and along the public paths and roads near the ejidos.[25] This new campesino group had no intention of being driven from the area.

Dr. Reyes responded boldly to the campesino threat. First, he shored up his political strength among the Liberal party hierarchy. According to campesino activists and the CGT, he allotted some land to his friend and ally, Irma Guerrero, the rising star of Chinandegan Somocista politics. Within Liberal party circles, Guerrero struggled against Mayor Alfonso Callejas, a Campuzano-Deshon sympathizer who had begun to support the campesino fight for the ejidos.[26] Next, Reyes consolidated his base of support among the medium-scale peasants of La Grecia. Just as the poor campesinos attacked Reyes's ejidal possessions, twenty medium-sized peasants signed a letter protesting a Campuzano action against the ejidatarios, accusing them (among other things) of poisoning the local water supply.[27]

Reyes then turned the intra-elite conflict into a bitter, potentially violent battle. He took the offensive by agitating among the landless campesinos to seize the lands of his elite antagonists. *La Prensa* wrote of the Guardia physician's tactics against the individual members of the Campuzano group. "He has gone all over saying that the government will distribute land to the poor. He says [the campesinos] can take land from Campuzano, Dr. Timoteo Baca's Obraje, Edmundo Deshon's Llano Verde (Las Cuchillas), Eduardo Deshon's La Laguna, Dr. Hugo Astacio Cabrera's La Mora and La Virgen, and the lands of Juan Bautista Espinales known as Santa Isabel. [Reyes] is ordering the campesinos to take those lands."[28] The journalist also blamed Reyes for an increasingly dangerous situation: "Class hatred is arising."[29] But the campesino mobilization against Deshon and the Alvarados was not the result of Reyes's manipulations, for the San José campesinos had been waging their own battle against the Campuzano group for over four years.

When the Guardia evicted the campesinos from the Nuevos Ejidos, the San José leaders revamped their efforts against their old antagonists, the

Campuzano group. Thus, on February 12, more than one hundred landless campesinos marched through Edmundo Deshon's and Dr. Astacio's haciendas. In a probable reprisal for that march, arsonists burned the hut of Justino Pérez, on the edge of Mundo Deshon's land. Moreover Deshon persuaded Colonel Pereira to block campesino access to their fluvial water supply.[30]

Rather than intimidating the campesinos, Deshon's reprisals consolidated the unity of the San José campesinos and the residents of the Nuevos Ejidos who were fighting Reyes. In fact, Justino Pérez, a member of the Nuevos Ejidos group, following the arson, approached Escobar and Suazo about supporting him and other landless campesinos in an invasion of the hacienda Santa Isabel, which was owned by a member of the Campuzano group. A majority of the San José community then joined Pérez and others from the Nuevos Ejidos group in the takeover of Santa Isabel.[31] The owner, Juan Bautista Espinales, immediately set off for Chinandega to look for Dr. Astacio. The same afternoon Astacio arrived with twelve Guardia to evict the campesinos and to arrest Pérez and Juan Chico Rostrán, another leader of the Nuevos Ejidos group.[32]

By February 1961, the San José del Obraje organization had become the vanguard of a regional campesino movement. The movement both thrived on and aggravated the split in the agrarian bourgeoisie. It was neither entirely spontaneous nor, on the contrary, formed principally through the involvement of external agents. The campesinos, moreover, did not limit themselves to a specific material objective.[33] Rather, the San José group had inspired a class consciousness that led the campesinos, regardless of their own immediate gain, to organize their landless brethren against the entire agrarian elite. But as rapidly as they assumed the leadership of the regional movement, they ceded authority to a remarkably different kind of ally—Andrés Ruíz Escorcia.

Andrés Ruíz Escorcia Takes Command

In September 1960, by a 36 to 35 vote, Andrés Ruíz Escorcia, former officialist secretary of conflicts, defeated a leftist candidate in order to become secretary general of the CGT, succeeding Roberto González. Although the Left had convincing evidence of vote fraud, there was no doubt that both Escorcia and Somocista unionism had built a sizable base in the CGT.[34]

From 1948 to 1958, the union movement, under Somocista control, had little success in their organizing drives, for the regime was interested in consolidating bourgeois support. The dynamic sectors of the bourgeoisie in control of the cotton, sugar, and modernized cattle industries in Chinandega and León had no tolerance for the unionization of the countryside or for the burgeoning campesino movements. Their support for the regime depended on the repression of popular movements. For the Somozas, then, trade unionism had become something of an obstacle to development rather than an aid to the consolidation of political power. Roberto González, then CGT chief, aptly described the Somoza regime in 1958 as "a government of three legs: guns, the clergy, and the Yanquis."[35]

González and other Somocista labor leaders had attempted to push the regime toward a renewed alliance with labor. Between 1958 and 1960, the regime's probusiness bias began to change slightly as a result of an economic crisis and the uninterrupted growth of the opposition movement. In order to politically bolster the regime and divide the opposition, the government opened new channels to labor leaders and began to tacitly tolerate the non-Castroite Left.[36] However, this new opening of the Somoza regime was narrower and more tentative than that of the 1940s and was subject to closure by the ever-present machine guns of the Guardia.

As in the 1940s, the growth of the labor movement involved an increase of leftist influence among Nicaraguan workers. The Somocista response to the leftist challenge a decade earlier had been to call for repression of the PSN. Escorcia, upon assuming office in September 1960, chose in contrast to carry the battle for control of the CGT into the countryside, where the Left was still relatively weak. Escorcia's decision to develop campesino and labor movements in the countryside was conditioned by more than a desire to combat leftist influence in the CGT. Through his contact with the San José organization, Escorcia, himself of campesino extraction and with family ties among the Chinandegan rural poor, had developed a commitment to the campesino cause independent of its political ramifications. Escorcia eventually came to value the struggle of the rural poor for land, decent wages, and working conditions more highly than he valued the regime.

Escorcia had been in contact with San José campesino leaders since his visit to San José in September 1959. Until his election in 1960, he had limited his involvement in the San José conflict to several visits to government ministries in the company of Escobar and Suazo. Thus, while still in a subordinate role in the union, he managed to establish a good working relation with the two campesino leaders.[37] To Escorcia, the land occupations of February 1961 announced the dawn of a regional agrarian protest movement, and he thus set out to gain control of the movement, not only to capture a base of support, but also because he believed that only his own leadership would guide the campesinos to victory. Within two months, Escorcia would in fact become the unquestioned leader of the Chinandegan campesinos.

Regino Escobar and Juan Suazo ceded their authority over the movement because they needed tactical advice and legal assistance on how to advance in the face of the overwhelming Guardia support for both factions of the agrarian elite. Although they had been constantly frustrated on their march through the Somocista institutions, they still could not conceive of an alternative to an alliance with an outside force. Their acceptance of Escorcia's leadership was therefore the result of an appraisal of his capacity to struggle within the Somocista system. At the same time, the CGT began to offer important free services to both sectors of the movement (San José and the Nuevos Ejidos group), apparently with no strings attached. Beyond their view of Escorcia as a man who delivered, the San José campesinos appreciated the fact that as a workers' leader he was far more compatible with their agenda than were Fredi Callejas, Marcelino Reyes, Colonel Rodríguez Somoza, or Dr. Osman Buitrago.

Regino Escobar and Juan Suazo's acceptance of Escorcia's authority was both gradual and informal. Regino, by acting as an authoritarian leader, had to a certain extent paved the way for Escorcia's rapid ascent. A certain degree of *caudillismo* was endemic in Nicaraguan political culture. In both ISA and the workshops of Chinandega, however, that authoritarianism was tempered by the rank and file. The same was true in San José. Eventually Regino had to face increasing democratic constraints imposed by Juan Suazo and the dissidents. But democracy in the San José organization was essentially consultative. Once an action was agreed upon, Escobar acted as a military commander. Neither the campesinos nor the CGT leaders could envision an organized fight against enemies like the agrarian elite and its Guardia allies that did not reproduce on some level a military chain of command. Leadership, whether of the strike in the ISA cane fields in 1936 or of an occupied cotton field near San José in 1961, was an all-or-nothing proposition. Escorcia thus became the commander in chief of the agrarian protest movement, albeit with a provisional appointment.[38]

Taking San José del Obraje to Managua

Following a brief visit to San José in February 1961, the CGT head informed President Luís Somoza in person of the agrarian problem and urged his intervention on the side of the campesinos.[39] Several days later, Eduardo Deshon responded to the CGT initiative. Deshon wrote a letter to the President Somoza defending his brother against Escorcia's "calumnious attacks." The hacendado then urged the convocation of a "round table" to deal with the Chinandegan agrarian problem. He underlined this suggestion by arguing, "This land conflict with the campesinos is taking an alarming turn."[40] Escorcia immediately responded by publicly accusing Edmundo Deshon of expropriating the land of the San José community and of closing the paths to the Estero Real. Similarly, the CGT leader insinuated that Edmundo Deshon was guilty of burning Pérez's hut. Nevertheless, Escorcia also supported the proposed round-table discussion.[41]

President Luís Somoza responded immediately to the contrary pressures of his supporters by naming a congressional commission to investigate the Chinandegan agrarian problem. He announced through the offices of the CGT that he favored the prompt convocation of a round table in Chinandega that would bring together representatives of the campesinos, the CGT, the Deshons, Reyes, and government officials.[42] While not committing himself to the campesinos, Somoza's pronouncement created the distinct impression of favoring the campesino cause. In addition to Somoza's apparent sympathy, Escorcia's credibility among the Chinandegan campesinos was enhanced by his special dedication to the San José struggle. The San José leaders had been willing to sacrifice their immediate interest, if necessary, for the good of the broader campesino movement. The CGT's willingness to meet Campuzano and Deshon head on was thus especially appreciated.

The union confederation organized a commission of lawyers to study the San José-Campuzano problem. The lawyers traveled to Chinandega and conducted the first serious investigation of the land conflict. After studying the relevant court documents and conducting interviews with area residents, the commission concluded that Campuzano had expropriated campesino land first in 1895 and then again in the 1950s. Moreover, they argued (somewhat speciously) that the campesinos had lived on Las Cuchillas uninterruptedly for over fifty years and thus had acquired legal rights to the land. Finally, they recommended:

1. The return of the 800 manzanas to the campesinos.
2. That the Guardia stop supporting the landlords.
3. That if the landlords believe they have a right to the land, they should sue the campesinos through judicial process.

4. That the campesinos of the region must have unrestricted access to the sea coast, to the estuaries, and to the springs and rivers.[43]

Escorcia immediately sent the lawyers' findings to President Somoza and to the Chinandegan deputy named to the presidential commission. Moreover, he encouraged the San José group to protest the president's failure to convene the round table.[44] Although Escorcia was eager to organize around the ejidal issue, he was careful to give priority to the San José struggle at this initial stage of CGT involvement. This special attention to San José derived from the prestige of its leaders, its organizational history, and the consequent general belief among Chinandegans that the San José campesinos deserved to win.

In March, Juan Suazo replaced Escobar as the leader of the San José group during the latter's hospitalization, resulting from many Guardia beatings over the previous four years. Escorcia's degree of influence over the new leader can be detected in a telegram dated April 22. "Remember to mobilize the largest number of *compañeros* to attend May Day in capital. President Somoza will be there and we can solve the problem."[45] Juan Suazo responded to Escorcia's appeal for support by organizing among the Nuevos Ejidos group as well as his own base in San José. One journalist wrote that a "large delegation" from the San José del Obraje area attended the demonstration. Oral testimony suggests that Juan Suazo and others mobilized perhaps four hundred campesinos to participate in the May Day rally, the largest since 1946.[46] Such extensive campesino participation in the labor celebration was unprecedented. Through the streets of Managua, the Chinandegan campesinos carried signs about their struggles and shouted slogans in favor of agrarian reform. Although most speakers called for an agrarian reform law, none did so as forcefully as PSN leader Domíngo Sánchez, who decried "the genocide in San José del Obraje" and praised the Cuban agrarian revolution. Indeed, most speakers voiced support for the Cuban revolution only days after the Bay of Pigs invasion, actively supported by the Somoza regime.[47]

Despite the leftist rhetoric of the May Day orators, Luís Somoza met with labor leaders of all tendencies after the rally. At an unpublicized conference, the President offered support for the principal CGT demands, including agrarian reform, minimum wage legislation, and an end to the repression of unions.[48] Although Somoza did not specifically endorse the Chinandegan campesinos' demands, his private and public commitment to agrarian reform could be interpreted as an endorsement of the goals of the agrarian protest movement and its charismatic leader.

The Right Kind of Target

The CGT-led campesinos who marched through Managua belonged to two distinct but similar groups. The geographical backgrounds of the two groups were quite similar: 50 percent of the Nuevos Ejidos community came from La Grecia, and 35 percent hailed from los Pueblos del Norte, the same two areas from which came over 80 percent of the San José residents. The occupational structures of the two groups were also comparable. As with the San José group, more than 80 per cent of the Nuevos Ejidos adults were laborers or tenant farmers who also worked the cotton harvest. Unlike in San José, smallholders were technically excluded from the Nuevos Ejidos group, which defined itself as an organization of the landless. Nevertheless, activists made so many exceptions for the landholding kin of community members that the proportion of small-scale peasants was roughly the same in both communities.[49]

Despite their common backgrounds, the objects of the two struggles were quite different. Those differences became extremely important in light of the regime's new agrarian reform commitment, which, inspired by the Alliance for Progress—the Kennedy administration's ambitious aid and development program for Latin America—aimed at dividing unproductive latifundios. The goal of the Somoza and Alliance programs was to distribute enough unproductive land to quell rural unrest, to increase agricultural production by increasing cultivated acreage and by converting latifundistas into capitalists, and at the same time to expand the domestic market by creating a rural petit bourgeoisie out of the rural poor. Large, efficient plantations were rarely targets of this model for agrarian reform.[50]

Under this program, the prospects for a legislative solution to the San José agrarian problem were dim. Las Cuchillas, the focus of the San José campesinos' struggle, had become a prosperous cotton plantation. Its owners, the Deshons, were an important Liberal family who had made the successful transition to capitalist agriculture. Indeed, Mundo Deshon's modernization of Llano Verde luxuriantly masked its illegitimate origins. The Nuevos Ejidos campesinos faced an easier target precisely because the land they fought for belonged to the Reyes group, which was guilty of what influential agrarian reform theorists considered to be feudal practices. Ironically, despite the middle-class backgrounds of Dr. Reyes and his associates, they committed the sin of renting the land they had appropriated, rather than turning it into a capitalist farm (a difficult task considering the relatively poor and hilly quality of much of their land). The case against Reyes was also legally clear-cut. The Conservative Congress of 1916 had set aside two thousand hectares of land on the southern flank of Campuzano as municipal, communal land reserved for poor peasants. The original intent of the legislation was probably to punish Liberal-owned Campuzano and also to develop a Conservative political base in the area. Reyes's legal victory against Campuzano had been as an ejidatario—a renter of municipal land.[51] His fight against the campesinos would oblige him to prove ownership of the ejidos. Reyes's transparent abuse of his power as jefe político between 1956 and 1958 placed the regime in an awkward position. Although Reyes was well connected in Chinandegan political and military circles, he did not have the clout of the Deshon family. Escorcia calculated that with enough campesino pressure, Reyes's ejidal "fief" would fall apart. Later, the campesino movement, supported by a revitalized CGT, might tackle Llano Verde.

Different collective experiences, related to different objects of struggle, conditioned different forms of social consciousness in the two groups of campesinos. The San José campesinos' long battle with the agrarian elite and the authorities had been an intense educational process. They had learned to be skeptical of elite motives. They had come to understand that their necesidades were not limited to one strip of land; their larger fight had much to do with a sense of their moral right to a just society. As a result of that class-rooted understanding, the San José campesinos wished to make horizontal, rather than vertical alliances with the CGT and with the Nuevos Ejidos organization. In contrast, the Nuevos Ejidos campesinos had experienced their initial stage of mobilization only in 1961. Although both the San José leaders and Escorcia stressed broader issues, the Nuevos Ejidos rank and file was not prepared to fight for any goal beyond the ejidal land.[52]

Shortly after the May Day demonstration, Escorcia informed Juan Suazo of his decision to mobilize against the Reyes group before moving against Deshon. Suazo accepted Escorcia's decision. The new San José leader considered Escorcia's real motives irrelevant. Suazo supported Escorcia because he believed that the CGT was capable of leading and defending a successful campesino movement; immediate victory over Deshon was less important than this long-term goal.[53] Escorcia moved quickly. On May 10, 1961, several hundred campesinos organized by the CGT peacefully demonstrated in the municipal palace in Chinandega, demanding that the mayor of Chinandega fulfill the government's promise to hold a round table as a preliminary step to the distribution of the ejidal land. The campesinos then marched through

Chinandega to the mayor's home. The recently installed Mayor Rodolfo Zelaya, perhaps intimidated by the hundreds of angry campesinos in front of his home, promised that the surveying of the ejidos would commence on May 21.[54]

As if to magnify the impressiveness of the campesino mobilization in Chinandega, the following day three groups of over two hundred Sutiava Indians, armed with machetes and shotguns, invaded the haciendas within their ancestral territory. Squadrons of heavily armed Guardia ready for war stormed the haciendas, but they found only cows, pigs, and horses. The invaders had slipped away. The Guardia comandante interrogated the Sutiavan leaders to no avail. They maintained that their community had nothing to do with the armed invasion, but they added that those particular haciendas were perched on Sutiavan land.[55] As in May 1959, the simultaneous actions, in 1961, in León and Chinandega illuminated the threat of a militant national campesino movement. The regime had no choice but to respond. At first it leaned toward supporting the Nuevos Ejidos group and Deshon against Reyes.

Mayor Zelaya's promised surveying and distribution of the ejidal lands calmed the Chinandegan campesino movement momentarily. But faced with a virulent defense by Dr. Reyes and his political allies, the Somoza regime hesitated before the conflicting demands of the Deshon and Reyes groups. The government delegated Francisco Argeñal Papi, a landowner and Somocista politician, to try to reach some sort of compromise. Argeñal Papi, a fairly typical Somocista functionary, portrayed himself as the savior of the campesinos even as he cut deals with their adversaries. When his game was discovered, he would deny everything but continue to present himself, with journalistic backing, as "the friend and protector of the campesinos."[56] His act was usually convincing.

In early June 1961, Argeñal Papi accompanied the minister of agriculture, Enrique Chamorro, on a trip to a Chinandegan village, where they were to meet with campesino representatives. The fifteen campesinos who met with the functionaries assumed that the minister and Argeñal had come to reiterate a government promise to distribute the ejidal land. They were quite shocked when Minister Chamorro stated instead, "I have come here today to find a solution to your problem. I do not wish you to continue to be victimized by agitators, who daily come here to offer something they cannot possibly deliver. These ejidal lands belong to proprietors who have their legal deeds in order. There is nothing to be done about that."[57]

The shocked campesino militants replied that the only agitators were CGT leaders who possessed letters from the president and the minister of development that promised the distribution of ejidal land. The campesinos also pointed out that the Chinandegan mayor, directly in charge of the municipal lands, had already ordered the surveying of the ejidos.[58] Argeñal Papi stepped into the dispute, posing as a mediator. "Whoever has used the name of the president is wrong and is perhaps trying to trick you. These lands have owners with properly registered deeds. So you people should not be careless. You should believe what the president—through us—wishes to tell you. That is that the government is willing to pay the rent for 120 hectares, that will be distributed to sixty heads of family . . . so that you can plant this season."[59]

Argeñal Papi's first intervention in the Chinandegan agrarian conflict was quite astute. He insinuated that Escorcia, by then the undisputed leader of the campesino movement, had deceived them. Argeñal Papi's official role lent credence to his principal charge against the union leader, namely that Escorcia had drastically misrepresented the government's position on the ejidal question. Moreover, the minister of agriculture had attacked the CGT leader as an agitator—a dangerous epithet in Somocista Nicaragua. Both Somocista functionaries strove to separate the base from their leader so as to deflate the campesinos' dream of ejidal land. At the start of the planting season, they offered to pay for the land of perhaps one-quarter of the Nuevos Ejidos families, obviously including those in attendance. By renting the land, they would split the movement and legitimize the Reyes group's control over the rented land. Despite such a shrewd tactic, Argeñal Papi found no takers. According to an eyewitness, "A chorus of voices of protest followed the speech by Sr. Argeñal Papi."[60]

The campesinos rejected Argeñal Papi because they knew that he had not spoken the final word on the ejidal question. If Chamorro and Argeñal Papi seemed favorable to Reyes, that reflected a tactical uncertainty in the Somoza regime. The lack of a clear governmental policy on the agrarian question arose out of the disunity of the Chinandegan elite. The split between the Reyes and Campuzano-Deshon factions, exacerbated by the campesino agitation, produced tensions throughout the Somocista power structure. In Chinandega, Liberal party boss Irma Guerrero and the jefe político, Ernesto Pereira, aligned themselves openly with Dr. Reyes. The Deshons and the Alvarados enjoyed the support of the Liberal sector of the agro-export elite, heavily represented in the national government. The two factions openly struggled to define regime policy toward the campesino movement, but were for the moment stalemated.

The campesino movement provoked but also took advantage of the growing antagonism within the Somocista power elite. The San José and Nuevos Ejidos organizations were united, in large part, because of the class-rooted perspective of Juan Suazo, the ailing Regino Escobar, and the other San José grassroots activists who had struggled together against Campuzano since 1957. The inexperienced Nuevos Ejidos group, however, grew quickly both organizationally and intellectually, in part thanks to the instruction of the San José leaders and Andrés Ruíz Escorcia. Moreover, they learned from the intra-elite conflict: once a marble wall of authority, the oligarchy now seemed composed of grasping, mean individuals whose notion of hegemonic rule was increasingly symbolized by a fat wad of dollar bills.

6

Sacred Rights and Social Peace:
The Struggle for the Nuevos Ejidos, 1961

A class culture or class discourse is never given; it must be constructed from the cultural raw material presented by history, from the "tradition" that is used to construct both the dominant and emergent forms of culture.

—William Roseberry, "Images of the Peasant"

Between June and September 1961, the Chinandegan campesino movement engaged in four mass actions to win back the ejidal lands. Yet by mid-September the situation in the Chinandegan countryside had come to a stalemate: no social force could successfully impose its will. Nevertheless, the campesino movement did gain important terrain on another front. Although it won no material victories, the campesino movement intensified elite divisions and forced a redefinition of the terms of political discourse.

Between 1958 and 1961 the San José campesinos had begun in practice and in thought to break away from traditional patrón-client relations. Reflecting on this transformation and on their sense of belonging to a new social group spawned by agrarian capitalism, the San José campesinos began to create a form of class consciousness. The development of consciousness was uneven both within and between the campesino groups, with the San José group generally in the vanguard of their class. Through their own agrarian struggles and with the aid of the CGT leader, Andrés Ruíz Escorcia, many campesinos began to codify in the realm of language and ideology what they had begun to achieve in practice. They transformed themselves from a pitied or scorned group into an autonomous political subject, thereby forcing the agrarian elite and the government on the political and ideological defensive. This symbolic victory in discourse would eventually have significant political consequences.[1]

Symbolic action and the struggle for symbolic power became so crucial to the agrarian struggle in Chinandega because the transition to cotton-based capitalist relations of production created a crisis of legitimacy for the agrarian elite. Before the cotton boom of the 1950s, the authority of the hacendado over the peón went largely unquestioned. Since the 1920s, Chinandegan hacendados had not needed to rely on any form of forced labor. The power of the hacendado resided fundamentally in the patrón-client relation. Until the 1950s, laborers received payments of cheese, milk, or land use as "gifts" that they were to reciprocate with their own and their children's lifetimes of labor. The transformation of Chinandegan productive relations arose when the patrón denied the campesinos' access to hacienda land and jobs, thus snapping the material underpinnings of patrón-client reciprocity.[2]

The mechanization of cotton cultivation progressed rapidly during the 1950s. Cotton growers increased Nicaragua's total number of tractors from five hundred in 1950 to twenty-five hundred in 1955. One tractor performed the work of ten laborers and twenty oxen, at less than 20 percent of the cost.[3] With the elimination of oxen as work animals and the successful mechanization of cotton cultivation, producers needed manual laborers mainly during the three-month harvest period. Thus, seasonal laborers grew from a small fraction of the rural laboring population in the late 1940s to over 90 percent of the agricultural labor force by 1960.[4] Furthermore, extremely favorable cotton prices from 1950 to 1955 made it highly profitable to plant cotton on every inch of hacienda land. Hence, the massive introduction of tractors and the high profitability of extensive cotton planting prompted the hacendado to evict most of his work force and to rely on seasonal labor. Those evicted laborers formed villages like San José along strips of land bordering their former haciendas.

The eviction of hacienda laborers caused dramatic changes in the social relations of the Chinandegan countryside. The crisis of elite legitimacy was directly tied to the birth of a new social group. Although many of these campesinos shared common roots on the haciendas, they first entered into social relations with one another as a direct consequence of capitalist development. Their communities came into existence during the late 1940s. In this sense the Chinandegan campesinos resembled the Costa Rican coffee farmers studied by Lowell Gudmundson and the Venezuelan Andean peasants analyzed by William Roseberry; they were "precipitates" of capitalism.[5]

Among their many contributions, Roseberry and Gudmundson have underscored the role of agrarian capitalism in the formation of social classes and the importance of such precipitates in any analysis of modern national and regional politics. This study continues these scholars' questioning of the prevalent model of agrarian revolt as the necessary consequence of capitalism's destructive impact on precapitalist communities.[6] In Chinandega, capitalism created rather than destroyed communities, and campesinos could appeal only to a selective portrait of their past. Notwithstanding, the Chinandegans did rebel and many eventually became revolutionaries.

The landed elite had no effective allies in its struggle to legitimize the new economic and social order and thus to debilitate this social force. It lacked the customary means to legitimize control over land and labor, for the church was organically weak in the Chinandegan countryside. Moreover, campesinos could not read newspapers, another mode of elite expression. And the schools, in the few hamlets where they existed, were but impoverished parodies of educational institutions. Hence, the oligarchs had to face their evicted peons directly and convince them that only the elite had a right to the land. The struggle for control of resources thus became inextricably bound up in a battle for "symbolic authority."[7]

The campesino movement's success in its struggle for symbolic power was the result of its ability to forge ideological and political arms out of inherited cultural forms. In Chinandega the campesino leaders, as well as their elite antagonists, attempted to manipulate what Raymond Williams has defined as residual culture: "experiences, meanings and values, which cannot be . . . substantially verified in . . . the dominant culture." The leadership of Andrés Ruíz Escorcia was decisive in shaping the discursive and practical use of those diverse forms, inherited from campesinos with varied sociological and geographical backgrounds. Out of a myriad of traditional images, Escorcia helped to create a common language of protest, one that found common ground with the authorities, thereby providing a degree of legitimacy for the campesinos' action.[8] By demonstrating the elite's inability to rule through custom and obligation, the campesinos' appeal to hacienda-rooted cultural forms reinforced the movement's conviction that its cause was just. Finally, the elite's demonstration that it was unable to perform its traditional functions, coupled with the campesinos' strengthened conviction of their rights, forced the *terratenientes* (landlords) onto the defensive, after decades of almost unquestioned authority.

From the Courthouse to the Fields and Back

On June 25, 1961, several hundred campesinos, led by Escorcia, occupied the Chinandega court house. The CGT leader declared that the occupation was a symbolic protest against the government for failing to survey and distribute the Nuevos Ejidos, as the mayor had promised several weeks earlier.[9] One week later, the agrarian elite dramatically responded to the occupation. On

July 4, Doña Tesla de Alvarado, the owner of Campuzano, addressed a distinguished audience of government officials and neighboring hacendados. She announced that she was donating 6,588 manzanas of Campuzano land to the government, to be distributed to the campesinos.[10]

The CGT and the Chinandegan campesino movement did not immediately respond to Doña Tesla's donation, despite its inclusion of ejidal land. Two weeks later, on July 19, Escorcia organized the largest popular demonstration in Chinandega since 1946. Over two thousand campesinos from San José and La Grecia marched to Chinandega in support of the struggle for the ejidos and to demand an agrarian reform law. Escorcia was the principal speaker and gave what is remembered by many as a powerful speech.[11] The CGT leader made no reference to Doña Tesla's donation, but he lashed out strongly against Dr. Reyes, the National Guard doctor and expropriator of the ejidal lands, and, more generally, against the unscrupulous elite that was corrupting the Somoza government and driving the Nicaraguan people into misery.

Three days after Escorcia's speech at the Chinandegan demonstration, the Somoza regime awarded the Order of Rubén Darío medal to Doña Tesla, in recognition of her "noble" land donation. The government also announced that land surveyors would be sent immediately to divide up the land included in Doña Tesla's donation.[12] A week later, Escorcia appeared to change course. He ordered a temporary halt to the campesino demonstrations in Chinandega and publicly stated, "After six years of conflicts, peace has returned between potentates and peasants."[13] The timing of Escorcia's statement made it clear that he was responding to the regime's award to Doña Tesla and to the announcement that it was going to survey the ejidal land; he was not responding directly to the oligarch's donation.

The peace that Escorcia celebrated was very short lived. On August 16, 1961, Regino Escobar, the San José del Obraje leader, died. The CGT issued a communique, pointing an accusing finger at the "gift-giver."

> In the León Hospital on Wednesday, the 16th Regino Escobar died. He was
> not only an inspired fighter, he was the pioneer of the organization that the
> Chinandegan campesinos have built so as to defend themselves from the vora-
> ciousness of the landlords. His premature death was the inevitable conse-
> quence of the repressive methods daily employed by the land-grabbers against
> the campesinos . . . to expel the campesinos from their own land, the señora
> Tesla de Alvarado ordered Regino to be beaten brutally on repeated occasions
> until he finally lost his health. Peace to the remains of Regino Escobar and one
> hopes that there may be peace in the conscience of Doña Tesla de Alvarado.[14]

On September 3, embittered by Regino's death and angered by the government's pro-elite favoritism in its survey of the ejidos, the campesinos prepared to occupy the donated land. Five days earlier, Escorcia had asked Deshon to pay for Regino's funeral expenses. Deshon had replied by telegram, "While I have no obligation, I will gladly pay for the funeral expenses and the casket for the first leader, the *caballero* Regino Escobar."[15] Alerted to Deshon's positive stance towards the movement, the Nuevos Ejidos leaders (not those from San José) asked Deshon to let the campesinos take lumber and palm fronds from his land. He granted the request, perhaps not expecting the campesino response. The next day, hundreds of campesinos joyously chopped wood and cut palm leaves on the uncultivated part of Deshon's land. By dawn on September 4, over three hundred ox carts, filled with palm fronds and wood, left Deshon's property and began the five mile trek down the road to the ejidos.[16]

Moments after the first campesinos reached the ejidos, Dr. Reyes, armed with an automatic rifle and dressed in battle fatigues, arrived with fifteen Guardia.[17] Dr. Reyes, a Guardia captain, ordered the campesinos off the land. The campesinos stopped piling the palm fronds and lumber, but they did not leave. As the caravan of ox carts stopped in front of the Guardia, Dr. Reyes made a difficult choice between violent repression or compromise. He must have realized that, given regime support for Doña Tesla's gift, a violent solution to the problem could result in serious difficulties. Several hundred campesinos, machetes in hand, stared sullenly at the fifteen Guardia, who nervously fingered their automatic rifles. Argeñal Papi, official delegate of the ministry of agriculture, arrived in a jeep and urgently pleaded for calm. Then, he suggested to Reyes that he order the principal campesino leaders to appear the next morning at Guardia headquarters in Chinandega. Argeñal Papi told the campesinos that they should keep their building materials, but, for the time being, they must remove them from the ejidal land.[18]

The next morning, on September 5, two hundred campesinos accompanied their leaders to Chinandega, where they met with the Guardia comandante, Francisco Rodríguez Somoza. Rodríguez, a movement sympathizer like his brother, the former León comandante, promised to allow the campesinos to occupy the ejidos. Rodríguez made it clear that Reyes had no choice but to obey his orders.[19] That same night, the campesinos, with the backing of the Guardia comandante, regrouped in San José del Obraje and marched on the ejidos in order to pile up their lumber and palm fronds once again. The following morning, they were surprised to see Dr. Reyes arrive again. This time the Guardia arrested the campesino leaders and hauled them off to Chinandega.[20] Later the same day, the Guardia arrested Escorcia near San José del Obraje. Newspaper reports indicated that the CGT leader was unaware of the earlier arrests.[21] According to *La Prensa*'s correspondent, Comandante Rodríguez admitted going back on his word because, "The landlords are extremely worried and bothered by the actions of the campesinos. They are afraid of worse to come. The campesinos responded [to Rodríguez] that, without a doubt, such nervousness was due to an over-burdened conscience because the campesinos had no thoughts of violence."[22]

When Escorcia arrived at the Guardia headquarters, he joined in a heated discussion. Rodríguez was adamant that because of Reyes's pressure, the campesinos could not continue even to store the building materials. Escorcia urged the campesinos to accept a one-week truce but added a crucial condition. Recognizing the urgency of planting corn and beans during the last months of the rainy season, he called on Rodríguez to support a demand for the immediate allotment of two hundred manzanas of land to be farmed collectively, while awaiting the formal distribution of the ejidal lands. The campesinos and the comandante agreed to these terms.[23]

Andrés Ruíz Escorcia: The Shaping of Campesino Consciousness

As the above narrative reveals, Escorcia was a crafty, opportunistic tactician, constantly weaving through governmental and elite obstacles. His attitude toward Doña Tesla and Deshon shows two dramatic about-faces in the space of several weeks. He ignored Doña Tesla's gift, then proclaimed peace with Campuzano, and then issued what amounted to a declaration of war against both elite factions. Escorcia's role in shaping the movement's attitude toward Doña Tesla's gift was indeed fundamental. Although in his July 19 speech, Escorcia did not even mention the gift, he did implicitly suggest ways in which the campesinos should understand the actions of the agrarian elite. He spoke of three interrelated themes: sacred rights, citizenship, and violated social pacts. In the speech, the CGT chief, perhaps only subconsciously, manipulated important Chinandegan cultural symbols.

> Dr. Marcelino Reyes has used Insults, Slander and Cruelty against the just claims of the campesinos. However, his attacks against the campesinos are being resisted by them thanks to their solid and disciplined organization; it is not easy to break the morale of more than three thousand campesinos and it will be that much more difficult when all the campesinos of this department and then of the entire nation [*patria*] Organize themselves in order to defend their Sa-

cred Rights. . . . This social peace has only served a small group, who, day by day, enrich themselves more and more, while the people . . . become morally, materially, socially, and economically impoverished. It is time that our highest governmental authority consider all of us as Nicaraguans, with equal rights to a better life.[24]

For the campesinos, access to land had been the cornerstone of oligarchic legitimacy.[25] That sacred right allowed many campesinos in 1961 to look back at their past in a quite selective manner and see it as a time of a moral economic order. In this speech and in his daily conversations, Escorcia verbalized a particular version of the campesino past by drawing on those unifying aspects of the heterogeneous rural traditions.

The heterogeneity of rural Chinandegan social history was far more complex than a simple patrón-client hacienda model would suggest. At the most basic level, social relations varied enormously from hacienda to hacienda. Moreover the region's agrarian history included late nineteenth-century Indian rebellions, episodes of spontaneous campesino resistance to Conservative oligarchs, rural laborers' organized resistance at Ingenio San Antonio, and the organization of five campesino unions during the 1940s. For participants in those movements, the hacienda did not appear to be the embodiment of anything sacrosanct. Yet many other Chinandegans were born, lived, labored, and, until the 1950s, thought they would die on the same hacienda. What then constituted the moral economy of the past, to which Escorcia appealed?

Escorcia wove his tapestry from one common thread of Chinandegan popular discourse. Most rural residents recognized the image of pre-1950 social harmony, even if they had not directly experienced such traditional relationships. Even the minority of Chinandegan campesinos who had participated in unions or other forms of anti-elite resistance understood the rural language of deference, reciprocity, and obligation. Moreover, for the thousands of evicted hacienda workers, that language evoked a recent past that seemed substantially more abundant and fertile than the present. In addition to past abundance, most campesinos remembered a traditional code of social rights and obligations. Judged by this code, the local elite had become morally reprehensible.[26]

Escorcia thus helped frame a historical vision that provided an effective critique of the present order. In his July 19 speech, Escorcia also enunciated a previously inconceivable notion—that campesinos themselves could change history. He elevated "the three thousand disciplined and organized campesinos" who resisted Dr. Reyes to the status of autonomous historical actors, independent of outside influence or manipulation; in doing so he announced the maturity of a new social and political force in Nicaragua. By placing the campesino movement at the center of Nicaraguan politics, Escorcia sent a strong message to the Somozas. He castigated the Somocista elite but not the well-intentioned Somozas who, he suggested, still wished for social justice and social peace. His theme of social peace was an implicit appeal to the regime still draped in the *Gran Pacificador* (Great Pacifier) imagery of the dynasty's founder. To the brothers Somoza, Escorcia offered some implicit political advice: if they wished to buttress their regime and maintain ideological coherence they should cut their losses with Reyes and his ilk and take serious measures to resolve the agrarian crisis.

Whatever Escorcia's hopes of reaching Somocista ears, by starkly proclaiming the campesinos as autonomous historical subjects, Escorcia demarcated the possible meanings of sacred rights and social pacts and thus defined the real historical movement. The landlords had forced the campesinos to abandon the ground that was the basis for their understanding of the social pact. Now Escorcia's words resonated against the actions of their changed patrons—who now poisoned their water sources, burned their huts, and sent the Guardia after them. For four years the former peons had been fighting back. Now, with the campesinos as protagonists of their own social movement, neither oligarch nor campesino could expect the restoration of a social order in which a hacendado named a campesino child or in which a peón would bow down and ask for a blessing from a landlord.

In light of this analysis of Escorcia's speech, his subsequent actions seem more comprehensible. Shortly following the regime's award to Doña Tesla—the Somoza stamp of approval on her donation—Escorcia publicly accepted the gift. Probably most elite groups connected to the Somoza regime interpreted quite literally Escorcia's remark that the donation would bring peace between "potentates and peasants." Most of the campesinos, however, interpreted the declaration as part of Escorcia's discourse on social justice and social harmony. The "donation," they realized, only returned what rightfully belonged to the campesinos and it came as the result of their own pressure. Thus, most campesino militants read Escorcia's remarks as a public statement of their own interpretation of the donation, peace returned between potentates and peasants precisely because the potentates had given back what they had stolen. The elite's and the campesinos' differing interpretations of Doña Tesla's act and Escorcia's declaration of peace would quickly become apparent. While the government and media showered effusive praise on Doña Tesla, the campesinos immediately began to use the gift as part of their legal and ideological arsenal against the landed elite.

Escorcia may have framed the campesino acceptance of the gift in a politically useful way, but his mode of acceptance constrained the tactical options of the CGT. Three weeks later, in response to Regino's death and the government survey, Escorcia's tone changed dramatically, though without altering the substance of his earlier argument. Rather than another declaration of peace, the communique issued on August 21 resembled a call to battle. The object of CGT anger was no longer the politically isolated Dr. Reyes. Rather, the federation attacked government complicity with the entire local elite, including Doña Tesla:

Everything was going well, until the survey reached the mojón known as "Espino." Beyond that mojón, the campesinos use the springs and the woods. . . . Despite the protests of the (accompanying) campesinos, Ingeniero Tijerino moved the compass, and instead of going straight to the mojón "Tasa," he went on an angle, leaving the campesinos without water and without woods; taking from them 300 manzanas—benefiting Lolo Deshon . . . Juan Bautista Espinales and Tesla de Alvarado. Now they add this injustice to the old ones, and this one has the aura of legality because the survey is official. To deny the campesinos their right to cultivate land, no method is immoral for the terratenientes: Eduardo Deshon destroyed the mojón La Lagunita; Mundo Deshon destroyed La Barca; Astacio destroyed El Tionaste. They act with such impunity, it seems that we are living in a state without laws.[27]

Once again, Escorcia adeptly manipulated images of the immediate and distant past. The contrast revealed a systematic violation by the elite of the social pact, rooted in the idealized paternalistic past. In conjunction with the July 19 speech, Escorcia's message was clear: the government must support the campesinos, the only social group capable of restoring harmony and legality to society. The communique's accusation of the Campuzano group, the putative gift givers, was a direct expression of the campesinos' anger at the death of Regino Escobar. His death forced the issue of San José del Obraje back on the movement's agenda. No matter how recent their recruitment, Chinandegan campesinos knew the story of Don Regino and his battle with Doña Tesla and Deshon. Whatever the intentions of the CGT leaders, Regino's martyrdom severely limited their ability to compromise with the Campuzano group.

At this stage of the conflict, the remaining San José leaders, the Suazos and Cándia, were operating with a qualitatively different set of goals and values than the other campesino militants. The Suazos, Ramón Cándia, and their community-based organization had fought bitterly against Deshon and Doña

Tesla for nearly four years. Their experience had shaped a consciousness that conceived the movement in class, not localist terms. Thus, although they were willing to fight under CGT command, they, unlike their campesino allies, could not accept, let alone solicit, gifts from Doña Tesla or Deshon.[28]

Piling Palm Leaves and Lumber

Ironically, when Deshon did open the gates, the campesinos entered the very land on which Regino Escobar had become the first leader of the campesino movement four years earlier. Deshon acted wisely by paying for Regino's funeral expenses. But calling his deceased enemy "the first leader" and a "caballero," was an audacious, perhaps brilliant, act and an effort to project an image of solidarity with the campesino movement and thus suppress his own repressive role in its history. By giving away the wood and palm, he emphasized that solidarity and tried thereby to defuse a potential threat. As late as June 1961, Deshon had denied San José campesinos their traditional right to gather palm leaves and wood on the land he claimed. But in July, faced with the growth of the movement and taking his cue from Doña Tesla's ploy, Mundo gave in to the San José demand. In doing so, however, he turned what the campesinos had demanded as their right into a "gift." Ironically, San José's victory came in a form that seemed to require gratitude and reciprocal obligation—a form that undercut the autonomy and class consciousness that had made the victory possible. The campesinos' acceptance of Deshon's gift thus revealed the cracks in their "symbolic authority."

Deshon and his government allies probably speculated that the campesinos would successfully attack his antagonist, Marcelino Reyes, occupy the ejidal land, and convert themselves into a base of social stability and seasonal labor for local cotton plantations. In addition, Deshon, whose family had lived in the area for several generations, seized an opportunity to regain some of the prestige he had lost during the course of his battle with Regino Escobar and the San José campesinos.

Although it is possible that the campesinos needed Deshon's palms to build their ranchos, given the resources of the CGT, this particular material need was probably Escorcia's pretext, for the CGT leader viewed Deshon's role as politically crucial. Deshon's "gift" thus added legitimacy to the occupation of the ejidal land—Doña Tesla's "gift." Nevertheless, for the campesinos, the acceptance of Deshon's gift could not be merely a tactical ruse. In Chinandega, as in other rural cultures, gifts had always played an important part in social relations. In this regard, we may recall the campesinos' insistence that Las Cuchillas was a gift from Manuel Antonio Baca. To accept a gift of land or building materials was to accept certain obligations of reciprocity. When the Chinandegan campesinos accepted the elite gifts, it was understood that they could repay them only through some form of personal deference.[29]

The gifts of Deshon and Doña Tesla, like Baca's before them, were immediately used to justify an occupation of elite-claimed land. The campesinos' acceptance of the gifts played on the key theme of Escorcia's discourse: the elite violation of a traditional, moral economy as legitimation for campesino militancy. Thus the action of storing the palm leaves and lumber on the ejidal land can be interpreted as both a defensive ruse and a significant variation on past themes of struggle. The threat of Guardia violence against the campesinos was real and required defensive tactics. Before the first confrontation, rumors circulated about a Guardia massacre of hundreds of campesinos, but the symbolic and ritualistic quality of the action permitted no pretext for violent repression. The campesinos did not destroy fences, nor did they commence the building of the ranchos. Rather, like a humble suggestion based on the supposed assumption of elite benevolence, they only stored palm fronds and lumber on the ejidal land. The act of storing materials, obviously in preparation for a future date of occupation, recalls an earlier campesino action in San José del Obraje in the spring of 1958, when they set up small boundary markers along Las Cuchillas, in symbolic preparation for future cultivation. In the Nuevos Ejidos, a similar activity—the storing of materials—which projected an image of docile, ignorant, trusting but somehow methodical peasants, probably prevented a massacre on the ejidal fields in 1961.

The campesinos' choice of actions could not guarantee that the Guardia would not fire on them, however. Internal divisions in the Guardia leadership resulting from the military's contradictory roles as ideological and physical defenders of the law and the system as a whole and as participants in the formation of a particular segment of the bourgeoisie (of which Dr. Reyes was a member in good standing) made institutional violence both unpredictable and arbitrary.[30] Ideological splits between rightists, such as Juan Angel López, and moderates, such as the Rodríguez Somoza brothers, made the Guardia's use of force even more erratic. In these uncharted, choppy waters, the campesinos had to navigate with extreme caution: fatal consequences might result from a tactical blunder like building huts instead of storing materials.

Comandante Rodríguez withdrew his support from the campesino movement because the Guardia hierarchy opted to back Captain Reyes. Reyes undoubtedly received important backing from those Guardia officers who had also been involved in the expropriation of ejidal lands or in similarly shady dealings.[31] The Somoza regimes distinguished themselves from their Central American and Caribbean counterparts by fostering the development of a key faction of the agro-industrial bourgeoisie, and many members of that faction were officers in the Guardia Nacional. Support for Reyes was thus somewhat akin to an act of class solidarity. If, however, the pro-Reyes forces in the Guardia possessed the power to reverse Rodríguez Somoza's position, they did not have the political power to crack down on the campesinos as a solution to the ejidal problem, since President Luís Somoza insisted on portraying himself as an ally of the workers and campesinos.

From Oligarch to Oppressed, Guardia to Agrarista: The Changing Terms of Political Discourse

The Reyes group managed to stop the movement temporarily but not before the campesinos had transformed the struggle for ejidal land into a national issue. Taking advantage of media attention, the CGT attacked both Reyes and Doña Tesla as expropriators of the poor peasants' lands. Dr. Astacio, Doña Tesla's lawyer and neighboring terrateniente, was the first to respond to the CGT charges. He admitted that 2,000 of the 6,588 manzanas, were municipal land, but he argued that Campuzano really did have a legitimate right to the disputed land. He then artfully accused Reyes. "Precisely when Doctor Reyes appropriated the 'ejidal' lands by use of false titles and the use of force, he grabbed away the land that my client pacifically possessed. He also despoiled poor campesinos of the claim that they had over these lands. Both the poor campesinos and my client have thus been victims of Dr. Reyes."[32] Astacio did not attack the CGT, but instead tried to link his client with the campesinos. He pleaded that the Guardia physician and Doña Tesla not be categorized together and that Reyes be recognized as the only oppressor of the campesinos.

Reyes, in turn, responded by accusing Astacio Cabrera of libel. The Guardia doctor cited land deeds suggesting that Doña Tesla's entire donation was fraudulent. Reyes argued that such fraud was made possible because Campuzano had never been surveyed legally. Then he reminded the public that twice Campuzano had lost court cases against him. Finally, he argued that *he* belonged with the campesinos, not Doña Tesla. "My detractor's confession [about the ejidos] will benefit me and the fifty or more campesino families who, all of us, the *ejidatarios*, rightfully occupy those two thousand manzanas."[33]

Thus, the two principle expropriators of the Chinandegan campesinos presented their arguments against each other on the basis of their supposed identity with the campesinos. The aristocratic Doña Tesla, of course, could not plausibly be presented as a campesina. Nevertheless, Astacio portrayed her as both the benefactor of campesinos and the victim of the practices of Dr. Reyes. The Guardia doctor, on the other hand, clearly identified himself as a victimized ejidatario who had been attacked, along with fifty other campesinos, by the latifundista. The two elite antagonists, Astacio and Reyes, thus followed the tactics laid out by Deshon. For it was Mundo who had adulated the campesinos' "first leader," the very man whom the landowner had sent to prison so many times. What appears to be the crudest of cynicisms, in fact, represented a serious effort to write about particular elite interests in a new political language. In the course of four years of struggle, the campesino movement had not only driven a wedge between the two elite factions, it had also redefined the terms of political discourse.

Deshon, Reyes, and Doña Tesla were compelled to identify themselves with the campesinos primarily because of the social and political strength of the movement and the internal divisions of the Guardia and the elite. Through their actions, the Chinandegan campesinos had transformed themselves from objects of patronage, pity, and condescension into an increasingly autonomous political force. By mid-September 1961, the elite gifts had been marked, as it were, "return to sender." The campesinos had transformed the gifts into rights. They had been prepared to accept the gifts graciously and settle down on the Nuevos Ejidos. But, for all their wealth and influence, Deshon and Doña Tesla could not fulfill their side of the bargain. The Guardia intervention interrupted the exchange and shifted the terms of the struggle.

By accepting the gifts, the campesinos would have reaffirmed the moral authority of Deshon and Doña Tesla. But instead, the intervention created a new situation in which Deshon, Reyes and Astacio were obliged to legitimize the struggle of the campesinos. Above all, this victory in the struggle for symbolic authority was the fruit of the campesinos' labors to forge tools of class struggle out of a heterogeneous cultural tradition. The agrarian elite could no longer manipulate those cultural forms because it now functioned under new restrictions on its use of land and labor. The elite's need for all available land and a seasonal labor force caused the local population to suffer.

The hacendado could still speak to the local campesino, his former dependent, with the same sharp tone of authority, but his words now sounded hollow and crude. The Chinandegan movement continued to expand, and the elite's inability to pacify or control the campesinos troubled all sectors of the dominant classes.

Chinandega peasant woman making tortillas
near Tonalá, ca. 1920

Army headquarters in Chinandega following attack by Liberal
insurrectionary troops led by Ernesto Pereira, 1922

Alfredo Pellas (1850–1912), founder and first president
of Nicaragua Sugar Estates, Ltd. (Ingenio San Antonio)

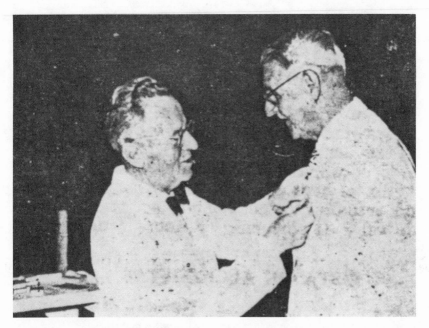

Ingenio San Antonio president Silvio Pellas presents an award
to former general manager Constantino Lacayo during company-
sponsored festivities of March 2, 1947

New ISA factory inaugurated in 1949

149

Clarifiers and evaporators on the top floor of the new ISA mill, 1949

Main plaza in Rancherías, 1989

150

Éntimo Sánchez, with granddaughter, at his *milpa* (corn patch) in Rancherías, with San Cristóbal and Chonco volcanoes in the background, 1989

Juan Suazo, *right*, president of a cattle cooperative at the hacienda
formerly called El Obraje, 1988

Juan Suazo's grandchildren in front of his rancho in San José del Obraje, 1989

Juan Suazo's twenty-five acres in San José del Obraje, 1989

Esteban Barcenas, former president of the Comunidad Indigena of Sutiava, 1988

Mariano Escorcia, Tonalá campesino leader, in El Viejo, 1989

154

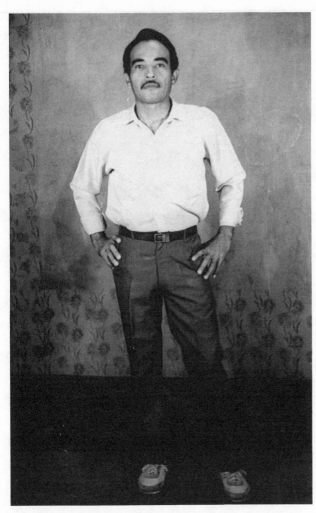

Oscar Osejo, Sirama campesino leader, 1989

Chinandega, 28 de Junio de 1977

"C O M P R O M I S O"

Nosotros los abajos suscritos en representación de más de
(100) Compañeros Campesinos que ilegalmente habiamos Invadido
tierras de la Sociedad Agropecuaria " LOMA VERDE SA." Quien Repre-
senta el Sr Edmundo Deshóm Morazan, y Propiedad del Sr Angel Molie-
re Bqca, LLamada " Santa Cristina" Contiguo a LLano Verde, nos
comprometemos ante el General (Ing) Ulises Carrillo R, GN. Es-
tando presente el Sr Juez de Policia Carlos Chavez Soza, de Esta
Ciudad, Don Edmundo Deshóm Morazan, y el Subt- (P- Inf) Fermin
Molina C. GN. A Desalojar de Inmediato dichas tierras nosotros los
abajo Firmantes y Resto de Campesinos.

En Gaso de no Cumplir este Convenio dejamos a las Autoridades en
el Derecho de el Apremio Corporal para nosotros y resto de Compañeros Campesinos que pretendieramos seguir en esta Invasión tratado de boicotear las siembras futuras de sus propietarios pues las
tierras invadidas por nosotros éstan listas para la Siembra.

*****
_____
Boris Castellón

_____
Ramón Panuagua Rodriguez.

_____
Alberto García Meza

_____
Felix Pedro Cancia Montalván

_____
José Angel Hernández Miranda.

"Compromiso" of June 28, 1977. San José campesinos, in return for their release
from prison, signed this National Guard document in 1977, stating their willingness
to submit to corporal punishment if they trespassed on Deshon property. It was similar
to an agreement signed in 1959.

7

The Village of Tonalá Combats
Its Destiny, 1961–1962

The movement was just spreading and spreading, like fireworks on the night of the *Gritería*. When they stop going off here, they start exploding over there.
—Éntimo Sánchez, Nuevos Ejidos campesino leader

Every time the elites and the campesinos would settle one land dispute, another wretched Chinandegan hamlet would rebel. Located ten kilometers west of the Nuevos Ejidos, the village of Tonalá became the next important base of the expanding agrarian protest movement. Like San José del Obraje, Tonalá was founded, during the late 1940s, on former hacienda land. Hacendados designed Tonalá as a residence for seasonal workers who once had lived in the haciendas as permanent laborers but had been forced to vacate to allow for more export crop acreage.[1]

From its origins, Tonalá's destiny seemed determined by its function in agro-capitalist development, which, like industrial capitalism, instituted the radical separation of work and community. Just as large factories replaced small family-based workshops, the agrarian bourgeoisie transformed haciendas from places of residence and labor exclusively into work sites. In the United States the separation of work and community diversely affected the development of the labor movement. The separation of work and neighborhood often facilitated the development of divisive ethnic and political loyalties among the working class.[2] Nonetheless, American workers also transformed communities into sites of resistance to negative changes in the workplace.[3] Similarly, during the course of the agrarian struggle in Tonalá during the early 1960s, work and community identities and attitudes became increasingly reintegrated, independent of the will of the hacendados. Tonalá came to know itself as a community of workers condemned to work for subsistence wages in the surrounding cotton fields. The reintegration of work and community directly stimulated the Tonalá workers' entrance and instilled a new radical content into the Chinandegan campesino movement.

On the Trail to Tonalá

Before its rechristening in the mid-1940s, Santa Rita de Tonalá, located a few kilometers to the south of the town's present location, had been a small Indian community. As part of his Liberal revolution, President José Santos Zelaya had ordered the distribution of communal land to individual Indian families. In 1906, however, five thousand of the approximately ten thousand acres immediately passed into the hands of Liberal politicians.[4] Although perhaps twenty indigenous families received a portion of the remaining land, the following report suggests that, in general, the Pacific Coast Indians lost out in Zelaya's social and economic revolution. "Santa Rita de Tonalá is the name of the *sitio* of the Indian Community of El Viejo, Chinandega; a legislative decree ordered these lands to be distributed among the Indians. But they had the same luck as the rest of the Indian communities of the Republic: there was something for everybody except the true owners of the land."[5]

Following the expropriation of the indigenous land of Tonalá, the new Liberal agrarian elite, excluded from political power following Zelaya's fall in 1910, failed to develop the region. Constant political and economic crises made it difficult for hacendados to obtain sufficient credit or a reliable labor supply. The region stagnated. While the few remaining descendants of Tonalá Indians engaged in subsistence agriculture, the elite let cattle roam freely through the hacienda land.[6]

Somoza García's rise to power in 1936 led to radical changes in the lives of rich and poor alike. During the mid-1930s, Campuzano and other haciendas in the area increased their production of cotton, bananas, and corn.[7] In addition, along the Estero Real, local hacendado entrepreneurs founded a mangrove bark industry. They paid wages to the *mangleros* who extracted the bark, and then they sold the product to tanneries. Such increases in regional production, as well as the promise of renewed Central American trade, prompted the Somoza regime to invest in a railroad from Chinandega to Puerto Morazán.

In 1938, Somoza García took a sledgehammer and drove in a gold spike to inaugurate the thirty kilometer Morazán railroad line.[8] This symbolic act signaled a new era of social change and relative prosperity for the Tonalá area. Although Puerto Morazán never handled more than 5 percent of Nicaragua's exports and imports, the railroad line dramatically transformed the region of Tonalá, driving up land values on neighboring properties since the farmers could for the first time ship their produce cheaply and rapidly to Chinandega, Puerto Morazán, or the port of Corinto.[9]

Local planters immediately took advantage of the new infrastructure by planning a strategic shift from traditional, extensive cattle raising to export agriculture. The transformation of the four-thousand-acre hacienda El Paraíso, purchased around 1915 from Campuzano, became the model for economic development in the Tonalá area.[10] The original owners of El Paraíso eventually had to sell the hacienda to the Horvilleurs, a Conservative family from Granada, in order to pay their debts. Because of its fertile soil, the availability of seasonal labor, and its prime location on the railroad line, El Paraíso became the leading corn and sesame producing hacienda in Nicaragua during the 1940s. In 1943, El Paraíso produced a record crop of three million pounds of corn. Favorable export prices for corn and sesame produced one million dollar profits annually during that decade.[11] From the sale of its produce, the Horvilleurs helped found the first large-scale factory (INA) in the city of Chinandega, a mill for processing corn, sesame, and cotton. In short, the Chinandega-Morazán railroad, by cheapening and speeding up transportation, enabled the Horvilleurs to decisively transform the countryside, six years before the start of the cotton boom.

When the Horvilleurs made the shift to intensive agro-export production, they experienced the same labor problem that others of their class would confront during the cotton revolution. El Paraíso needed more acreage for sesame production and the owners wished to control the corn cultivation scientifically. Hence, they cut back traditional land parcel allotments to their fifty permanent laborers. At the same time, the hacienda had high seasonal labor needs during the planting and harvesting of corn and sesame. El Paraíso managed to recruit its seasonal labor force without having to resort to the expulsion of hacienda workers by letting the workers live on the hacienda without land allotments. As their opportunities to plant corn and beans dwindled, some of the laborers voluntarily moved to the strips of land on either side of the railroad. Thus El Paraíso accomplished its goal of recovering the land once ceded to its permanent laborers with a minimum of force.[12] The problem of creating a seasonal labor force also appeared to resolve itself during the late 1940s. Urban and rural Chinandegan families, faced with a rapidly rising cost of living, stagnant salaries, and the need for living and planting space set up their huts along the Morazán railroad. Many of these families moved with the intent of finding work in El Paraíso and of clearing and cultivating a few acres of land along the edge of the line. El Paraíso's "solution" to its labor problem, however, was less than ideal for the squatters.

On a campaign trip to Puerto Morazán in 1946, President Somoza stopped near El Paraíso. Given the president's instrumental role in building the Morazán railroad, it is not surprising that the local residents, many of them squatters along the line, gave Somoza a warm welcome. Ruperto Mayorga, a young, local, Liberal party activist, made a brief welcoming speech. Ruperto, an *apuntador* (production clerk) at El Paraíso and the son of a medium-scale peasant, was well liked, though hardly typical of the poor campesinos in the crowd.[13] Ruperto used his brief moment in the national spotlight to address an issue of concern to all those at the rally. After expressing the people's thanks to Somoza for building the railroad, he pleaded with the president to provide basic services such as water, electricity, health services, and education to the growing community of squatters and small-scale farmers. Ruperto suggested that Somoza might donate national land to found the village of Tonalá, which would allow people to live in a civilized manner.

Somoza heard in the sound of the Tonaleños' cheers the promise of easy political points. The impressive growth of the opposition movement during the mid-1940s made every political gain significant, so he talked with Roberto Horvilleur about the request, and they quickly struck a bargain. El Paraíso donated some fifty acres to Somoza, who, in turn, made a gift of a village to the people of Tonalá.[14] Somoza's action was extremely successful politically and cost him little financially. Through the donation Somoza bolstered his regional and national image as a generous father figure and as a sponsor of economic development.

The Horvilleur family also prospered immensely from its gift to Somoza and Tonalá. El Paraíso rid itself of a minuscule fraction of its land whose boundaries were quite imprecise and had probably been appropriated illicitly from the indigenous population four decades earlier. Ruperto Mayorga later commented that the Horvilleurs gave away communal land. Thus the Horvilleurs were able to convert their property into a modern capitalist hacienda while projecting themselves as kind-hearted patrons. In both design and practice, Tonalá became, in the words of one resident, "nothing more than a barracks" for the hacienda's seasonal labor force.[15] Years before other oligarchs became aware of the difficult transition from permanent to seasonal labor, the Horvilleurs had already engineered a solution to the rural labor problem.

"There Was Great Beauty on the Land":
The Dispossession of Tonaleño Smallholders

The area's smallholding farmers, often descendants of the Indian community, experienced several prosperous years during the 1940s. In the recollections of peasant smallholders, that prosperity came with the founding of the village and the railroad, both important outlets for their produce, and halted abruptly with the advent of the cotton industry. In 1950, probably fewer than one hundred smallholders farmed Tonaleño land, almost all in the area on the west side of the railroad, south of El Paraíso.[16] Although it is virtually impossible to calculate the quantitative effect of the cotton boom on this group, perhaps only one-half of the peasants farming in 1950 were still farming in 1960.[17]

The cotton elite in Tonalá did not always have to resort to blatant forms of expropriation to acquire more land. When elite cotton growers needed more land they generally purchased it with cash, and peasants often opted to sell their farms. Behind the peasants' willingness to sell their lands were often hidden, structural changes that had rendered their economy unproductive during the 1950s. Unlike during the export bonanza of the late 1940s and early 1950s, corn production had become a more precarious venture. Lack of credit and monopsonistic marketing practices obligated the peasants to sell their harvest at artificially low prices. Under such conditions, farming often did not produce sufficient income for the peasant to be able to resist the hacendado's cash offer. If the peasant had acquired credit to cultivate cotton, the severe drop in cotton prices during the mid-1950s increased the debts.[18] Thus, whether farming cotton or corn, the small-scale peasant was often prepared to sell, although even cash from such a sale was not always sufficient to avoid a gradual socioeconomic decline.

Although the sale of farms to the bourgeoisie was a legitimate practice, peasants' memories of the loss of land, accompanied by the sight and sound of tractors uprooting trees, opened a wound that time alone would not heal. Engracia Zapata recounted her early years on her grandmother's forty-two acre farm during the late 1940s and early 1950s. "I grew up on my grandmother's farm. We never went hungry there . . . we always had what we needed . . . there was great beauty on the land . . . woods and lovely, abundant fruit trees. Then one day, we had to leave. . . . She sold the *finca* to the Horvilleurs . . . she said they gave her a good price. You should have seen how they sent in the tractors to uproot all the lovely fruit trees. What did they care? And then they planted cotton. . . . Then my grandmother died and I was all alone, in Tonalá.[19]

Although El Paraíso did not expropriate the Zapata finca and in fact had paid for it, young Engracia sensed that there was more injustice committed than the destruction of her beloved fruit trees. Elite landholders' purchases of peasant land did take advantage of the few cultural, legal, and financial resources at the peasants' command. In the most honest of cases, the cash paid probably amounted to several years' income from the farm's produce, an amount that dazzled the peasant into overlooking the true market value of the land or the cash cost of living without the farm. Mariano Escorcia's tale is similar in its raw outline of painful loss.

> My father was from around here. He worked for a long time on Campuzano. Old man Alvarado was good friends with him. He made my father his foreman . . . they went hunting together. . . . So one day, when I was a small kid, General Alvarado gave my father a present, a fifty-acre farm. I remember that day we had a big fiesta. . . . My father didn't have enough money to fence off the whole property, but he fenced off twenty-five acres. Now one day, the General was on the run . . . some political problem or a fight. He was getting out by way of Puerto Morazán . . . somebody overheard the General talking to my father about getting him the deeds. So they told Doña Tesla. . . . Years later, when I was sixteen, after spending my whole youth working that land with my father and brothers, Virgilio Alvarado, the son, shows up with a bunch of Guardia and kicks us off the farm. . . . He said we had no legal deed to the land. We got a lawyer, but it was no use . . . we had to leave. . . . My father died just a short time later.[20]

For Engracia Zapata and Mariano Escorcia, the experiences of dispossession were bitter—all the more so because they were singed with the memory of the loss of loved ones, victims by association, of elite greed. Not surprisingly, both Engracia and Mariano cultivated their anger for the expropriators of their land long after they had left the countryside. The loss of the land and relatives also forced Engracia and Mariano to become economically self-sufficient in a new, urban environment. Mariano moved to Managua and became a barber; Engracia moved to Tonalá and worked as a seamstress. Although the smallholding peasant background and artisanal occupations set Engracia and Mariano apart from the majority of the Tonaleño population, the destinies of the two peasant youths and the village proletarians would nevertheless become intertwined, for the objects of Engracia's and Mariano's personal revenge were also the principal employers of Tonaleño seasonal labor. Thus, Engracia's and Mariano's personal losses prefigured—and thereby allowed them to better comprehend—the collective problems of the Tonaleños.

"We Are Forgotten by the World, the Government, and the Sanitation Authorities": The Siege of Tonalá

The founding of the Puerto Morazán railroad and the village of Tonalá at first generated strong worker support for Somoza and the Horvilleurs. Rather than live in huts along the railroad tracks, subject to eviction at the whim of a hacendado or a Guardia officer, the new villagers of Tonalá now lived on their own property. Even if they still resided in thatched huts, the Tonalá workers planted gardens and fruit trees on their own half-acre plots. Beyond their new sense of pride and security, the minimal services of running water, electricity, nonhacienda grocery stores, and an elementary school were significant improvements in the lives of most Tonaleños.[21]

The optimism of the postwar years, however, soon became tempered by new economic hardships. The cultivation and harvest of both corn and sesame had once provided work for the local population for nine or ten months of the year. The conversion to cotton (and in some cases cane) production usually reduced that annual employment to no more than five months. That change did not involve expulsion from the haciendas as it did in other areas, such as San José, since most of the work force already resided in Tonalá, but it did threaten to create a serious problem of seasonal unemployment.

The thousands of acres of wooded land claimed by the haciendas mitigated the unemployment problem during the early years of the cotton boom. Typically, the hacendados would allow the Tonaleños to clear the land and raise corn for a two-year period. The campesinos would pay 312 pounds of corn per manzana as rent, roughly 15 percent of their production. Then the hacendados would legally reappropriate the land, now ready for cotton cultivation. While this was an extremely cheap way for hacendados to convert *la montaña* (the bush) into cotton land, local campesinos also benefited from the arrangement. Families often earned as much from their corn plots as they did from yearly wage incomes. For campesinos, access to the agricultural frontier was vital since their wages during the 1950s represented only 50 percent of the minimum income necessary to feed a family of four.[22]

Thus when Doña Tesla's son, Virgilio Alvarado, offered the Tonaleño community 860 acres of uncultivated land, rent free for a two-year period, their response was enthusiastic. "Virgilio was a *rico*, so we were all happy because we figured that no one would dare dispute our right to cultivate and harvest the land because it belonged to a *rico*. We also thought that it was good of him not to ask for rent."[23]

During preceding years, Tonaleño efforts to cultivate national land—efforts analogous to the San José attempt to cultivate Las Cuchillas—had been rebuffed by the agrarian elite. In Tonalá, however, the campesinos did not initially resist the agrarian elite. The Tonaleños' passivity partly reflected their relative security in their ownership of the village plots, greater hacienda employment opportunities, and the existence of an agricultural frontier between Tonalá and the Estero Real. The Tonalá workers' sense of security, however, was soon dashed by the terms of the Virgilio Alvarado deal. One Tonaleño laborer recalled, "The first year, after we had cleared the land and planted corn, Virgilio sent in the tractors to plow up our crops. Then he planted cotton. So there was no more land left and nothing we could do."[24]

Why did Virgilio Alvarado, a man of refinement, find it necessary to so callously break the agreement with the Tonaleños? The principal explanation is economic: the Alvarados probably obtained at least $50,000 in annual profits from cotton planted on the land prepared by the Tonaleños. Considering that Campuzano, with its reliance almost exclusively on cattle raising, probably never grossed more than $10,000 in annual profits during the 1930s and 1940s, Virgilio's appropriation of the land was what allowed the Alvarados to afford a life-style in accordance with their aristocratic social standing.[25]

Virgilio's unscrupulous treatment of the peasants, however, also underscored a fundamental change in the quality of Tonalá-elite relations. Although minimally decent living conditions for agricultural laborers seemed a real possibility during the 1940s, the quality of life in Tonalá rapidly declined at the end of the following decade. The view from the village changed from verdant, lush forests and hilltop pastures into brown, barren hills and blinding white fields of cotton. Where a few years earlier, men had hunted birds to provide extra protein for the family diet, small propeller planes now sprayed insecticide, poisoning men, women, children, animals, and water supplies, and, indirectly, the milk of nursing women. In one boom year alone, several hundred cotton pickers died from inhalation of the poisonous fumes; but the cotton buds sprouted and the hacendados prospered beyond their forefathers' wildest dreams.[26] The cotton growers shut off most of the peasants' sources of agricultural income by converting land to cotton. The widespread use of insecticides and the stripping of surrounding foliage similarly devastated the household economy by harming livestock and garden plots. As a result, by 1960, the Tonaleños' nonwage income was drastically reduced.

The changes in the regional social relations of production that accompanied the development of the cotton industry were difficult for not only the former hacienda laborers but also for their employers. The employing class did not become fully aware of the changes in workers' lives until the Tonaleños began to fight back. For those hacendados who had supervised all aspects of their workers' lives, it must have been both confusing and unpleasant to see the same laborers show little or no deference. The hacendados also had grievances against the workers. Laborers living in town now found themselves in a position to play one hacendado off against another in order to try to obtain better jobs and higher wages. To the hacendado, this lack of loyalty meant that a worker might decide to take a job at better wages elsewhere just as the cotton was ready for harvest.

A relative shortage of laborers, in turn, raised the specter of competition among the hacendados. No intelligent member of the agrarian elite could help but remember that the single greatest problem that had faced their forefathers was a scarcity of labor caused by the availability of nonwage sources of income, so it was in their interest to keep the workers dependent on the hacienda. Throughout the 1950s, Chinandegan cotton growers complained bitterly about labor shortages, particularly at harvest time. In 1954 and again in 1959, cotton producers actually lost income because of a shortage of pickers.[27] The lack of Tonalá's population growth indirectly affected that labor shortage. Despite the greatest surge, from 1950 to 1963, in capitalist develop-ment in the area's history, the percentage of wage laborers in Tonalá's labor force remained approximately 60 percent.[28]

It is quite likely that the agrarian elite saw Tonalá's village economy, along with migration to the city, as the chief causes of their labor shortage. A significant but indeterminate number of young Tonaleños, like Mariano Escor-cia, migrated to Chinandega and Managua in search of new economic opportu-nities. Other sons and daughters of hacienda laborers strove to find alternative forms of employment closer to home. In 1963, for example, perhaps twenty-five families (less than 8 percent of the total population of the village), still managed to produce basic grains on rented or family parcels.[29] These peasants provided some refuge for kin or friends during the dead season and thus served as functional supports to the haciendas.[30]

The same local peasants, however, were also a source of social friction. Like other Tonaleños, they needed grazing land for their animals, firewood for cooking, and lumber and palm for building repairs. The hacendados, however, claimed nearly all uncultivated lands. Peasants and other Tonaleños resisted elite claims by trespassing and stealing materials.[31] Finally, the peasants competed with the hacienda economy because their very produce—corn, milk, and cheese—constituted an alternative to the hacienda store. In addition, the circulation of peasant products provided employment for petty merchants, usually female, who accounted for an additional 10 percent of Tonalá's labor force.[32]

Tonalá's artisanal community constituted another 10 percent of the town's active population. Tailors and seamstresses, who formed the largest group of artisans, supplied the area's working population with clothing. Indeed, the clothing sector of the town economy thrived in the early 1960s. Many of these artisans, with their shared campesino roots and the economic independence to withstand elite blacklisting, became union militants. Mariano Escorcia, who became a union leader, with little experience as a tailor, purchased a sewing machine with savings from his job as a barber in Managua and set up a workshop in Tonalá. "I set up my shop in my ranchito right in town. All I had was my Singer. I found that if I worked just on Saturday and Sunday, I made more than enough money, so that I could devote the week and sometimes the weekends to the union."[33]

Mariano was joined in the union leadership by two other artisans with peasant roots, Leoncio Martínez and Engracia Zapata. In addition to their ties to the local peasantry, the daily work of the artisans kept them in close contact with their working-class neighbors. Although artisans did not compete economically with the haciendas, most of their customers were hacienda workers. Their fair treatment of customers provided a sharp contrast to the hacienda stores—the RATAS—which pumped the laborers' wages into elite bank accounts.[34] The village economy, despite its size, posed a challenge to the agrarian elite. It provided Tonalá workers with limited employment alternatives and consumption opportunities. Elite anxiety about potential labor shortages and dwindling RATA profits turned to anger when the Tonaleños organized a union and began protesting to labor department authorities.

In 1960–61, the village suffered three new catastrophes: storm-produced isolation, an attempt to rob Tonaleño land plots, and the emergence of a corrupt local power structure. Nature dealt the first blow with the great rainstorm of October 1960, which intensified the land shortage to the south and east of Campuzano. The storm also destroyed the railroad line, Tonalá's only link to the world beyond the haciendas. The government-owned rail company decided not to repair the track and bridges, thereby devastating the small-holders of Tonalá and the mangrove bark and shipping industries of Puerto Morazán, ten kilometers to the north.[35]

The elite reaction to these problems exacerbated class tensions.[36] In 1961, local hacendados recruited armed men to patrol their property and prevent Tonaleños and their livestock from trespassing on hacienda property. In part, the elite obsession with protecting private property reflected economic realities. To the north of Tonalá, thousands of acres of elite-claimed land, unsuitable for cane or cotton, remained uncultivated. Many Tonaleños wished to utilize such land for wood gathering or subsistence farming; by preventing them from doing so, the elite fostered greater village dependence on the haciendas.[37] Moreover, some villagers felt that the hacendados' use of armed guards reflected their fears that the nearby protest movement might soon infect Tonalá.

The reappearance in 1960 of Dr. Enrique Cabrera, an important Somocista Liberal politician, may have inadvertently fueled those fears. In 1951 Cabrera, Hugo Astacio's first cousin, had visited Tonalá in his capacity as departmental land registrar. Cabrera, accompanied by a Guardia officer, had ordered the townspeople to pay him thirty córdobas (a week's salary) in order to process their titles to the land which they had received a few years earlier. In return for the money and the only property documents the residents possessed, the registrar had given the villagers a temporary title for one-eighth of a manzana, instead of the original one-quarter manzana each. Despite Ruperto Mayorga's protest of the swindle to President Somoza García, Cabrera's political influence had blocked an investigation.[38]

In 1960, Cabrera appeared once again in Tonalá, ready to auction the land he had expropriated. Confronted by an angry crowd, Cabrera changed his mind and promised that President Luís Somoza would soon arrive to distribute the property titles.[39] Cabrera perhaps thought that, given the pressure for rural housing caused by the October 1960 storm, his private land distribution program would be applauded. He evidently possessed little regard for the memory of the Tonaleños. But Cabrera's visit not only opened an old wound, it also came at a time when some Tonaleños had discovered a vehicle of protest—the weekly CGT meetings at the nearby hamlet of Ceiba de Arenal.

In February 1961, shortly after Cabrera's second visit, about a dozen Tonaleños traveled to one of the first agrarian protest meetings in La Ceiba, several kilometers northeast of Chinandega, where they denounced the official swindle. Andrés Ruíz Escorcia promised the Tonaleños the CGT's full cooperation in return for their participation in the Nuevos Ejidos movement.[40] In response, increasing numbers of Tonaleños took part in the protest demonstrations in Chinandega from April to July 1961. In late July, during a lull in the Nuevos Ejidos battle, Andrés Ruíz Escorcia made the journey on horseback to Tonalá. The CGT leader addressed hundreds of villagers who packed the local cinema. Agricultural laborers constituted the overwhelming majority at the meeting. Escorcia denounced both Cabrera and the illegal payment practices of the local hacendados. The answer to both of those problems, Escorcia argued, was to unionize. A week later, Escorcia returned to preside over the founding meeting of the Sindicato de Obreros Agrícolas de Tonalá. The union elected local Liberal party leader Ruperto Mayorga as president.[41]

Since approximately 60 percent of the population had worked for decades as wage laborers on the neighboring haciendas, a labor union seemed like a reasonable solution to Tonaleño problems. Nevertheless, it was in the spheres of consumption and community that the Tonaleños recognized their common plight. They worked on at least five different haciendas, and within each, individual workers engaged in widely different relations with the hacendados, ranging from the total anonymity of the seasonal cotton picker to the day-to-day personal contact and trust experienced by permanent workers like Ruperto Mayorga. Relations of production often divided the outwardly homogeneous laboring population. But Cabrera's assault on private property and the armed guards along hacienda fences affected the overwhelming majority of Tonaleños.

Andrés Escorcia understood that the new union had to confront community as well as labor issues. He initiated a campaign of demonstrations and press releases through which the union denounced Cabrera's swindle, the RATA system, the armed guards, and the abysmally low wages on the haciendas. Under the guidance of the CGT, Tonalá workers began to file a barrage of complaints with the labor ministry about infractions of the labor code ranging from failure to provide vacation pay to the lack of drinking water in the fields. More than 150 of the 250 local hacienda laborers responded enthusiastically to the union. But the rapid growth of the union and its defiant public presence enraged the agrarian elite. On September 16, 1961, the Tonalá comandante arrested Andrés Escorcia and banned union meetings in the village. Following a week of national pressure by the CGT, including the threat of a general strike, the Guardia released Escorcia.[42] The union reemerged unscathed, but its repression highlighted the elite bias of the local power structure.

The bias of the local power structure was inextricably tied to the haciendas' assault on Tonalá's autonomy. The campesinos' ownership of homes, live-stock, and gardens, as well as their participation in local economic and cultural institutions, constituted that autonomy. While Cabrera's swindle and the arrest of Escorcia had threatened the Tonaleños, it was an outside threat to village autonomy that illuminated the issue of local power. Ruperto Mayorga, the union leader and town father, recalled the activities of Alejandro Acevedo. "Acevedo was corrupting our daughters. He was trying to turn Tonalá into a recreation center for the haciendas. The laborers would come here Saturday night to whore, drink and gamble. . . . We were honorable, hardworking families."[43]

Ruperto and the union membership saw Acevedo's prostitution business as the most flagrant example of the elite effort to reconquer Tonalá. For many union members of both sexes, prostitution was an illicit extension of the haciendas' control of workers into the life of Tonalá. It was an "outsiders' business"—directed at migrants for the profit of those who did not live in the village. In a public denunciation, the union members showed that, beyond the issue of morality, they also resented the abuse of political and economic power that accompanied the new businesses of prostitution in Tonalá.

> Sr. Luís Gutiérrez, a Civil Reserve auxiliary to the comandante is involved in the gambling racket. Whenever he loses he refuses to pay up so as to provoke the Campesinos. Then he has them arrested. . . . Acevedo is the owner of two brothels (and is) also responsible for Gutiérrez's outrages. Saturday at noon Acevedo has thirty prostitutes from Chinandega parade down the street and they create an evil atmosphere in town. . . . These women say that they have the right to do what they please since they pay a thirty córdoba tax to Acevedo, who claims that he turns it over to the sanitation authorities. . . . He is also a *curandero*. Given our meager resources and his constant threats we cannot legally defend ourselves against him.[44]

For the unionists, prostitution and gambling were dramatic examples of the hacienda assault on the town's physical and cultural integrity. Acevedo, an outsider connected to the Guardia and to some hacendados, had become the informal but absolute political boss of Tonalá. His wealth and power emanated from his control over the prostitution racket and the local Guardia. Many villagers were offended by Acevedo's disregard for public morality: thirty prostitutes, under his command, walked right through town every Saturday and Monday. This weekly parade of prostitutes symbolized Acevedo's particular brand of power. Acevedo projected a crude machista vision of an amoral world. Even more striking was his practice as a *curandero* (healer); the man who embodied depravity in Tonalá was the only doctor available to the Tonaleños. Acevedo's poor performance as a curandero did not enhance his prestige, but his practice angered and intimidated the villagers.

In early October 1961, several hundred Tonaleños gathered to denounce Acevedo and the local power elite. Speaker after speaker rose to the front of the stuffy meeting place to criticize Acevedo, the swindler Cabrera, the local comandante, the RATAS, and the haciendas. While no one pointed to the interconnectedness of the community's grievances, all spoke of them as outside threats to the community.[45] Mariano Escorcia saw in that union meeting the gestation of an anti-elitist community consciousness. He had returned to Tonalá after reading about the new union in a September newspaper article, and he was excited by what he saw at the October meeting. "It was amazing to see the change. I mean before everyone was so quiet, like living your life scared. Now there was so much effervescence among the people. Everybody got up to talk at the union meeting and argue against this rico or that rico and the pain they were causing us. I just couldn't believe my eyes. I figured Andrés Ruíz Escorcia had a lot do with it. He really broke down the walls here in Tonalá."[46]

For Mariano, Escorcia had knocked down the walls of fear constructed by the agrarian elite. The vivid example of the growing movement in Chinandega, just ten kilometers away, facilitated the CGT's success. Tonaleños had witnessed and participated in the protests in Chinandega, made up of people who, like themselves, had rarely challenged elite domination before. Escorcia's integration of Tonalá into the campesino movement had helped to produce the liberating atmosphere witnessed by Mariano. Despite Andrés Escorcia's immense prestige, he did not seek to impose any particular agenda on the Tonalá agricultural workers' union. Rather, he encouraged the Tonaleños to identify with the broader agrarian protest movement while carrying out their own community-oriented protests. Moreover, the CGT leader also helped the workers win concrete victories like receiving vacation pay and punctual wage payments. Thus the union's first months of existence were a time of multi-faceted activity in which the majority of the town's residents discovered ways to resist the constant encroachment of the haciendas on Tonaleño life.

The unique style of the Tonalá union is reflected by a petition drawn up in late October 1961. Mariano Escorcia and Ruperto Mayorga wrote the statement following a meeting; sixty-four union members, daring management reprisals, signed it: "WE ARE FORGOTTEN BY THE WORLD, THE GOV-

ERNMENT AND BY THE SANITATION AUTHORITIES! We are surrounded on four sides by cotton fields. The cotton producers drain off their water onto town, drowning our chickens and making huge puddles, where malarial mosquitoes breed. They patrol their fences and shoot at our animals. We are cut off completely from the rest of the world. . . . The mayor of Puerto Morazán only comes over here to collect taxes."[47] Although these union complaints seemed quite moderate, they posed a problem for the regime, for the guilty landowners included two cabinet ministers and several friends of the Somozas. Hence, even the straightforward problem of drainage could not be solved by a simple dike because it might flood the property of a Somocista.

The union manifesto's style of complaint was politically dangerous for the regime because of the Somocista connections of the Tonaleños' elite adversaries. The union leaders framed deceptively mundane community problems in a series of radical oppositions between Tonaleños and terratenientes that created the image of an elite siege of the town: they cause malaria, they kill animals, they block roads. In conjunction with previous union declarations, these stark oppositions delivered the message that the cotton haciendas were systematically harming the welfare of the villagers. The government "forgot" about Tonalá's plight for the same reasons of corruption and political favoritism that led the sanitation authorities to ignore the "pimp" Acevedo's practice as a "healer." Despite their own modest objectives, the union activists had created a radical language of conflict with which to describe the siege of Tonalá.

The Origins of Private Property and Campesino Consciousness in Tonalá

Just as the hacienda pressure against the workers of Tonalá came from all sides, so too the Tonaleños resisted on a number of fronts. By October 1961, the union had denounced all the political and social activities of the procurer Acevedo and the hacendados' armed patrols. In addition, it had participated in more traditional union struggles for the enforcement of the labor code in the haciendas. This broad range of union activities primarily addressed issues of interest to hacienda workers, but they also elicited the support of those Tonaleños who were not members of the work force. The active participation of artisans, petty merchants, and smallholders, side by side with the agricultural laborers in their struggle against hacienda abuses, was both economically beneficial to the union and politically significant.

Several Tonaleño artisans played key roles in the union movement. Mariano

Escorcia, Engracia Zapata, and Leoncio Martínez all shared peasant backgrounds and had been driven off the land by the rise of agrarian capitalism. Their collective experience of losing their farms and their accompanying feelings of antipathy for the agrarian elite provided an important stimulus for their union participation. Mariano, for example, left his comfortable job as a barber in Managua to join the Tonalá workers' union. "I already had an ironic kind of bitterness towards the Alvarados when I came back to Tonalá. I thought that the union was the last chance I had to get revenge . . . bueno . . . but nobody was talking about the land question. So I threw myself into the struggle—a kid without experience—to lead the people. I suggested a plan to take the Island of Bonete, claimed by Campuzano."[48]

Mariano wished to avenge the expropriation of his father's farm with an almost biblical notion of an eye for an eye. What is striking is that Mariano could so quickly transfer his personal vision of social justice onto a union which was at the time preoccupied not with land expropriations but with obtaining biweekly wage payments and vacation pay. Although supportive of the agrarian protest movement, the union had no space available on its agenda for land problems. Moreover, November and December were months of increasing seasonal employment in the cane and cotton fields, tactically the most inappropriate time to launch a land protest in Tonalá.

Mariano Escorcia began by gaining the support of other artisans who shared his sense of autonomy and resentment against the agrarian elite.[49] His relationships with his fellow tailors led him into contact with an aged tailor who lived on a small farm just outside Tonalá, Rafael Cantillano, a man reputed to be an authority on the region's history. Indeed Cantillano possessed many local historical documents, including land titles. After several visits, Cantillano agreed to share the documents with the union. "Sr. Cantillano did not get involved but he was real good to us. After showing us all his maps and documents . . . for example, I'd ask him for a document to show the compañeros of the union or even to some official, and he'd hand it to me and say, 'Return it to me,' and I'd answer, 'Count on it.' And that's the way it was with Sr. Cantillano."[50]

Cantillano's documents played a key role in the development of the agrarian struggle in Tonalá and in the entire Chinandegan campesino movement. Most important, they provided legitimation for the movement's immediate goals. Several Zelaya-era documents substantiated the San José campesinos' claims to Las Cuchillas and demonstrated, moreover, that Campuzano currently possessed other land that it did not own. One document purported to be the text of

Zelaya's wife Blanca's farewell address. Although Blanca Zelaya had probably intended her speech only to gain political support among the Chinandegan peasantry of 1911, it came in 1961 to provide ammunition for both the San José and the Tonalá campesinos. The speech read: "Señores and Señoras: The Cofradía de la Virgen de Santa Ana is independent of my haciendas since it was granted as a *Colonia Creditaria* by the colonist José Antonio de Castilla and his wife Manuela Rodríguez together with Las Cuchillas. . . . The Island of Bonete is also independent because it belongs to the ejidos of El Viejo and Chinandega—in the Map it is all engraved in its corresponding spot. Adiós to my country, Adiós to my children and to the noble Liberals of Nicaragua."[51]

The campesinos of Tonalá and San José enthusiastically cited Blanca Zelaya's speech as evidence of their right to land claimed by Campuzano. In response to union requests, Cantillano also wrote a brief outline of Chinandegan agrarian history, based on his own oral and documentary sources. The following excerpt gives the flavor of the text and suggests its importance to the campesinos.

Since Don Arturo Baca died of fright from the earthquake that occurred on Friday at eleven on the 29th of April 1898, Don José Manuel Antonio Baca no longer had a partner; nevertheless he once again tried to acquire the same lands of the Cofradía. . . . This time the Junta of the Cofradía appealed to the Minister of Hacienda, Dr. Julián Irias. He communicated to General Zelaya what was happening to his neighboring lands; so the General ordered his son-in-law Claudio Saravia to call on the Junta. Then he showed them how he had arranged the land titles: "The Cofradía de la Virgen, Las Cuchillas and El Bonete are independent of my hacienda and they have their corresponding colonial boundary markers" . . . and so he nullified Don Manuel Antonio Baca's attempt to usurp the sons of the people.[52]

Although of limited value in a court of law, Cantillano's writings were politically important precisely because their messages were immediately accepted by and incorporated into the consciousness of the Tonalá union members. Tonaleño workers eagerly accepted Cantillano's version of history, in part because, whatever their private thoughts about the Somoza regime, Tonaleños, by tradition, defined themselves as Liberals and possessed a rudimentary knowledge of the Liberal version of Nicaraguan history, in which General Zelaya played the role of creator and tragic hero.[53] Furthermore Cantillano's well-known family connections to Zelaya provided an aura of authenticity to the documents.

Tonaleños also discovered a source of ideological inspiration in Cantillano's writing. In particular, Cantillano's writings articulated the vague popular notion that General Zelaya founded private property. Zelaya had indeed, in one sense, originated the concept of capitalistic private property. Both in Campuzano and throughout Nicaragua he had attempted to stimulate the growth of agrarian capitalism, and in the process he had privatized many indigenous, church, and communal lands.[54] The titling of lands, to which the above excerpts allude, was an important aspect of Zelaya's program of rational land use and capitalist development. Perhaps the Chinandegan campesinos' collective memory of the Zelaya period had conveniently repressed the expropriation of lands and the forced labor they had endured and transformed it into a powerful image of Zelaya "discovering" private property on behalf of the campesinos. At the very least, Chinandegan campesinos seized upon Cantillano's idea that Zelaya's notion of private property was anti-oligarchical. One Tonaleño commented, "Before Zelaya, the *ricos* had no respect for our land. He founded private property to give us rights and protect us from the *ricos*."[55]

Through their interpretation of Cantillano's writings and other Zelaya-era documents, Tonaleños and other Chinandegan campesinos developed their own unique concept of private property and of their right to defend themselves against illegitimate oligarchical claims. Inspired by the Zelayista message of Cantillano, Chinandegan campesinos began to use the words "private property" to refer to a social right bestowed on them by Zelaya to communal or private land. For, in those documents, Zelaya had established the limits of both forms of property and demonstrated to the campesinos that most of the contemporary elite possessed their land fraudulently. The campesinos thus came to legitimize communal and family forms of land ownership and production, while at the same time viewing the elite haciendas as the illegitimate result of robberies.

The Zelaya parentage in combination with the label "private property" made the campesino concept extremely palatable to Somoza, fond as he was of both Zelaya and private property. Thus, the campesinos' notion of private property created a common ground with the regime by appealing to its stated political and ideological values.[56] Indeed, the campesino version of private property could claim as its inspiration a strand of Liberal doctrine. The 1950 Constitution, approved five years before the first symptoms of agrarian unrest, had established the principle of the social function of property: "The right of property, as far as its exercise is concerned, is subject to the limitations imposed by the maintenance and progress of the social order."[57]

The campesinos thus found legitimation for their notion of private property in the Constitution, itself a legacy of Zelayista principles. Furthermore, by defining their struggle in terms of private property, the campesinos created ideological problems for the regime by revealing an inherent contradiction in Liberal ideology between the inviolability and the social function of property. Moreover, the campesino struggle for private property meshed quite smoothly with the ideological content of the Somoza regime's agrarian reform legislation, sponsored by the Alliance for Progress.[58] While music to the ears of Alliance for Progress technicians, the campesinos' concept of private property, articulated by early 1962 in concert with their notion of "necesidad," nevertheless had a number of quite radical implications.

Like the notion of private property, the campesino use of the term "necesidad" was part of a search for common ground with the authorities. For decades, the landed elite, the church, and the government had defined their own obligations as a function of the needs of the poor. But the experience of agrarian struggle and the leadership of Regino Escobar had infused new meaning into the campesinos' usage of "necesidad." The Spanish word's meaning includes both of the English words "need" and "necessity." In the course of their struggle, the campesinos came to use the word not only to signify material deprivation but also deprivation of the political rights necessary to fulfill their needs. In other words, the campesinos' desire for social justice—decent living and working conditions—imposed certain imperatives, including the necessity to defy the power of the landed elite. For the Chinandegan campesino activists, that necessity seemed closely related to their notion of private property. Indeed, "private property" and "necesidad" became pivotal terms within the evolving discourse of campesino struggle.

The Tonaleños' commitment to the struggle for land should not be attributed to their peasant consciousness or background.[59] Rather, Tonalá workers initially forged their notion of private property and began the fight with Campuzano out of nonpeasant motives. Their idea of private property derived from a conscious political reflection on an unequal distribution of landed wealth and power in a society where private property was sanctified. Cantillano's writings, in this sense, helped union members to articulate and justify pre-existing criticisms of the landed elite.

The workers' desire for elite land was heightened, but not determined, by the problem of seasonal employment. One Tonalá worker claimed that the land struggle derived from "a need to work."[60] This view of land as a solution for unemployment closely parallels the experiences of Cuban rural workers in the late 1950s and Mexican field hands in the 1970s.[61] In both Cuba and Mexico rural workers consciously struggled for land in order to cope with seasonal unemployment. The laborers valued land as a necessary substitute for wage labor. But in Tonalá, as we shall see, the workers' struggle was more an effort to ensure the survival and integrity of their community than a defense against seasonal economic difficulties.

In addition to validating the intuitions of many Chinandegan campesinos, Cantillano's writings and documents told the secrets of the ill-begotten wealth of the haciendas surrounding Tonalá. Of immediate interest to Tonaleños was evidence that Campuzano had illegally expropriated land, including nearby Bonete Island (actually a peninsula). The union members vividly remembered Campuzano's appropriation of five hundred manzanas of land cleared by the Tonalá community. Many union members thought that reclaiming Bonete, a two-thousand-acre hilly section of Campuzano bordering on the Estero Real, would be well-deserved retribution.

Cantillano's documents allowed Mariano Escorcia to rapidly attain his goal of waging a battle against Campuzano. Even before meeting the aged Zelayista tailor, Mariano had planned to mobilize the union against that very personal antagonist, the Alvarado family. However, when Mariano had first cautiously suggested, in November 1961, the possibility of a union struggle for land, he received no support from the rank and file. The field workers refused to support Mariano, for they were about to be engaged in full-time seasonal labor. Most workers had agreed that the union's scarce resources would be best utilized in the fight for the implementation of the labor code on the cotton and sugar haciendas. Yet with the Zelaya manuscripts in hand, Mariano Escorcia was able to alter dramatically the union's perspective. Within a few weeks of circulating and discussing the documents, the union agreed to change its program radically and to invade the Island of Bonete.[62]

Union workers so rapidly adopted Mariano's peasant goals because the haciendas' earlier encroachments on Tonalá had framed their formative community and union experiences. The informal siege of Tonalá had taught local workers that although the struggle for a fair work situation and a decent community entailed two different forms of resistance, the enemy was the same. The multifaceted nature of the hacienda-Tonalá conflict had broadened the vision of the union members and deepened their sense of irrepressible conflict with the landed elite, while at the same time reinforcing their solidarity. Thus, when Mariano used Cantillano's documents to show that all campesinos had the right to private property and that Campuzano had no right to the island, the workers readily, if not eagerly, accepted that language and that argument as their own.

On Leaders and Necessity, January 1962

In December 1961, at the start of the sugar and cotton harvests, the union membership met and formally endorsed the decision to reclaim land from Campuzano. Only Ruperto Mayorga, the Somocista founding father of Tonalá, objected to the organization's change of course. The remainder of the leadership asked for the support of the CGT. Andrés Ruíz Escorcia readily offered his backing and tactical counsel. He viewed the proposed invasion of Bonete as an integral part of his own plan to force the regime to resolve the campesinos' conflict in the Nuevos Ejidos with Dr. Marcelino Reyes. Escorcia believed that the regime was close to capitulating over the ejidos issue and that additional campesino pressure would convince Somoza to pacify the region by undermining the Reyes group. The CGT leader therefore argued that the Tonalá union should publicly claim their right to Campuzano's island, not on the basis of Cantillano's documents, but rather as an "acceptance" of Doña Tesla's gift.[63] Phrasing their demands as the acceptance of gifts would tactically unify the two groups of campesinos, defuse the threat of repression, and hurl back into the spotlight the promises of the agrarian elite and the Somoza regime.

Although Mariano and his compañeros readily accepted the CGT argument about linking their action with those of other campesinos, they had a much more difficult time concurring with his proposal to accept Doña Tesla's gift. The attitudes of the Tonaleño campesinos were quite different from those of the Nuevos Ejidos organization. The Tonalá workers' uniformly negative experiences with Campuzano had prompted their decision to invade the land. They did, however, appreciate the irony of the ploy: they did not have to believe in the gift in order to use it against Campuzano.

Mariano argued for one change in the plan. He wanted to claim the campesinos' right to the island based on 1903 and 1917 agrarian laws that stated that land one kilometer inland from any body of water belonged in the public domain. The law was still on the books in a slightly modified form. So, Escorcia agreed that the union defense could refer to the water law as well as to the gift.[64]

At dawn on New Year's Day, 1962, 150 men and women, roughly one-half of Tonalá's adult population, began the five-kilometer trek from town across a dry river bed to the Island of Bonete. The Tonalá invaders, including twenty men mounted on horseback, must have presented an intimidating sight to the two National Guardsmen stationed at the island's gate. Virgilio Alvarado, Campuzano owner, described the scene based on the Guardia's testimony. "Carrying all kinds of arms, blowing on *cachos*, and shouting Viva Fidel Castro, the campesinos invaded private property."[65]

Whether or not the Tonaleños were shouting "Viva Fidel," they were indeed noisily joyful as they disarmed the Guardia and streamed onto their liberated territory. The campesinos behaved as if the occupation was permanent even though they expected Guardia reprisals and, moreover, planned to leave only ten families on Bonete, while the rest returned to Tonalá until the May planting season (to work and support the settlers).[66] One union activist evoked the communal nature of the occupation: "We stayed for three days. . . . We divided up the land but we all worked as a community. . . . There was so much faith in the people's work that in one day we prepared ten manzanas, cut clean and ready, from one end to the other."[67] This communal labor in early preparation for May planting stands out in many union members' memories of the occupation. Despite the extremely harsh conditions on the island (whose still accurate indigenous name, Moyotepe, means land of mosquitoes), the occupation was an enjoyable experience precisely because of the excitement of their communal experience.[68] Another unionist recalls, "We all enjoyed building our *ranchos*, clearing the parcels, hunting, fishing and cooking. . . . We did this altogether sharing all the labor. We were doing well . . . and we enjoyed to fight against harshness and for justice . . . even though we knew the Guardia was going to come back . . . we wanted to stay and struggle."[69] The union activists drew radical conclusions from their new experience of working and living in a community, freed of the social, political, and economic hierarchies of Tonalá. Yet they continued to express their politically novel thoughts through the concepts of rights, private property, and necessity.

This experience was the culmination of months of experimentation with communal and democratic forms of struggle within the Tonalá union. From the beginning the union's activities had been characterized by an integration of labor and community concerns. The tactical flexibility of the union struggle had been a very effective democratizing influence, since no one leader could have possessed the proven capacity or expertise to manage all the arenas of conflict. Moreover, this strategy was implicitly predicated on active participation by the rank and file, not just to ratify the leadership's decisions but to expand constantly the domain of union activity and to create collective responsibility. The conscious and deliberate involvement of all members made the leadership less relevant and less vulnerable, thus strengthening the campesino movement.

During the occupation of the island, the integration of community issues and economic issues became even more evident, since the social distinctions between family residence, community, and work crumbled. Although Mariano Escorcia had played a key role in preparing the community for the occupation, on the island everyone's immediate survival was directly contingent on the others' activities, and his voice became but one among many engaged in a perpetual state of assembly. "We talked about everything out there. We voted about everything, but there weren't hardly any disagreements or fights."[70] In this new situation, the agrarian rebels collectively confronted the immediate needs of the community by hunting, fishing, crabbing, and cooking together. They performed that labor not to earn wages or to satisfy the material needs only of their families but to symbolize their claim to the land and to satisfy the needs of the community as a whole, as revealed by the union members' decision to voluntarily leave jobs in the cotton and sugar harvests and homes in Tonalá to occupy this mosquito-infested island. Nevertheless, the Tonaleños did perceive the invasion as a direct result of their necesidad.

In this new context, the meaning of necesidad became as clear as the land they stripped of jungle undergrowth. Necesidad was expressed in productive labor from dawn to dusk on land that the Guardia would surely reconquer. And yet they worked harder than they had ever done on the haciendas because now labor was infused with a desire to forge different social relations and a new democratic community. On Bonete, for a brief moment until the Guardia led them all to jail, necesidad became removed from the web of material need that had defined it, so that the Tonalá workers could glimpse that which they immediately recognized as freedom.

On January 3, the Chinandegan police chief, Miguel García, Dr. Hugo Astacio Cabrera, and six soldiers arrived at the campesino encampment. García reported, "I saw about 126 campesinos, 20 of them on horses. I announced to them that they had to leave, that these lands did not belong to them. I said that these lands belonged to Tesla de Alvarado. So the guy who acted like the leader said, 'No, Doña Tesla donated 6,000 manzanas, so this is part of the donated land.'"[71] García and the soldiers seized Mariano Escorcia and appeared to be going to beat him. The entire rebel force, stroking their machetes, encircled the eight representatives of lawful authority. García said to the menacing crowd, "Don't worry, I'm just taking your leader down to Chinandega to talk this thing over. You all go on home."[72] No one moved an inch, except for one man who stepped forward from the ranks of the campesinos and addressed the police captain, "Pardon me, my captain. But this man you wish to take to Chinandega is not our leader, for our only leader is our necessity. If you take him, you must take all of us prisoner. *Nuestro jefe se llama necesidad.*"[73]

Unwelcome Settlers and Their Struggles

If after two decades of repression the informants seemed to glorify what indeed was only a three-day occupation, it only underscored the point of the narration: the moment of Escorcia's arrest *was* a seminal moment in their collective lives, a moment that resembled nothing in their past, but one they would often try to recreate in the future. This particular experience on the island was an important part of the radicalization process of the campesinos. After a few days in jail, the campesinos returned to Tonalá to regroup. The very next month, in February 1962, by linking up with other campesino communities, the Tonaleños successfully spearheaded Nicaragua's first strike of cotton pickers, and in March 1962 they returned to occupy Bonete. For the next fifteen years, they continued to combine community-rooted and agrarian styles of struggle despite increasing Guardia repression. Indeed, the collusion of the Guardia and the agrarian elite only served to sharpen the focus of the campesinos' evolving democratic consciousness.

Although the Tonaleños established a link with Andrés Ruíz Escorcia, the transformation of their political beliefs with respect to the regime and the elite was essentially endogenous, deriving from their own reflections on their struggles. Those struggles infused elite concepts with new meanings that allowed the Tonaleños to better understand the role of the landowning elite in their own community plight. Terms such as necesidad and private property became pivotal concepts in the evolving collective identity of the Tonaleños and the larger movement.

These campesinos could only use elite culture as they did because they brought their own particular experience to bear on it. That experience, by the late 1950s was dominated by conflictual relations with the local landowners. Moreover, those conflicts over land and labor conditions were themselves the direct results of the formative development of the community of Tonalá—like San José del Obraje, a creation of the agro-export economy. Its birth amid the upheavals of cotton development precluded its residents from calling upon and adapting previously formed traditional cultural repertoires, to which the Indians of Guatemala or Sutiava may have had access. Thus the modern capitalist origins of the Chinandegan communities made them more prone to operate within the symbols of the dominant culture.

The Chinandegan campesino struggles surely have relevance for other Latin American rural communities that were "precipitates of capitalist development."[74] For throughout the region there have been numerous uprooted and unwelcome settlers on the terrain of agrarian capitalism who, like those of San José del Obraje and Tonalá, with neither an autonomous past to draw upon nor urban allies to instruct them were similarly obliged to defend themselves with the few materials at hand—a palm leaf for a hut or a decaying scrap of paper for a manifesto.

8

The Growth and Limits of
Labor-Campesino Solidarity, 1962

No me pidas que los saque.
—Andrés Ruíz Escorcia to President Luís Somoza, 1962

When the Guardia led the Tonaleños off to jail, most of them believed that they would be protected by the CGT. Indeed, Andrés Ruíz Escorcia helped obtain their prompt release. Such concrete acts of solidarity helped create a worker-campesino alliance. Although labor and campesino solidarity tended to increase the militancy and autonomy of both social forces, that solidarity also frightened the agrarian elite and the Somoza regime.

During the early 1960s the Partido Socialista Nicaragüense (PSN), or Socialist party, bitterly contested the Somocista faction, led by Escorcia, for control of the CGT. The Chinandegan countryside became not only an arena of class struggle but also a battleground of factional strife. While Escorcia concentrated on organizing campesino unions, like the one in Tonalá, the PSN strove to organize banana plantation workers in Posoltega and El Realejo. Despite regime sponsorship of the Escorcia faction, the period 1960–62 was one of steady if unspectacular growth for both factions of the CGT. From the perspective of organized labor, the early 1960s resembled the mid-1940s. Both periods witnessed U.S. emphasis on democratic foreign policy goals, the growth of a powerful anti-Somocista opposition, and the regime's tolerance, as a consequence, for the labor movement. Yet industrial expansion in the 1950s and 1960s outstripped the capacities of union organizers, and much of the new working class remained unorganized.

Industrial Development and the Labor Movement, 1950–1962

Propelled by the rapid expansion of the agro-export industry, Nicaraguan manufactures grew at an annual rate of 7.8 percent during the 1950s. Industrial development depended in great measure on the success of agricultural exports since many industries were directly tied to the agro-export economy. Indeed, the ownership groups of the industrial and the agro-export sectors were interlocked. Thus, for example, the Banco Nicaragüense (BANIC) financial group founded in 1952 by some ten León and Chinandegan families, controlled, by 1972, four cotton ginning mills and two cottonseed-oil processing plants directly tied to the agro-export market. At the same time, BANIC controlled a significant proportion of the beer, milk pasteurizing, plastics, and chemical factories. The other key financial groups, the Conservative-dominated Banco de America (BANAMERICA) group (including ISA) and the Somoza clan, possessed a similar balance of interests among agro-exports, domestic manufactures, and commerce.[1]

As the old landed oligarchy formed itself into these powerful financial groups, it lost sight of neither the priority of export earnings nor the agricultural roots of its wealth. The overwhelming majority of industrialists also had major investments in coffee, cattle, sugar, and cotton operations.[2] The Nicaraguan bourgeoisie was thus divided between its collective interests in the agro-export economy and in manufacturing. The same person, at once banker, industrialist, and cotton exporter, had conflicting economic interests on issues such as agrarian reform and labor union rights. Their agricultural operations had traditionally depended on extremely low wage costs. Yet they could only continue to accumulate industrial capital through the expansion of the domestic wage goods market. A more autonomous industrial bourgeoisie might have favored a thoroughgoing agrarian reform as a mode of deepening the domestic market. With the exception of a small progressive minority, however, the policies of the economic elite and the regime favored agro-export businesses over the development of national industry.[3] Thus, most employers had little incentive to raise wages. As a consequence, in 1961, 90 percent of industrial workers earned less than five hundred córdobas a month, the minimum wage necessary to meet basic family needs.[4]

Construction workers led the urban working class in the struggle against their poverty-level wages. In June 1960, three thousand construction workers went on strike for nineteen days, visibly inspiring other Managua workers. A PSN spokesmen commented during the strike: "Our impoverished people are prone to emotional behavior and wishful thinking and easily fall into the extremes. For example, a month ago, it was difficult to find any group of workers who were ready to go on strike. Today, the picture has changed. Spontaneously, the workers of the glass and venetian blind factory . . . and those of the Aceitera Nacional [vegetable oil factory] want to go 'on strike' . . . this is very dangerous."[5]

The PSN recognized that the first priority of the labor movement was to win the construction strike, the largest sustained labor conflict in the country's history.[6] The Left feared repression if the movement began to expand beyond the construction industry. It is probable that the regime tolerated the strike in part because the principal contractors, Cardenal-Lacayo and Villa-Pereira, belonged to the Conservative-led BANAMERICA group and were involved in the anti-Somoza opposition.[7] Moreover, the regime did not wish to alienate potential support from labor at a time of growing student and Conservative opposition. Still, the regime's tolerance for strikes had limits. Days before the outbreak of the strike, the Guardia had arrested shoe workers on strike against wage reductions.

The construction workers' union, Sindicato de Carpinteros, Albañiles y Armadores (SCAAS), however, won a dramatic victory. The union had demanded 60 percent wage hikes, and the contractors agreed to 50 percent raises. Journeymen carpenters' and brick masons' hourly wages went up from $C1.50 to $C2.25 and those of helpers rose from $C1.00 to $C1.50.[8] Given the absence of inflation during the period, this victory increased the purchasing power of at least three thousand workers and set an example for thousands more. In addition to improving wages, SCAAS's triumph consolidated the most important union in Nicaragua. At the start of the strike, only thirty-four workers participated in SCAAS activities. Yet these militants succeeded in organizing and coordinating workers at eighty-four construction sites. The organizational skills of the PSN, the dominant force in the union since the 1940s, played a key role in the victory. Of course, in the end, the construction workers won because the regime decided not to repress the strike. Yet it was the organized solidarity of the construction workers that eliminated the classic pretext for government repression: the protection of strikebreakers. Thus, the workers' solidarity and discipline increased the potential costs of repression for the regime.

As the PSN statement underscored, rank-and-file workers' attitudes towards collective action were changing dramatically. With the exception of a 1958 printers' walkout, the labor protests of 1960 were the first strikes in Managua since 1953.[9] The period of dormancy between 1953 and 1960 coincided with a recession, but the emergency laws aimed at the political opposition also weakened labor. In 1960 Managua workers very quickly shed what both leftist and conservative observers had called their "submissive attitudes."[10] For example, the glass factory workers engaged in their own brief, successful walkout during the construction strike, despite the PSN's discouragement. Vegetable oil factory workers waited until mid-October but then launched a strike, which also resulted in a wage hike.[11] In Matagalpa, on October 17, 1960, construction workers engaged in building a large coffee processing plant launched a strike for higher wages against the firm of Cardenal-Lacayo. Workers in the region's major manufacturing industry—coffee processing— also declared a strike for higher wages. At that point the PSN-dominated labor federation declared a general strike in the city, and Matagalpa's powerful coffee growers' association mobilized against the general strike.[12] Only the lethal rainstorm in Chinandega on October 25, 1960, ended the general strike, for the Matagalpa workers, dependent on group solidarity, did not wish to compete with the homeless campesinos for public financial support. Nonetheless, the Matagalpa workers' movement gained significant victories. Coffee plant workers, in particular, won 20 percent increases.[13]

The storm in Chinandega thus marked the end of the largest strike wave since the mid-1940s, involving close to one-fourth of Managua's working class. Less than a month after the storm, Luís Somoza dealt the unions an even greater setback, when he declared a state of siege in response to the fourth opposition insurrectionary movement since May 1959.[14] Nonetheless, the large turnout for the May Day rally of 1961 indicated that the effects of the previous year's labor mobilization had not dissipated. The orators' insistence on radical agrarian reform sent a strong message to the Somoza regime: the labor movement, clearly capable of substantial growth, was in danger of falling under leftist control. The PSN, in turn, might prove capable of bridging a major divide in Nicaraguan political culture by allying with the middle-class opposition.[15] To guard against such an eventuality, Luís Somoza called a meeting with both factions of the labor movement. He promised to end the state of siege, guarantee full rights to urban and rural labor organizers, and introduce agrarian reform as well as pro-labor legislation. In return, Somoza reportedly asked only that the labor leaders discourage violence as a form of protest.[16] Although there is no record of the labor leaders' response, their subsequent activity indicated at least a tacit acceptance of the first major Somocista offering to labor since the mid-1940s.

The labor movement benefited significantly from this informal pact with the regime. Once again, the government hoped to use the unions as a buffer against increasingly powerful opposition. Union organizers began to experience the kind of freedom they could only dimly recall from the mid-1940s. Between 1960 and 1962, the CGT increased its membership from roughly

Table 2. Growth in CGT Membership, 1960–1962

Union	Number of Members 1960	1962	Faction (1962) Somocista	PSN
Managua Workers' Federation[a]	1,000	2,500		X
Highway workers	300	500	X	
Railroad workers	300	230	X	
Corinto Workers' Federation[b]	500	1,200	X	X
ISA workers	75	300	X	
Chinandega Workers' Federation[c]	100	500		X
Masaya Workers' Federation	—	200		X
Hospital workers	—	800 (1963)	X	
Federal district employees	—	325		
Tonalá farm workers	—	125	X	
Other provincial unions	200	1,000	750	250
Total	2,475	7,680	3,030–4,230	3,450–4,650

Sources: CGT archives; U.S. Department of Labor, "Labor Conditions in Nicaragua" (Washington, D.C., 1964); "Memorias del Ministerio del Trabajo 1962–1963" (Managua, 1964).

[a]Managua Workers' Federation included unions of construction workers, liquor factory workers, printers, mechanics, textile workers, drivers, shoemakers, as well as three rural workers' unions.
[b]Corinto Workers' Federation included a stevedores' union, a dockworkers' and warehouse workers' union, a customs house employees' union, and a sailors' union.
[c]Chinandega Workers' Federation included unions of construction workers, shoemakers, mechanics, bakers, and agricultural workers in Posoltega, Chichigalpa, and El Realejo.

2,500 to 7,700 members (see Table 2). Unlike during the 1940s, however, the Somocistas matched the PSN stride for stride, with both factions in control of roughly one-half of the CGT membership between 1960 and 1962.[17]

The Somocista faction was more successful than it had been in the 1940s primarily because Escorcia, rather than devoting his energies to combating the Left, led the CGT into struggles against the agrarian and industrial elites. Although labor and agrarian conflicts were problematic for the regime because of its alliance with key sectors of the agro-export bourgeoisie, Escorcia continually gained prestige and followers precisely because of his aggressive tactics.

Juan Lorío, the PSN chief, sharply criticized the Somocista union leaders, arguing that they represented the "new form that the national capitalists use to divide and pacify the union movement," and Lorío attacked Escorcia's "opportunism."[18] Moreover, memories of blatant fraud in the September 1960 CGT elections, which the Somocistas won thirty-six to thirty-five against the PSN candidate, were still quite fresh. Yet despite his strong criticism, Lorío issued a call for labor unity, primarily because the PSN recognized that the majority of the thirty-six union delegates who voted for Escorcia did actually represent the will of the membership. At this point, therefore, it was practically impossible for the Left to win over the rank and file of those unions dominated by the Escorcia faction. Lorío underscored this when he grudgingly acknowledged the Somocista unionists' success, even before Escorcia's major organizational advances in the Chinandegan countryside. In 1961, Lorío wrote, "The group which runs the Executive Committee of the CGT is not, as some *compañeros* believe, only a gang without prestige or following. That is a sectarian and unreal belief. One cannot deny that in Nicaragua there are thousands of authentic workers, of Liberal affiliation, who belong to unions. It is upon this worker base that Ruíz Escorcia, Jiménez, and the Medinas operate . . . and the truth of the matter is, they have a lot of political prestige."[19]

Lorío's analysis reflected his own thirty years in the urban labor movement. Regardless of political ideology and party lines, Lorío acknowledged Escorcia's membership in a common political culture of the urban working class, and he realized, as we shall see, that because of their cultural commonality it would be easier for the PSN to forge a tactical alliance with the popular Escorcia faction than with the middle- and upper-class opposition. Indeed, there are strong indications that the Left and Escorcia agreed not to interfere with one another's organizing work. Such tacit cooperation, to some extent encouraged by Luís Somoza, contributed significantly to the growth of the CGT.[20]

Although vital for the advance of the labor movement, PSN-Somocista cooperation involved a politically curious alliance between Communists (PSN) and the supporters of Luís Somoza, a man who personally supervised the launching of the Bay of Pigs invasion.[21] The anti-Somoza movement, also on the rise between 1959 and 1962, indirectly encouraged this alliance of Communists and anti-Communists, for Somoza, out of fear of the opposition's strength, supported this odd marriage in a fairly desperate move to gain popular support.

Another Kind of Silence: The Anti-Somoza Opposition and Popular Movements

In 1960 and 1961, the anti-Somoza opposition encompassed Castroite students, moderate members of the Liberal Independent party (PLI), and centrist and rightist members of the Conservative party. Despite its social and political heterogeneity, the anti-Somoza opposition lacked any significant base in the labor or campesino movements. Indeed, a formidable barrier of political culture separated the leaders of the opposition from the popular movements. Opposition writers and intellectuals rarely could see beyond the political contradiction between Somocistas and anti-Somocistas. Intellectuals and politicians therefore had difficulty in understanding the Chinandegan agrarian movement. Their incapacity to understand the movement, in turn, derived from a key historical feature of Nicaraguan political culture: the wide gulf between middle-class and elite political dissidents on the one side, and the majority of the laboring population on the other.

Shepard Forman has defined political culture as "the meaningful context in which political ideology is forged and politics is played out."[22] The gulf in Nicaraguan political culture, however, was not "ideological," insofar as that implies two wholly separate, formal, and organized sets of political beliefs. Marxists, social democrats, and liberals, for example, could be found on either side of this political barrier between the working populace and the anti-Somoza opposition. People with opposing political notions and dispositions, at the same time, might share a wide range of cultural assumptions about religion, sports, community, sex, drinking, social aspirations, and family responsibilities. In general, membership in a political subculture depended on social class and geography—factors that in turn conditioned exposure to decisive historical events.

Obrerismo, for example, although an important part of popular culture in Chinandega and León, was largely ignored by the elites. Ironically, the birth of the modern labor movement, in 1944, weakened obrerismo as a tool of the regime, while strengthening obrerista political culture among workers. Indeed, during the 1940s, the obrerista version of populism, heavily accented with artisanal social pride, became the dominant political idiom among urban workers throughout western Nicaragua.

Nevertheless, from its beginnings obrerismo had been with a few exceptions largely incomprehensible to middle- and upper-class anti-Somocistas. While the worker militants focused on economic problems and social inequalities, the oppositionists concentrated on the issue of fair suffrage and honesty in government. Moreover, the middle- or upper-class origins of most professionals, the backbone of the anti-Somoza opposition, led them to dismiss working-class pride. The Somozas, on the contrary, were quite conversant with the vocabulary of labor's struggle for social justice and against social prejudice. Somoza's ability to address urban workers did not necessarily earn him their unequivocal political support. Yet many workers tolerated Somoza to a degree the middle-class and elite opposition found, at best, distasteful.

These workers' perceptions regarding the apparently antagonistic class interests of Somoza and the opposition infused the entire political culture. Although the agrarian protest movement battled both the Somocista and Conservative economic elites, Somocista trade unionists who led the campesinos tended to camouflage the economic interests of the Somoza group. For example, by sacrificing individual Somocista landowners like Marcelino Reyes, progovernment union leaders kept the movement from focusing class resentments on the regime itself.[23]

On the other hand, Conservative class interests in the Chinandegan countryside provided easy targets for Somocista propagandists. Graphic denunciations of Conservative landlords, industrialists, and businessmen sent a clear message to urban and rural workers: you may not be thrilled with the Somoza regime, but give these Conservatives power and they will take us back to colonial times all over again. One fairly typical example of anti-elitist rhetoric by Somocistas read, "The hacienda Candelaria, also run by a Conservative Agüerista, Ramiro Gurdian, is a place which resembles a Russian or Cuban concentration camp. One of the most incredible abuses of these Conservatives is to make their payments every 12 weeks . . . after a long, hard day's work, they make the campesinos sleep outdoors . . . after being exploited through miserable wages, then they're exploited at the company store where they have to pay fifty centavos [an hour's wage] for a capsule of quinine."[24]

With rare exceptions, the Conservatives replied in a different language. They attacked the regime as a corrupt dictatorship, but that issue did not yet relate to the Nicaraguan workers' and peasants' struggle for survival. Even a man like Fernando Agüero, a popular Conservative leader from 1961 to 1971 and known for his effort to address social issues, phrased his social critique in strictly political terms, with little reference to the agonies of daily life for workers and peasants. In 1961, Agüero, unconsciously betrayed his concerns for the "people's social necessities" when he revealed that they were rooted in his fears of social revolution. "The Castroite hordes are attacking churches, profaning religious symbols and persecuting the anointed of God. But this tragic political experiment taking place in Cuba is the direct result of the Batista dictatorship and social inequality. . . For this reason, the Conservative party, as a people's party. . . unifies abstract principles of Democracy with the material ones of the people's social necessities."[25]

Both the Somocista and Conservative statements convey partisan messages to a mass audience—the Nicaraguan people—by exploiting anti-Communist rhetoric aimed particularly at Cuba. Nevertheless the Somocista propagandist addressed an audience specifically defined as "the workers," who could identify with those who labored on the supposedly Cuban-style hacienda Candelaria, where workers who were unable to afford quinine were forced to suffer the ravages of malaria. Thus, the Somocista document drew political inferences from concrete social and economic realities. Agüero, on the other hand, inferred social and economic necessities from political realities.

While the Conservative party was the largest opposition party nationally, in Chinandega and León, the Liberal Independent party (PLI) was the strongest opposition organization. Founded in 1944, the PLI was led by middle-class professionals who espoused political notions ranging from democratic socialism to liberal democracy. With the exception of the fact that its leader, Adan Selva, had a close relationship with the Sutiavas, the party was largely isolated from the urban and rural working classes. Part of that isolation, like that of the Conservatives, had to do with the PLI's class situation. The educated middle class in Nicaragua, perhaps 35–40,000 out of the country's 475,000 adult population, experienced a period of rapid social and economic ascendancy during the 1950s and 1960s. Many middle-income professionals invested in cotton and shared in the crop's jump in annual earnings from $7 million in 1951 to $34 million in 1956, making it the country's leading export.[26] As a result of their new wealth, many professionals took a direct interest in the cotton business and participated in growers' associations. This participation tended to win the middle-class professional social acceptance among the agrarian/business elite. Moreover, their participation in cotton-based activities recast their own political beliefs toward the right.

Although PLI militants still adhered to an essentially social-democratic agenda, they actively protested taxes levied on the cotton growers, which might have benefited workers and peasants. Thus, many PLI militants' opposition to the regime began to find a new economic grounding, one that increased their social distance from the rural and urban working classes. The Chinandegan PLI leader, Dr. Hugo Astacio Cabrera, provided a particularly graphic example of this distance. In his capacity as attorney for Campuzano, the largest hacienda in Chinandega, Astacio personally supervised Guardia operations against the agrarian movement. The politician, who had spent three months in prison for his democratic convictions, saw no contradiction between his professional duties and his political activities. Even more astonishing, PLI militants were silent about their leader's collaboration with the Guardia against the rural poor.[27]

Further to the left, we can detect the same inability to understand and address the urban and rural labor movement adequately. Ignacio Briones, a prominent journalist linked with the pro-Castro Juventud Patriótica (a branch of which would merge with the Frente Sandinista in 1961), for example, explained the failure of a 1959 call for an insurrectionary general strike to coincide with a guerrilla invasion as follows. "The CGT refused to participate in the strike. On the contrary, its militants, and some of its leaders received arms from Somoza, so that they could patrol the streets. The leadership command of the CGT has tight ties to the Somocista Popular Fronts . . . and as we have already said the leadership of the CGT are members, some of them very active of the Socialist Party, alias Communist."[28]

Although writing from a more radical political perspective than the other opposition spokesmen, Briones could still only envision the labor movement through an anti-Somocista political lens. His attack on what he called Communist and Somocista collaboration reflected his own exasperation with a working class that did not spontaneously assume its broader revolutionary duty. Briones and many other Nicaraguan progressives failed to confront the serious question of why workers and peasants refused to participate in the anti-Somoza movement? With the exception of a few PSN or (later) Sandinista intellectuals, most progressives were prevented from addressing this issue by their own political convictions, which framed every issue within the antinomy of Somoza versus anti-Somoza.[29]

Workers and peasants, however, operated within a profoundly different cultural universe during the early 1960s. Beyond their immediate family realms, urban and rural workers focused their attention on questions of property rights, unions, and labor codes. Thus, the narrowness of anti-Somoza political discourse created a growing social distance between middle-class dissidents and laborers. When middle-class democrats confronted what they perceived as political apathy among workers, their explanation was that the workers were vulnerable to Somocista manipulation.

They did not see that the campesino and labor movements had to develop within the boundaries constructed by Somocista political culture, for the alignment of national political discourses and conflicting class interests virtually precluded any significant interaction between the broad spectrum of opposition forces and the Chinandegan laboring classes. Some opposition militants, in particular those of Movilización Republicana (founded in 1959), were aware of the need to forge alliances with the working class, but they simply had no idea how they might penetrate what they perceived to be Somocista control over the labor and agrarian movements. Moreover, the spread of union organization further complicated the possibility of restructuring political alliances.

From February to June 1962, Chinandegan union militants made significant progress in the countryside and on the Corinto docks. Yet, unlike the campesinos in Tonalá, Nuevos Ejidos, and San José, the port workers' union had to face economically powerful sectors of the Conservative party. Indeed, this new economic conflict between the labor movement and the elite opposition reinforced the major barrier of political culture that had long segregated the Nicaraguan polity into two noncommunicating spheres, with the Somozas artfully moving between them. The Somozas were content with this barrier, a masterful piece of political architecture designed to isolate urban workers and the rural masses from the opposition. Yet, they astutely recognized that this barrier was always vulnerable to acts of sabotage.

Somocismo held a kind of prophylactic discursive power: other political forces could not operate within the worker/campesino world unless, like the PSN, they accepted the rules of the game. Yet the Somozas enjoyed neither great popularity nor the ability to mold directly the evolving consciousness of the rural poor. Therefore, beyond the coercion of the National Guard, Somoza's strength resided primarily in the social and political distance between campesino and union militants, and the opposition. Most anti-Somocistas still saw the campesino movement as a class threat manipulated by the regime. Yet, although the campesinos still interpreted the world through Somocista/obrerista language, they were rapidly creating their own meanings. By mid-1962, the mobilizing storm of the labor movement swept workers and campesinos into the field of vision of the political opposition. Consequently, when, the Corinto port workers and the Tonalá cotton pickers struck simultaneously, both the regime and its opposition, for the first time since 1947, had to take the working class seriously.

The Corinto Port Workers' Strike, February 1962

The dockworkers of Corinto occupied a strategic position within the agro-export economy and within the working class. Since the turn of the century, the stevedores and warehouse men of Corinto had handled the overwhelming majority of Nicaragua's international commerce. Taking advantage of their numerical strength, their community cohesiveness—an island of workers not dependent on companies for housing or food—and their key economic role, Corinto workers had engaged in six strikes since 1911. The latest took place in 1957, when 450 stevedores won a 15 percent wage hike from the Port Authority, raising their average daily wage to twenty-four córdobas, the highest in the country.[30]

Major improvements of the port facilities tended to help consolidate labor organization. During the 1950s, the International Bank for Reconstruction and Development financed the construction of two new piers. Before 1955 only two ships could dock at Corinto at a given time. With the completion of the second pier in 1961, the port's capacity for handling cargo increased more than threefold.[31] More efficient use of the piers and the introduction of cranes contributed to the greatly increased tonnage handled by the port workers, and despite such mechanization, the new piers required more workers. Twice as many blue-collar workers labored on the docks in 1963 as in 1950. Significantly, Corinto inhabitants, with deep union traditions, absorbed virtually all of the new job openings. On the crest of the wave of work force expansion, five Corinto unions, with over twelve hundred members among them, joined together in the Corinto Workers' Federation. That same year, the unions won contracts that included carefully worded closed-shop provisions.[32] By 1962, Corinto was unrivaled as a union stronghold in Nicaragua; in Central America, the dockworkers' strength was matched only by the banana plantation workers of Costa Rica and Honduras.

The Somocistas had a relatively firm control over the Corinto unions based, in part, on thirty-five years of port workers' support for Somocismo, as elsewhere in Chinandega, an outgrowth of earlier forms of liberalism. The very structure of the port was conducive to the perpetuation of Somocismo among the residents of Corinto. Port employment was fairly evenly divided between private companies and semi-autonomous agencies of the government. Although occasionally under severe budgetary constraints, the government could usually afford to use some of its revenues from the port to augment wages in return for worker loyalty. Similarly, when workers pressured the private shipping firms owned by prominent Conservative families such as the Palazios and the Vassallis, the Somoza regime had enough stake in keeping the dockworkers happy that it at least appeared to side with the union. There were, however, limits to the regime's support, since any wage increase in the private sector inevitably would lead to pressures for similar increases from the state Port Authority.

Although Corinto was largely Somocista, leftists were not excluded from the unions. In a script played out repeatedly around the world, the corruption of some port-worker leaders allowed leftists to obtain influence among the rank and file and gain a foothold in the union hierarchy.[33] However, rank-and-file port workers probably cared less about political ideology than about the efficacy of their leadership. Between 1960 and 1962, the united leadership of the Corinto federation was quite successful, guiding its unions to a series of victories. The stevedores' union started the drive by winning a 21 percent increase in its first contract with San Antonio in December 1960.[34] In 1961, the white-collar employees' union followed suit, winning wage increases that averaged more than 40 percent. Of equal importance, the federation defended such gains by actively supporting workers in on-the-job conflicts. In June 1961, for example, when the Casa Molieri, a shipping agency, fired seven employees, the federation won their reinstatement. With similar aggressiveness, on August 30 of the same year, the federation threatened a general strike to remove the local labor judge who, the unionists claimed, sided with management on contract violation disputes. In sum, the federation successfully expanded the domain of union power on the docks.[35]

The multimillion dollar governmental and private investments in Corinto infrastructure and mechanization, however, made management increasingly unwilling to cede any more of its control over the labor process. Management, in particular, wanted to avoid any union resistance to the increasing mechanization of the port. The Port Authority was planning to fully mechanize the piers and to avoid conflict with the federation it promised no job reductions when it began to introduce cranes in 1961. But the union leadership perceived the mechanization of cargo handling as a threat to their jobs. In February 1962, the port workers' union (private sector) demanded a revision of its contract, to insure job protection. The Maritime Agencies' (the consortium of private shipping companies) negotiating team signed an agreement acceptable to the union. However, when the management association published the contract, the union denounced the changed wording of one key clause relating to job security. The Maritime Agencies accused the union of trickery. The port workers' union, with verbal support from the Workers' Federation, replied on February 23 with a strike declaration.[36]

Within two days, the other Corinto unions voted to strike in solidarity. The general strike tied up seven ships and millions of dollars worth of cotton and other goods.[37] Just as the shipping firms resolved that their principled stand was worth more than any immediate losses, the shippers stood their ground for the right to mechanize, regardless of the social consequences. Key sectors of the agro-export bourgeoisie lined up behind management's position in Corinto (sugar and cotton producers had themselves encountered union opposition to their plans to introduce mechanical harvesters). Reflecting the fears and goals of the agro-export bourgeoisie, the Managua Chamber of Commerce issued a statement that summed up the importance of the conflict and defined its class strategy. "The conflict has revolved around the attempt of the workers of the *Sindicato de Agencias Marítimas* to insert a clause in the collective bargaining contract which stipulates that workers will be paid for operations performed by automatic machinery, without any human labor. The Assembly [of the Chamber of Commerce] unanimously agreed to reject 'featherbedding' [in English in the original]. Featherbedding only serves to discourage investment for the . . . industrial development of the country.[38]

What the chamber of commerce termed "featherbedding," the Workers' Federation of Corinto called "the equitable use of machinery." The unions, in particular, challenged the threat of the *mulas mecánicas* to the port workers' jobs. These electrical tractors hauled goods from the ships to the warehouses and therefore greatly reduced the need for human labor. The union argued that any solution to the conflict would have to safeguard union jobs. Thus, the port workers demanded an increase of 50 percent of their share of the shipping proceeds to divide among the crew, most of whom were working fewer hours. From management's point of view, such a work-sharing scheme would reduce the return on investment in machinery. For both labor and management, then, the strike had portentous, long-term as well as immediate, strategic implications.

The Corinto unions recognized that their fifty-year struggle for power on the docks might be lost through mechanization. Both factions of the CGT realized that the crippling of the federation would be a devastating blow to the resurgent Nicaraguan labor movement. At this decisive moment in February 1962, labor solidarity began to sprout in the Chinandegan countryside.

From Campesinos to Proletarians: Solidarity and Strikes in the Countryside

After five days of the port workers' strike, with no sign of a change in management's intransigent position, the Corinto federation and CGT leaders looked for ways of putting additional pressure on management. They approached the local union leadership of El Realejo and Tonalá about initiating actions in solidarity with the Corinto strike. In Tonalá the union had already been preparing a strike to demand higher wages for cotton pickers. Following the Guardia removal of the occupants of Bonete, most of the union members had taken jobs picking cotton. Not losing sight of their goal to acquire new land for the community, the two artisan leaders, Mariano Escorcia and Leoncio Martínez, began to consolidate key groups of union members in the cotton fields. Demonstrating a sophisticated understanding of the relationship between profit margins and wages, Mariano Escorcia and Leoncio Martínez noted that the price of cotton had risen nearly 20 percent between 1958 and 1962, while the growers continued to pay the same wages. During the 1961–62 cotton harvest, producers generally paid six córdobas a quintal, often a day's work for an experienced picker.[39] Higher wages in the new banana plantations and the sugar plantations, together with the short duration of the seasonal work, made the cotton wage seem particularly inadequate to the workers. Thus, when the appeal for solidarity with the Corinto workers arrived in Tonalá, the union was poised to strike. Mariano explained, "There was a strike in Corinto when they called on me . . . but we had already decided to go on strike for another córdoba. . . . The idea of the strike came from our own union meetings where people discussed how their situations were getting more critical every day."[40]

Mariano Escorcia's statement implies that the strike, although set off by events in Corinto, developed autonomously. However, as we saw in the previous chapter, the transition in the Tonalá union from trade-union to agrarian demands was both rapid and profound, and the union's demand for land enriched and broadened the union's preexisting working-class consciousness. By the same token, the union's renewed interest in hacienda labor activities did not indicate that it was abandoning its goal to reappropriate Bonete. Rather, it reflected a tactical retreat on the agrarian front as well as the union membership's participation in the cotton harvest. The maneuverings of the Tonalá militants represented a bold, and perhaps almost instinctive attempt to develop flexible, interrelated forms of organization concordant with their double status as peasants and seasonal workers. Indeed, the occupation of Bonete, by legitimizing collective struggle against the agrarian elite, prepared the union for another form of resistance: a strike.

The Tonalá union leadership seized the opportunity to strike simultaneously for a raise and in solidarity with the workers of Corinto. Sixty union members attended a meeting in Tonalá, where they voted unanimously in favor of Nicaragua's first strike in the cotton fields. Then, the assembly discussed the problem of how to implement the strike decision, given the fact that the entire union membership represented less than 20 percent of the total number of cotton pickers in the Tonalá region. Taking into consideration security precautions, the union opted for a strike form that—although they may well not have known this—typified strikes in the San Antonio sugar mill. Mariano Escorcia recounted the tactic. "We placed a group of eight or ten campesinos at all the exits, because to tell the truth, Tonalá was like a big workers' dormitory for the hacendados . . . so all the people left town at the time, at dawn. We shouted: 'No work today! Hey! There's a strike for a one peso raise!' Sometimes we had to get pretty tough: 'Look, man, don't go to work! If you go, you're going to screw us!' "[41]

The union tactics were extremely successful, with virtually the entire labor force on the six major cotton haciendas ceasing to work. Mariano Escorcia suggested that the coercive picket lines were necessary because of the dangers involved in an open, systematic strike campaign. Although the majority of workers probably accepted the strike action, the union leadership believed it necessary to enforce the strike both to convince the rank and file to take the risk and to minimize the danger of violent repression. The image of a unified movement might dissuade a Guardia unit from attacking. Moreover, in the Tonalá strike as well as in other protests, there was a curious relation at once authoritarian and democratic between the leadership and the rank and file. In one sense, the leaders responded directly to the needs and ideas expressed by their constituency. Yet the leaders also felt compelled to push the rank and file into action. In this way, workers abdicated full responsibility for their actions.

Although the Tonalá strike involved both democratic and authoritarian styles of action, the local agrarian elite was probably more intimidated than intrigued by the phenomenon. The Guardia normally could have been counted upon to defend the national economy and the strike breakers' right to work. However, all available units were in Corinto, protecting the warehouses from the threat of "Communist saboteurs."[42] Faced with a mass strike throughout the cotton belt and the danger of a prolonged dock strike, the six principal cotton growers caved in to the union demand for a one-córdoba wage hike.[43] The cotton pickers' strike thus ended after two days but not before revealing the potential of the campesino-worker alliance.

The agrarian elite in the Tonalá region ceded ground to its workers in part to avoid the strike's unification with a rural movement in El Realejo that was organizing at about the same time. Since 1958, rural workers in that village, a few kilometers to the north of the port, with the aid of the Corinto federation, had organized a union among the local banana and cotton workers. In 1962 the three hundred members of the El Realejo Agricultural Workers' Union responded immediately to the call for solidarity. Two days after the outbreak of the dock strike, Manuel Campos led one hundred union members on a march from El Realejo to Corinto, where they joined with fifteen hundred port workers in a solidarity rally. Andrés Ruíz Escorcia and leftist union leaders from Managua then met with the Corinto strike committee and the Realejo leaders. Inspired by the solidarity rally, the Realejo leader, Manuel Campos, vowed publicly to "call out the workers of the cotton fields in a solidarity strike."[44] The urban leaders applauded Campos's decision and offered suggestions about using labor code violations as a legal pretext.

Manuel Campos was a most unusual union leader. As a youth in the 1930s, he had been involved in illegal activities ranging from counterfeiting to moonshining. During the mid-1940s, Campos briefly participated in a union organizing drive in El Realejo. His union experience may have opened his mind to ideological alternatives, for in the late 1940s he became Chinandega's first Baptist preacher. Campos's new religious calling revealed a gift for eloquent words and rhetoric, despite his illiteracy. Whether or not his claim to have memorized the Bible was true, he certainly could spellbind a crowd with lengthy passages from the Scriptures or from his own astoundingly fertile imagination.[45]

Campos's religious conversion was a serious affair; in some respects, however, it merely changed the form of his rebellious stance. Local authorities and religious figures combined to repress Manuel's successful evangelizing. In 1950, the mayor of El Realejo ordered the Guardia to arrest him on charges of not cleaning up trash in front of the Catholic church. Campos made the case for freedom of religion all the way to Managua. Not only was he released, but the national government also ordered the removal of the mayor and the local Guardia comandante. According to Campos, in order to protect him from future harassment, a sympathetic cabinet minister also bestowed on him the somewhat honorary post of Comisario.[46]

More than a decade before Catholic activists began to speak of a theology of liberation, this illiterate ex-moonshiner found that Christianity and class struggle were inextricably linked. Living among the field workers of El Realejo, Campos preached messages of dignity and earthly salvation. When the Corinto dockworkers helped reorganize the Realejo farm workers' union, Campos not only joined but also, with his eloquence, persuaded twenty or thirty members of his congregation to do so as well. Moreover, after a decade of Campos's preachings, the bitter anti-Protestant feelings of the village's Catholic majority had noticeably subsided. In 1961, the predominantly Catholic union members elected the Protestant preacher to its leadership and then followed him on the Corinto march.[47] He recounted the union's solidarity strike as follows. "As Secretary of Conflicts I shut down all the haciendas. I went to the Comandante of El Realejo and as Comisario I informed him of violations of the law on the haciendas. So together with . . . [other union officials] and the Comandante, I went out to Las Lajas. I stated that this hacienda is violating the labor code in the following articles . . . vacations, overtime, schooling, health and so on. Sr. Comandante, I said, it is your sacred duty as the enforcer of the laws to shut this hacienda down. He was a bit amazed but he went along with it. I was like a two-colored leaf. He thought that I was with the Guardia, but I was really working to change the whole system. And from there the strike spread like a fire."[48]

Indeed, Manuel Campos, playing on the local comandante's ignorance, managed to manipulate him into behaving as if he were ordering the strike of cotton pickers—and the movement did spread rapidly throughout the zone. The cotton growers of the Realejo area correctly interpreted the strike as an act of solidarity with the Corinto port workers. They also reasoned that, given the Guardia's commitment in the port, massive repression was not a viable option. Thus, the Realejo hacendados ceded a wage increase as the only means of ending the costly and potentially dangerous strike.[49]

The Realejo action was similar to the Tonalá cotton pickers' strike. Both appeared to the elite and to the rest of the labor movement as solidarity strikes, yet the strikes focused on local wage and labor code issues. In part, the difference between elite and campesino perceptions about the field workers' strikes derived once again from the fusion of democratic and authoritarian forms of popular politics. Whether through minority picket lines or through the ingenious manipulation of the Guardia, the rural union leadership pushed the rank and file into actions to win shared goals. The union leaders knew that worker solidarity beyond the local level was a far more serious offense in the eyes of the elite than local self-interest. With this in mind, they purposefully underplayed to the media and the Guardia their highly significant gestures of solidarity to the Corinto strikers.

The field workers did, however, express solidarity with the Corinto workers, most notably during the El Realejo march. When the Realejo cotton pickers marched to Corinto, they were returning the favor of the assistance in organizing they had received from the port workers' union. By demonstrating their solidarity, they were also stating the expectation of reciprocal action in support of their own goals of land, better working conditions, and higher wages. In a similarly pragmatic vein, the campesinos of Tonalá and El Realejo were quite prepared to take advantage of the fact that the attention of the Guardia was focused on the docks of Corinto.

More important than this pragmatism, however, was that after a decade of breaking away from vertical relationships with the agrarian elite, the Chinandegan campesinos established their first horizontal relationship with urban workers, based on a familiar code of reciprocal obligations. Reciprocity with the elite had implied labor and deference on the part of the workers in exchange for "gifts" of land and food. Reciprocity with the urban working class, on the contrary, involved neither expressions of deference nor material gifts, but rather genuine mutual aid. This shift in the concept of reciprocal obligations was part of a process in which campesinos began to see themselves as independent social actors, while recognizing a commonality of interest with others of their class that overrode differences of residence and occupation.[50]

The campesinos' sense of identity with the dockworkers created a collective social pride and sense of equality. For example, Campos said of the solidarity march, "We agreed to participate in the Corinto strike."[51] For the rural workers, solidarity with the port workers literally meant to *participate* in the strike, as equals. By joining the solidarity parade, they merged with the strikers. This heightened sense of identity with the port workers was revealed even more emphatically when the Realejo union went on strike. Campos then stated, "We represent the Corinto strike."[52] Identification with the Corinto workers reinforced the campesinos' social pride after centuries of elite scorn; it also strengthened what might be called the "proletarian" component of campesino consciousness. Florencia Mallon's discussion of the unity of rural proletarian and peasant groups in the Pernambuco campesino movements during the early

1960s provides a useful point of comparison. She writes, "Neither the peasants as a whole nor the rural workers by themselves, were the most revolutionary force; rather it was the alliance of poor peasants and rural laborers. By allying with the rural proletariat, the poorer peasants gained the economic power and the political connections that their class position might give them. By allying with the peasants, rural laborers expanded their demands beyond trade-union issues."[53]

As in Pernambuco, a rural proletarian/peasant alliance operated in Tonalá, Realejo, and San José del Obraje.[54] Among the Chinandegans, rural wage labor did not provide economic power or political connections, but it did foster an identification with the dockworkers. The rural workers' immediate link with the urban workers was their common dependence on wage labor and on the agro-export elite. Through their active solidarity with the Corinto strike, campesino militants began to reflect on broader questions related to capitalist social relations, class alliances, and power. Rural class consciousness did not involve a zero-sum game in which the addition of proletarian ideas canceled out peasant ideas. Rather, as campesinos developed a more acute awareness of their role as wage laborers in agro-export capitalism, the greater political knowledge and perceptual range involved in that awareness enhanced their peasant-style struggle for land. At the same time, as Mallon underscores, the fight for land expanded the rural proletarian perspective beyond trade union issues, such as higher wages and enforcement of the labor code. The struggle for land in Chinandega invariably questioned the legitimacy of the agrarian elite in ways that the struggle for trade union demands often could not, since the assumption behind the latter was the acceptance of the elite's right to the land. The Corinto strike, by appealing to agrarian rebels as workers, stimulated this fusion of campesino and proletarian consciousness.

Conversely, the solidarity from the fields had a strong impact on the union members of Corinto. They devoted entire communiques of thanks to their rural allies. Moreover, powerful gestures of rural solidarity broadened the scope of the port workers' own immediate concerns. The union strike committee reiterated their new sense of solidarity during talks with the labor ministry by presenting this argument. "When have feudal lords remembered about the campesino? Do they care about endless waits in the scorching sun, on the Chinandegan sidewalks, waiting for their patrón to pay their miserable wage? . . . Do the Lords care that the campesinos have to sleep under trees like animals and that their children die of starvation? When will you declare this system of campesino life to be illegal?"[55]

The solidarity strikes in the cotton fields and on the docks sent a message to the government and to the elite that the new labor movement was no longer weak, divided, and isolated. Rather, the unions had infested the countryside like a plague of locusts, and in harmony with a unified Corinteño proletariat they might well threaten the entire agro-export edifice.

The Terms of a Settlement, the Limits of a System

The Somozas recognized imminent danger in the development of this new labor movement. For the Somoza regime, the strikes meant first a loss of customs revenue. Far more serious, however, were the political challenges posed by the strikes. Although technically acting within the boundaries of Somocista unionism, the Left had played important roles in Corinto and El Realejo. Moreover, the worker-campesino alliance, by its very constitution, had created a movement too broad to be manipulated. Since Somoza did not have a firm base of support among the agro-export elite, he still needed the backing of the labor movement. Thus, the regime's political interest in self-preservation contradicted the strategic interests of the agro-export bourgeoisie, which Somoza also sought to represent.

As individual employers, key members of the agro-export elite had given in to the strike demands of their field workers, but as a class they vigorously opposed the goals of the Corinto dockworkers. Industrialists, shipping companies, and plantation owners all quite accurately recognized that the dockworkers' demands for job protection in the face of mechanization "would block increases in labor productivity and make any attempt to lower costs a sterile effort."[56] For the elite, whose vision of economic progress was a technological utopia, the fate of development indeed seemed to be dangling by a thread in the sea breeze of Corinto.

On March 1, 1962, Luís Somoza conceded victory to the strikers in order to forestall a further erosion of the political situation. Chinandega was increasingly volatile, and Managua braced for a March 2 solidarity demonstration that some leftists planned to convert into a general strike. While considering the long-term interests of the elite, Somoza may well have reasoned that there might be no future for the elite if he did not defuse the situation. The President forced an agreement on the shipping firms. They granted a 30 percent wage hike and promised employment security against displacement by the machines.[57] This was indeed a great victory for the labor movement.

Yet Somoza did not exactly cave in to the strike movement, as some elite oppositionists implied, for the Somoza group also had economic interests in the profitable introduction of labor-saving machinery. Somoza announced that the guaranteed employment/payment clause was a temporary solution to the mechanization problem pending an exhaustive study by the labor ministry. As if to deflect any charges of weakness, Somoza also ordered the jailing of Andrés Escorcia, believed to be responsible for the solidarity movement in the countryside, and of Campos, who was surely guilty of agitation in the cotton fields.[58] Those arrests, however, were symbolic gestures, and the Guardia released both unionists shortly after the strike.

The strike victory energized the campesino movement. Days after the settlement of the Corinto strike, hundreds of campesinos invaded the ejidal land claimed by Dr. Reyes. Following twenty arrests by the Guardia, hundreds of campesinos returned to occupy the ejidos. Animated by their new sense of power and militancy, the campesinos began to build huts, rather than merely store materials—clearly increasing the symbolic and real stakes. Once again, Reyes went over the head of Comandante Rodríguez Somoza and obtained military support to evict the campesino rebels.[59] The acceleration of turmoil set off by the strikes again pitted an important segment of the Guardia against CGT-led campesinos. This conflict between groups that both nominally supported his regime compelled Luís Somoza to journey to Chinandega to try to settle the issue.

The campesino movement thus exacerbated class tensions within the Somocista alliance: a faction of the agrarian bourgeoisie joined by sectors of the Guardia and the state bureaucracy aligned themselves against the rural and urban laboring classes under the leadership of the Somocista unionists. Although Andrés Ruíz Escorcia tried to prevent the rupture in the Somocista alliance, he fully understood that his own leadership (and by extension the leadership of all Somocistas) in the labor and agrarian movements depended on his capacity to extract concessions from the elites. This was no easy task, for the regime had a different agenda: it wanted to avoid alienating elite supporters while projecting a populist image that would bolster the regime against the opposition.

In March 1962 the latent tension between Somoza and the popular movement flared up in a personal confrontation. Fresh from the picket lines, 150 Tonalá activists reoccupied Bonete.[60] Somoza called on the CGT leader for an urgent conference. The conversation between Somoza and Escorcia, recounted here by Andrés Ruíz Escorcia, revealed the limits of this new form of Somocista populism and underscored the relative autonomy of the CGT and the campesino movement. Escorcia's pointed remarks to Somoza implied tribute to the power and independence of the organized rural poor; Somoza, in turn, realized that he would have to find other ways to control the rebellious campesinos.

SOMOZA: Get those campesinos off that island!
ESCORCIA: Mi jefe, do you look on me as the leader of the campesinos?
SOMOZA: Of course I do, that's why I'm telling you to get them out of there.
ESCORCIA: But Sr. President, do you want me to remain the leader of the campesinos?
SOMOZA: Of course.
ESCORCIA: Pues no me pidas que los saque [Then don't ask me to get them out of there].[61]

9

Andrés Never Understood:
Educating the Liberator, 1962

You've made my man Escorcia a Communist!
—President Luís Somoza to PSN leader Domingo Sánchez, 1962

In the first six months of 1962, the labor and campesino movements began to undermine the stability of the Somoza regime. The militancy of the campesino movement and leftist-led rural laborers' unions threatened to drive Somocista and neutral members of the agrarian elite into the opposition, for the regime seemed incapable of protecting their interests. Moreover, campesinos, workers, and students were beginning to chip away at the class and ideological barriers that divided the popular movements from sectors of the anti-Somoza opposition.

Somoza dealt with the agrarian crisis by granting a limited victory to the Nuevos Ejidos group and then sending in Colonel Juan Angel López to crush the campesino and labor organizations throughout the department of Chinandega. The regime would attempt to employ a similar strategy on a national level when it implemented labor and agrarian reforms in late 1962 and 1963. The national strategy, however, hinged on its successful application in Chinandega, the center of the agro-export economy and the vanguard of Nicaraguan popular movements.

Return to Bonete, March 1962

Andrés Ruíz Escorcia's response to Somoza's order that he clear Bonete of the campesinos made it clear to the president that he had to look for another intermediary with the campesinos. The president turned to a trusted local functionary of the agricultural ministry, Ernesto Cervantes, to warn the campesinos that if they did not leave Bonete peacefully, the Guardia would come in shooting. Cervantes, in turn, looked for assistance to his friend Domingo Ramírez, who had been a labor leader in Chinandega from the 1920s until the late 1940s and was now attempting to challenge Escorcia's role in the campesino movement. Ramírez hoped to use leadership of the campesinos to launch his political career; thus he accepted the presidential mission, assuming that Somoza's removal of Escorcia would increase his own prestige among the campesinos. The obrerista leader had earned a modicum of popularity among some campesinos for his role in the successful struggle of the Palacios group near Puerto Morazán.[1] Moreover, Ramírez had gained a small but loyal campesino following through his criticisms of Escorcia and the CGT, and he was able to recruit two of his campesino followers for the journey to the occupied land.

The four men traveled by car to the Bonete, and then went the final eight kilometers by horseback and on foot. When they reached the camp, they saw two large banners, one carrying a quotation from Somoza that promised land reform, and another that stated, The Campesinos Ask for a Solution to this Problem of Life and Death for Nicaraguans. An exhausted Domingo Ramírez looked at that slogan and then at the hardened faces around him. He was friendly with many of the Tonaleños but felt intimidated by this group. Ramírez explained that he had traveled to the island on a presidential mission to avoid bloodshed. By his own account, the response of the Tonaleños was very negative. "The majority were of the opinion that it was better to get gunned down by machine guns than to go on suffering so much [without land]. . . . Others said, 'We, the campesinos, are alone. All politicians are shameless. . . . Where are Somoza's promises now?' "[2]

The Tonalá campesinos' anger was politically significant because it was the most forceful and direct statement that the movement had yet made against the regime. Tonaleño rage welled up on that dusty, barren strip of land because Somoza was directly threatening the lives of the union members for carrying out their own version of the promised land reform. Escorcia could not stop the regime's repression because Somoza was more responsive to the agrarian elite, who were ready to withdraw their political support if Somoza did not crack down on the campesinos, than he was to the movement. Moreover, as Escorcia pointed out in his conversation with Somoza, there existed a growing contradiction between his position as mediator between the regime and the campesinos, and the autonomous direction that the movement was taking. The CGT leader's consequent refusal to carry out Somoza's order damaged a previously essential mechanism of mediation. Rather than mediate, Domingo Ramírez could only offer the Tonaleños unconditional surrender. Although Ramírez did not appreciate it, these campesinos looked at him as no more than the messenger of the regime. Without Escorcia's skillful mediation, the campesinos stared directly and angrily at the regime.

Despite their expressions of bitterness, the campesinos were not about to bring on their own massacre. Without any firearms, resistance would entail a purely symbolic sacrifice of lives. Moreover, during this second occupation, the Tonaleños had come to recognize that the land on Bonete was of poor quality and was not worth any more sacrifices. The union agreed on a strategic retreat. They would leave the island but only to look for new land. Some militants still recall that as the Tonaleños gathered up their belongings, they looked up at the receding figures of Ramírez, Cervantes, and the two other campesinos. A black cloud suddenly descended from the sky and enveloped the group. They started shouting in agony as hundreds of mosquitoes sucked their blood and turned their flesh into swollen lumps. A few of the rebels chuckled and joked that maybe they were not so alone after all.[3]

Leaders and Factions

President Luís Somoza was particularly angered by the Tonaleño occupation of Bonete since he had journeyed to Chinandega to put out a different fire—the fight over the ejidal land. One week after the Corinto strike, 260 campesinos had occupied the land claimed by Marcelino Reyes.[4] After the Guardia evicted the agrarian rebels, the President arrived to negotiate a settlement with Dr. Reyes and his allies.[5] The Tonaleño occupation in the same week warned Somoza that if both groups of campesinos attained their objectives, other campesinos would be encouraged. Nevertheless, Somoza, after one year of unmitigated pressure, had made up his mind to redistribute the ejidal land claimed by Reyes. There he would draw the line.

Putting out the ejidal fire by granting victory to the campesino rebels required the regime to negotiate with sixteen families who claimed ejidal land (see Table 1 in Chapter 5). Since staking their original claims in 1954, the ejidatarios (those with ejidal land claims) had acted in unified fashion. Nevertheless, they represented a socially heterogeneous group including both urban professionals and middle peasants, with different economic interests and family alliances.

Estanislao Cáceres was one of the peasants, and, like the other peasant ejidatarios, he thought of himself as a struggling campesino. "I am neither a *terrateniente* nor a *rico*. My only source of income to support the needs of my large family is my [100 manzana] farm."[6] Estanislao Cáceres's claim was, of course, self-serving. Faced with the threat of expropriation by the campesino movement, Cáceres presented himself as just another *campesino*, but in actuality he was a member of an economically powerful family in the region of La Grecia. He was, however, a more convincing campesino than Dr. Reyes and some others, who had urban properties and professional positions. Movement activists viewed Cáceres and his peasant allies as "campesinos ricos."[7] Contrary to the activists' intention, such a categorization, in particular the use of the word "campesino," tended to legitimize the sixteen families' claim to the ejidal land. Beyond their knowledge of agriculture and local labor, the peasant faction of the Reyes group thus played a vital political role. As we have seen, these wealthy peasants had legitimized the ejidal claims of the entire Reyes group, first against Doña Tesla and then against the campesino movement.

For the movement activists, who stood by the 1916 decree that designated the land for poor campesinos, rich campesinos had no right to the ejidal land. Nevertheless, some of the campesinos ricos had actually purchased land from Dr. Reyes, and others continued to pay rent to the municipality in order to farm the ejidal land. Those peasants, all professed Somocistas, often had the sympathy of both government and opposition politicians. Moreover, their land titles and rental agreements had been validated in three court cases brought against them by Doña Tesla and Campuzano. Hence, they often presented themselves publicly as peasants in battle against the latifundistas. Nevertheless, each time Luís Somoza promised to resolve the ejidal issue by giving land to the landless, he ran up against the legal and political problems posed by these well-off, but nonetheless, authentic, peasants.

On March 20, 1962, shortly after Somoza had dispatched Cervantes to Bonete to evict the Tonaleños, the president met with the sixteen ejidatarios. Somoza proposed that the government indemnify all improvements (*mejorías*) made to the ejidal land, including clearing, planting, and building, at the rate of two hundred córdobas for every manzana. Apparently, all of the ejidatarios agreed to the deal, with the exception of Dr. Reyes, who held out for a total indemnification of C$360.000 ($51,400), roughly double the government offer. Still, Reyes agreed in principle to Somoza's proposal that he give up the ejidal claims in return for cash payments.[8] When the meeting adjourned, only one other ambiguity remained: the status of the ejidal land actually purchased from Reyes by his cohorts. In 1957, Dr. Reyes, then the acting jefe político, sold four lots of seventy manzanas of land at roughly thirty-five córdobas each. Although the price seemed quite high for uncultivated land, the wealthy peasants possessed legal bills of sale.[9] Somoza apparently did not wish to rule on the issue of whether they could keep the land. By not taking a position, the president suggested that the peasants could remain on the purchased land.

Despite Reyes's holding out, *Novedades*, the semi-official daily, announced that Somoza had persuaded the sixteen to turn over their land to the government for immediate distribution to landless campesinos.[10]

Escorcia, the campesinos' representative at the negotiations, took his cue from the *Novedades* article and passed the word on to the campesinos that the movement was victorious and they could now move onto the ejidal lands—this time to stay. During the first days of April, several hundred campesino families moved onto perhaps two hundred manzanas of the two-thousand-manzana ejidal tract. Most of the land remained fenced off, since the government had not yet indemnified the sixteen ejidatarios or settled the pending issues. But the campesinos built dozens of thatched huts every day, radically transforming the space from pasture and underbrush into a village. The campesinos named their new community Rancherías, which literally meant hamlet of thatched huts.[11]

The campesinos of Rancherías (previously the Nuevos Ejidos group) immediately organized a production cooperative. Escorcia, who remained the overwhelmingly popular leader despite Ramírez's efforts, supported the idea of cooperatives as a politically and economically sound project, but he did not force this idea on the rank and file. In fact, some campesinos opposed the cooperative, and some politicians linked it to Communist subversion. But the organization of the cooperative was an essentially local creation. As with the Tonaleños during the occupation of Bonete, the cooperative on the ejidal land emerged as a result of a collective struggle and the evolving campesino definition of private property. Significantly, the campesinos named the production cooperative in honor of the martyred campesino leader, Regino Escobar.[12]

Every day, Juan Suazo, Ramón Cándia, and other San José militants rode on horseback from San José to the new village to assist in everything from building ranchos to discussing strategy. In gratitude, the campesinos of Rancherías offered those of San José the right to join the community and receive land or to collectively use a portion of the land they expected to win from the sixteen ejidatarios. Several San José families accepted the offer of land in Rancherías.

The San José organization had not directly contested Edmundo Deshon's claim on Las Cuchillas since May 1959. Nevertheless, the leaders and many rank and filers participated in CGT-sponsored activities in Rancherías, Tonalá, and Corinto. They expected that the growing power of the popular movements would some day allow them to return the favor. In April 1962, as they helped build the thatched huts of Rancherías, Juan Suazo and Ramón Cándia thought that their time had come. When Juan and Ramón proposed that the next action against the ejidatarios, who still controlled most of the contested land, coincide with an invasion of Las Cuchillas, the Rancherías group accepted the idea. Moreover, the two neighboring organizations convinced Escorcia to support the plan for two simultaneous invasions.[13]

Juan and Ramón spent a busy few days reactivating the old organizational network in San José. The social, economic, and demographic situation had not changed significantly over the preceding two years. Some families had emigrated to Chinandega or Managua. Four or five families joined the Rancherías community. The majority of village inhabitants, however, remained in San José, on the edge of desperation at the close of every cotton harvest. Although three years of inactivity and broken promises had bred apathy and cynicism, especially toward the CGT and the government, perhaps one quarter of the San José organization had participated in the larger campesino movement, which was now more powerful than the days in 1959 when Juan, Justo, and Regino had signed away their right to resist Campuzano.

After several days, the renewed San José organization had the participation of one hundred families, over three-quarters of the village. Unfortunately, shortly after the decision had been made to invade Las Cuchillas (which had been renamed Llano Verde by Deshon), an inebriated young cotton picker boasted of the impending invasion to a soldier. The next day, on April 7, 1962, the Guardia came to San José to arrest Juan Suazo, Justo Vega, and Ramón Cándia.[14] Escorcia promptly came to the aid of the jailed campesino leaders, and CGT lawyers arranged their release.

Several days later, Escorcia sent orders canceling the planned invasion of Deshon's land and urging the San José campesinos to bolster the forces of Rancherías. Escorcia's order dismayed the militants of San José. In May 1961, the campesinos had willingly accepted Escorcia's original justification for deactivating the San José movement, when he had argued that the campesinos should concentrate their forces on the most obtainable target, the ejidos. Suazo and Regino had accepted this argument because they had already taken a stand in favor of supporting the Nuevos Ejidos (Rancherías) group at the temporary expense of San José's objectives. In April 1962 the Chinandegan campesino and labor movements were on the offensive in the towns and villages of Corinto, Posoltega, Realejo, Rancherías, Tonalá, Morazán, and Cañanlipe.[15] Yet, despite the force of the movement and President Somoza's command to distribute the ejidos, the Reyes group continued to hold out. Hence, the two assumptions behind the CGT policy with regard to San José—that the movement was too weak to fight on two fronts at once and that Reyes would fall without a prolonged struggle—were no longer valid. For Suazo and Ramón Cándia, there was now no justification for holding back the campesinos of San José del Obraje. As Cándia expressed it, "We were only used to back-up Rancherías."[16] Nevertheless, the San José leaders accepted Escorcia's decision without protest, recognizing that their protest could only endanger campesino unity.[17]

Escorcia's opposition to the San José invasion, though no doubt influenced by the cotton picker's breach of security, was based primarily on his evaluation of the two regional elite factions. Politically, the Campuzano and the Reyes groups belonged to the two main factions of Somoza's local party organization. Reyes was a close political friend and reputedly a lover of Irma Guerrero, the rising star of Chinandegan Somocista politics. Irma was the daughter of Salvador Guerrero, Chinandega's mayor during the 1940s. Although an outsider from León, old obreristas like Ernesto Pereira had considered Guerrero an ally. His daughter inherited a warm, popular, perhaps even vulgar touch. Fortunately she moved into a political void; most of the surviving obreristas had long since lost their political legitimacy, due to their corruption and their lack of responsiveness to popular demands.[18] In fact, Irma's only serious competitor for the mantle of obrerismo was Domingo Ramírez, who lacked credibility among the political elite because of his unpredictable behavior and had also lost prestige among many campesinos because of his attacks on Escorcia.

At a time of rising opposition and popular movements, when Somocista politicians were in short supply, Irma was an attractive leader. Her firm alliance with Reyes virtually guaranteed that the sixteen ejidatarios would not relinquish the land without strong resistance. In the best tradition of obrerismo, Irma could simultaneously rail against the landed oligarchy, rhetorically turn professionals into campesinos, talk intimately with the better-off peasants, and lead others into battle against her enemies within the elite. In fact, she did all of this while accumulating large landholdings and running for Congress.[19]

Families of the agrarian elite—the Deshons, the Callejases, and the Montealegres—dominated the other faction of the Somocista Liberal party. During the 1930s, the Callejas family, whose members had occupied nearly every departmental and municipal office, had lost much of its power to the obreristas. With varying degrees of intensity, the elite-obrerista factional battle had dominated Chinandegan politics ever since. Although defeated in the municipality, the Callejas family, in league with the Deshons and Montealegres, maintained an important national influence. During the 1960s, for example, these families supplied the Somoza regime with several cabinet ministers and a vice president.[20] Moreover, in 1957, Alfonso Callejas once again assumed the mayoralty representing the agrarian elite. Not surprisingly, it was under the Callejas administration that the municipality gave support to the campesino claims against the ejidatarios, thereby deflecting the movement away from Deshon and Alvarado. Additionally, Meza y Salorío, Doña Tesla's first attorney, served as city councilman, inclining the political balance even more against the Reyes group. It was during this period that Regino Escobar and Juan Suazo, and then the CGT, chose to concentrate their forces against Reyes.

Ironically, the very growth of the popular movements favored Irma Guerrero, despite the campesino rage against her friend Dr. Reyes. The Guerreros, unlike the Deshons and the Callejases, could in some way claim to represent the resurgent popular classes, if only through her indigenous countenance and plebeian accent. Irma's popular appeal thus sparked yet another shift in the local power structure. In 1961, the regime appointed Rodolfo Zelaya, a follower of Irma, as mayor of Chinandega.[21]

The jurisdictional boundaries between local and national government in Nicaragua were not clearly laid out. Through special taxes, the municipalities achieved a significant degree of financial autonomy from Managua. Nevertheless, municipal functionaries, as appointed officials, were politically beholden to the federal government. The regime usually did not intervene in day-to-day municipal and departmental operations. However, the threat of intervention was always present since any offended party would not hesitate to denounce local officials, especially for illegal acts.[22] When an important dispute like that over the ejidos reached Managua, the role of the municipal government was to provide information to the executive and to carry out the executive's directives. While dependent on the political will of Managua, Chinandegan politicians possessed considerable power precisely because the central government lacked the capacity to organize political life on a local level. The importance of the local administration did not derive from a federalist conception of government, but rather revealed the persistent weakness of the Nicaraguan state despite twenty-five years of Somocista efforts to strengthen it.

Although the export boom of the 1950s had created revenues sufficient for a 300 percent increase in government employment, agro-industrial development also had created and intensified contradictions between and among elite and popular classes.[23] The Somocista state was bogged down by countless conflicts of interest. Yet the regime's most powerful contradiction was within the state itself—between the economic interests of the Somocista bourgeoisie and the state's goal of hegemonic control over the Nicaraguan polity. Such economic and political entanglements meant that from one day to the next the regime would consider the same businessman or oligarch first a political enemy and then a distinguished patriot. Given the shifting winds of alliance, the regime found directing local politics to be politically inexpedient.

Irma Guerrero's hold on town hall therefore strengthened the resolve of the sixteen families of the Reyes group. Nevertheless, once Somoza made his deal, Guerrero could not appear to oppose it. Her elite opponents, situated in the highest realms of national and departmental government, would take advantage of any opportunity to catch her willfully disobeying the presidential decree to vacate the ejidos. "La Irma" could thus only offer discreet support to Reyes. In this treacherous terrain of factional politics, Escorcia reasoned that the presidential directive was the only key to success and that actions that used Somoza's deal as their justification would be victorious regardless of La Irma's role. Escorcia thus chose not to attack Deshon's property because at that moment such a tactic would involve alienating the elite faction of the Somocistas, cabinet ministers, and, given his reaction to the Tonalá invasion, the president himself.[24]

Juan Suazo's Blues and the Problem of Representation

Although Juan Suazo counseled the other San José militants to participate in the imminent Rancherías action, doubts began to plague him about Andrés Ruíz Escorcia. Vague notions of deception wove themselves into a mental tapestry of pain and confusion. But he dared not confide in any of his comrades, for the campesino movement had ceded its leadership to Escorcia, and questioning that direction could jeopardize the whole struggle. Without an alternative, Juan Suazo forced himself to accept Escorcia's orders. Nevertheless, he carefully dissected the leader's motives for the volte-face. Suazo doubted that Escorcia's decision was based on the cotton picker's drunken indiscretion, although he was sure that Escorcia wanted the rank and file to believe that the paralysis of the San José organization was its own fault.

Suazo thought back to the previous rainy season, when Escorcia had talked publicly about Doña Tesla's noble donation and Deshon's gifts of palm and wood to the campesinos who wanted to settle on the ejidos. At the time, those words had stung Suazo like so many red ants. Now Suazo understood the "gifts" as emblems of the CGT's alliance with the Campuzano group to crush the Reyes group. The question that now plagued Juan was whether this tactical alliance that was paralyzing the San José organization would become a permanent feature of CGT strategy even after a victory over Reyes. Suazo's own observations of Escorcia in the company of enemies of San José, Deshon and Argeñal Papi of the agricultural ministry, reinforced his suspicions. "I saw Andrés with Papi and with Mundo Deshon in Chinandega. They were just too friendly. Maybe I could understand why Andrés said all those flattering things about Mundo, you know—politics. But I couldn't understand why he had to be friends with them. I sure didn't like it."[25]

In April 1962, Suazo thought that the most likely explanation for such signs of friendship between the CGT leader and the enemies of the campesinos was so disturbing that he tried to hold back the thought: "Mundo Deshon had him in his hip pocket."[26] Suazo's loyalty to the campesino movement forbade him from mentioning this suspicion. Indeed, Suazo continued to act as though he believed Escorcia was merely engaged in tactical maneuvers. Despite his fundamental opposition to the CGT policies, Juan Suazo agreed with other rank-and-file leaders that Escorcia deserved his leadership role. Mónico Avilés, a key member of the Rancherías group, expressed, twenty-four years later, their collective assessment of Escorcia. "We carried out orders because he came and put those decisions into practice, because he wasn't about to throw us into a fire and sit back and relax. We knew that he would defend us, no matter what. . . But of course we couldn't say that Andrés led us . . . that would have been the end . . . we all had to take responsibility. You could see that Andrés had something of genius as a leader."[27]

The problem that gnawed at Juan Suazo was linked to the organizational structure of the campesino movement. Escorcia had played a major role in Tonalá, where the agricultural workers' union engaged in more democratic practices than did other campesino organizations, primarily as a result of its greater isolation, its varied forms of struggle, and its literate, artisan leadership. But the Rancherías and San José campesinos depended more directly on the clandestine directives of Escorcia. Suazo understood that rigid organizational discipline was a necessary defense against the ricos and the Guardia. The cotton picker's boastful words had certainly driven home that point. Nor could he deny the validity of Avilés's assessment that Escorcia had earned his authority. Suazo had seen how Escorcia talked down the oligarchs and spoke directly and meaningfully to the campesinos. In the words of one activist,

"Andrés Ruíz Escorcia was that great man who came to the Western lands [León and Chinandega] and all those campesinos who heard his voice resonate in the government palaces, in the police headquarters, and in the Guardia headquarters will always remember him."[28]

Escorcia achieved this kind of hero worship because, unlike the politicians, he was always on the front lines of the struggle. Nevertheless, as Avilés pointed out, the campesinos had to assume increasing responsibility and suffer the consequences for their own participation in the struggle. The rank-and-file leaders therefore held an important consultative position. Since the CGT leader rarely made a decision without consulting the local leadership, his veto of the San José action was quite extraordinary. Whether or not Suazo's suspicions of corruption were true, they nonetheless underscored the tension between liberator and political opportunist implicit in the CGT leader's relations to the campesino rebels. By fighting on the front lines, through speeches, lectures, and friendly conversation, Escorcia performed a remarkable job of political education and mobilization. As the Rancherías leader, Éntimo Sánchez, stated, "Before Andrés came to Chinandega, we were mute."[29] Sánchez thus expressed the impotence and inarticulateness of illiterate campesinos in a world dominated by an educated elite. The power of the patron's word had condemned peons to centuries of silence. For to speak directly and truthfully to an *autoridad* or a *señorito* was considered an act of impudence. Silence therefore had become a means of survival for many Nicaraguan campesinos.

The agrarian revolt challenged the social structure that had perpetuated the silence of the campesino. Escorcia helped to generalize and to unify the revolt and thereby deepened that challenge. The voice of Escorcia, resounding in protest throughout authority's prohibitive spaces, was so powerful because it articulated the long-repressed ideas and feelings of the campesinos. Moreover, by fusing such political concepts like *oligarchy*, *feudalism*, and *working class* together with campesino images of sacred rights and violated social pacts, Escorcia helped the rebels create a new language of their own. Hence, Mónico Avilés, an illiterate campesino, awakened by the movement, found these words to explain the struggle. "We inherited the land. Through our inheritance of nature we had a right to the land."[30]

Such an eloquent expression of natural rights derived indirectly from the teachings of Andrés Ruíz Escorcia, for it was he who taught them to speak a language of pride and protest, which the campesinos continually enriched. Urged on by their need to organize, the campesinos rapidly became fluent and creative in their emerging idiom. Indeed, these formerly inarticulate rural folk could argue their land claims through the Liberal version of history or through ideas about natural rights. As they overcame their muteness and mastered this language, the campesino students had less need for Escorcia's instruction. Nevertheless their continuing illiteracy kept them politically dependent on the CGT leader.

Suazo and other campesinos have suggested that being illiterate is like being blind. Although a terrible impediment, blindness and illiteracy force people to develop other senses. Perhaps that is why Juan Suazo was so uneasy when Escorcia asked him to sign letters. The CGT leader would explain in general terms what the letter contained and why he needed Suazo's signature. Without having a direct knowledge of the letter's contents, the illiterate San José leader signed but always felt uneasy about it. Suazo resented Escorcia's letters both because the act of signing made him feel ashamed of his own ignorance and because Andrés's repetitive explanations did not sound convincing. And Suazo's suspicion about the letters and other texts was well founded. On January 23, 1962, for example, Juan Suazo and five other San José leaders signed the following letter. "We put our problem in the hands of Dr. Osman Buitrago who got us two rulings, one in Chinandega and one in León. But it turned out to be a C$20,000 swindle. . . . After all of these failures we went to the CGT and they have been aiding us without asking for a cent. Thus, once and for all we are denouncing and rejecting the calumnious accusations made against Andrés Ruíz Escorcia, the secretary general, to the effect that he is being paid for his work on our behalf."[31]

Juan Suazo did not know its contents when he signed this letter. Had he known, he would have refused to sign it, for the statement about Buitrago had been at the heart of his bitter dispute with Regino Escobar. Since he knew of Suazo's support for Buitrago, the CGT leader purposefully avoided mention of the issue. For Escorcia, the veracity of that slice of campesino history was far less important than its use in his own defense; one week earlier Marcelino Reyes had publicly accused Escorcia of robbing the funds of the campesino movement.[32] For the CGT chief, on several occasions, strategic as well as personal considerations dictated his manipulation of the illiterate leadership of San José into stating something in writing that they did not believe.[33]

Andrés Ruíz Escorcia, the voice of the voiceless, the man who helped to free the campesinos from the shackles of elite-imposed silence, nevertheless felt compelled to muzzle his subjects. Ironically, it was the campesinos' profound gratitude and esteem that obscured Escorcia's field of vision. The CGT leader lost sight of the difference between his own language, ideas, and interests on the one hand, and those of the campesinos on the other. With the line between himself and the others so blurry, Escorcia had difficulty seeing that the campesinos also could educate the educator and that his own genius depended on the nurturing environment of the organized rural poor. Escorcia's inability to interpret the campesinos' thoughts and actions outside of his own vital role prompted him to violate the campesinos' right to create their own history.[34]

Despite Escorcia's invaluable services to the campesino movement, his personal interests and his tactical vision did not always mesh with the desires and needs of the rank and file. Although he sincerely believed in the radical agrarista goals of the campesinos, he also had personal ambitions to perpetuate his power in the CGT and to gain a congressional seat. Suazo and perhaps others sensed that there was a contradiction between Escorcia's personal agenda and his commitment to agrarian struggle. Indeed, the San José leader recognized that part of Escorcia's genius was his brand of opportunism, which the CGT chief had readily admitted. Suazo remembered an important incident, one of the very few times that Escorcia discussed politics with the local campesino leaders. Alluding to Luís Somoza, Escorcia whispered to them, "You're going to see me standing next to that big *hijueputa* [son of a bitch], but don't believe for a second that I'm with him!"[35]

Such an astounding revelation, which Suazo personally appreciated, demonstrated a high degree of confidence in the campesino leaders: a leak might have destroyed the CGT leader. Yet the admission also showed that Escorcia was capable of tricking the highest authority in the land and that he might be capable of similar duplicity toward the campesinos. Suazo's inability to follow Escorcia's actions and declarations outside of Chinandega exacerbated his sense of uneasiness about the relationship between the representative and the represented.

The CGT leader, nevertheless, also seemed to recognize that the campesino movement had a life of its own. His reply to Luís Somoza about the Bonete occupation had cogently summed up such an understanding of campesino autonomy. Escorcia was as complex and contradictory as the movement he strove to represent. Although extraordinarily sensitive to the needs of campesino liberation, he also needed and demanded the obedience due to a patrón. Although he led the campesinos into war with the elite, he also had to serve the regime as its labor lieutenant, a role that encouraged his authoritarianism. Escorcia's personal conflicts were the direct consequence of the contradiction between his role as a Somocista union leader and his own social-democratic, procampesino objectives. Indeed, Luís Somoza had unkindly accused Domingo Sanchéz, the PSN leader of "making my man, Escorcia, a Communist." Escorcia, nonetheless, made a heroic and largely successful effort to prevent his Somocista commitments from damaging the overall course of the agrarian protest movement. But the CGT chief was somewhat less successful in controlling his own authoritarian style of leadership. Juan Suazo came to bemoan that area of silence between them: "Andrés never understood that we understood."[36] He never grasped that the campesinos were not only capable of reasoning on his level, but, moreover, that they were willing to sacrifice their own immediate goals in the interest of future class unity.

The Ejidos Revisited

On the night of Holy Monday 1962, Andrés arrived in the settlement of Rancherías. Éntimo Sánchez remembers that "Andrés brought along *un alicate bárbaro* [a huge wire cutter]." That same night the Rancherías militants stripped thousands of yards of Marcelino Reyes's fence, which divided their land from the Reyes claim. Silently they rolled up the wire and hauled it off to the thickly wooded slope of the Chonco volcano. On Holy Tuesday, hundreds of Rancherías and San José campesinos began to burn underbrush on the ejidal land in preparation for May planting.[37]

Thanks to the recent completion of a paved highway from Chinandega to a few kilometers beyond San José, a Guardia patrol arrived within two hours of the first signs of smoke. The patrol evicted the campesinos and later issued warrants for seven campesino leaders.[38] Dr. Reyes had relied on Irma Guerrero's power to evict and arrest the campesinos. Because La Irma controlled the mayor and the chief of police, he chose to disregard the still informal presidential directive and turn the question of land rights into a criminal case against the campesino leadership, charging them with trespassing, robbery, and arson.[39]

In response to mass campesino demonstrations and the threat of a nationwide general strike, Somoza intervened once again on the side of the Rancherías campesinos. In the space of one month, the Somoza regime had now vetoed local power twice in favor of the insurgent campesinos. Yet the regime could not definitely resolve the conflict between the Rancherías campesinos and the Reyes group. Indeed, the ejidal issue was becoming a kind of symbol of the contradiction between the local and national dimensions of the Somocista state—between regional elite interests and those in the government and the private sector who strove for hegemony on a national level.

Castroites and Bananas: The Left Threatens to Make Its Own Agrarian Reform

May Day demonstrations in Managua and Posoltega, Chinandega added drama to the dilemmas of Somocismo. Although a long way from building a counterhegemonic force, in 1962 the Left paraded in greater numbers than at any time since 1946. In Managua, fifteen to twenty thousand marched under banners celebrating Fidel Castro and the Cuban agrarian reform.[40] In Posoltega, a few miles east of Chichigalpa, hundreds of banana plantation workers demonstrated together with a large delegation from the Chinandegan Workers' Federation, including Manuel Campos and the Realejo unionists.[41]

The local Guardia reacted violently against the Left's unprecedented demonstrations of strength in the countryside. Alberto Orozco, Socialist leader of the Chinandegan bakers' union since the 1940s, remembered the event. "Guido, a young militant from El Viejo, a campesino himself who the Party helped get some schooling, began to give a speech to the hundreds of banana workers, almost all of them in the union. And there was the Guardia lined up on the edge of the plaza facing the crowd. So Guido starts talking about the Cuban agrarian reform which everyone was very excited about. And some Guardia start firing at Guido. Everyone ducked and then scattered. You could see the impact of the shots on the pabellón nacional, where Guido had been standing."[42]

The near massacre of leftist-led banana workers underscored the seriousness of the situation in Chinandega. For the Somoza regime, the unionization of the new banana plantations threatened a vital development project, produced new tensions within the ruling elite, and once again demonstrated the organizing capacity of the Socialist party. In 1961, the government development agency, Instituto de Fomento Nacional (INFONAC), had signed an agreement to sell bananas to the United Fruit Company. INFONAC financed the banana production operations in their entirety, providing more than $1 million in credit to twelve Chinandegan landowners.[43]

The Somoza regime had encouraged banana exports, along with the meat and sugar industries, in response to the fall in cotton prices during the late 1950s. The government hoped, too, that jobs created by the new industry would address the problem of seasonal unemployment, considered by many politicians and journalists to be at the root of agrarian unrest. Over 80 percent of banana plantation jobs were permanent. According to INFONAC projections, by the mid-1960s, some thirty-five hundred permanent workers, more than 20 percent of the Chinandegan rural working class, would be employed on the plantations. The INFONAC-financed plantations were located primarily in the zones of rural insurgency in Chinandega.[44] Beyond expected increases in governmental revenue, the Somoza regime also expected a social and political return on its investment.

The Socialist party's forthright and systematic organization of the new permanent work force changed the regime's thinking about the Chinandegan agrarian conflict. The Escorcia faction of the CGT had attempted to organize the banana workers of Posoltega in 1961, but the CGT's failure to respond to the first wave of anti-union repression on the plantations had damaged the prestige of Somocista unionism. Somocista union leader Leonídas Morales's, negotiations with the plantation owners, which resulted in an unsatisfactory wage increase early in 1962, had further opened the way for leftist organizers. Throughout the labor conflict in Posoltega in 1962, the CGT national leadership had played a role that drove the workers toward the PSN. Morales, for example, appeared on the largest plantation, San Pablo, accompanied by the Guardia, a hitherto unresponsive labor inspector, and the plantation owner. Playing the part of a regime-backed union boss, Morales red-baited the union, which had held together despite the intimidating shots of the Guardia.[45] Thus, the PSN, exploiting similar contradictions as had existed in the 1940s, could once again develop important bases of support in the Chinandegan countryside.

The three plantation owners directly involved in the conflict with the banana workers' union were all prominent members of the anti-Somoza opposition. As in Corinto and elsewhere, the Conservative owners were willing to rely on the regime's repressive muscle while simultaneously making a political issue out of its inability to maintain labor peace. When the union's job actions halted the first harvest of bananas in Posoltega, the labor conflict not only threatened INFONAC's investment but also alienated all factions of the bourgeoisie. Pressured from both sides, Luís Somoza seemed unable to decide whether to back the Left or the Right. However, as a businessman and a card-carrying member of the elite, he wanted to maintain the active cooperation of his class allies.[46]

The events of May 1962 also revealed that the Left was on the verge of unification. The May Day demonstration in Managua included not only pro-PSN workers but also large delegations of students and middle-class Castroite sympathizers, organized in the Movilización Republicana.[47] Previously, the largely working-class PSN had maintained cold relations with the student and middle-class movements, in part as a reflection of Soviet-Cuban conflicts over revolutionary strategy in Latin America, and in part as a result of their separate, class-based political cultures. Thus, not only was the May Day rally a momentary dismissal of sectarian differences, but along with the demonstration in Posoltega, it also revealed an opening in the barrier of political culture, an opening through which an anti-Somocista *popular* movement would emerge.

As the Left began its recomposition, across town some Somocista labor leaders hinted that they might become part of that process. Although they applauded Luís Somoza's announced labor code reforms, which included paid Sundays and a minimum wage, many saw the reforms as too little and too late. One CGT orator after another attacked different aspects of the regime. Luís Somoza must have wondered about the counterinsurgency role of Somocista labor leaders when one veteran proregime leader stated that the Liberal and Conservative parties marched "toward the cemetery of failed ideologies."[48]

"Tell President Somoza We Will Continue to Invade the Land"

Two weeks after Comandante Rodríguez Somoza had engineered the campesino leaders' release from prison following their destruction of Reyes's fences, the Rancherías and San José campesinos returned to knock down fences on the ejidal battlefield. Once again the Guardia units, led by Nato García, the police chief, arrived swiftly and arrested campesinos from both villages. This time Escorcia escaped immediate arrest and led the activists to Chinandega. In front of the courthouse, two hundred campesinos began to chant, "Freedom for our compañeros" and "Down with the police director!"[49] The police chief, a Reyes ally, then had to ask for protection from Comandante Rodríguez (a Deshon sympathizer) in order to enter his own office. The Comandante telephoned his cousin, Luís Somoza, and urged a definitive solution to the ejidal conflict, undoubtedly citing the danger posed to the institutional order by a struggle that involved two governmental party factions and their representatives in the Guardia. President Somoza ordered the release of the campesino activists and the cessation of repression against the Rancherías group. The day following the release of the prisoners, the movement tested the president's orders by occupying an area of the hacienda called El Maneadero, which included ejidal lands. The hacienda owner, Juan José Zavala, denounced the invasion, but the police chief explained that he could do nothing because of the presidential directive.[50]

On the surface, the faction represented by Deshon and Rodríguez Somoza had won the regime's support for their struggle against the Reyes-Guerrero group and in favor of pacifying the campesino movement by ceding the land to Rancherías. The police chief provided graphic evidence of the regime's bias when he broke ranks with the Reyes group in order to carry out the orders from Managua.

The victory in Rancherías inspired other Chinandegan rural folk. Just as the campesinos marched onto the land claimed by El Maneadero, Posoltega threatened to erupt. The union engaged in an undeclared work stoppage. INFONAC, afraid of losing its investment, urged management to negotiate. The plantation owners declared that they would "never negotiate with Communists." Instead, they fired fifty suspected Communist union members, then offered a 50 percent wage hike to the remaining workers if they disassociated themselves from the "subversive" union.[51] Luís Somoza surely appreciated management's tactics, which so closely resembled his father's tactics during the 1940s.

On June 1, the Guardia announced that the moderate Rodríguez Somoza, a Deshon ally, would be reassigned to Managua as part of a nationwide rotation of departmental commanders. The Guardia replaced Rodríguez Somoza with the infamous Colonel Juan Angel López, the hardline rightist who as a captain had terrorized protesters in Sutiava in 1959.[52] A leading ejidatario, Manuel Cáceres (himself a colonel in the Guardia reserve), must have interpreted the Guardia change as a positive sign. Together with other ejidatarios, he persuaded García to move against the Rancherías campesinos, and the Guardia hauled in more than one hundred campesinos in the space of a few days.[53] Walking from the police van to the jail, one campesino questioned Somoza's credibility, telling a journalist, "Please tell the President that we will continue to invade the lands because they belong to us since he himself authorized our claim when he came to Chinandega."[54]

The gentle threat to the president was hardly news. Since March the Rancherías organization had staged five land invasions, each one using the pretext of presidential approval. This last reference to the presidential promise and the campesinos' desire to make it a reality was backed up by the actions of what amounted to unarmed, but extremely disciplined battalions, each composed of hundreds of rural protesters. The jailed campesinos did not have to wait long for their freedom. Escorcia and Argeñal Papi conferred with Rodríguez Somoza. They agreed on a compromise solution that might, with presidential support, placate the Reyes group. The compromise would grant the sixteen ejidatarios the land they currently had under cultivation. The remainder of the ejidal land would be distributed immediately to the Rancherías group. The departing Comandante agreed with the proposal and made one final phone call from Chinandega to his cousin. Somoza reiterated the point of view he expressed in March and gave Rodríguez instructions "to resolve the conflict as he deemed fit."[55]

Comandante Rodríguez Somoza ordered Manuel Cáceres, a major antagonist of Rancherías, to appear at his office, where he explained the compromise, appealing, no doubt, to his sense of self-preservation. By this time, Cáceres must have known that the Rancherías campesinos could only be stopped with bloodshed, a poor option since many campesinos were excellent shots with hunting rifles and even better with their machetes. Cáceres wisely dropped the criminal charges against the campesinos and agreed to the proposal. Cáceres and his family allies represented the most intransigent sector of the ejidatarios, so when Cáceres agreed to the compromise, the rest of the wealthy peasant faction of the Reyes group followed suit. Since Dr. Reyes, his family, and the other professionals did not actually cultivate the land themselves, Rodríguez Somoza excluded them from the new agreement, leaving them with the option to accept payment for the improvements or lose everything. On June 13, 119 campesinos joyfully left prison, and Escorcia, Argeñal Papi, and Colonel Rodríguez Somoza drew up the formal agreement that brought a halt to the hostilities in the Rancherías area.[56]

During the negotiations, Escorcia acted both in his union capacity and "in special representation of the campesinos." Escorcia's word obliged them to respect the boundaries of the hacienda Maneadero and the six cultivated areas of the campesinos ricos, who collectively held 234 manzanas of the best land.[57] The agreement left the Rancherías campesinos with the remaining hilly and rocky land. Although they did not particularly like the concessions, Escorcia convinced the campesinos that this was the best agreement they could get and that he therefore had signed it in their names.[58] Escorcia continued thereafter to be the undisputed leader of the Rancherías campesinos, and he helped them celebrate by immediately distributing five-manzana parcels to 150 campesino families. Although about 200 Rancherías families did not obtain parcels, the campesino movement celebrated an important victory.

The champagne glasses were surely clinking on the seaside villas of the Deshons as well. The Campuzano group had finally exacted retribution from Reyes. Moreover, like Somoza himself, Deshon, Argeñal Papi, and especially Hugo Astacio Cabrera (who was briefly the defense lawyer for Rancherías) now received politically important accolades as "defenders of the campesinos."[59] Finally, they could rest assured that the new comandante, Juan Angel López, would take care of any remaining conflicts.

The appointment of Colonel López would inaugurate a new era of repression against the campesinos. The movement's partial victory over the Reyes group contained the seeds of evil times to come. As a condition of the agreement, the Rancherías campesinos were obliged to dissolve their organization, breaking ranks with their Chinandegan compañeros. One Rancherías activist summed up that condition: "So then both Rancherías and Palacios [Puerto Morazán] had won land, though their problems were far from over. But because we had won land, the organization had to end. Not because we wanted to, but just because that was the agreement."[60]

The Rancherías activist thus cogently described the true design of the Somocista agrarian reform program—to pacify an increasingly militant campesino movement and crush any sign of leftist influence. Yet the terrifying repression to come, while momentarily silencing the movement, would at the same time tear apart the structures of authority that had tormented Juan Suazo and allow for the creation of new, more egalitarian forms of campesino leadership.

Beyond the May Rains: Women and Leadership in the Time of Juan Angel López, 1962–1964

A leader must feel that she is just one more person in the group. . . . When she speaks, she feels she is not alone, but that all are speaking because she is expressing the thoughts of others. . . . Here a woman's patience is important; because it is much harder among men, since men are authoritarian.
—Anonymous Mapuche leader, quoted by Ximena Bunster, "The Emergence of a Mapuche Leader"

After 1962, the Chinandegan campesinos met with increasing violence from the Right, and for the first time death squads were used as a counterinsurgency technique to squelch the reform movement. Shortly after arriving in Chinandega, in June 1962, the infamous Juan Angel López journeyed to Rancherías where he told a group of campesinos, "If some bastard shouts viva Escorcia, I'm going cut off his head without touching his shoulders."[1] The new comandante then condemned Andrés Ruíz Escorcia and the local campesino leadership to death. Although many campesino rebels escaped to Managua, for the next eighteen months Chinandega lived under the constant threat of Guardia torture and assassinations. Although it is impossible to state exactly how many times Juan Angel López ordered his *patrulla fatidica* (death patrol) to kill, he most certainly merits the dubious distinction as the mastermind of the first death squad in Nicaraguan and probably in Central American history.[2]

Nevertheless, under the gun of Juan Angel López, the agrarian movement engaged in three major land takeovers and one strike. Indeed, the most extreme forms of repression in twentieth-century Nicaraguan history could not silence this movement of illiterate, inarticulate campesinos. At the same time, López's fury inadvertently broke the anti-Somoza opposition's silence about the campesino movement, a silence that had alienated the popular movements from the middle-class dissidents. Colonel López's brutality, by itself, did not bring together the labor and anti-Somoza forces. The habits of mind and political dispositions separating the two groups were too deep to be overturned immediately. But eventually the Somoza regime's violent repression against both groups gave them something in common. Moreover, many campesino activists, whatever they felt about the anti-Somoza opposition, had realized by 1963 that they would not gain further support from the regime: they had become an opposition force. More important, they came to believe that land reform with Juan Angel López was worse than no reform at all, and they renewed their struggle for dignity, as well as for land. Once they understood that the appointment of López was deliberately undertaken to squelch the campesino movement, the campesinos realized that they would ultimately have to take on the Somozas.

Under the reign of Juan Angel López, the tensions between rank-and-file democratic aspirations and authoritarian structure would continue to inform the development of campesino organization. However, after López drove out the original male leaders, women began to guide the movement in a strikingly new direction: female militants added democratic dimensions to the ideology and practice of campesino leadership.

Women and Class Power

The forced exile of Andrés Ruíz Escorcia from Chinandega did not have the pacifying effect planned by Somoza. On the contrary, the departure of Escorcia, although mourned by the campesinos, forced them to clarify their own thoughts and to plan their own actions in spite of severe local repression. The Tonalá union, for example, operated clandestinely after Mariano Escorcia, Leoncio Martínez, and others escaped to Managua. Experienced women activists began to fill the leadership void in Tonalá, Rancherías, and San José.

Scholars have suggested that women participated actively in mass movements on a national level during the 1960s and 1970s because increasing numbers of single mothers sought to defend their children physically and economically through these movements. Similarly, they have explained the growing proportion of single mothers (women heads of household) as a result of the growth of agrarian capitalism, which relied on migratory labor that often divided families.[3] In Chinandega, however, there was no correlation between the proportion of single mothers and the rapid development of agrarian capitalism during the 1950s. Women headed 26.8 percent of all Chinandegan households in 1950, before the cotton boom, and in 1963, after a decade of unbridled capitalist development, the percentage had dropped to 20.7.[4] This decline during the agro-export boom does not negate the fact that agrarian capitalism prompted the break-up of peasant family units, and indeed in absolute terms the number of single mothers rose sharply. But the increased likelihood of female-headed households others ascribe to the agro-export boom seems in Chinandega to have occurred in an earlier phase of agrarian capitalism before 1930.

Fragmentary evidence suggests that the number of illegitimate births increased significantly in Chichigalpa between 1901 and 1919.[5] Since the Ingenio San Antonio's massive appropriation of land and labor occurred during the same period, a correlation between the two phenomena seems probable. Moreover, data from the 1920 census substantiates the hypothesis that the development of capitalist social relations had affected the peasant family well before the 1950s. In seven out of ten departments where the *jornaleros* (seasonal or permanent wage laborers) constituted more than 60 percent of the rural labor force the illegitimacy rate was 40 percent or higher.[6]

Rather than see the disintegration of the nuclear family as a direct consequence of migratory labor, the increase of single mothers derived indirectly from peasant strategies to resist proletarianization through the urban migration of their daughters. Some evidence suggests that female migration from the surrounding countryside to the urban centers of Chinandega contributed to a significant gender imbalance in both the towns and the countryside. In 1920, for example, women made up more than 56 percent of the urban inhabitants of Chinandega and El Viejo, while in the surrounding countryside they accounted for only 45 percent of the population.[7] By 1950, the gender imbalance increased significantly, with women making up 62.5 percent of the adult urban population of the municipality of Chinandega.[8]

Between 1900 and 1950, many peasant fathers sent their daughters to work in the urban centers of Chinandega. Whether to sell produce or to earn income, fathers used daughters to buttress the household economy. Although most of this migration was short-term, many peasant girls went to work as domestic servants on a long-term basis. Domestic service often resulted from patron-client relations that obligated the rural folk, in particular hacienda peons, to provide their daughters for such labor. In addition, at least since 1940, income from women's wage labor became a vital weapon of peasant resistance against full-scale proletarianization.

Commenting on an occupational pattern dating from the pre-Columbian era, a Chinandegan observer in 1916 wrote of "women's domination of the marketplace."[9] Although elite immigrant males, between 1890 and 1920, gained control over commercial capital, women dominated the lower and middle echelons of commerce. During the late 1920s and early 1930s, women owned thirty-one of forty-five small shops and market stalls, five of eight middle-size shops, and three of the four largest stores in Chinandega.[10] Moreover, several women profited greatly from the small import-export trade to El Salvador. The relative success of women shop owners probably did not diminish male sexism. Nonetheless, men were forced to view the marketplace as a relatively autonomous area of economic activity for women. To a limited degree, men came to recognize *vivanderas* (market women) as at the very least an interest group. Thus, for example, twenty vivanderas offered their support to the merchant Luís Venerio's 1920 campaign for mayoral reelection, in return for promises of lowered commercial taxes and better market hygiene.[11] A Chichigalpan correspondent noted in 1922 that ISA exploited "the poor vivanderas who come here to sell their small articles."[12] Those same vivanderas would play a key role in support of ISA workers during the 1936 strike. Nonetheless, the diminutive size of the market limited its political or social importance. In 1950, the Chinandegan markets employed only 152 women, a mere 6 percent of the female work force.[13]

The agro-export boom of the 1950s, however, contributed to a spectacular rise in the number of vivanderas. By 1963, markets employed 1,525 vivanderas in Chinandega, 20 percent of the female labor force.[14] Also during the 1950s, the vivanderas began to act as a visible and cohesive force. In 1956, for example, both urban- and rural-based vivanderas protested against taxes on market products. In 1960, more than five hundred vivanderas staged a protest against the "dictatorship" of "La Crema" Martínez (of 1940s obrerista fame), the manager of the market.[15] Moreover, Irma Guerrero viewed the vivanderas as a vital constituency in her effort to take control of the Somocista Liberal party.

Although more numerous than vivanderas, domestic servants formed a far less cohesive group. In 1950, 526 Chinandegan women labored as domestics, 37.8 percent of the total female municipal work force. By 1963, 1,268 domestic servants formed 39 percent of the female labor force in the city.[16] Domestics tended to maintain rural ties longer than the rapidly urbanized group of vivanderas. Indeed, many domestic servants each year returned to the countryside to pick cotton. Their *patronas* had to accept the seasonal departures, since their husbands needed the women's labor in the fields even more urgently than it was needed in the house. In any event, the Chinandegan elite usually had a few servants to spare.

Anna Rubbo and Michael Taussig have analyzed the role of patriarchal ideology in the exploitation of domestic servants. They write: "The role live-in female servants play in bridging the class structure and in buttressing hegemony is not a small one. They act as a conveyor between city and country, ruling class and exploited, and female servanthood is especially conducive to the reproduction of the patron-client power theme that runs through most if not all, hierarchical relationships in Latin America."[17]

In Chinandega as well, the employment of rural domestics undoubtedly served as a "conveyor" between country and city and perpetuated paternalistic ideology. However, Rubbo and Taussig also argue that the increasing "commodification" of domestic service has continually undermined patrón-*empleada* (domestic) harmony. Whatever the precise role of commodification in the process, during the past two decades domestic workers in Brazil, Chile, Colombia, Mexico, and Peru have challenged paternalist ideology and exploitative working conditions by organizing trade unions. In Chinandega, as well, the fit between structural role and ideology has been neither static nor tidy; as early as the mid-1940s, the city's empleadas attempted unsuccessfully to organize a union.[18]

In the era before cotton, members of the agrarian elite, like their brethren throughout Latin America, tended to compare and evaluate their wealth and status by counting servants. The Deshons, for example, probably employed more than ten female servants.[19] The wealthy thus prized domestics not only as household laborers but also as objects of conspicuous consumption. Moreover, it seems that another form of social status was involved in the acquisition of female domestic labor: elite males used and abused their servants sexually and often boasted about their "conquests." Sexual liaisons between an elite man and his female domestic often continued until the woman became pregnant. That pregnancy "dishonored" the lady of the house, who often demanded that the servant be fired and expelled.[20]

The dismissed domestic servant could usually find work only as a seamstress or in the marketplace. Her family often would not accept her home again (when village morality was not an issue, economy always was). In the dense, steamy barrios stretching out toward the countryside from whence they came, the often stigmatized women would raise their children in extreme poverty, the *hijos por fuera* (outside children) of the elite.

Michael Jiménez, in analyzing the social history of early twentieth-century Colombian coffee estates, cautions against viewing elite abuse of women, "a cruel partnership of class and sexual oppression," as a vestige of precapitalist social relations. Rather, Jiménez argues that sexual coercion was indeed a logical extension of "managerial arbitrariness," in turn predicated on prejudices and fantasies about the poor that "merely affirmed for the landowners their own sense of superiority and gave them license to rape and seduce lower class families. . . . Sexual coercion represented perhaps the most powerful weapon at the disposal of the planters in imposing their will on their workers. The possibility of forced intimacy kept the families of the rural poor in a state of anxiety and demoralization."[21] Jiménez goes on to demonstrate how elite sexual abuse of women seriously disrupted the sexual hierarchy of the peasant family by making peasant men look powerless with respect to women. Elite abuse of women also provided an important focus for peasant protest during the 1920s.

Jiménez's astute insights help us to understand the history of domestic service in Chinandega since the empleadas, as Rubbo and Taussig suggest, lived and worked at the intersection between the country and city. Thus, what happened to them was relevant to their rural families. Moreover, as in Colombia, the sexual relations between servants and their masters often poisoned the relations between Chinandegan working-class men and women. The male workers' reaction to the women's liaisons with the señores was one of scorn rather than compassion. As Jiménez notes, between master and servant there was a "certain degree of reciprocity in these [sexual] relations"; some Chinandegan domestics may have sought such relations with their masters as a means of material advancement. The following testimony of a male worker, typical of his class, overlooked the strong element of coercion in master-servant relations and emphasized the opportunism of some women. "But you know a lot of them are just putas. Maybe they start out with the señor, and then that's what they become."[22]

While male workers and campesinos bitterly resented what they perceived to be female acquiescence to the elite conquista, they also detested elite men's "deflowering of women." Finding it difficult to confront their own feelings of inadequacy and powerlessness directly, many working-class men reproduced elite machismo and promiscuity.[23] In making their own conquistas, working-class males added to the number of single mothers while at the same time stigmatizing them. Working people resented the Chinandegan elite for their liberties with domestic servants and for their contribution to deep hostilities between working-class and campesino men and women.

In Chinandega, elite men's abuses of domestics did not directly contribute to the agrarian rebellion, but in Sutiava, these abuses may have contributed at least indirectly to the peasants' mobilization against the elite. Leonese elite males, like their Chinandegan counterparts, also raped and seduced many *nodrizas* (wet nurses) and domestics and then fired those that became pregnant. Unlike Chinandegans, however, the Sutiavas accepted the single mothers back into their community. This acceptance was based on a unique history of ethnic solidarity and community cohesion in urban neighborhoods (although most Sutiavas worked in the countryside). The community's acceptance of illegitimate mestizo children, in turn, strengthened the community at a time when other indigenous communities were disintegrating. That Sutiavas considered the mestizo children Indians was important; by transcending a strictly physical notion of ethnicity, the Sutiavas strengthened their own ideological concept of *indio*. During the 1950s, this elastic notion of indio became a vital force in the Sutiavas struggle with the agrarian elite. Finally, some of the elite's illegitimate offspring may have been particularly predisposed to rebellion. Many Sutiavan mestizos grew up knowing their fathers' identities, and some often waited for years to repay them the favor: on several occasions, at least, the sons burned the fields of their fathers.[24]

In Chinandega, the greater physical distance between domestic servants and their families, and the fact that families did not generally accept single mothers back into the community, meant that elite men's abuse of peasant women did not usually become a factor of class resentment. Nevertheless, elite men did not confine their sexual conquests to the town house. Beyond proving their manhood through sexual conquest, elite men abused women to reassert their right to rule over peasant men as well as women, in mansions and in huts. Mundo Deshon, for example, used one such conquest as a conscious political action, as if to boastfully demonstrate the convergence of sexual and class oppression.

Beginning in 1958, Mundo Deshon had been engaged in a battle with the San José campesinos over his purchase and development of land claimed by the community. The symbolic tactic Deshon chose to assert his power was as strikingly original as his gifts of palm to found the village of Rancherías: he started a long and public affair with Cándida Pastrán, the widow of "the first leader," Regino Escobar. Deshon's sexual conquest of Cándida was a directly political act, and it was clearly perceived this way; it stung the entire San José community. Deshon's affair, including many expensive gifts to his mistress, wounded the pride of the community, particularly that of its male members. Since Cándida and her children through Regino Escobar embodied the spirit of the fighting community, her "selling out" to the enemy seemed to show the organization's bonds of solidarity to be illusory. To the campesinos, Cándida's behavior suggested that loyalty to the martyred leader was secondary to her own material advancement.[25] What had now become a main goal of the movement—dignity—seemed abandoned for material well-being or (worse yet) sexual pleasure.

To the agrarian elite, the conquest was even more laden with symbolic connotations. Twenty-five years later, Hugo Astacio Cabrera, Campuzano's lawyer and Deshon's in-law, gloated over the affair, using it to buttress his argument about the illegitimacy, lack of leadership, and weakness of the San José organization. "You know Regino's woman started living with [sleeping with] Mundo. She was a chela [blondish] and good-looking and she just took up with him. Mundo's wife was Maria Luisa López. . . . Well, you see those campesinos didn't have a leader or any real orientation."[26] Astacio Cabrera mentioned Cándida's blondness in unspoken contrast to her fellow Indians. Thus, he hinted that she was "racially" superior to the rest of the campesinos. Although better than the other San José women, she was still "no good." Moreover, Astacio falsely implied that Mundo Deshon's conquest took place before Regino's death. In any case, as the lawyer viewed it, the affair showed the community to be immoral and without honor. The conduct of Regino's wife revealed the late San José leader to have been less than a man, a weak cuckold. The attorney's discourse therefore merged gender and class ideology into a single indictment of the community. Moreover, Astacio Cabrera's statement substantiates Jiménez's work and the above analysis of Chinandegan domestics, for the attorney revealed how elite males operated in a discursive universe where sexual conquest symbolized class power and where the latter was experienced passionately.

Although deeply hurt by the betrayal, most campesinos probably did not share Astacio's vision of the affair. Many San José militants, both men and women, were able to adapt a different perspective precisely because of the transparency of Deshon's unification of sexual and class power. The elite assertion of power over the body of a female servant had exacerbated male proletarian hostility toward female proletarians primarily because of the arbitrary style of conquest. Elite men's violation of poor women had thus symbolized elite class domination, female complicity in its rule, and, by implication, male proletarian impotence. However the effectiveness of Deshon's conquest as a symbol within elite male discourse was mitigated by the San José community's conceptualization of the act as a direct political attack, the moral equivalent of Mundo's use of bribery, imprisonment, and torture against the San José community. Regardless of Cándida Pastrán's real motives, the community ostracized her as a traitor like Fredi Callejas. More importantly, the community refused to internalize Mundo's conquest and did not allow Cándida to represent all San José women.

Women and the Agrarian Protest Movement

Despite campesino attitudes of paternalistic protectiveness and patriarchal hostility toward women, women participated in the movement in increasing numbers. Campesinos viewed female militants, usually unmarried mothers, from a multidimensional perspective that had emerged during the course of struggle. One pervasive attitude toward women leaders was what Deborah Levinson has called "masculinization."[27] A man commonly admired a woman militant for her putative "male" qualities, such as physical courage or verbal skill. Irma Guerrero, the Somocista political leader, was a model of such "masculine" political style. She combined her father's important political contacts, obrerista rhetoric, and her own charismatic personality to ascend the staircase of Somocista success. Although she was one of very few important female politicians in Nicaragua, she developed good relations with the growing numbers of working women, who admired her ability to manipulate the male power structure. Moreover, unmarried and childless herself, Irma denounced the plight of single mothers and railed against the wealthy who would "borrow" (and put to work) the children of the poor. In 1956, La Irma organized the Frente Popular Femenino (a Somocista political organization of women); by 1961 she was cultivating support among men as well.[28] Recognizing her boastful and popular discursive style, Somocista males often viewed La Irma as a real macho and, thus, as a woman who did not threaten their own values. Thus, although Irma Guerrero certainly helped to legitimize women's participation in politics (and in this sense paved the way for revolutionaries and Somocistas alike), she could do little to crack the machista core of male consciousness.

Women, however, developed their own consciousness in reaction to masculine attitudes and stereotypes, a reaction further influenced by the male workers' imitation of elite male sexual behavior. Engracia Zapata, the Tonalá seamstress, summed up a generalized feeling among urban and rural women, "If in Nicaragua today, the fathers are not very honorable, it was much worse back in that (pre-revolutionary) era. Fathers just picked up and left as casually as if they were going to the corner store. They never worried about supporting their children."[29] Zapata's complaint explains one of the bases for women's participation in the agrarian protest movement. As heads of village families, they demanded the right to participate as equals. When Juan Angel López came to power and drove Escorcia and the local leadership away, campesinos of Tonalá and San José turned to experienced, literate militants like Zapata. Indeed, under the reign of Juan Angel López, women's participation in the rank and file and the leadership increased from between 15 and 20 percent to between 40 and 50 percent. Increased female participation signified at least a partial rejection of the elite male discourse on sex and power.[30]

In Sutiava, women not only participated in the agrarian protest movement from its inception in 1954, but they also created their own organization to support the movement to reclaim community lands. While the Sutiavan women did not formulate their own demands, they played an effective role by using their condition as mothers and wives to protect Sutiavan protesters from serious harm at the hands of the Guardia. Sutiavan women, in addition to doing domestic chores and seasonal agricultural labor, supplemented family income by harvesting wild fruits and plants (especially the calihuate for making tamales). The agrarian elite's fencing off of large sections of communal land seriously affected these subsistence activities and served as a focus of the Sutiavan agrarian struggle. Consequently, while women fought for men's goals in ways that may have reinforced patriarchal relations, they at the same time fought for their own immediate economic interests.[31]

Dora Medina and Ernestina Roque, through their activities on behalf of the female harvesters, achieved leadership positions in the general Sutiavan protest movement. Besides accepting women's participation as appropriate to women's vital economic activities, Sutiavan men also had a cultural predisposition to accept specific female leadership roles. Ernestina Roque became the community's official "guardian of the land titles," far from a ceremonial role. In addition to thwarting several attempts to rob the community documents, Roque organized rank-and-file meetings and served on the directorate of the Comunidad Indígena. Moreover, she, along with Medina, rejected monetary bribes from León's mayor in 1958 to withdraw from the struggle.[32] Like Roque, Dora Medina was an important cultural representative—she studied and taught about Sutiava's language, customs, and history. She also served frequently as an eloquent orator at Sutiavan protest rallies. Whether or not Roque and Medina effectively changed patriarchal ideology is hard to determine. However, they did set a precedent, however limited, for the incorporation of women into popular leadership positions.

As in Sutiava, Chinandegan campesino militants eventually chose women as their leaders because of their movement experience and their literacy, which was in part a reflection of their middle-peasant origin. State repression, however, accelerated the "feminization" process in Chinandega. The more cohesive and militant development of the Sutiavan agrarian struggle, and perhaps its Indian identity, during the 1950s prevented the regime from mounting a prolonged campaign of violent repression as it did in Chinandega. Those male activists who remained in Chinandega, understandably terrified of Juan Angel López, had a compelling reason for relying on female leadership: they assumed that López would not cut off the heads of women.

Female leadership also provided an excuse very much in keeping with the Chinandegan movement's defensive tradition of not taking responsibility for their actions. The activists' hope was that López might excuse or at least not condemn women who cited the hunger of their children as their motive for occupying land. Even if there was some truth in this analysis of López, it nonetheless took a great deal of courage for women to lead movement activities during his reign of terror. Women were willing to assume leadership roles in part to prove themselves to communities traditionally prone to devalue and denigrate single mothers. More significantly, there were fewer possibilities for these women to return to normal life when López cracked down on the campesino movement. Male rank and filers certainly had more options to choose from, including migrating from the villages. Single mothers, with family responsibilities, had fewer options and in this sense had less to lose than did men.

Engracia Zapata and others became very good campesino leaders. Their experience in surviving in a patriarchal world prepared them for the task of popular leadership in Somocista Nicaragua. They had to strive to meet their individual needs while operating within a patriarchal hierarchy. They had to meet their family needs, while allowing men to define them as virginal, masculine, or whorish. They already knew how to manipulate authoritarian language and structures. For generations, women had exerted their will through a patriarchal straitjacket far more rigid than Somocismo or obrerismo.

Two scholars, Temma Kaplan and June Nash, have made important theoretical contributions to the study of women and popular movements, which help us to understand the impact of female leadership in Chinandega. June Nash, through a study of women's activities in support of Bolivian tin miners, arrived at the following conclusion. "Women's entry into the resistance movements signals the breakdown not only of a normal social structure but also of the personal relationships that underlie it. Because women are the dependent subordinated sector of most societies their acts of resistance threaten men's public role as protector. Thus the same acts of resistance that men may perform have a different significance when performed by women. Women's resistance heightens the sense of social breakdown and shakes the very foundation of the dominant-subordinate hierarchy which has its roots in the home and family network."[33]

Temma Kaplan, through an analysis of specifically female mass movements in Barcelona from 1910 to 1918, offers a sharply distinct perspective on women's participation in popular movements. She argues that rather than debilitating the gender hierarchy as Nash suggests, "Women with female consciousness [appropriate to female popular movements] demand their rights that their obligations [within the sexual division of labor] entail."[34] Moreover, Kaplan concludes that "the logic of female collective action in early twentieth-century Barcelona demonstrates an implicit language of social rights that emerges from a commitment to the sexual division of labor."[35]

The analyses of Kaplan and Nash illuminate different facets of the Chinandegan campesino movement (suggesting a common thread linking these opposing perspectives, rooted perhaps in different objects of study). Female participation in the leadership of the campesino movement, as Nash argues, did challenge the male-dominated hierarchical relations that characterized both elite and peasant society. But the challenge to male authority did not involve an attack on the sexual division of labor, which according to Kaplan grounds women's convictions that they must defend "their right to feed and protect their communities."[36] Indeed, the Chinandegan women joined the organization precisely to meet the survival needs of their families, in Kaplan's view a defense, rather than a challenge, to the sexual division of labor. In sum, female leadership of the movement had a "different significance" that challenged patriarchy, and at the same time, through a defense of their traditional nurturing role, female activists developed "an implicit language of social rights." Chinandegan women in both ways buttressed the expansion of democratic ideology and organization. Moreover, they were able to forge horizontal or egalitarian modes of communication. Living on the fringes of an essentially male-defined conflict allowed women to value and enrich community sources of understanding.

To Lead As Equals, To Learn As Equals

In early November 1963, Engracia Zapata and 140 men and women invaded the uncultivated land of the Hato Grande hacienda, constructed huts, cleared away jungle growth, and began to plant corn. The Guardia intervened quickly, evicted the campesinos, and hauled off three militants, including Engracia. In a letter, another Tonalá female activist explained the action to Escorcia, "We campesinos have no defense against los ricos, or against the authorities. . . . We were trying to take care of our hungers, our needs, but when one tries to defend one's necessities without anybody to support you, the campesino just gets screwed. . . . That is why the campesinos think a lot about Andrés Ruíz Escorcia—because he was and could still be the defender of the humble campesinos. If we had had a leader maybe they wouldn't have kicked us out of the land we occupied. The campesinos of Tonalá greet him, waiting for him as we await the rain which begins to fall in May."[37]

Until the time of Juan Angel López, authoritarian leadership had played a catalytic role in changing the campesinos' consciousness. First, Regino Escobar's showdown with Doña Tesla and his subsequent decision not to buy back their land led to a new definition of the campesinos' struggle. Regino had pushed the campesinos towards a new understanding of their own "necessity." Then, Escorcia, another authoritarian leader, drew upon campesino cultural symbols in order to construct a discourse accessible to all the various members of the agrarian protest movement. In each case, the authoritarian initiative of the leader provided the rank and file with a passive cover, a protection against Guardia and elite reprisals, and encouraged the rank and file not to feel guilty about offending the patrón. The residue of paternalistic social relations in the Chinandegan countryside was still strong in the 1950s, and many campesinos had a very difficult time turning against their former "benefactors." The ability of the rank and file to psychologically shift the responsibility to the leader thus aided significantly in their development of new ideas and meanings. Yet these new forms of consciousness did not necessarily reproduce authoritarian relations. On the contrary, the rank-and-file militants increasingly infused their new language and activity with democratic meanings, despite their authoritarian shell.

The woman's letter to Escorcia recalls this previous mode of transforming consciousness, for the author invoked an image of helpless, dependent campesinos: "If we had had a leader maybe they wouldn't have kicked us off." Here she cited the absence of leadership as the reason for failure. To a limited extent, the failure resulted from a need for that intermediary ground between themselves and the authorities previously occupied by Escorcia. Nevertheless, that phrase was profoundly misleading. For, on the contrary, the Hato Grande invasion was planned down to the most minute detail by the campesino union under the leadership of Engracia Zapata. The union had wisely targeted Hato Grande, an uncultivated latifundio that was subject to expropriation under the agrarian reform legislation enacted in April 1963. Hato Grande had a bad reputation because of a land dispute with another hacienda. Finally, the land invasion was so well planned that the union had even infiltrated the Guardia, following its plans and troop movements.[38] Short of arming themselves for combat, there was little more that the campesino organization could do. So why this plea for leadership?

The reply to this question probably lies in the act of writing to Escorcia, the man who had always defined his own writing as part of his power over the campesinos. Through it he controlled the space between his own private agenda and the voice of the campesinos. It is unclear to what extent the campesinos, at the time, evaluated the gap between their speech and Escorcia's writing. But it is clear that this letter, one of the first written expressions of the campesino movement, was initiated with a great deal of seriousness, for despite their desire for Escorcia's leadership, the campesinos now had to think and act on their own. In 1963, the campesinos took a major step forward by cloaking their autonomous expressions and actions in words that would not offend Escorcia, even as their actions pushed beyond his political horizons.

A different variation of the process developed in San José del Obraje, where several women assumed leadership responsibilities after Juan Suazo and Ramón Cándia fled from Juan Angel López. During Holy Week of 1963, the Obraje campesinos organized an occupation of Las Cuchillas. Before invading the land, one female militant wrote the following handwritten message to President Luís Somoza.

> The land which for many years belonged to us was usurped by the latifundista without shame, Edmundo Deshon, who used both the force of his capital and of his influence . . . he took over our lands through his influence and then threw the Guardia Nacional at us, yanking us off our land with our hands tied behind our backs. . . . Deshon's outrages and abuses were so numerous that the compañero Regino Escobar lost his life. . . . In order to keep us off of our land he has to keep a permanent command post along our land. In order to clarify our rights that we have to these lands we would like to submit that the very General Zelaya, then owner of Campuzano, respected our rights. . . . As an honorable and hard-working man please do what you can to see that our lands are returned because we are ready to defend them by any means necessary . . . so that in the future they won't lie about us and accuse us as guilty

when we reclaim our lands because the hunger and misery we suffer each day will not permit us to wait any longer.[39]

Before attacking elite property, a dangerous crime during the reign of Colonel López, the San José campesinos wisely attempted to justify their action to Somoza, not because they expected a gift of land but rather because they hoped he might prevent a potential massacre. They framed their principal justification in terms of traditional rights to feed their community. The San José women also appealed to Somoza's honor, manhood, industriousness, and Liberal lineage; but in 1963 they knew the limits of Somocista reformism.

The San José campesinos employed Escorcia's vocabulary of "latifundista," "capital," and elite political "influence." But Escorcia had introduced these terms as ideological weapons for use within the political and discursive boundaries of Somocismo. The CGT leader had used these terms selectively, to serve the interests of one elite faction (Deshon and Campuzano) against another. Thus, he had consistently portrayed Reyes as a usurper who obtained political influence through his capital.[40] But when he also attacked Campuzano in more subdued tones as a "latifundio," he clearly circumscribed the meaning of the term. He did not use the term "latifundistas" to describe Campuzano's elite political and economic allies to whom it had sold thousands of acres of land on the plantation's eastern flank. On the contrary, Escorcia saw the Deshon, Molieri, and Astacio Cabrera families as part of a modernizing bourgeois faction and therefore as tactical allies in the struggle for an antifeudal agrarian reform. The San José women, by contrast, implicitly rejected Escorcia's strategy and proposed campesino struggle against the agrarian bourgeoisie. Thus, the women's use of Escorcia's language to attack the Deshon faction was a radical departure, for it challenged the very boundaries delineated by Escorcia in his use of that same language.

Through their communication with the Tonaleños the San José organization developed a natural rights-based concept of private property that legitimated their claim to the land. As in Tonalá, the evolving campesino notion of private property was at once tolerant of collective forms of production and vigorously skeptical about the legitimacy of elite ownership. Thus, by 1963, Chinandegan campesinos shouted "the land belongs to everyone" when they invaded elite haciendas.[41] Previously, vertical knowledge could in part glue meanings to particular objects, for example the militant vocabulary used against Reyes. Campesinos and workers had tended to accept the fixed meanings in part because they often ceded a sense of responsibility for their thoughts and actions to the authoritarian leader who bore the burden of guilt for the community. Under predominantly female leadership, the campesinos' egalitarian forms of communication broke with the established pattern of vertically instituted changes of consciousness.

The forging of these new modalities of communication had two important consequences. First, the experience of repression and the creation of horizontal ties gave San José campesinos the intellectual confidence and the sense of collective responsibility necessary to question the meanings of Escorcia's political vocabulary and program. Second, as we have shown, the new forms of communication and leadership enabled women to articulate a new theoretical understanding of anti-elite private property and to deploy the old political vocabulary in ways that went beyond Escorcia's definitions.

On Holy Friday 1963 the San José campesinos engaged in their first collective action against the Deshon-Campuzano group since 1959. One day after the campesinos had built their ranchos and broken the sun-baked ground for spring planting, a large contingent of Guardia arrived at Las Cuchillas. Despite the Guardia's orders and the machine guns pointed at them, the two hundred women, men, and children refused to move. Argeñal Papi, the executive delegate, by now renowned for his pacification of Rancherías, arrived with the property titles, explaining that this land was not involved in the conflict because "it did not belong to Campuzano but to Molieri." Another friend of Deshon, Fredi Callejas, the journalist, reported that the "famished campesinos" were so obstinate that, "in order to remove these campesinos it was necessary to burn the ranchitos they had just built."[42] Callejas might have added that the Guardia's physical brutality expedited the removal process. After burning seventy-six huts, the soldiers forced the entire community onto trucks. Seven kilometers from Chinandega, the Guardia unloaded most of the prisoners, leaving them stranded twenty kilometers from home. Then they drove the remaining thirty-four protesters, including many women, to jail in Chinandega. Later, another woman militant wrote to Escorcia and to Juan Suazo, hiding out in Managua, about their experience in the Chinandegan jail. "Juan Angel López kept on asking us who told us to go on to that privately owned land? Who had tricked us? We answered that we all led as equals, and that we had no leader. . . . the Judge asked us the same thing and we declared that Regino Escobar had started everything, but ever since he died *mandamos iguales* [we lead as equals]."[43]

Colonel López had a psychopathic hatred for popular leaders, and the San José campesinos knew this well. With Escorcia and Juan Suazo out of the picture, the comandante was looking for the next culprit. Juan Angel shared with all security agents and many social scientists a conviction that campesinos only act under the command of a leader. Indeed, the fact that the woman militant wrote the letter to Escorcia might suggest that her expression, "*mandamos iguales*" was, in part, a defensive ruse. In other words, the prisoners had declared "we lead as equals" precisely because it was not true, so as to protect the leader. But who was the leader they sought to protect? To many, Escorcia was still the leader of the Chinandegan campesino movement, and in fact he was personally protecting most of its rank-and-file leadership, in Managua. But Juan Angel López had snapped the chain of command; Escorcia was not giving the orders. The San José prisoners collectively formed and protected their own leadership.

The San José woman's declaration may also be read as part of the evolving campesino discourse of necesidad. Since Escobar's death, if not before, the campesinos had taken collective actions on the basis of decisions made in democratic assemblies. No one ordered them to invade Molieri's land or put their lives on the line to support the struggles of fellow campesinos. The San José letter stated that abject physical misery dictated such sacrifice. Nevertheless, the very concept of necessity, a constant in campesino discourse, referred to those political, economic, and cultural measures necessary to alleviate that suffering. In this sense, mandamos iguales articulated the campesino concept of necesidad and igualdad into a coherent class discourse. For once conscious of necessity as a collective problem, the movement transformed the character of its leadership. The expression mandamos iguales, like the phrase uttered on the island—*nuestro jefe se llama necesidad*—referred above all else to a new definition of individual responsibility for the class movement. The transcendence of authoritarian forms of consciousness was neither total nor permanent. Those campesinos who did break loose from the fetters of imposed language, however, felt that the long-awaited rains of May had finally arrived.

Part III
Campesinos and the Sandinista Revolution, 1964–1979

11

The Campesinos and Agrarian Reform, 1964–1973

Solo muertos nos sacarán.
—Apolonio Carrasco, Rancherías leader, 1963

Esos señores Somoza, con palabras no se entendían.
—Pablo Guido, Tonalá union activist

Luís Somoza's administration terminated on what must have seemed to Alliance for Progress technocrats to be an upbeat note: the promulgation of an agrarian reform in April 1963 in the midst of a sustained economic boom. As it had been during the early 1950s, cotton was the domestic engine of Nicaragua's economic resurgence, following the recession of the late 1950s. Between 1961 and 1965 cotton export earnings jumped from $18.3 million to $66.1 million, accounting for roughly half of the increase in total export earnings, which went from $68.4 million to $149.0 million in the same period. Foreign investment, facilitated through the Central American Common Market, provided the other major stimulus to the Nicaraguan economy; from 1959 to 1969 investment leaped from $18.9 million to $41.5 million.[1]

During the early 1960s, the Alliance for Progress drove home the point to the Somoza regime that economic investment and aid would be contingent upon political and social reform. Luís Somoza and René Schick, who became president in May 1963, and was one of the more technocratic and less corrupt of the Somocistas, responded to that challenge by placing land reform at the center of a program of social, economic, and (to a lesser degree) political modernization. However, sectors of the agro-export elite resisted the reform program; in particular hacendados and businessmen refused to pay the minimum wage to rural workers, repressed their unions, and fought any attempt to finance social projects by taxing owners' profits. The reign of Juan Angel López was, in effect, the fruit of such elite antireformism. Yet the Schick administration did usher in a timidly reformist era, perhaps best symbolized by the trial of Colonel Juan Angel López for the murder of four campesinos near Posoltega. Though convicted, López served no time in prison.

The Labor Reform and Labor Repression, 1962–1965

From 1960 to 1964 some eight thousand Nicaraguan wage laborers, primarily port, construction, textile, and shoe workers, participated in twenty-eight strikes. The bulk of this unprecedented strike activity preceded an important labor law reform. In October 1962, in response to the labor offensive, the government established minimum wages and a paid day of rest and legalized sympathy strikes.[2]

On June 11, 1963, the customs house employees of Corinto launched a strike, demanding a 60 percent wage increase. The following day a government tribunal declared the strike illegal. Ostensibly to protect against "leftist sabotage," the Schick administration sent 175 elite troops of the Somoza Battalion to occupy the port facility. On June 13, the rest of the Corinto labor force launched strikes not only in solidarity with the customs employees but also against the "new modalities of port labor," in particular against the management's new attempts to mechanize the loading of cotton bales directly from trucks to ships. Despite the protective labor laws, the Guardia proceeded to arrest labor leaders and crush the strongest union in Nicaragua. The victorious employers were now powerful enough to institute a "black list," which effectively eliminated at least 120 militant unionists and leftists from the docks.[3]

The repression of the Corinto dock workers induced paralysis throughout the Nicaraguan labor movement. In Chinandega, through arrests and terror, Colonel López drove the leftist labor leadership underground. On December 4, 1963, *Novedades* triumphantly announced the end of "the extreme left's" influence in the Chinandegan labor movement.[4] Although López's terror drove militants underground, it did not rid the fields of labor protest. In December 1964, during the first post-López zafra, the canecutters of San Antonio demonstrated to the rest of the country that the Chinandegan workers' movement was still alive. Ten days after a pay delay caused by a computer malfunction, more than fifteen hundred canecutters marched from the colonias to the mill, starting the first major strike at ISA since 1936.[5] The same day, the company supplied the IBM pay cards and thus argued for the termination of the strike. The canecutters did not, however, consider the cards to be the main issue. Rather, they made three demands of the company: a 25 percent increase in the piece rate for cane; improvements in the weighing system for cut cane; and the firing of two administrators, the Coronel Kautz brothers, for their "maltreatment of field workers."[6]

The same day as the strike broke out, ISA called for government aid. The regime again deployed its infamous Somoza Battalion. The Guardia protected the numerous strikebreakers and ordered strikers to leave ISA, but the canecutters defied them, shouting: "We are not moving from here!"[7] After four days of major financial losses, ISA granted the salary and weighing demands but would not negotiate their "principle of authority": the Coronel Kautz brothers would stay on. Although angered about their failure to remove the administrators, the canecutters returned to work with more than just an impressive wage hike; for the cutters had shattered the aura of ISA invincibility, acquired valuable organizational experience, and inspired other Nicaraguan workers.[8]

The Schick administration engaged in selective repression against the labor and campesino movements, ranging from individual arrests to the deployment of the Somoza Battalion in Corinto and ISA. Schick's death in 1966, however, cut short what may have been a slow process of democratization. That process included an official toleration for labor, peasant, and even leftist groups. Under the Schick administration, the Frente Sandinista de Liberación Nacional (FSLN) could organize and participate in popular struggles in the cities and in the countryside under the cover of the Movilización Republicana (MR), a progressive political alliance. Tomás Borge, one of the founders of the FSLN, received an amnesty and began to edit the MR's weekly newspaper in Managua. FSLN leaders have since described this period of semilegal mass struggle as the product of an ideological deviation; it was nevertheless a time when Sandinistas made organizational inroads among the urban poor and learned to work with agrarian rebels.[9] Moreover, many campesino rebels throughout Nicaragua, thanks to their experiences with the Somocista agrarian reform, were becoming ready to listen to the Sandinistas.

The Somocista Agrarian Reform

Leoncio Martínez, a Tonalá activist, remarked: "We made the Agrarian Reform and then they clipped our wings . . . it was all a trick to demobilize us."[10] Martínez's statement aptly characterizes the Somocista agrarian reform. For if the political and economic pressure of the Alliance for Progress stimulated the reform, the wave of campesino land invasions in León and Chinandega forced the regime to redistribute land in the heart of the agro-export economy. Yet, as Martínez's comment suggests, although the campesinos made the agrarian reform, the regime used it to suppress the movement. To the campesino militants, the Instituto Agrario Nicaragüense (IAN), the agrarian reform agency, became but one more autoridad to cope with and combat. Dr. Rodolfo Mejia Ubilla, the director of IAN, recognized this conflict when he stated in 1965, "The general opinion of labor and campesino leaders is that by now, the Nicaraguan Agrarian Institute should have confiscated all the lands which peasants have denounced, and it should have already divided up those lands; but in Nicaragua there exists the respect for personal possessions."[11] Although the Somozas counted on creating more peasant proprietors as a bulwark against Castroite subversion, the campesinos' struggles with IAN prepared the field for an alliance with the FSLN.

The regime initiated the agrarian reform with the aim of ending the campesino movement, modernizing agriculture, and obtaining funds from the Alliance for Progress. The main objectives of the agrarian reform bill of 1963 were to relocate landless peasants from the populated Pacific to the undeveloped Atlantic region of the country, to provide land titles to peasants who had settled on the agricultural frontier in the east-central region, to settle individual disputes over squatters' rights, and to expropriate latifundios.[12] From 1964 to 1976, IAN implemented the non-redistributive objectives with the following results: the resettlement of 2,651 families (17,479 people), the granting of 16,500 land titles to peasants on the eastern agricultural frontier, the legal resolution (with mixed outcomes) of over 28,000 squatter-proprietor conflicts.[13]

In the 1960s, more than fifty thousand Nicaraguan campesino families lacked any land to cultivate and another fifty thousand families possessed insufficient land for their survival.[14] Thus, the transfer of 2,600 families to land on the Atlantic coast made little difference. The settlement of the agricultural frontier did, however, help to ease pressure on Pacific coast lands and thus could be considered a minor success of the Somocista agrarian reform.[15] Similarly, the resolution of squatter conflicts undoubtedly assuaged, however slightly, class tensions in the countryside.

Contrary to what most scholars have argued, the Somocista agrarian reform program was quite consistent with similar legislation throughout Latin America.[16] For in addition to its socially conservative colonization policy, the Nicaraguan version contained an explicit and forceful assault on latifundios. The act called for "the expropriation and division of uncultivated latifundios and of lands with low levels of productivity due to inadequate exploitation." Moreover, in Article 19, which rapidly became the most quoted section of the Agrarian Reform Act, all lands of more than five hundred hectares were subject to expropriation when, "in a determinate zone, the excessive concentration of property . . . is damaging to the campesinos because they lack land or other means of subsistence."[17] The agrarian law required the government to compensate the owners of all expropriated land. In Chinandega alone, IAN could have legally expropriated more than one hundred properties and distributed some 200,000 manzanas of land to 20,000 families.[18] Such a redistribution program would have eliminated land hunger among the Chinandegan campesinos, but IAN only expropriated a minute proportion of the available land in Chinandega.

IAN's failure to effectively confront latifundismo in Chinandega and the rest of western Nicaragua was not the result of a total lack of political will. The two principal officials of IAN, Rodolfo Mejia Ubilla and Ricardo Hidalgo, sympathized with progressive Latin American social thought that gravitated around the concept of "integral agrarian reform," first elaborated at the Punta del Este conference in 1961. Mejia Ubilla wrote in 1965, "What we want, within a new ideology, is that we keep the land as a means of production and we eliminate everything which makes it a means of exploitation."[19]

Ex-president Luís Somoza, a prominent member of IAN (representing cattle raisers), in 1965, argued vigorously in favor of expropriating uncultivated haciendas. "If yesterday the landlord didn't need the land, now when the campesino is on his land he needs it less."[20] Moreover, leading representatives of the Chinandegan agrarian elite, such as Dr. Astacio Cabrera and Callejas Deshon, strongly endorsed the breakup and distribution of latifundios and harshly criticized IAN for its "fear of applying the law rigorously."[21] These representatives of the cotton elite urged, moreover, that titles immediately be granted to squatters. Luís Somoza and the representatives of the agro-export elite were against the latifundistas because they viewed such archaic forms of property as a brake on the progress of agro-export capitalism. Most of the Somoza properties on the populous Pacific coast were quite efficient, even if the Guardia had to provide a substantial part of the labor force.[22] In Chinandega, Astacio, Callejas, and the Deshon family had no uncultivated land and had already evicted rebellious campesinos before IAN's institution in June of 1964. Moreover, they understood that since Juan Angel López had failed to destroy the campesino movement, land distribution was the best method of pacifying the Chinandegan countryside.

Nevertheless, despite the political will of IAN and a sector of the agro-export elite, the government did not redistribute latifundios to any significant degree in Chinandega. IAN, a semi-autonomous institution, blamed the Executive and Congress for not providing it with adequate funds. In 1965, IAN operated on a budget of slightly more than $500,000, approximately 2 percent of the national budget. After meeting expenses, however, it had only $50,000 with which to purchase land.[23] Hence, IAN's director argued that without such funding, the attack on latifundismo could not be effective.

Although Presidents Luís Somoza and Schick believed in the redistribution of latifundios, other elite groups blocked land reform. Luís Somoza's brother, Anastasio (Tacho), commander of the Guardia and presidential aspirant, was one major opponent of the expropriation of latifundios. Tacho was undoubtedly afraid of losing some the estimated 10 percent of Nicaraguan farm land which belonged to his family, but it is also possible that a different political perspective informed Tacho's anti-reformist stance. Tacho Somoza probably rejected land reform for fear that it would alienate important elite sectors and that it might provoke even more campesino insurgency.

Since the introduction of the agrarian reform bill, the Somoza regime had been harshly criticized by hacendados who feared expropriation. Between 1961 and 1963, elite pressure had instituted a radical change in the bill originally proposed by the executive to Congress, which allowed the government to expropriate without indemnification any property of more than three hundred acres. The 1963 legislation more than tripled the expropriation to over nine hundred acres and added the key obstructionist clause mandating prior cash indemnification for the expropriated landlord, which of course would have necessitated a significant budget increase for IAN. The same forces that had transformed the legislation continued to exercise political persuasion and indirect budgetary pressure against IAN.[24]

Tacho Somoza was probably more responsive to these conservative sectors than was his brother; as commander in chief of the Guardia he saw that the labor and campesino movements had already escaped the boundaries of Somocista populist discourse. Unlike his brother Luís, he would make no serious effort to develop or control popular movements. Tacho did, however, cultivate the support of many hacendados, inside and outside of the "Somocista clique."[25]

Although the vanguard of the agro-export bourgeoisie supported land reform, other powerful sectors of the elite adamantly opposed it. The antireformists ranged from Somocista politicians who had illegally expropriated land to latifundistas on a slow march towards modernization. Three Somocista politicians in Chinandega who had become important antireformists were Augusto Terán, long-time mayor of Chichigalpa, Irma Guerrero, congressional deputy since 1963, and Paulino Nororí, jefe político since 1963. Terán, had in 1950 illegally appropriated more than one thousand manzanas of ejidal land. By renting the land near Chichigalpa, he had financed the purchase of other properties.[26] Irma Guerrero similarly used her political power to acquire properties. Paulino Nororí was an exceedingly corrupt official specializing in fraudulent tax collection and land sales to campesinos.[27] These three Somocista politicians were targets of the campesino movement (although La Irma artfully cultivated a clientelistic relationship with one faction of the campesino movement).

The other groups of antireformists reflected the uneven development of capitalism in Chinandega. The difference between reformists and antireformists was not simply between backward and advanced sectors of the agrarian bourgeoisie, for some of the principal elite families had interests in both sectors. Sugar and sesame had first developed near the center of the department in the areas northwest of Chichigalpa and Chinandega. Cotton production pushed capitalist social relations east to the Obraje region and north to Tonalá. Finally, during the 1960s, cattle raisers outside of the cotton and sugar zones struggled to join the export economy. Thus, during the 1960s it would have been hard, if not impossible, to locate pure latifundistas unconnected to agro-export capitalism. Indeed, the antireformist landlords generally operated both inside and outside of the cotton industry. Thus, for example, the Gasteazoras, Ricardo Frissell, the Barberenas, and some of the Deshons belonged to the agro-export elite but also possessed thousands of acres of undeveloped land on the peninsula of Cosigüina, in the northwestern corner of Chinandega.[28]

Since the late 1950s, a United States-approved slaughterhouse had been constructed in Managua, and as a result, Nicaraguan beef exports more than doubled between 1960 and 1963.[29] The Chinandegan oligarchic families thus quite rationally sought ways to incorporate their uncultivated estates into the agro-export economy. In keeping with a common Central American practice, they typically would rent land to campesinos, who would then clear and sow the land for one or two years. Once the campesinos had prepared substantial portions of the land, the oligarchs would evict their tenants and bring in cattle.

The Chinandegan oligarchs opposed the agrarian reform for several compelling reasons. First, their tenuous legal claim made them fear that they would lose all of their land. Second, their inability to immediately put the land into production made them more vulnerable to expropriation according to the 1963 law. Third, they suspected that the reform might deprive them of laborers or, even worse, convert their tenants into peasant proprietors. Even more ominous to the elite, between 1963 and 1965 their own tenants and numerous squatters, inspired by the campesino movement and by the reform law, began to resist their authority; the growing protest movement confirmed their worst fears about the political effects of the reform legislation.

The agro-export bourgeoisie was therefore deeply divided on the agrarian reform issue. Although the Callejas and Deshon families and Astacio wished to accelerate the reform, the politically and socially heterogeneous rank and file of the agrarian bourgeoisie attempted to sabotage it. The increasingly powerful General Tacho Somoza sympathized with the antireformist group, which included some of his key regional political allies such as Irma Guerrero, Terán, and Nororí.[30] Thus, the coalition of Tacho Somoza, the *nouveau riche* politicians, and sectors of the agrarian bourgeoisie combined to cripple land redistribution programs throughout Nicaragua. Still, the reform process set in motion by the campesinos could not be turned off so easily.

The Campesinos' Agrarian Reform

On June 15, 1964, Geraldo Suárez, an official of the agriculture department, journeyed some forty kilometers northwest of Chinandega to investigate a land dispute in the area known as Petacaltepe. Since the arrest of Colonel López in February 1964, agrarian conflicts seemed to erupt daily throughout the department. In the Petacaltepe dispute, the *jefe político*, Nororí, had apparently sold authorizations to campesinos giving them the right to settle on national lands; but two powerful families, the Deshons and the Lacayo Montealegres, claimed those same lands. During the previous few years, some fifty campesino families, most of them dispossessed hacienda workers, had settled on the lands of Petacaltepe.

Suárez recognized that the dispute had serious political implications; Nororí and Irma Guerrero, leading Somocista politicians, were accusing the Lacayo Montealegres and the Deshons of being "land-robbing latifundistas." Suárez was probably also concerned with his own job security: his boss, "Tommy" Lacayo Montealegre, minister of agriculture, was a close relative of the owners of Petacaltepe.

When Suárez arrived at Petacaltepe, he realized that the campesinos would not accept yet another dispossession. Suárez urgently reported, "The situation is grave, extremely grave . . . those campesinos are ready to resist the Guardia Nacional."[31] Suárez managed to negotiate a temporary truce in Petacaltepe, nonetheless his warning of violent confrontation both reflected and stimulated elite fears of campesino militancy.[32] The creation of IAN badly divided the elite. To one group, only land reform would quell campesino militancy; others pointed to Petacaltepe as a portent of violent revolution, the bitter fruit of agrarian reform.

The language of agrarian reform was indeed the final dialect of Somocismo: it provided the regime with its last effective means of communication with the campesinos. IAN represented the last strip of common ground between the campesinos and the regime. Mejia Ubilla, IAN director, stated in 1965, "We must accept the truth that private property has a social function to fulfill which does not only benefit the owner, but rather the surrounding community. . . . The social interest stands above the absolute right to private property; and one can place restrictions and limitations on property when it does not fulfill the community's expectations, . . . This concept is still not accepted very well by many large landowners."[33]

The Chinandegan campesinos, in contrast, were quite willing to acknowledge the "social function" of private property. As we saw earlier, the movement had constructed a concept of private property which anticipated the official language of agrarian reform. Official discourse attempted to restrict the meaning of social function to uncultivated latifundios; campesino meanings were more open-ended. Socially responsible private property for campesinos included individual and cooperative forms of production but excluded capitalist cotton plantations that operated among the landless poor. Nevertheless, after two years of Juan Angel López's silence by violent repression, the campesino militants were quite willing to communicate in the official language of agrarian reform.

Return to Tonalá, 1964

In February 1964, shortly after the arrest of Juan Angel López, Mariano Escorcia, Leoncio Martínez, and Engracia Zapata returned to Tonalá. They immediately set out to reorganize the union, seriously weakened by the repression of the Hato Grande invasion the previous November. Although in 1962 the union had had some 150 members, in 1964 the militants could only persuade thirty people to attend meetings. Now that the Tonaleño pickers had turned the waves of blinding white cotton into a dead brown plain, the union members discussed what land they might plant. Having studied the agrarian reform law in Managua, Mariano Escorcia and Martínez argued that Isaac

Montealegre, minister of development, had no right to the land south of the Estero Real, around the abandoned port of Tempisque. Mariano and Leoncio explained that the same law regarding coastal land by which they had claimed Bonete in 1962 would apply to the Tempisque; only this time the newly created IAN would enforce the law.[34] Hence, the Tonaleños could claim a sizable portion of the Montealegres's hacienda, La Chunga.

Shortly before the first May rains, the union helped ten settler families move onto the Tempisque lands. At first, the Montealegres apparently did not notice the Tempisque settlers, as they were physically isolated from the rest of La Chunga (locally called La Chingada). For the next six weeks, the settlers cleared the land and planted corn, fruit trees, and *chaguites* (plantains). By mid-June the "port" of Tempisque, dotted with ranchitos, gardens, and *milpas* (corn patches), resembled any other remote, muddy, and miserable settlement.

On June 19, the Montealegres reported that campesinos had invaded La Chunga.[35] The next day, Ernesto Cervantes (the government official who had suffered the mosquito attack on Bonete in 1962) journeyed to the inhospitable Estero Real. His mission was basically the same as it had been in Bonete—to convince rebellious Tonaleños to leave occupied land. The fourteen Guardia who accompanied Cervantes gathered the squatters together and ordered them off the land.[36]

The Tonalá union leaders helped the squatters return to the Tempisque and then sought aid from IAN, basing their petition on the agrarian reform law, which they could now cite chapter and verse as grounds for the expropriation of the surrounding latifundios, including La Chunga.[37] Two weeks later, instead of an official reply, the union read the answer to their petition in the ashes and smoke of their smoldering huts, as the Guardia evicted the Tempisque squatters. Several days later, Fanor Argüello, owner-operator of San Miguel on the western border of Tempisque, also burned his tenants' huts.[38] After consulting with the local Guardia comandante, Argüello acted to prevent potential tenant claims to land given the bias of the agrarian law in favor of tenants and squatters.

The appointment of Horacio Montealegre, the nephew of Tomás Lacayo Montealegre, as secretary of the executive board of IAN represented another piece of bad news for the Tonaleños.[39] Two antagonists now occupied key positions on the board which would rule in the Tempisque-Montealegre conflict. Despite the odds, the Tonalá union members rebuilt their huts. Then, on August 12, 1964, the Montealegres ordered workers to tear down the fence between La Chunga and Tempisque. Subsequently, the Montealegres' lawyer cynically filed charges against seven union leaders for "damages to property." The Chinandegan police chief led the Guardia, armed with machine guns, into Tonalá and arrested the union militants in their homes.[40]

The presence of machine guns in Tonalá was symptomatic of the heightening of class tensions throughout Chinandega in August 1964. Land conflicts broke out not just in Tonalá but all along the agricultural frontier on the peninsula of Cosigüina. For the establishment of IAN sounded like a bugle calling the campesinos to battle. From the passage of the agrarian reform law in April 1963 and the institution of IAN in July 1964, demands for immediate land reform rang out throughout Nicaragua. Yet IAN lacked the organizational coherence, the funding, or the political capability to respond quickly and favorably to such demands. Chinandegan campesinos, rather than waiting for bureaucratic action, occupied contested land, presenting IAN with fait accomplis.

The mechanization of cotton production also contributed to rising tensions. In 1964, major cotton producers announced the introduction of mechanical harvesters.[41] The new minimum wage and union pressures to enforce the labor code in the countryside had prompted the cotton growers to attempt to mechanize the harvest in order to save on labor costs. Indeed, the harvesters would have eliminated some fifty thousand seasonal jobs. The labor movement, however, reacted angrily to this new threat to the livelihood of agricultural workers, and the PSN immediately organized a large protest demonstration in Chinandega.[42] The PSN influence over the movement worried the authorities and hacendados. The campesinos now seemed to be contesting all aspects of elite rule, from land rights to production decisions. Moreover, the authorities took very seriously rumors that the machinery would be sabotaged.[43]

Between August and October, like the ebb and flow of the Estero Real, the campesinos would enter to work on the lands of the Tempisque and would leave with their hands bound by the Guardia.[44] By October 1964, the Montealegres' resistance to the Tonalá union was becoming a problem for the regime. Images of burnt huts and thirteen-year-old prisoners cast blame on a prominent family of the Somocista elite, thus compromising any political benefit the government might have reaped from the agrarian reform. What made the situation even worse was that the Montealegres themselves recognized that their claim to the Tempisque was, at best, extremely dubious. Tommy Montealegre, the minister of agriculture, was undoubtedly hard-pressed to explain his family's behavior in the context of his duty to implement the agrarian reform. The cabinet minister's legitimacy was particularly important in light of the Schick administration's concerns to project an image of honest, civilian, and progressive government.

The Montealegres agreed to a deal in mid-October. They withdrew their claim to one hundred manzanas of Tempisque land and agreed to sell to IAN two hundred manzanas of land they did claim as part of La Chunga. IAN then entered into negotiations with the Tonalá workers' union. Initially Mariano Escorcia and Leoncio Martínez opposed the deal because it acknowledged Montealegres's possession of national land. Moreover, three hundred manzanas represented less than one-half of what they had been fighting for in the Tempisque: there would simply not be enough land to distribute. After conferring with IAN, Andrés Ruíz Escorcia, now a congressional deputy, made a special trip to Tonalá in order to convince Mariano and Leoncio. Escorcia brought only one argument: to reject the agreement would be to invite a reprisal and to lose even the three hundred manzanas. The union leadership accepted Escorcia's argument and drew up a list of beneficiaries, forty-four Tonaleños who had participated in the union since 1961.[45]

Ruperto Mayorga, the founder of Tonalá, led a minority of Tonaleños in denouncing the "irresponsible union" for an agreement that only served to "satiate the avarice of the terratenientes."[46] Fighting to retake the union leadership, Mayorga chose an opportune moment to strike out against his adversaries; an implicit part of the agreement with IAN and the Montealegres was the prohibition of union activity for land recipients. Mayorga could thus attack Escorcia and Martínez but they could not defend themselves.

Escorcia and Martínez were willing to accept the formal logic behind their removal from the union leadership since they had become peasant proprietors and were no longer workers, but they vehemently rejected Ruperto Mayorga's effort to take over the union and paint them as "sell-outs."[47] After all, they, and not Mayorga, had been on the front lines of the Tonalá workers' struggle for three years. Ironically, the union's victory at the edge of the estuary, the culmination of years of danger and hardship, isolated the militants from those Tonaleños. Although not among the 44 beneficiary families, Escorcia and Martínez began to lose touch with some of those 150 to 200 Tonaleño families left out of the bargain. Many of those families began to look to Ruperto Mayorga for leadership.

Mayorga's critique of the Tonalá union leadership was trenchant. He argued that the union allowed the Montealegres to get away with the ruse of selling national land. The sale, he said, allowed IAN to legitimize the Montealegres' claim to fifteen hundred manzanas of national land that should have been distributed to the remaining landless families. More seriously, according to Mayorga, the union's deal with IAN had given the local agrarian elite valuable ammunition, a pretext for announcing the "completion" of agrarian reform in the area.[48]

Although harshly criticizing Andrés Escorcia and his distant relatives in the local leadership, Mayorga nonetheless demanded assistance from the CGT to carry on the struggle:

> Relating what has happened in this town of Tonalá the struggle is completely off course. The needs of three hundred campesino families have been destroyed with one blow. You know how hard we've struggled for the land and we blame the CGT because it supports and instructs the Tonalá workers' union, . . . They put their foot in their mouths and hairs in their conscience when they accepted the . . . three hundred manzanas of fourth- and fifth-class land . . . from IAN without caring about the sacrifice of the other families of Tonalá. Only because your parientes [relations] are looking out for their own leadership and not the well-being of the cause . . . IAN now sabotages our efforts and tries to fool the great mass of campesinos of Tonalá. . . . We hope that you will give us orientations so that we may reach some conclusions . . . we need to hammer even though the nail is always bent.[49]

It is ironic that Ruperto Mayorga, the man who in 1961 had argued against occupying Bonete, should become a radical agrarista three years later. His letter reveals his anger at the Escorcias—the three brothers who stole his leadership and their powerful (if distant) relative who helped them do it. But the letter also suggests that Ruperto had been converted to the agrarian struggle, although his conversion did not involve questioning Somocista politics or his own habit of clearing everything with the comandante. Thus, since Mayorga's leadership activities inevitably would involve conflict with the Somocista political and economic elite, his efforts would indeed resemble hammering a perpetually bent nail.

From the point of view of elite landowners, serious division in the campesino ranks was clearly the most successful and purposeful outcome of the Somocista agrarian reform in Tonalá and elsewhere. The partial campesino victory in the battle against the Montealegres divided the Tonalá campesino organization into an officially inactive group of forty-four families of small proprietors on the Tempisque lands—the movement veterans and beneficiaries—and the landless, several kilometers away in Tonalá. Ruperto Mayorga's takeover emerged from that structural division and from the "clipped wings" of his opponents in the union. His leadership also deepened the split in the campesino ranks, for the Tonalá movement had already surpassed in theory and practice Mayorga's style of clientelistic Somocismo. For several years, the Tonalá militants had been forging a radical language of struggle within the authoritarian shell of Somocismo. Despite the sincerity of his commitment to win the fifteen hundred manzanas for the community, to accept Mayorga's leadership seemed to many campesinos like gaining shelter from the searing dust storms of April only to await forever the rains of May.

Campesinos Splits, Somocista Factions, 1964–1971

Engracia Zapata challenged Mayorga's leadership, for she wished to keep the campesino movement along the course that she and other union leaders had charted between 1961 and 1964. Although personal animosities were part of the conflict between Engracia and Mayorga, the underlying tensions were fundamentally political. Engracia argued that the division was Mayorga's fault. "The division was so deep that it has lasted until today. You see Mayorga believed in himself a lot, but he knew next to nothing. You can learn a lot in universities, but if you haven't developed a consciousness about compañerismo, then you just can't lead a campesino movement. Ruperto, you know, was well-off. He always had plenty to eat. So his vision of the struggle was a lot different . . . talking things over with the political bosses of Chinandega. Taking personal credit for everything. . . . We believed that the struggle wasn't about one group or another in Tonalá but about the whole campesinado."[50]

Engracia Zapata's questioning of Mayorga's authority soon prompted another division of the campesino organization. Starting in 1965, Mayorga's group, some forty to sixty families, concentrated their efforts on claiming one thousand manzanas of the hacienda San Miguelito, owned by the Argüello family. Engracia Zapata, beginning in 1966, led another group of eighty families in a struggle to win the same land, located to the west of the Tempisque settlement. When the Tonaleños unleashed two-pronged land invasions, their organizational division worked to defeat their common adversary.[51] At other times, however, the campesinos' factionalism undermined the movement; in 1966 and 1971, Mayorga asked the Guardia to intervene against the group led by "esa mujer loca," Mayorga's description of Engracia.[52]

Ruperto Mayorga relied heavily on his connections to the Chinandegan power structure to obtain concessions for his organization. He thus received the political backing of a Chinandegan lawyer, Dr. Noel Pereira. The son of the late jefe político and long-time obrerista boss, Pereira headed a faction of the local Somocista party opposed to both Irma Guerrero's group and the elite Callejas-Deshon faction.[53] Through his family name and his pro bono legal efforts on behalf of the Corinto dockworkers and Tonalá campesinos, Pereira had sought to reactivate the old obrerista politics. Although far short of the "thousands of campesino followers" that Pereira claimed for himself, Mayorga's group in Tonalá provided the lawyer with a symbolically important political base.

Engracia Zapata's campesino organization received some support from Irma Guerrero, who sought to counter Pereira's political success in the countryside. Although Mayorga argued that Irma Guerrero ran the Tonalá organization, Engracia and her followers apparently offered nothing in return for Irma's occasional gestures of sympathy.[54] On the contrary, the Tonaleños looked for material and political support from the ex-union members who now resided on the Tempisque lands, for Engracia never resented their acceptance of the IAN deal. "I would have joined them if I hadn't already moved with my kids to Corinto. It was better to have some corn planted than none at all. Now the Tempisque business did cause some division, but that wasn't the end of the struggle for those compañeros, they kept on helping right up until the triumph."[55]

Although the Somocista agrarian reform split the Tonaleño movement, it did not attain its goal of creating a pacified petty bourgeois group of colonists politically divorced from the landless proletariat. Moreover, the younger generation in the Tempisque colony—the children and younger siblings of the original union members—not only joined with Zapata's group in occupying Argüellos's land, but also they spearheaded an invasion of La Chunga in 1966. Through these actions, supported by the entire colony, the Tempisque group demonstrated that they had not rejected their own tradition (however brief) of union struggle. Indeed, IAN rekindled that sense of antagonism by attempting to oust Mariano Escorcia and Leoncio Martínez from the colony's directorate, by vetoing a production cooperative, and by interfering in the campesinos' lives and work.[56]

The colonists, even if they had wished to, could not fulfill the role of pacified petty bourgeois (proprietors who do not need to sell their labor) because IAN did not provide them with the necessary land base. On the contrary, the Tempisque group, while better off than the landless, still had to survive on three or four manzanas of poor quality land, with limited bank credit and highly exploitative commercial outlets. Pablo Guido summed up their plight.

So we had to make do with a few manzanas of this lousy land. But no one could live on that. So we all got by working for *el rico*, during harvest. You see, the bank gave such little credit it only covered the preparation of the land. So lots of people had to sell their harvests to some *acaparador* [buyer] before even seeing the crops. And even if we made it through to the end of, say, a sesame harvest, they'd get us with real low prices. Once we thought we'd get by all these acaparadores by selling cane to the sugar mill. We worked out a deal with Monterrosa, we planted it and then had to chew it, probably because the Montealegres [related to the owners of the mill] still had it in for us. It was like the rain. Instead of enjoying it, we had to curse it, because it meant fighting off these little lakes filled with mosquitoes which would form on the paths. They wouldn't even build a road so we could get out. It was all one big trap.[57]

Tacho Somoza argued that the agrarian reform, by making proprietors out of proletarians, created "a seawall against the waves of Marxism-Leninism that are trying to sink our continent."[58] But Pablo Guido's testimony, substantiated by the other Tonalá veterans, suggests, on the contrary, that a limited land reform, when brought about by the agrarian movement itself, tends to stimulate and broaden the radicalization process. The Tonaleños' radical-democratic ideology combined with their poor quality lands, insufficient credit, lack of transportation, and exploitative commercial outlets made it difficult for the campesinos of El Tempisque to become the conservative yeomen farmers envisioned by the agrarian reform.

The forty-four families on the Tempisque received 409 manzanas of land (according to IAN). Nevertheless, since most of the land was not cultivable, most families could work on only three or four manzanas. At most seven families (with slightly better land) attempted to survive exclusively by cultivating their parcels without selling their labor. Twenty colonists worked as canecutters in La Chunga, and more than thirty families worked in the cotton harvests. Hence, rather than yeomen, the Somocista land reform in Tonalá merely aided in the creation of a more stable seasonal labor force. The new semiproletarians did not often become conservative; nothing changed in their material situation so dramatically as to affect the consciousness they had developed over the years of struggle against the agrarian elite. Indeed, the campesino consciousness forged in Tonalá, on the haciendas, and on Bonete was further developed by the experience of agrarian reform. For in addition to working once again in the harvests for el rico, now the colonists experienced the arbitrary impositions of the state, which quite literally tried to run their lives. Rather than becoming Somoza's barrier against revolution, the new Tonaleño proprietors would come to recognize that a real agrarian reform would require overturning the state and its elite allies. As Pablo Guido posed the problem, "Esos señores Somoza, con palabras no se entendían" (Those Somozas, they didn't understand with words).[59]

"One Dagger in My Gut and Another in My Back":
Reform in Rancherías

As it had in Tonalá, land reform in Rancherías responded to the regime's counterinsurgency strategy. In both zones the regime expected that the conversion of landless peasants into a peasant petty bourgeoisie would end the campesino movement and create a political base of support. Such expectations were quite in keeping with the theory and practice of agrarian reform throughout Latin America during the 1960s.[60] The regime's strategy was largely unsuccessful in Tonalá because it failed to provide the necessary land base. At the same time, seasonal wage labor, authoritarian administrators in the colony, palpably unequal market relations, and contact with neighbors actively involved in the agrarian protest movement all served to reinforce the Tonaleños' radical-democratic tradition. The regime's limited success in Tonalá was the result exclusively of the organizational split in the movement outside of the Tempisque colony. Land reform in Rancherías produced relatively more positive results in part because of its more adequate land base and credit. As in Tonalá, however, the accumulated political experience of the campesinos would be the decisive factor both in the regime's limited success and ultimately in the failure of the Somocista agrarian reform.

The campesino movement had waged its principal battle against Marcelino Reyes and his allies. The land distribution in Rancherías ratified this decisive victory. Officially the government ceded 4,396 manzanas to 288 families. The reality, however, was less impressive: more than 250 Rancherías families received approximately 1,250 manzanas (five manzanas per family). Nonetheless, the Rancherías group did receive land of slightly better quality than did the Tempisque colonists. In addition, the government gave more, if still insufficient, credit to the Rancherías group. In 1964, the Banco Nacional provided C$298,000 of credit to finance 1,138 manzanas of corn, bean, and sesame cultivation. The following year, the bank financed 350 manzanas of cotton, although the government provided neither technical assistance nor enough credit to cover fumigation costs.[61] The insufficiency of land and credit in Rancherías, as it had in Tonalá, inhibited the formation of a petty bourgeoisie. Still, perhaps one-fourth of the Rancherías families achieved a tenuous petty-bourgeois status—in good harvest years they did not have to work for el rico.

The divisions that came to plague the Rancherías group derived only partially from the emerging class differentiations between petty bourgeois and semiproletarian, for divergent political experiences preceded this class stratification and continued to play an equally important role. Like the Tonaleños, the Rancherías campesinos broke apart following their victory. In July 1962, Domingo Ramírez and Irma Guerrero helped organize a faction within the Rancherías organization to combat Andrés Ruíz Escorcia's influence. Aided by Juan Angel López, who drove Escorcia from Chinandega, Tomás Castañeda led a bitter campaign against the veteran pro-Escorcia leaders, accusing them of being Communists and Hondurans. By 1965, Castañeda's group included some eighty-five families.[62] In particular, Castañeda and his group opposed cooperatives, a key part of the pro-Escorcia program. Éntimo Sánchez recalled the roots of the schism in Rancherías. "Castañeda got his group together because of anti-Communism. We wanted to start cooperatives. We wanted to work in community. And they said that sounds like communism."[63]

The division in the Rancherías organization had much to do with the different types of experience and consciousness among the campesinos. Among the 250 colonists many had not previously been active participants in the movement. Castañeda, aided by Ramírez, established his base of support among those more conservative, inexperienced elements who desired neither cooperatives nor more conflict with the neighboring terratenientes. In a letter to Escorcia, Abraham Carrasco, the president of the Rancherías organization, referred to three antagonists—Castañeda and a wealthy peasant formally allied with Carrasco (the two daggers), and Colonel López."I've got one dagger in my gut and the other in my back. . . . You tried to do us some good by pushing for me as president, but with Juan Angel López watching me all the time, I'm screwed."[64]

Despite Carrasco's predicament, his faction of the Rancherías campesinos continued to resist those wealthy peasants among the sixteen who broke the June 1962 agreements. Defying the iron rule of Juan Angel López, in March 1963, the Rancherías militants began to occupy and cultivate land claimed by the wealthy peasants. In response to Manuel Cáceres's threats, Apolonio

Carrasco, Abraham's eldest son, proclaimed, "Manuel Cáceres is no campesino. . . . Seven of his group have seized 400 manzanas of land, and Cáceres poses as Commander of the Civil Reserve; he does not respect our private property. . . he threatens to shoot us. . . . We campesinos will march 10,000 strong to Managua . . . because from this land which belongs to us—solo muertos nos sacarán! [we will only leave dead]."[65]

The Rancherías organization's militant challenge under the rule of Colonel López underscores a central point about how the campesino movement reacted to its partial victories: the distribution of land did not automatically override the nascent class-conscious perspective forged during the previous agrarian conflict. Carrasco's defiant letter clearly referred to a broader movement than that of the new smallholders of Rancherías. When he appealed to those ten thousand campesinos who would march to Managua, he called on the solidarity of all rural Chinandegans, who, regardless of whether they benefited from the land reform, still desired "the unity of our class."[66] Over the next fifteen years, the Rancherías group would maintain informal ties of solidarity with this campesino class composed of workers, tenant farmers, and smallholders.[67]

Although the Rancherías organization would continue to struggle on a number of fronts, the Somocista land reform clearly registered a political success with the consolidation of the Castañeda group. Within Colonia San Luís (for "Saint" Luís Somoza) the militants, like those of Tonalá, had to confront the IAN administration over many issues, including the formation of a production cooperative. However, the Rancherías group also had to contend with Castañeda's faction, allied with the IAN administration. The alliance of Castañeda's group with IAN permitted the consolidation of a limited Somocista base that functioned in Rancherías until 1978.

The limits of the reform impeded the complete pacification of Rancherías, however, and antagonisms born in the heat of the conflict in the early 60s did not disappear. Indeed, after the settlement, most of the Reyes group still kept their properties. Along the borders of Colonia San Luís, campesino militants continued to fight with their old antagonists over everything from land claims to fishing and hunting rights on the "island" of Bonete. Such conflicts would flare up into major confrontations with wealthy peasants and hacendados in 1963, 1965, 1968, and 1977.[68] The Rancherías campesinos continued to resist elite pressures on their land and resources, in an effort to escape the plagues of poverty, indebtedness, and field labor for el rico. In Rancherías as in Tonalá, many campesinos found the agrarian reform at once too stingy and too arbitrary with the campesinos and far too generous with the agrarian elite. The regime's land reform had succeeded in dividing the agrarian movement, but it failed to suppress the campesinos' organization altogether. Indeed, the campesinos' experience of counterinsurgency reform would by the 1970s help generate the conditions for a revolutionary movement in the Chinandegan countryside.

Agrarian Reform and Revolution in Sutiava

In Sutiava the origins of the agrarian protest movement and the immediate consequences of the counterinsurgency reform were quite different than in Chinandega. The development of agrarian capitalism in the Sutiava area since 1940 had tended to stratify rural society, as many small farmers and especially tenant farmers became proletarians. Moreover, the process of subdivision of family plots through inheritance and sales to the elite forced most Sutiavas, like their Chinandegan counterparts, to work seasonally in the cotton fields. But at the same time, perhaps 40 percent of Sutiavan families survived as smallholders, far more proportionately than in San José del Obraje or Tonalá. Not surprisingly, the social and ideological origins of the protest movement in Sutiava diverged from the Chinandegan experience. In the 1950s the agrarian movement started as a defense of the traditional land-use rights of propertied cattle ranchers. The mass participation of landless Sutiavas changed the movement's focus; its target became the reappropriation of some forty thousand manzanas of indigenous territory occupied by the elite following Sutiava's annexation to the municipality of León in 1902. Rather than seeing this as a shift in class focus, the Sutiavas conceived of this new stage of agrarian protest as a reaffirmation of their traditional right to communal land.[69]

Their particular notion of *derechos* unified diverse Sutiavan social groups against the ricos. That same notion was not, however, pertinent to the Chinandegan campesinos. Whereas some eight to ten thousand Sutiavas of diverse social classes lived in one geographically circumscribed urban community, the Chinandegan activists lived in much smaller, largely landless villages like San José or Tonalá, socially and economically cut off from smallholding communities such as La Grecia. Hence, rather than appealing to a notion of traditional common rights, Chinandegan campesinos had to construct and define their own concepts—campesino class, private property, and necessity. In Sutiava, in contrast, a discourse of ethnic unity represented by the notion of traditional rights preceded and then guided the agrarian movement. The Sutiavas recreated their identity through a struggle to overcome their internal class differences, while combating an elite who defined them all as a single class— Indios.

The ethnic dimension of Sutiava's struggle complicated the regime's efforts at pacification. Following four consecutive springtimes of agrarian unrest, in May 1961 groups of armed Sutiavas simultaneously occupied five haciendas, destroying fences and crops and stampeding cattle and then disappearing into the surrounding brush. To put an end to this "insurrectionary state" among the Sutiavas, Somoza promised land redistribution.[70] As they had in Chinandega, Somoza's land concessions aimed to quell the agrarian insurgency. In Sutiava, however, the land reform had an additional objective—to roll back leftist gains. Unlike in the politically insulated Chinandegan countryside, since the 1940s, progressive students and labor leaders in León had maintained at least informal contact with some Sutiavan artisans and students. Between 1958 and 1960, independent progressives gained control of the communal organization, the Comunidad Indígena (CI); the regime then set out to plug such a dangerous leak in the Somocista ideological dam between the popular movements and the opposition. Every regime concession to the Sutiavas in the early 1960s was thus accompanied by a symbolic demonstration by the Indians of their loyalty to the regime. Following yet another successful agrarian mobilization in 1963, for example, the CI awarded its Bartolomeo de las Casas medal to Argeñal Papi—the man who had left a trail of broken bones and promises all the way from San José to Sutiava.[71] The Somoza regime played its political cards well in order to obtain such obsequious performances from the Sutiavan rebels. As the regime distributed land, Somocista agents would pack CI elections with non-Sutiavas. Although the Somocistas captured the CI leadership and took credit for land reform, they still had difficulty pacifying the protest movement.

Paradoxically, the Sutiavan response to the initial stage of land reform was more prolonged and militant than it was in Chinandega, while at the same time, the Somocistas in Sutiava established greater control over the communal campesino organization. These contradictory tendencies were, however, interconnected. In much the same way as Andrés Ruíz Escorcia had operated earlier in Chinandega, the Somocista group, from 1961 to 1965, by continuing to confront the regime and the agrarian elite increased its legitimacy in the CI and countered any leftist suggestion that support for the regime was equivalent to selling out the community. Thus, in April 1962, after the regime had distributed more than one thousand manzanas, the CI organized an occupation of Nagualapa, a hacienda belonging to a distinguished member of the Somocista elite. After several arrests in this new stage of postdistribution insurgency, one Sutiava warned, "We want freedom for our Indian prisoners and we want land to work. One day we're going to end all this!"[72]

The Sutiavas' sixty-year-old struggle to reclaim their communal lands from the elite shaped their militant response to the initial stages of land reform. Responding to the clamor of the rank and file, the proregime leadership, in turn, pressured the regime into purchasing more than one thousand manzanas of Nagualapa. By 1965, the regime had distributed roughly 2,600 manzanas of land to some 300 Sutiavan families. In one colony, 139 families received seven manzanas each and grazing rights on 400 manzanas of pasture. In another colony, the Banco Nacional financed basic grains with C$514 credit per manzana, more than twice the rate in Rancherías. Moreover, the government promised to invest more than $500,000 in electricity, housing, and schools.[73]

The Sutiavas indeed benefited more from agrarian reform than did the Chinandegans. By rejecting the regime's initial land offers with armed mobilizations, the Sutiavas forced the regime to choose between bloody mass repression or substantial reform. The question remains why there could be such an option in Sutiava and not in Chinandega. Juan Angel López's rule no doubt stunted the growth of the Chinandegan movement, but why was López (or an equally hardline commander) there and not in León? Perhaps the regime viewed the Chinandegans by 1962 as politically suspect, but retained their faith in the Somocista-dominated Sutiavan organization. A more compelling, complementary conclusion is that the Sutiavas were more capable of violent resistance than the Chinandegans. Some ten thousand Sutiavas in one geographical area with a centuries-long tradition of collective violence formed a more menacing force than did the relatively dispersed Chinandegan militants. Finally, considering his particularly ruthless reputation in the Guardia, it is important to recall that Juan Angel López's dispute with Colonel Rodríguez Somoza had forced him out of León in 1959, when he violently repressed the Sutiavas.

Whatever the reasons for the regime's choices in Chinandega and Sutiava, the Sutiavas paid a political price for their success. In October 1964, in the official ceremony inaugurating two colonies, the CI awarded Anastasio (Tacho) Somoza the medal *Cacique Adiact*. As the Sutiavan Felix Pedro Hernández placed the medal on Somoza's uniform, he exclaimed, "Just as we place this medal on you, in 1967 we will place upon you the presidential sash."[74]

While it is difficult to measure the sincerity of the applause that followed those words, the regime's political gains from land reform in Sutiava were clearly more substantial than those from Chinandega. The solidification of Sutiavan ethnic unity through the nominally apolitical agrarian struggle initially bolstered the Somocista leadership. Indeed, the Somocista leaders took credit for strengthening the community by creating more Sutiavan landholders. Moreover, the Somocistas argued that any leftist challenge would imperil the community's gains and undermine the CI's unity.

Despite the initial success of the CI leadership, the subversion of Somocista control commenced with the final stage of agrarian reform in 1964 and 1965. First, the Sutiavan colonists refused to indemnify the former landowners, as IAN required. A Sutiavan schoolteacher argued on behalf of the colonists, "These lands are vestiges of the land over which we have full legal rights . . . so we should not indemnify anybody."[75] Many Sutiavas also resisted paying indemnification because they believed the regime had purposefully paid inflated prices for the land to its elite supporters. Moreover, many beneficiaries refused to recognize IAN's authority in the colonies, claiming that the CI was sovereign over its lands. In 1965, the colonists of Nagualapa levied another serious charge against the land reform. They claimed that the hacienda lands that the regime had purchased "were totally useless." Moreover, they argued that IAN had given the good lands to the "only real beneficiaries . . . those closest aligned to the regime."[76] The dissidents reported that one Somocista received thirty manzanas of excellent land.

In Rancherías and Tonalá the land reform had divided the campesino leadership; in Sutiava the Somocistas maintained firm control over the CI from 1961 until 1973. But their monopoly of power also facilitated corruption and spawned resistance. Indeed, many Sutiavas recognized the interconnection between Somocista corruption and the failure of the agrarian reform. The indigenous leaders had an exemplary model of deceit and corruption in "Pancho" Argeñal Papi. In addition to manipulating the politics of the CI, Papi avidly practiced the art of vertical *compadrazgo* (fictive kinship). His crowning success, a fusion of his political talents, was the installation of one of his Sutiavan godsons, Ismael Bárcenas, as president of the CI.

Initially, the Sutiavas viewed their Somocista leadership in a historical perspective that tolerated opportunism in defense of communal unity. During the early 1920s, for example, radical leaders had allied with the Conservative regime in order to win back their municipal status and lands that the Zelaya regime had stripped away in 1902. But the Sutiavas could no longer tolerate their Somocista leaders when they began to undermine the community through the palpably unfair creation of privileges, directly exacerbating the economic problems of most CI members. Many Sutiavas then began to consider a leftist alternative. In the words of Tomás Perez, a militant in the progressive alliance of the 1950s and a founding member of the FSLN in Sutiava, "The cunning [*vivos*] and the servile [in the CI leadership] always got gifts and money from the regime. So we presented an alternative, by combating the abuses and the errors that they committed."[77] In 1971, when the Frente Sandinista established a base in Sutiava, its first in western Nicaragua, it seemed that the Somocista leadership was in firm control of the community. Yet the Sandinistas soon discovered that they were organizing on surprisingly fertile ground prepared by an inadequate and unjust agrarian reform managed by corrupt Somocistas.[78]

In September 1973, Ismael Bárcenas, sold two hundred manzanas of land that many considered to be "usurped from the community." Two hundred Sutiavas journeyed twelve kilometers to the site, known as Las Lomas de Panecillos, where Hildebrand Hernández, a Guardia officer, and some workers were putting up fences. Hernández or the Guardia fired a rifle at the crowd. A Sutiava responded by fatally shooting Hildebrand Hernández.[79]

The Guardia issued warrants for the arrest of the leaders of the Lomas demonstration. In response, the new organization that had emerged within the shell of the old CI gathered sixteen hundred names on a petition blaming Bárcenas for the incident and demanding his resignation. The Somocista elite, in an attempt to pacify the Sutiavas, pressured Bárcenas to resign.[80]

The assault on "Las Lomas" and the resignation of Bárcenas signaled the end of Somocista reformism in Sutiava. One week after his resignation, hundreds of Sutiavas, "dressed like Indians," marched through downtown León. The parade demonstrated the community's solidarity with their new leaders, accused of Hernández's murder. As in the 1950s, women took center stage in the demonstration. The Sutiavan banners read, "The People of Sutiava turn over their sons and take responsibility for their actions. . . . Women of dignity are in the struggle."[81] Another banner, directed at Bárcenas read, "If you want to keep your skin, go to where no Indian can see you." In front of the courthouse where the insurgent leaders turned themselves in to the authorities, several Sutiavas hoisted an effigy of Ismael Bárcenas, once a symbol of Somocista success and now of its bankruptcy. Flames quickly engulfed the effigy, but before Bárcenas's image turned to ashes, one could discern in each hand a one-thousand-córdoba bill and taped across his mouth the words,

"Salváme Por Favor, Panchito Papi!"[82] In 1973, Congressman Argeñal Papi could neither save Bárcenas nor resurrect the politics of agrarian reform in western Nicaragua. As in Chinandega, Somocista reformism in Sutiava had created revolutionaries. By 1979, Congressman Papi could save only himself—by boarding a jet plane to Miami.

12

Toward Revolution in the Countryside, 1974–1979

For as soon as the distribution of labour comes into being, each man has a particular, exclusive sphere of activity, which is forced upon him and from which he cannot escape . . . while in communist society, where nobody has one exclusive sphere of activity but each can become accomplished in any branch he wishes, society regulates the general production and thus makes it possible for me . . . to hunt in the morning, fish in the afternoon, rear cattle in the evening, criticize after dinner . . . without ever becoming hunter, fisherman, shepherd or critic.
—Karl Marx, 1845

Since the 1930s, Chinandegan proletarians and anti-Somocistas had evolved radically different political-cultural perspectives. By recognizing their common enemy, campesinos and Sandinistas finally came to bridge this barrier in Nicaraguan political culture during the 1970s. The key to this bridge resided in the campesinos' ability to understand and appropriate the revolutionary language of the Sandinistas and to accept the subordination of their own class struggle to the national revolutionary movement. That acceptance, in turn, was possible because the struggles in the countryside had virtually emptied Somocismo, the other principal political language, of its once potent content.

By confronting the agro-export elite, the campesinos came up against the Somoza regime, whose combined reformist and repressive responses spurred the movement's autonomous development. In so doing, the campesinos came to recognize the limits of Somocista reformism; their experience with IAN revealed the growing breach between Somocista rhetoric and practice. By the mid-1960s, the obrerista content of Somocismo was becoming a stale joke. When the campesinos saw the Somozas, the great "peacemakers," send troops to crush their movement for "sacred rights," they began to chart an independent course in search of land and dignity.

From the vantage point of the late 1960s, however, there was nothing inevitable about the campesinos' eventual support for the Sandinista revolution. For although many campesino militants had worked through the vagaries of Somocismo, they had little or no knowledge of the FSLN, and they were not ready to throw in their lot with an armed revolutionary movement. Thus, the start of the political transformation from Somocismo to Sandinismo in Sutiava could well have remained an isolated phenomenon. However, two events—a Guardia massacre of an opposition demonstration in 1967 and an earthquake in 1972—sparked a realignment of the opposition and helped to energize a radical Christian movement that became the Sandinistas' most valuable ally— precisely because it provided a common language and an organizational bridge to the campesino movement.

The Guardia massacre of dozens (or hundreds) of anti-Somocistas on January 22, 1967, as many commentators have argued, significantly changed the political contours of Nicaragua.[1] The massacre of anti-Somoza demonstrators discredited not only the regime but also the opposition leaders. The Left, spurned by the opposition, blamed the Conservative candidate Fernando Agüero for provoking the Guardia by attempting to stage an armed rebellion in the streets of Managua. Whatever Agüero's true intentions and actions in 1967, he quickly shied away from confrontation with Somoza. By 1971, he signed a pact with Tacho Somoza that granted 40 percent of the seats in Congress to the Conservative party. Moreover, Agüero agreed to serve as a member of a triumvirate executive from 1972 to 1974. His capitulation to the regime removed his own charismatic leadership and his Conservative faction from the opposition movement and precipitated a political realignment to the left.

On December 23, 1972, an earthquake killed ten thousand people and destroyed fifty thousand homes in Managua. Besides inflicting pain and misery primarily on the poor, the earthquake, in the words of Sergio Ramírez "was more than a physical trauma, an economic trauma for the national bourgeoisie: they came to the alarming realization that Somoza and his clan were not only committing armed robbery and stealing the humanitarian aid which was coming into Nicaragua, but they were beginning to invade all of the fields of business they had before left alone, starting with construction, real estate, concrete, aluminum, cement blocks, bricks."[2]

All sectors of the bourgeoisie thus began to reassess their economically comfortable relationship with the Somoza regime. However, despite the increased political tension, Nicaragua's key financial groups, BANIC (the cotton elite) and BANAMERICA (led by ISA) did not join the opposition. Dr. Eduardo Montealegre, president of BANIC in 1978, lamented the group's previous loyalty to the regime in these self-critical terms. "Our country is already paying a high price for the lack of principles in political activity. . . .

It gives the sensation that we are trapped between not doing anything . . . or accepting the dangers of action. Our past, filled with errors, has led us to this point."[3] In 1974, while the haute bourgeoisie remained politically neutral, middle sectors of the bourgeoisie, professionals, the Social Christian party, the Independent Liberal party, a Conservative faction, and the Socialist party formed the Unión Democratica de Liberación or Democratic Liberation Union (UDEL). Yet this moderate opposition group failed to broaden its base, despite the growing popular resentment against the regime reflected in the unprecedented 50 percent abstention from Somoza's 1974 presidential election.

The earthquake of 1972 not only reanimated the bourgeois opposition, it also directly precipitated a labor offensive, for the Somoza regime imposed a sixty-hour work week on construction workers engaged in rebuilding efforts. In response, the PSN-led Sindicato de Carpinteros, Albañiles y Armadores (SCAAS) guided two victorious strikes involving thousands of workers. SCAAS rolled back the sixty-hour edict and moreover obtained wage increases sufficient to cope with a 40 percent rise in food prices in 1973 (the first serious inflation since the early 1950s).[4] SCAAS became powerful enough so that by January 1974, thirteen hundred union members engaged in a successful solidarity strike to aid construction workers at five small sites.[5] Moreover, SCAAS expanded its organizational focus beyond Managua, to Chinandega, Masaya, and León, where it helped revitalize a dormant urban labor movement.[6]

"Free Us From The Yoke!" The Rise of Radical Christianity

The spectacle of regime corruption following the earthquake also alienated the church hierarchy from the regime. The archbishop of Managua, Monsignor Obando y Bravo for example, rejected a regime offer to rebuild the cathedral because of an attached condition that he appear publicly with Somoza. In 1974, the bishops issued a statement denouncing "all of these abuses" and declaring "the necessity. . . for structural changes and changes of governmental authorities."[7] Similarly, for Christian community activists, the earthquake meant " 'a certain disarticulation' [for many existing barrio organizations were literally wiped out], but also a leap in consciousness."[8]

It would be wrong, however, to ascribe to the earthquake the same politically catalytic effect on Christian activists as it had on business sectors. The radicalization process inside the Nicaraguan church had started at least four years earlier, at the Medellín Bishops' Conference in 1968, where the hierarchy endorsed a "preferential option for the poor."[9] Before the earthquake, clergy in Nicaragua had already helped to found some fifty Christian Base Communities (CEB), each involving at least two hundred parishioners. The CEBs served as a forum for liberation theology, a training ground for lay preachers (Delegates of the Word), and as community improvement organizations. Although in Nicaragua liberation theology did have different tendencies, they were united in their hostility to capitalism and to Somocismo. Hence, the CEBs, organized in poor barrios and hamlets, became vital links between popular struggles and the opposition.[10]

The Delegates of the Word, usually selected by the CEBs, played an important role in this convergence process between the two movements. The Delegates, Catholic missionaries in a nominally Catholic country, often preached where priests had never set foot. After centuries of neglect by the church, campesinos responded eagerly to these Delegates, who discussed religious themes in a peasant dialect. A report from a Chinandegan hamlet underscores this reception. "The first communities showed tremendous enthusiasm for the evangelical message. They left their homes to go to the celebration no matter . . . the distance, the time, nor the physical conditions . . . usually 100 adults and children attended. Most Sundays the celebrations lasted up to . . . eight hours, due to the abundance of personal testimonies, songs, games, dinner, and finally the explanation of the Bible by the Delegate."[11]

Initially the lay preachers, many of whom learned to read through the CEBs, emphasized personal testimony and direct understanding of the Bible, but they also strove to meet communal needs. As the political and social context for biblical understanding hardened under the repression of the mid-seventies, the Delegates began to organize meetings with more political themes. One Chinandegan Delegate recounted questions asked at one such meeting. "Why are there so many poor people? Why is this country's wealth in so few hands? What will Nicaragua's true liberation be like? When and how is mankind saved? . . . After we studied passages from the Bible, we . . . explained them . . . and they began to see that among our people there was a great deal of injustice, and that there was a man or better yet a system who caused this inequality."[12]

The Guardia soon began to treat the Delegates as subversives and assassinated scores of them. The repression of the Christian activists hardened and radicalized their commitment to their communities. By the late 1970s, a large majority of the five thousand Delegates had become FSLN militants or sympathizers.[13] These religious Sandinistas became more than revolutionaries with a decent cover; rather, they helped to merge regional popular struggles and the national revolutionary movement. The testimony of Edgar García, a founder of the pro-Sandinista rural workers' union called the Asociación de Trabajadores del Campo (ATC), reveals this linkage process. "When the other organizational forms began to be repressed, then we could still denounce [the regime] through the celebration of the Word of God. For the Word of God illuminated and strengthened the struggle of the . . . campesinos and rural workers. They found in their faith in God, motivation to struggle for their demands. . . . There came a moment when I stopped being just a Delegate of the Word in my community and I came to coordinate the campesino movement in the region [Carazo] and then I visited Chinandega. In other words there came a time when, in addition to my religious work, I organized unions and then became involved in clandestine and semiclandestine organizations [connected to the FSLN]."[14]

Radical Christians and Sandinistas organized the ATC in Carazo and Chinandega in 1977. Carlos Centeno, a founder of the ATC in Chinandega, for example, was both a Delegate and a Sandinista. Centeno had spent much of his youth on the Palacios colony (near Tonalá), the fruit of one of the first campesino victories. During the early 1960s, he befriended many of the Chinandegan activists including Mariano Escorcia and Leoncio Martínez in Tonalá and the Carrascos in Rancherías. In the mid-1960s he migrated to León, where he found work in a variety of jobs. His last job in León, as a government distributor of antimalarial medicine, took him into the León and Chinandegan countryside, where he came into contact with both Sandinistas and radical Christians. Unlike many others who initially experienced a strictly religious conversion, Centeno simultaneously became a Christian activist and a Sandinista.[15]

In the early 1970s Centeno moved to El Realejo, where he earned his living in construction but dedicated himself full-time to his political-evangelical mission as a Delegate of the Word. He immediately made contact with the remnants of Manuel Campos's agricultural workers' union from the early 1960s in El Realejo. Indeed Campos's own brand of Christian radicalism provided an important precedent for Centeno's mixed religious and political message. Centeno recalls his method of proselytizing in El Realejo. "I often used the text Isaiah where it talks about breaking the chains and liberating the slaves, by using the people's force against iniquity. The folks would start to murmur, and then someone would ask for more explanation and I'd say that here in Nicaragua God is against the suffering of the oppressed and for that we have to struggle. God's struggle is not in Heaven but here on earth."[16]

Centeno managed to attract workers from different plantations who, while working on community projects such as a consumer cooperative, would also begin to clandestinely organize unions. The Christian radicals organized rural workers around trade union demands quite similar to those of the 1960s. In one hacienda near El Realejo, the ATC organized a *Junta de Lucha* (struggle committee) that made demands on the hacendado for better piece rates and better food. These juntas, groups of ten or fifteen workers on each hacienda, later became cells of the ATC and the FSLN. Salvador Ramírez recounts a typical meeting of a cell in early 1978. "I was working as *puntero* on the hacienda—I had to set the piece rate by the amount of weeds and underbrush I chopped. So in some ways I had the boss's trust. But because I tried to be decent with my fellow workers by not overdoing it, I earned their respect too. Well, I was very careful to only discuss salary and food questions on the hacienda. But then in the evening I would get a bunch a people from the junta de lucha together and go to the beach where we'd discuss religion and Sandinismo."[17]

The ATC drew on local union traditions, the appeal of radical Christianity, and the growing understanding that the FSLN represented the only alternative, since the Guardia repressed peaceful forms of popular protest. The ATC's greatest success was not, however, union organization but instead its formation of revolutionaries in the fields. In September 1978, when Sandinistas led an insurrection in Chinandega, they could count on rural support from some thirty-five guerrillas, first awakened by the Word in El Realejo. When the Guardia reconquered Chinandega through aerial bombing, the ATC also played a vital role in saving civilian lives and hiding Sandinista fighters.[18]

Centeno also reestablished his old contacts with the Chinandegan campesino militants. Many of those campesinos who had fought for land in the early 1960s had never ceased to defend their communities. Moreover, by the mid-1970s their sons and daughters were ready to continue that struggle. The children of Engracia Zapata in Tonalá, Juan Suazo and Ramón Cándia in San José, and Abraham Carrasco in Rancherías indeed rejuvenated the campesino movement. The second generation of activists had, of course, learned from their parents, and many remembered their own experience in the earlier battles with the Guardia and los ricos. Apolonio Carrasco, in particular, as a young teenager, had fought side by side with his late father. Yet beyond a sense of commitment to a movement they had known all their lives, reinforced by a recognition of the bankruptcy of Somocismo, the message of liberation theology called this new generation to action.

During the early 1970s, two progressive priests, Padre Alvarez Ortíz in

Tonalá and Padre Lovo in Rancherías, found fertile ground for Christian activism.[19] Ortíz and Lovo were the first priests to take any serious interest in the spiritual, let alone the material, existence of the villagers. Many Chinandegan campesinos, who had politically awakened to notions of the people's necessities and sacred rights, found that the radical interpretations of the Bible legitimated and reaffirmed their own beliefs. Moreover, liberation theology could build upon important popular religious beliefs in the countryside. Thus, the patron saint of the San José struggle, San Martín de Porras, symbolized both a recognition of the social dimension of Christianity and a desire for the religious legitimation of campesino thought and practice. Similarly, the belief of many campesinos that Campuzano (like ISA) had "a pact with the devil" was congruent with the radical Christian notion that an island of wealth in a sea of poverty was sinful.

In 1974, Apolonio Carrasco helped Father Lovo organize a CEB in Rancherías. An attorney, Zela de Porras, who worked with the Rancherías group recalled the early fruits of their evangelical activity. "The very campesinado came up against the hard reality and suffered repression because he fought for his rights. Then the campesinos said to us, 'Well now I know all about my dignity and know they are stomping on me. Now what? When is Moses going to liberate us?' "[20] The "Moses" these campesinos desired soon appeared in the form of the FSLN. Indeed, Zela de Porras (the mother of FSLN comandante Alonso Porras) commented, "Those campesinos who had been evangelized in the faith . . . were the first ones to join up when the Frente Sandinista appeared."[21]

In Rancherías, the radical Christians converted many who had not participated in the earlier movement. For those conservative campesinos even posing the question of deliverance from the regime involved a radical change in consciousness. Moreover, the content of liberation theology worked against the movement's dependence on external leadership and was in this way congruent with the egalitarian perspective that had evolved among campesino militants in Tonalá and San José. In particular, the radical priests and lay activists directly addressed the issue of personal responsibility in collective activity. For the evasion of personal responsibility—an evasion based on an acute sense of individual vulnerability, poverty, and powerlessness in the post-hacienda world—had thrown up major roadblocks on the path to campesino liberation. That sense of vulnerability had often defined the particular forms of struggle that were used, as it had in the 1936 ISA strike and in the 1962 Tonalá strike, where union militants had used coercive tactics to mobilize their members. From its inception liberation theology emphasized "an ethical dimension of responsibility in the task of social transformation."[22] Indeed, many CEBs dramatized this sense of ethical engagement with a liturgical practice whereby, under the image of the crucifix, individuals would voluntarily pledge specific forms of commitment to their community. The campesinos first pledged commitment to the movement and then to the revolution, not as blind obedience to either God or the Sandinistas, but rather as a conscious decision.

In 1976 Carlos Mejía Godoy composed the song "Misa Campesina," which quickly became immensely popular throughout Nicaragua. The following excerpt illustrates its radical Christian dialectic of faith and conscious practice.

Christ, Jesus Christ, identify with us.
Lord my Lord, identify with us. Christ, Jesus Christ
Have solidarity not with the oppressing class that
Squeezes and devours the Community. Have solidarity
With us the oppressed, my people, thirsty for peace . . .
Free us from the yoke! Give us Freedom! . . .
Join together our hands, in this immense bond of
Brotherhood, of Nicaraguan love, join our hands to make
A powerful wall to defend the Community.[23]

Mejía Godoy's "Campesino Mass" invoked and reaffirmed religious faith, joined to a notion of human agency and social practice. When the campesinos pleaded for a Moses, they knew (or were rapidly learning) that they had to create and defend their own communities. When they prayed that Christ free them from "the yoke," the campesinos understood that emancipation must be the fruit of their own labor.

"In the Year 1977, We of San José del Obraje Invaded the Land for the Fifth Time"

Karl Marx wrote that history repeats itself "the first time as tragedy and the second time as farce."[24] In the hamlets of San José and Tonalá, history repeated itself the third time as social revolution. For the campesinos had *learned* from the tragicomedy of their parents' struggles, and the campesino movement launched its own offensive against the agro-export bourgeoisie in February 1977, while Somoza's state of siege still paralyzed the rest of the country. That offensive would stimulate and in turn receive impetus from the Sandinista forces.

In one sense, elite arrogance reignited the movement, dormant during the state of siege. In late 1976, Miguel Zavala, the owner of the neighboring hacienda Maneadero, arrived in Rancherías and presented a document to the community leaders. The document, signed by the Instituto Agrario Nicaragüense, awarded to the hacienda several hundred manzanas of land disputed since 1963 by the Rancherías community. The campesinos duly registered their protest with IAN, but their bitter experience with the Somocista agrarian reform—which included increasing examples of corruption in the "Colonia San Luís"—had convinced them not to expect any satisfaction from the government.[25] Apolonio Carrasco and the Rancherías leaders, in addition to mobilizing their Christian contacts, decided to respond to the Maneadero's latest aggression by contacting their old friends from San José del Obraje.

Carrasco found that the San José del Obraje network was still largely intact. More than 70 percent of the members of San José's organization that reemerged in 1977 had either participated or had a parent who had participated in the organization led by Regino Escobar and Juan Suazo in the late 1950s.[26] In February 1977, the San José campesinos began to hold regular meetings at which Juan Suazo and Ramón Cándia would give talks on the history of the "people's land." The size and enthusiasm of the meetings did not go undetected. Mundo Deshon sent word to the Guardia about subversive activities in San José. The Guardia responded by breaking up meetings, arresting several militants, and prohibiting organizations in San José and Rancherías.[27]

In April 1962, while the Rancherías group launched an assault on the ejidos, Andrés Ruíz Escorcia restrained the San José campesinos from carrying out a simultaneous invasion. Fifteen years later, Escorcia was still loyal to the campesino movement, but, like many others during this period, he no longer supported the regime. Moreover, the campesinos exerted far greater independence from outside control than they had in the 1960s; at four o'clock in the morning on June 13, 1977, 200 campesinos from Rancherías and 140 from San José took aim at their respective targets, Zavala's El Maneadero and Deshon's Llano Verde. The next day the Guardia arrested 53 campesinos from the two groups. Escorcia, still influential in high places, helped to win their release.[28]

Although Escorcia played a part in Chinandega, the campesinos were in full command of their own movement.[29] The words of one San José participant made it quite clear that although most of the actors were the same, both sides had new roles to play. "We were still thinking about our land, so we organized ourselves again. Some of our compañeros took our documents to IAN, but they did nothing for us. And so in 1977, for the fifth time we of San José del Obraje invaded the land. . . . The next day [following the first arrests] 120 of us invaded Mundo's land again. In the afternoon, Mundo sent up a plane which strafed us, shooting out poison. The next day Mundo sent the Guardia, who hauled off fifty men and women. . . . The Guardia told the women to go work in cantinas [as prostitutes] in order to support their families instead of invading land."[30]

On June 28, the Rancherías and the San José campesinos regrouped and unleashed yet another offensive. A *La Prensa* article described the campesino targets. "The campesinos already had [Bernardo Venerio's] land ready for planting and refused to leave . . . thus their huts were knocked down. . . . Since some campesinos resisted, they were arrested. . . . Campesino invaders were also captured in Bob Baca's El Obraje, Angel Molieri's Santa Cristina, Eduardo Deshon's La Laguna and Edmundo Deshon's Llano Verde. . . . These lands had been ploughed and the campesino occupation has paralyzed the planting."[31]

The campesinos, in June 1977, not only took up where the movement had left off in the mid-1960s, but they built upon their heritage in three important respects. First, in the early 1960s San José's solidarity with Rancherías was never reciprocated, but in 1977 both groups joined together in the occupation of several haciendas. Second, the rejuvenated campesino organization struck at the entire landed elite in the region, not merely at their traditional antagonists, such as Mundo Deshon, Molieri, and the wealthy peasants of the Reyes group. Particularly revealing of the deepening of class conflict was their assault on Baca, the longstanding friend and benefactor of San José. Finally, the campesinos audaciously invaded land prepared for planting and resisted arrest. Such actions went far beyond earlier forms of struggle that had projected ignorance and deference, such as the storing of palms on the Nuevos Ejidos or the takeover of uncultivated (and apparently unclaimed) land. In sum, the campesinos, inspired by their own traditions of struggle, by liberation theology, and by the failure of Somocista reformism to meet their most basic necessities gave a new face to the class movement. Months before the FSLN launched its first offensive, the campesinos had declared war, not on individual enemies, but on the agrarian elite.

The Guardia could still temporarily halt the movement through mass arrests. A confident Mundo Deshon dropped charges against the San José rebels after making them sign an agreement to respect his property. Deshon must have believed that the campesinos were a people without history. Twenty-eight years earlier, with the help of Fredi Callejas, he had forced Regino Escobar, Juan Suazo, and Justo Vega to sign a document of "honor." Now, with a Guardia command post on Llano Verde once again, he obliged the campesinos to respect elite property in the area or else suffer the "right of the Authorities to use Corporal Punishment."[32] This time the Guardia were armed to their teeth and did not leave on Saturdays to collect their pay. But the campesinos of San José had also learned from their history; they had no respect for Deshon's paper or property. They only respected his machine gun emplacements.

From the Fields to the Factory: ISA, 1974

The field workers of San Antonio also began to reorganize in the mid-1970s. During the years following the 1964 strike, thanks to the mechanization of field work, ISA increased sugar production to over 2.3 million quintals, earning annual profits of close to $5 million.[33] By the mid-1970s, ISA had transformed itself into one of the most efficient sugar mills in the hemisphere, doubling its output without a significant increase in its labor force (approximately five thousand workers).[34] Not content to rest on its laurels, the company applied for and received a $6.5 million loan from the International Finance Corporation to develop new cane lands on the north shore of Lake Managua.[35]

As a way of staving off salary demands during a period of stable world prices, the company had offered to raise salaries commensurately with the value of exports. In 1973, workers' salaries did not, however, rise along with a 30 percent leap in the sugar export price. The price rise did impel the company to plant and produce more cane. To fulfill its quotas, ISA needed some forty-nine thousand tons of cane cut every week. By the end December 1973, the company had met its new export obligations and decided to cut back to thirty-five thousand tons a week until February 12, for "the recuperation of the cane fields."[36]

As in 1964, field workers seized on a particular incident—the cutback—to wage a strike for broader demands, including a 20 percent salary increase, an improved weighing system, and free transportation from the colonias (their residences) to the mill area and to Chichigalpa.[37] Instead of joining the strike breakers as they did in 1964, many permanent field workers in January 1974 filled the ranks of the strikers—some three thousand canecutters, cane loaders, and irrigation workers. The canecutters spoke for them all when they accused the company of excluding them from "the many benefits it gives to its mill workers."[38]

The company could only be grateful that the division between factory and field workers still existed. The field workers reacted angrily at the strike-breaking factory workers by storming the mill gates. They ordered the workers to shut down the machines. Then a field worker made a speech to a silent audience about class solidarity and scolded the mill operatives for playing into the companies' hands. The occupation apparently stunned management; the strikers won their demands after three days of negotiations.[39]

1978: Class Struggle and National Crisis in San Antonio

From December 1974 to September 1977, Nicaraguans lived under state-of-emergency laws. The Somoza regime resorted to kidnapings, torture, and assassinations in order to combat the FSLN.[40] The enforced passivity of the ISA workers did not, however, eliminate the organizational gains of the 1974 strike. The FSLN, and to a lesser degree, the Frente Obrero (a Maoist-inspired group), managed to connect with an informal network in the fields. The assassination of Pedro Joaquín Chamorro, the famous opposition leader and editor of *La Prensa*, in January 1978, forced ISA to define its position with respect to the growing anti-Somoza movement. Managua businessmen and professionals, organized in the Frente Amplio (including UDEL), called for a national work stoppage in protest against the regime. ISA technicians and factory workers announced their participation in the protest strike. The following report to ISA's stockholders revealed the company's response to the political protest. "We told the workers that they should travel around for a day to see whether there really was a national strike on. They did not accept our suggestion. At 1:40 a.m. the mill shut down. It is important to clearly state that at no time did the Administration order or even suggest to the workers that they support the strike. Nevertheless, because of the vulnerability of our industry, and given the national effervescence and the degree of emotional involvement of the workers, our energetic and violent opposition to the strike would have put the whole zafra in jeopardy."[41]

ISA's owners possessed the single most valuable business enterprise in the country, headed BANAMERICA, one of the three main financial groups, and formed part of the leadership of the Conservative party. The assassination of Chamorro and the subsequent revulsion of all sectors of the population against the regime placed the company owners in a complicated position. They had worked efficiently with the Somoza regimes since 1936 and had negotiated an amicable division of the domestic sugar market with the Somoza-owned mills.[42] The 1970s had been the most profitable decade in the company's history; ISA had no incentive to provoke problems with the regime. But the owners—the Pellas, Benard, and Palazio families—also aspired to the economic and political leadership of their class. ISA's problem was that their own immediate economic interest conflicted with the political will of their class. Since the earthquake in 1972, cotton and coffee growers, stockbreeders, and construction contractors were responding to what they perceived to be unfair competition from the Somoza clan. Many cotton growers and stockbreeders resented the low prices they received for their goods and services from the Somoza-controlled meat packing plants and cotton gins.[43] Representatives of those groups had issued the strike call to protest the Chamorro assassination. ISA tolerated what it could not halt. But at least in February 1978 (as the company report indicated), ISA was less concerned with its leadership role than with the immediate impact of the turmoil on its physical plant and its profits.

Nevertheless, thanks to eighty years of political experience, the company emerged from the strike without endangering its ties to either the regime or to the opposition. The stockholders' report of February 1978 evidences the owners' self-confidence even when insurrectionary fighting raged in Masaya and in nearby León. "We emerged from the conflict smiling. Despite the tense and delicate situations . . . we managed to preserve the best worker/management relations that have always distinguished our company and we might be so bold as to add that these relations have even improved the communication between the workers and the administration."[44]

The owners' self-congratulatory tone may have been in order. Nevertheless, although the protest did not involve labor-management issues, the mill workers had collectively resisted company policy for the first time since 1948, for national events were politicizing workers, technicians, and even managers. In February 1978 the indigenous people of Monimbó, a barrio of Masaya, and the Sutiavas in nearby León fought pitched battles with homemade weapons against the Guardia, whose violent repression angered most ISA employees.

From March to September 1978 the Proletarian and the Tercerista factions of the Frente Sandinista, as well as the Frente Obrero, took advantage of the growing anti-Somoza sentiment among workers, employees, and management and began an intense recruitment drive throughout the plantation.[45] Both the FSLN Proletarian Tendency and the Maoists organized field workers to support immediate demands, as well as the strategic, long-term goal of socialist revolution. Many field workers were receptive to this message, in part because the FSLN and the Maoists linked up with the field workers' informal network of rank-and-file militants, which had led the 1964 and 1974 strikes. Despite their mutual antagonism, ISA militants of the FSLN and the Frente Obrero often collaborated. There was a limited ideological affinity between the Proletarians and the Maoists, and many saw no contradiction between the two groups. One San Antonio worker, a Sandinista, recalled, "All the militants of the Frente Obrero were real good compas. Some people belonged to both the Frente Sandinista and the Frente Obrero. We were fighting for the same proletarian revolution."[46]

Such sentiments began to seep into the mill area from the surrounding cane fields. Two Sandinista tractor drivers, in particular, began to organize the agricultural machinery maintenance workers. The workers of Repair and Maintenance of Agricultural Machinery (RYMMA) distinguished themselves from the rest of the mill labor force in several respects. As RYMMA grew during the 1970s, reflecting the increased mechanization of agriculture, management usually trained new workers (often the sons of mill workers) rather than transfer veteran workers. Thus, RYMMA workers were generally young, and after battling the youth of Sutiava and Monimbó, the Guardia treated everyone under twenty-five as a potential Sandinista. Moreover, RYMMA workers had not become part of the union leadership. Their contact with field laborers and their lack of ties to the conservative union thus freed the RYMMA workers for independent activity. Youthful, independent, and located between the mill and the fields, RYMMA workers became the vanguard of Sandinista organization at ISA. Most of the 120 mechanics and apprentices of that section organized the pro-Sandinista Unión de Trabajadores Independientes (UTI), which by September 1978 had become strong enough to challenge the established union leadership.[47]

Within the mill a different dynamic was at work. Many employees came to support the FSLN through their traditional anti-Somocismo. Even high-level managers had reached the conclusion that the only way to end the Somoza regime was through armed insurrection. Their willingness to ally with the FSLN led key management employees to permit Sandinista organization in the mill. Management was logically more sympathetic to the Tercerista faction of the FSLN, which stressed goals of national liberation, than to the local "proletarios" (members of the Proletarian Tendency), who called for the abolition of bourgeois property. Tercerista employees and workers thus began to forge a base in the mill. Despite the more moderate message of the Terceristas, however, perhaps one-half of the mill work force remained politically neutral.[48]

In late August 1978, following the FSLN's dramatic takeover of the Palacio Nacional in Managua, unions and opposition groups organized another nationwide general strike that shut down 85 to 90 percent of Nicaragua's businesses and industries. Guardia efforts to crush strike demonstrations sparked a spontaneous insurrection in Matagalpa. The FSLN then led insurrections in Masaya, León, Chinandega, Estelí, Carazo, and Managua. Resorting to aerial bombardment of the cities, Somoza managed to put down the urban rebellions after one month of fighting, which killed at least three thousand combatants and civilians.[49]

San Antonio workers played a role in the insurrectionary movement. They joined the nationwide strike in late August. On September 2, some ISA workers, organized by UTI, occupied the main plaza in San Antonio, set up barricades, and fought the Guardia in the streets.[50] The regime had to dispatch a battalion to ISA, which otherwise would have been used to crush the insurrections in Chinandega and León. On the morning of September 4, the ISA workers defied the Guardia by mounting another demonstration under the banner, For the Fallen Fighters of Matagalpa—Popular Revolution![51] The Guardia responded with systematic arrests and assassinations of suspected Sandinistas, including five strike leaders and ISA general manager Alfredo César, accused of collaboration with the FSLN.

While this remarkable process of revolutionary unification was taking place, linking the canecutter to the general manager, class tensions were nonetheless intensifying. Sandinista workers supported the Sandinista general manager, but they also made radical demands on the company. In September 1978, mill workers and field workers jointly forced the company to sign a contract that included salary raises of 20 percent, seasonal unemployment insurance, and a more generous pension plan. Moreover, the Sandinista workers, echoing the demands of 1936 and 1964, called for the removal of high-level employees, including Manuel Coronel Kautz, because of what the field workers considered to be his "abusive attitude."[52] The workers' call for the removal of Coronel Kautz was particularly significant since his brother Ricardo (a former ISA manager) belonged to the vitally important los Doce, a pro-FSLN group of twelve businessmen, educators, and professionals. The workers' demand thus revealed the limits of multiclass unity. Management's alliance with the FSLN conditioned tolerance of pro-Sandinista labor activity in the mill and in the fields, but the growth of the workers' movement in turn stimulated demands for fundamental changes in San Antonio.

The company gave in on all demands except the removal of its high officials. ISA continued to use language almost identical to that used decades earlier in response to similar challenges. "We accepted all the demands except those which went against the company's principle of authority, which is absolutely not subject to negotiation."[53] The company ceded ground on all economic demands perhaps only because of the large number of worker revolutionaries in their midst. But despite the willingness of high-level managers to take the large risks of supporting the Sandinista revolution, they (or at least the owners) were also ready to fight to preserve their control over the productive process.

The defeat of the September insurrections did not signify an easing of political or class tensions in San Antonio. In early December 1978, as most of Nicaragua waited expectantly for the FSLN's final offensive, field workers struck to redress historic grievances against ISA. On November 27, eight work crews of some 180 canecutters each marched toward the administration building. One canecutter climbed on the ledge of the veranda and shouted out a list of demands. The first demand conformed to canecutter tradition—an increase in the piece rate. After the cheering died down, the strike leader proceeded to read a list of twenty department heads, pausing after each name to let the strikers hiss and shout obscenities. The list included mostly foremen from the fields but also some notorious supervisors in the mill and RYMMA, as well as the interim general manager, Manuel Coronel Kautz. Then the speaker demanded their removal, charging them with "abuses and bad treatment" and asserting the workers' right to choose their own supervision.[54] The canecutters shouted their enthusiastic ratification of the demands and then divided into four groups. One squad marched through the administration building forcing the employees to leave and, in the words of a company report, "abusing company goods."[55] Some five hundred canecutters occupied the mill, shutting it down as they had done in 1974. This time, however, many of the young Sandinista mill workers actively joined the strike.[56]

By late morning, some five thousand workers had stopped work. The cane fields were nearly deserted since most of the workers were participating in strike meetings. But in one cane field, a slow, irregular chopping sound could be discerned amidst the sound of laughter. The canecutters were teaching Manuel Coronel Kautz how to cut cane. His hands were bloody, his face was cut and stained black from the burnt cane. Except for his hands, the general manager looked like a canecutter. "They got Coronel Kautz out there to cut cane. Of all the managers, he was hated by the canecutters for the arrogant way he treated them over the years. He was saved because of his politics. Everyone knew that his brother was in los Doce and that he helped the Frente in San Antonio. But even so, he needed that lesson. Man, those days out in the fields really changed the man. He lost that arrogance and became humble."[57]

No faction of the FSLN was involved in the kidnapping of Coronel Kautz, a spontaneous action initiated by field hands. Forcing the boss to cut cane did more than realize vengeful fantasies. In conjunction with the demands to fire the management elite it made a profound statement about the revolutionary process, for although the ISA workers sympathized with or were members of a multiclass revolutionary movement, they also sought to graft on to that movement their own class-based project. Even as they acknowledged the political value of the general manager and many of the department heads, the workers demonstrated that their revolutionary struggle involved not only the defeat of Somocismo but also the abolition of authoritarian relations of production.

The company president, Alfredo Pellas, correctly pointed out that the "radical posture" of the field workers derived from the "general crisis of authority" in Nicaragua.[58] Indeed, the political crisis of the old order also allowed revolutionary social ideas to flower on the plantation. Fearful of the catastrophic consequences of bringing in the Guardia to stop the strike movement, after eight days, management accepted most of the demands. Moreover, Coronel Kautz convinced many field workers that he had learned to respect the canecutters; to them that seemed an astonishing victory.[59]

During the strike, radical students, canecutters, and mill workers fraternized as they had never done before. Sandinista recruitment soared, and by the end of the strike perhaps about four hundred workers had joined the FSLN.[60] Similarly, the unity of factory and field workers created conditions for revolutionary social change in San Antonio. The workers' class consciousness—a desire for a deep transformation of the relations of production—animated a simultaneous revolutionary consciousness, a commitment to overthrow the Somoza dictatorship, strip power from the oligarchy, and fight for Nicaragua's national sovereignty. With a machete in one hand and a rifle in the other, the San Antonio field worker would help make a revolution that would know the human worth of cutting cane.

The Campesino Movement and the Sandinista Revolution

Once again the San José del Obraje struggle prompted a new campesino insurgency throughout Chinandega. The zones of rebellion—Sirama, Cosigüina, Tonalá—where IAN had in the 1960s promised reform but had at best delivered only partially, reignited in 1977. The case of Sirama, located in the foothills above Chichigalpa, is particularly important, since it became a base for the FSLN. The landless campesinos of Sirama in 1969 had occupied ejidal lands that Augusto Terán, former mayor of Chichigalpa, had expropriated in 1950.[61] Guardia repression ended the occupation. In 1976, following the trend of elite arrogance during the state of emergency, Terán's son evicted twenty permanent laborers from his hacienda. Oscar Osejo, a young man who had participated in the 1969 movement and the 1974 ISA strike, began to organize a response to Terán. He counted among his initial supporters several people with outside connections—two sons of a PSN labor organizer and a man who had worked with the Sutiavan movement.

After six months of organizational work, the group mobilized 220 families to occupy Terán's land. During the following month, on several occasions, the Guardia forcefully removed the campesinos. Fearing the political consequences of Sirama's resistance, the regime decided to let IAN's bureaucracy defuse the movement.[62] When the Guardia came to the campesino encampment known as El Porvenir to inform them of the truce, they warned Oscar Osejo, "Whatever you do here, don't ever let a Sandinista come through here. If they do, you have to inform us because they want Communism to come in. Now if you don't tell us, we're going to come back here and kill every last one of you."[63]

The Guardia lieutenant was a little late. While the soldiers had been beating campesinos to defend the land of a corrupt Somocista, Oscar Osejo and the Sirama militants had contacted pro-Sandinista lawyers and leftist militants. Material, legal, and moral support for Sirama's fight against the authorities had already created an environment in which any Sandinista would be an honored guest in any ranchito in El Porvenir. The Sirama organization also received advice and assistance from the rejuvenated campesino movements in San José, Rancherías, and Tonalá. Although the Guardia repression of July 1977 temporarily halted their land occupations, by May 1978 the campesinos took advantage of Sandinista attacks on the Guardia. The campesino movement pushed forward with varying degrees of independence from the national revolutionary movement. Yet throughout 1978—a year of insurrection and bloody repression—it became increasingly clear to both campesinos and Sandinistas that their mutual survival depended on a close alliance. From the Chinandegan campesinos, the Sandinistas needed food, logistic support, and an active mass movement from which to draw recruits and with which to distract the regime. From the FSLN, the campesinos needed the force necessary to overthrow the Somoza regime, which would enable it to implement its own agrarian reform.

The alliance between the campesino and the Sandinista organizations was, however, far more than an opportunistic partnership, for ideological affinities between the Sandinistas and the campesino insurgents indeed ran deep. Liberation theology played a vital role in fusing campesino and Sandinista ideologies. Similarly, through years of fighting in the northern highlands, the Sandinistas had become more knowledgable of campesino ways and more committed to agrarian revolution than most urban revolutionaries in the Third World. Moreover, veteran campesino activists and their children had learned to despise the regime, for they had intimate knowledge of its workings. The campesinos had originally fought under the protection and guidance of Somocista unions, and they had taken Somocista ideology seriously. Elite power and influence had blocked their constant search for common ground with the authorities, and the campesinos' repeated confrontations with the regime had sapped Somocismo of any traces of populism. Tacho Somoza could rail against a supposed alliance of los ricos and the Communists, but by 1978 few people were listening. Those campesino militants who had forged their own style of class consciousness had, a long time before, come to Pablo Guido's conclusion that the Somozas no longer understood the people's language. In the end, whether as an assassin of Sandino and thousands of other Nicaraguans or as the eternal betrayer of campesinos, Tacho Somoza was a despised man.

The strong ideological affinities between Sandinistas and Chinandegan campesinos converted San José, Tonalá, and Rancherías into strategic bases for the revolution. In addition to providing food and protection for the FSLN, many youths from San José, Rancherías, Tonalá, Sirama, and El Realejo joined the ranks of the revolutionary army. In Nicaragua, Chinandega, along with Estelí and Carazo, had the highest proportion of workers and campesinos in the revolutionary army.[64]

Equally important, the campesino militants played a vital political role in 1978 by dramatizing the antagonism between campesinos and the dictatorship. In May 1978, some five hundred families, led by Engracia Zapata's son Juan Alberto and Angel Escorcia, invaded the cotton fields of San Miguel.[65] In 1961, Fanor Argüello had shot at Tonaleños who were hunting iguanas to feed their children. Now Argüello faced five hundred families ready to settle an old score not only with him but also with his class. When the Guardia came to remove, arrest, and brutalize the peasants, they merely regrouped in town and invaded the land again, with the support of the ATC, the PSN, and Andrés

Ruíz Escorcia.[66] In a departure from past patterns of protest, as the bulk of the campesino population reoccupied the land, the village youths staged demonstrations in Tonalá and Chinandega. One young Tonaleño boldly exclaimed, "Tonalá is soon going to be the next Monimbó. . . . God save Tonalá or we're going to save it!"[67]

The Tonalá struggle quickly became a national symbol of the campesino movement's antagonism to the Somocista regime. On June 2, sixty Tonaleño families, many showing scars from Guardia tortures, entered the Managua Cathedral and announced that they would not leave until they won their demand for land. Several days later, a delegation from Sirama joined the occupation. The Sirama campesinos had recently occupied the town hall of Chichigalpa to pressure Terán to legally cede them the ejidal land. Moreover, they had organized two other land invasions on the slopes of the San Cristóbal volcano.[68] In this context, the message of the Cathedral occupation was clear: agrarian reform was impossible under the Somoza regime, and the battle of the campesinos, a sacred struggle, was part of the national revolutionary movement.

In San José del Obraje and in Rancherías, the campesinos took their cue from Tonalá. The San José militants invaded Deshon and Molieri's land while the Rancherías organization occupied El Maneadero and Venerio's hacienda. One young participant in the occupation of Deshon's Llano Verde stated, "In 1978 things were different. We returned, but with a lot of revolutionary consciousness, even though the Guardia took fifty-five prisoners including women and children. But we didn't give up because we had the support of the ATC (when it was clandestine), the CGT independiente [PSN] and Andrés Ruíz Escorcia. . . . who involved himself with all the land struggles in Chinandega. Since these people helped us we gathered up all our courage and protested the jailings and occupied those lands one more time. Twenty-eight days they were in jail and we kept up the pressure. Then one day these big convoy trucks pulled up to the fields, the Guardia dragged us onto the trucks and threw us out on the other side of León."[69]

The resurgence of the campesino movements in Tonalá, San José, and Rancherías, though closely tied to the revolutionary movement, nevertheless maintained independent class goals. The campesino militants, after all the pain and misery of their learning process, were not about to distinguish between good and bad members of the agrarian elite—between those who supported and those who opposed the FSLN. While the FSLN, including hundreds of Chinandegan campesinos, fought to overthrow the regime, the campesino movement also pushed to expropriate the land base of the agrarian elite.

As had the agenda of the ISA field workers, the campesinos' class agenda conflicted, to a degree, with the FSLN's strategy of class alliances. Rancherías campesinos, for example, attacked the property of Venerio, a FSLN ally. Similarly, the Tonaleños battled the Argüello, the Montealegre, and the Vilchez families, many of whose members were either neutral or supported the FSLN. Even Mundo Deshon was beginning to look for a new hook on which to hang his white sombrero. In Sirama, though the Somocista Terán was a marked man, the latest campesino antagonist, Julio Fornos, pleaded political neutrality.[70] Consequently, the campesino movement potentially endangered the strategy of the FSLN. But since the Sandinistas would not halt the rural upsurge, the Frente ultimately benefited enormously, for the campesino land occupations came to symbolize the popular character of the revolution, and the Guardia repression pushed many hesitant campesino youths to pick up a gun. Under such circumstances, the agrarian elite had to fend for itself.

During the early 1960s, the campesino movement reached higher levels of consciousness and efficacy when it merged proletarian and peasant forms of struggle. In the late 1970s, the same movement achieved an important threshold in its struggle for liberation when it acquired revolutionary and class forms of consciousness. As a result, Nicaragua's revolutionary movement gained ground. Nevertheless, it would be an error to reduce campesino class consciousness to Sandinismo. Many campesino militants became Sandinistas but also maintained the identity that they had forged over the past two decades of agrarian struggle. Moreover, through their participation in the national liberation struggle, students, intellectuals, and workers came to understand and respect the campesinos' class-rooted culture: in the Sandinista revolution, both the full representation of campesino class interests and the horizontal communication among the popular classes came to fruition for the first time.

Chinandega: 1979

On June 4, 1979, the FSLN issued a call for an insurrectionary general strike. Radio Sandino broadcast throughout Nicaragua, "The final hour has sounded. Let the despots, the assassins, the thugs and the Somocistas tremble. For the moment has arrived for the people to settle old scores."[71] The general strike was a success, and insurrections broke out immediately in the western cities of León, Chichigalpa, and Chinandega. Before the final insurrection, some sixty ISA Sandinistas joined with students from Chichigalpa to seek refuge from the Guardia on the slopes of San Cristóbal. They went to El Porvenir, received food and shelter, and told the campesinos of the final offensive. On June 5, Sandinistas in San Antonio and Chichigalpa attacked the Guardia. A force of three hundred fighters from Sirama, armed with M-16s and machetes, joined the attack. On June 22, the campesinos, students, and workers drove out the Guardia and liberated Chichigalpa and the Ingenio San Antonio.[72]

Following the latest occupation of the land the campesinos still called Las Cuchillas, Mundo Deshon sensed that he had to resolve his campesino problem before it was too late. He sent word to San José that he wanted to meet with the organization. The young militants went to Juan Suazo and asked him to accompany them to Chinandega. Deshon was disturbed to see Suazo. Less than a year earlier during an occupation, someone, apparently a Deshon agent, had given Suazo a poisoned soft drink, but he had survived. Now they stared at each other across a lawyer's conference table.

Deshon came quickly to the point. Claiming to recognize the difficult lot of the landless campesinos, Mundo offered them free of charge a large cultivated property to the west of Chinandega. Juan Suazo let him finish his remarks and then calmly pointed out that Deshon had taken the campesinos' land twenty years earlier, so he should simply give it back. Mundo angrily exclaimed, "Don't get involved in this because you have no business in it. This is for landless campesinos. You're a landowner so you have no right to speak."[73] As Juan Suazo replied, he raised his right hand to his forehead to wipe his brow. "You're right Mundo, I've got my land . . . Pero eso *si*, a mi sí me ha costado (it has cost me)!"[74] As he finished, Juan's hand thudded to the table, echoing a moment two decades earlier when Regino Escobar had out-talked an oligarch. Mundo, too, was speechless.

One dawn in July 1979, several hundred San José campesinos, carrying guns and work tools, occupied Las Cuchillas. They built ranchos; they thinned the cotton that was now people's cotton; they planted corn; and a few older folks began to put up the mojones, which had marked off the people's land before the cotton fever. Juan Suazo, glistening with sweat, tapped Ramón Cándia's shoulder. As the eighty-year old veteran militant looked up, Suazo spoke to him, "Mirá Moncho. Look up to the volcano, down to the highway, up there to the Estero. Mirá hombre, la Guardia. They're not coming back."[75]

And they went fishing in the afternoon.

Conclusion

This study spans seven decades of Chinandegan history. Only in the last chapter does it touch upon the most important event in contemporary Nicaraguan history: the Sandinista revolution. The vantage point of Chinandegan social history provides new insight into that revolution, however, precisely because existing interpretations have been constructed upon an underdeveloped historiography, one severely constrained by the Somoza dictatorships. The first part of the conclusion will thus engage existing interpretations of the revolution, in the light of the Chinandegan evidence. The failure to sufficiently consider the impact of Somocismo on the development of popular movements and consciousness has hampered our understanding of both the longevity and the downfall of the Somoza regime. The analyses of Carlos Vilas and others who stress the popular-political as opposed to proletarian-social character of the revolution are called into question by an emphasis on the class character of the community-based movements. Within the framework of theories of agrarian revolt and revolution—counter to the view that consciousness is a series of oppositions: revolutionary/reformist, political/economic, or popular/class— it is possible to conceptualize a multilayered consciousness that combines often-contradictory class and revolutionary elements.

Somocismo and Anti-Somocismo: A Reassessment

Most interpretations of the Sandinista revolution focus on three interrelated causal factors: the social dislocations caused by rapid capitalist development after 1950; the growing political opposition of all classes to a repressive, militarized regime that strove unsuccessfully to articulate its own interests as common with those of the entire bourgeoisie; and the tenacity, acumen, and growth of the Frente Sandinista, which united the various disaffected social forces against the Somoza regime. The contradictory nature of the Somocista state as the representative of the entire bourgeoisie *and* simultaneously as a small faction of the bourgeoisie, combined with the flexible class structure of the society engendered by an underdeveloped capitalism, led to a popular rather than a proletarian revolution.[1]

Conclusion

Most scholars agree that the Somoza regime ruled through repression and, to a lesser degree, cooptation. In the 1970s, when cooptation—a policy designed to divide opposition forces while unifying the bourgeoisie—no longer functioned, the regime had to rely exclusively on the Guardia. Carlos Vilas, an outstanding scholar of the Nicaraguan revolution, summarized this perspective when he wrote that Somoza's overtures to the working class in the 1940s were but a "subordinate" part of a strategy designed to unify the dominant class, and that after the Liberal-Conservative Pact of 1950, "repression became the dominant method of managing the popular question."[2]

My analysis challenges Vilas's conclusions, however, because it suggests that the Somozas created a populist political style that combined an anti-oligarchic discourse with appeals to the working masses. Simultaneously, the Somozas ruled a repressive regime that served the interests of the family and its domestic and foreign accomplices. Such strikingly antagonistic loyalties—to the working classes and to elite cliques—marked the limits of Somocista populism as a political project.[3] Workers and peasants largely accepted the Somozas' variant of populism and its corresponding rules of the game, but, at the same time, they shaped and transformed Somocista populism. Indeed, during the 1960s these social movements pushed Somocista populist discourse to its limits, sapped it of its value, and left the regime with nothing to defend itself but the National Guard.

Between 1910 and 1940, artisans and workers developed both a political movement and an ideology of obrerismo, which ennobled manual labor, fought for the rights of workers, and resisted the claims of the landed oligarchy and of the United States. Despite Somoza's assassination of Augusto Sandino and repression of the anti-imperialist movement, his regime managed, in large part, to coopt obrerismo and transform it into a tame discourse of labor/capital harmony. However, given the low level of economic development and business dependency on labor-intensive production, such rhetoric was often at odds with the reality of daily strife in the shops and in the fields. This tension between rhetoric and reality, however, transformed the obrerista discourse because rank-and-file Somocista workers and campesinos turned it against their elite antagonists.

A cultural barrier between anti-Somocista and popular political discourses helped to perpetuate Somocista populism. While workers expressed themselves politically within a language of social and economic rights, middle- and upper-class democrats operated with a bifurcated vision of reality, separating Somocista from anti-Somocista. This political blind spot impeded the democratic forces from understanding, let alone allying with, the struggles of workers and peasants during three decades of Somocista rule. Only the combined efforts of the campesino movement and the FSLN (in particular its radical Christian component) began to overcome this division in Nicaraguan political culture.

Until the last decade of the dynasty, the Somozas were able to direct the repressive apparatus against the political opposition precisely because, with the exception of a brief period in the mid-1940s, the anti-Somocistas lacked a mass base within the urban and rural working classes. As late as 1964, the regime tolerated popular struggles in order to defuse the threat of the growing opposition movement. However, by defining and struggling for their class goals within the framework of Somocista politics, the popular movements not only drove a political wedge through the Somozas' multiclass coalition, but also they exploded their populist discourse, thereby clearing the field for Sandinismo. Luís Somoza's speeches in the 1950s about the campesinos' right to the land and the workers' right to strike sounded plausible to Nicaraguans, but Tacho Somoza's railings, in the late 1970s, against the alliance of los ricos and the communists sounded stupid, hollow, and fraudulent.

Because scholars have failed to explore the different roots of anti-Somocismo, they have had difficulty understanding the origins of the revolutionary coalition welded together by the FSLN. No serious student can dispute the Sandinistas' leadership of the revolution; most analysts, however, confine their focus to the way in which the Sandinistas asserted their leadership over the elite and the middle-class opposition forces.[4] Implicit in the focus of these studies is the assumption that somehow support for the FSLN emerged naturally out of the workers' and peasants' innate hostility toward the regime. Vilas, for example, argues that the Frente gained legitimacy in the eyes of the people through "two decades of struggle."[5] Thus, Nicaraguans were prepared to grant such legitimacy precisely because they perceived an identity of interest with the Sandinistas. Vilas cites a political tradition of anti-Somocismo and anti-imperialism. "For broad sectors of the people the FSLN was the continuation, with new strategies and focus, of a war against imperialist aggression and dictatorial oppression that dated at least from the beginning of the century. The national consciousness of the Nicaraguan people was always nourished by anti-imperialist and anti-dictatorial components. . . . The FSLN . . . presented itself as the continuation of an anti-imperialist and democratic armed struggle profoundly rooted in Nicaraguan popular culture."[6]

Although this perspective is shared by most scholars, it nonetheless, simplifies the regionally varied, complex process through which the popular classes came to support the FSLN. Chinandegan workers and campesinos arrived at a revolutionary understanding of the political world through reflections on their own struggles, not through some immutable current of anti-Somocismo running through the veins of "broad sectors of the people." While there is strong evidence that most Nicaraguan workers and peasants shared anti-imperialist sentiments throughout this century, that such beliefs would merge with anti-Somocismo was never a foregone conclusion. Certainly, geographically and socially circumscribed Sandinista political subcultures did stretch back to the time of the "Hero of the Segovias."[7] Central highlands peasant families and several generations of university students passed on Sandinista traditions and thus played a vital role in forging a political base for the FSLN. Nevertheless, the majority of the working classes did not come to Sandinismo spontaneously. As we saw in Chinandega, many workers and campesinos joined the revolutionary struggle after first participating in organizations originally controlled by Somocistas. Indeed, only after working through populism and the system were those campesinos and workers able to discard first the Somocista discourse and then the dynasty.

Communities, Classes, and the Social Subject of the Revolution

Although Vilas comes to conclusions that differ from my own, his analysis of the popular subject of the revolution in Nicaragua and Central America has indeed opened up important areas for future investigation. Most significantly, Vilas has discovered that "trades-people" (petty commodity producers and merchants) formed the principal "social subject" of the insurrection. Moreover, he shows that the predominance of this sector in the urban economy and in the revolutionary army was not a vestige of a precapitalist society but rather "the product and central protagonist of the type of capitalism that developed in Nicaragua."[8] For Vilas, the tradespeople (*gente de oficio*) were particularly susceptible to revolutionary recruitment, for the Somocista state made unbearable what was already an insecure and unstable existence. "The decisive factors were the limitations, regulations, controls, and repression of the state directed at their survival tactics. . . . They have contact with the state on a daily basis [and suffer] . . . police brutality, the necessity of paying for 'security' in order to carry out their activities."[9] Anthropologist Carol Smith indirectly supports Vilas's argument when she argues that, because of its dispossession without proletarianization and its relative economic autonomy, the Nicaraguan petty bourgeoisie (a category including the tradespeople) "may not be necessary for capitalism, but . . . the continued existence of capitalism is not necessary for the survival of the petty bourgeoisie—as it is to the proletariat."[10]

Vilas and others are, of course, correct to underscore the urban center of the insurrectionary process and to point to its essentially "popular" rather than "proletarian" basis. Nonetheless, by failing to analyze the regional data more closely, they miss an important point: in the key agro-export departments of Chinandega, León, and Matagalpa a twenty-year-old agrarian movement created the conditions for a campesino-FSLN alliance, thus providing a large political and military base for the revolutionaries. That support, as Vilas's own statistics demonstrate, involved substantial revolutionary recruitment as well as material aid.[11] Oscar Osejo juxtaposed these two forms of revolutionary participation, referring to a 1978 occupation of ejidal land near Chichigalpa: "Our decision [to occupy the ejidal lands] was solid and firm: better dead than give back an inch of land. . . . We are saying all this so that you recognize our struggle, because you do not only struggle with the gun . . . but [you are] also cooperating in one form or another."[12] Osejo's point is not to elevate cooperation over fighting the Guardia as a form of revolutionary action. In fact, Osejo and several hundred Sirama campesinos used both of these forms of resistance. But Osejo's declaration and actions underscore a fundamental aspect of the 1977–79 period—national and regional movements involved similar levels of commitment and became mutually dependent. Indeed, it is difficult to conceive of the Sandinista successes in Chinandega, Sutiava (León), or Matagalpa without their alliance with a mature campesino movement.

Vilas's positing of the gente de oficio as the social subject of the insurrection is not in question. Yet, by deemphasizing the revolution's rural component, he stresses the political rather than social character of the revolution. James Dunkerley, for example, building on Vilas's analysis, argues that the revolution "was generated far more directly by a crisis of a political nature in which the determinants of oppression prevailed over those of exploitation."[13] Similarly, Tommi Sue Montgomery states, "Nicaragua is the first country in Central America where class conflict has followed rather than preceded the revolutionary triumph."[14]

The insurrections were political, and the relatively few strikes and the low level of union organization tend to substantiate the insignificance of class conflict. But these arguments give at once too much and too little credit to the FSLN. They give too much because the thesis that the FSLN did not need to root itself in social movements provides ammunition for the erroneous arguments that the Sandinistas artificially injected a social agenda into a strictly political revolution. They give too little because to the Sandinistas' great credit they welded together a broad coalition for national liberation, despite intense social conflict. In particular, the FSLN not only neutralized a besieged rural middle class but also incorporated it into an alliance with its two different class antagonists—those in the blistering cotton fields and those in the air-conditioned offices.[15] Representative of this alliance is the image of the anti-Somocista Bernardo Venerio among the campesinos of Rancherías and of Coronel Kautz among the ISA field workers.

The political/popular interpretation does, however, oblige us to consider the class character of the campesino movement, for it could perhaps be assimilated into a more broadly defined popular subject. This study has shown that the villagers of San José, Rancherías, and Tonalá created a group identity based on a shared antagonism to the agrarian elite. Although they used concepts, such as private property and necessity, that were acceptable to the elite, the campesinos infused those notions with radically new meanings, thus forming part of their class consciousness. If the Chinandegan campesinos possessed class consciousness, though, there is still the question of whether they structurally formed a class. If class is defined as a shared structural role in the relations of production, they did not. However, I would argue, using Carol Smith's concept, that these communities formed a class in a "relational" sense. "The classes that emerge . . . may or may not hold a single objective interest with respect to their material circumstances, but they will hold a single and opposed interest with respect to those classes that emerge in opposition to them."[16] For the tenant farmers, landless laborers, and village smallholders all shared an antagonistic relationship to the agrarian bourgeoisie. The campesino movement began to stimulate the formation of a social class by uniting these groups in their struggle for land and against different forms of labor and market exploitation. While the Somocista state sought to create a semiproletariat—seasonal laborers with a minimal access to land—the campesino movement struggled to create a politically unified and economically cooperative peasantry.

The villages of San José and Tonalá, like others in Latin America, were direct creations of capitalist expansion; a nascent agrarian bourgeoisie created these villages to meet its labor requirements. Community and class forms of struggle were intertwined for the campesinos precisely because as communities they resisted their assigned function in the reproduction of capitalist relations of production. Hence, communal relations reinforced the social ties formed through productive labor on the haciendas. The social ties among laborers illuminated the nature of agrarian bourgeois domination and provided important collective weapons to combat it—unions, strikes, and the threat of labor shortages. Village ties between smallholders, tenant farmers, and seasonal laborers enlarged the latter's resource base and allowed the community to resist elite claims on their land and labor.

Many scholars have emphasized the importance of the great horizontal movements of the Nicaraguan laboring classes, typified by the migrant cotton picker who worked and resided in an urban barrio during the dead season and eventually became integral to the insurrectional urban masses.[17] However, the Chinandegan campesino movements—composed largely of seasonal laborers—maintained a remarkably stable membership over two decades. Despite the recent origins of the Chinandegan communities, more than 70 percent of the San José fighters of 1978 belonged to families that had participated in the first battles of 1958. These figures do not challenge the numerical or qualitative importance of migrants, who did form the majority of the cotton labor force. Rather, the evidence suggests that within the campesino movements, residential stability, fostered by evolving communal ties solidified through a collective history of struggle, was a more decisive factor than migration and horizontal mobility. Moreover, through the communal ties that bound them together, the Chinandegan campesinos—wage laborers and direct producers—came to form a class (in Smith's relational sense) and to engage in a class struggle against the agrarian elite.[18]

The distinction between the class position and the class structure of the communities is key to understanding their ability to adopt forms of struggle that deviated radically from accepted norms of proletarian and peasant behavior (whereby workers organize unions and fight for trade union demands, and peasants struggle for land).[19] In contrast to these norms, in Tonalá, San José, and Rancherías, within the space of several weeks, the same group of "peasants" struck and seized hacienda land.[20] Such tactical flexibility countered some of the enormous political and economic advantages of the elite. The use of both proletarian and peasant tactics allowed the campesinos to enlarge the scope of their own demands and their recruitment base and, moreover, to achieve a fuller understanding of themselves and their class antagonist. Indeed, the combination of proletarian and peasant forms of consciousness and struggle led to the political maturation of the campesino movement.

Conclusion

Rural Communities and Agrarian Revolution

Theda Skocpol, in analyzing the work of four leading theorists of peasant revolution, has made a major contribution to the ongoing debate about rural classes and social change.[21] The principal thrust of her argument goes against ontological conceptions of class that assign specific revolutionary capabilities to particular groups, for example, to the middle peasantry or to the landless proletariat. She argues that scholars have mistakenly grouped together two very different kinds of rural revolutionary movements. The French, Russian, and to a lesser degree, the Mexican revolutions all involved high degrees of autonomous village mobilization that directly contributed to the overthrow of the regimes. Those villages with deep precapitalist cultural roots possessed strong communal organizations, enabling them to wield major blows to the old order. Nevertheless, such villages were incapable of replacing a national government. In each of these cases, therefore, a revolutionary movement seized power from a regime already reeling from peasant rebellion, and the institution of a new regime entailed containing the peasants not mobilizing them.

The Chinese, Vietnamese, and Angolan revolutions, Skocpol notes, involved a qualitatively different process, in that Communist or nationalist parties directly mobilized the peasantry against the regime. In the precapitalist village model, despite the scope of autonomous peasant action, the rural poor obtained few benefits from the revolutionary regime. In the second, more contemporary model, peasants sacrificed much of their autonomy by subordinating themselves to outside leadership, but nevertheless they received substantial benefits from their alliances with the revolutionaries. Skocpol's distinction between the two types of peasant revolutions clarifies much of the previous debate. For the autonomous peasant village—the core of the first type of revolution—becomes analytically marginal in Communist or nationalist mobilizations, the principal contemporary form of peasant revolution. Although the Chinandegan case substantiates Skocpol's distinction, it nevertheless suggests that she draws her categories too rigidly. The Chinandegans did not belong to traditional precapitalist communities like those where village history directly conditioned forms of revolutionary action.[22] Yet the Chinandegans' relatively autonomous struggle, like those of other rural Latin Americans, also falls outside of Skocpol's second category.

As social types, the Chinandegans more aptly fit William Roseberry's description of "precipitates of capitalist development."[23] Roseberry has underscored the necessity of studying communities that have sprouted across the Latin American landscape, responding to the dislocations and the needs of capitalist development, from Tonalá to the coffee highlands of Costa Rica and Venezuela. As Roseberry notes, when such communities rebel, they cannot justify their actions by appealing to a traditional moral economy. Yet neither are they a "dependent" peasantry (like hacienda peons). Roseberry goes beyond establishing peasantries as a subject of study, for he questions the notion of autonomous communities. He argues, "The very formation of anthropological subjects, even in . . . small and isolated villages, is caught up in historical processes (of regional growth and decline, state making and unmaking, economic development and underdevelopment) that cannot be analytically set aside. The setting aside of those actual historic processes . . . restores to anthropological subjects a fictitious primordial character."[24]

Roseberry cites Gavin Smith's case study of a traditional Peruvian village. While the villagers in different decades waged apparently similar struggles from 1870 to the 1960s, they nonetheless involved different projects. Roseberry notes, "The struggles themselves differed over time even as they shared a common language of land recuperation."[25] My Chinandegan study shares Roseberry's emphasis on historical analysis of the changing meaning of cultural forms. Just as the Peruvians understood and engaged in quite contemporary battles using traditional concepts, the Chinandegans worked through and transformed the meanings of inherited notions of private property and necesidad.

Like Skocpol, Craig Calhoun and Douglas Kincaid have made important advances in the study of communities and revolution.[26] Their studies show that in their vastly different fields of investigation—England during the industrial revolution and twentieth-century El Salvador—community was a far more important radicalizing factor than class. Although their notions of traditional communities are largely congruent with Skocpol's autonomous peasant village, Calhoun broadens the field of inquiry to include artisanal groups. Kincaid, moreover, establishes an important analytical category to account for the success of the radical Christians in the Salvadoran countryside during the 1970s. According to Kincaid, the Christians organized and helped form "recreated" community solidarities, "based on residual community social bonds."[27]

The evidence presented in my study confirms the importance of residence over occupation, and community over class (in a traditional sense) as factors in the formation of the Chinandegan movement. Nevertheless, the Chinandegan case also questions several methodological aspects of Kincaid's and Calhoun's studies. Following Roseberry, I have argued that a notion of community that depends exclusively on tradition or even on recreated "residual social bonds" would miss the active creation and recreation of the Chinandegan movement, which arose on historically vacant, uncultivated land. Moreover, the growth of that movement required the projection of a sense of communal solidarity on to a wider collectivity—other communities that shared a common sense of antagonism to the agrarian elite. These communities together formed a class *in relation* to that elite.

Calhoun's model of changing consciousness (similar to that of moral economy theorists) poses another problem, as well. Although he underscores the contextual and constructed nature of the tradition that welds these communities together, he does not completely escape from what Roseberry criticizes as the myth of primordial essence. For example, Calhoun argues that socialist ideas in France developed out of preexisting corporatist practices or "were incorporated [by artisans] to the extent that they could be fitted into the traditional structure of thought and action."[28] Calhoun's argument is fascinating and persuasive in the French context. But the Chinandegan case offers an alternative view of the evolution of popular consciousness in rural communities. Rather than fitting ideas into "traditional structures of thought and action," the Chinandegan campesinos first used elite notions to understand their reality and then overturned the meaning of those notions along with their associated forms of deference to the elite.

The Chinandega campesinos fought to create a new independence, where only dependence had existed before. The Chinandegan campesinos eventually engaged in collective action independent of local and national elites, despite their lack of an autonomous village structure or a precapitalist cultural fabric. When they created these communities, elite cultural forms dominated their lives so powerfully that many bowed down to the lords of the land. Hence, their struggle for cultural autonomy could not seek to preserve precapitalist forms, rather it sought to transform elite discourse into a campesino language of protest aimed at creating a new social order. At any point along their path toward a political class consciousness, then, campesino discourse exhibited many of the characteristics of one form or another of elite domination. The dialectical interplay between inherited dependency and discovered autonomy has been at the core of campesino action and consciousness. Not surprisingly, then, their participation in the revolutionary process of the 1970s and 1980s has involved an alliance, neither wholly dependent nor fully autonomous, with the Frente Sandinista.

Revolutionary and Class Consciousness: The Problem of Representation and Meaning

In traditional revolutionary theory the vanguard party represents the *historic* interests of the working class. The task of the vanguard party is to persuade the proletariat to cross a tangible boundary marker between "trade union" and "political class consciousness," between the immediate and the strategic interests of the proletariat.[29] Ernesto Laclau has blasted away the theoretical underpinnings of this political model by demystifying the notion that one can assign historical missions and meanings to specific classes.[30] Indeed, we cannot understand the trajectory of the campesino movement unless we accept Laclau's break with the notion of historical representation (that a class can be directly represented politically). For there was no class essence in the Chinandegan countryside that blossomed into social revolution. Nor was there a vanguard (at least before 1974) that generalized, transformed, or elevated the political consciousness of the dispossessed. Indeed, the Chinandegan movement developed in isolation from the anti-Somoza opposition. Although they shared certain goals with the Frente Sandinista and its peasant followers in the central highlands, the Chinandegans had relatively little contact with the revolutionaries until the mid-1970s. The campesinos eventually supported the Sandinistas through an informal alliance. But the political consciousnesses of the campesino and the Sandinista militant had evolved in different subcultures with different interpretations of Somocista and Sandinista discourses.

Laclau argues that "class struggle at the ideological level consists, to a great extent, in the attempt to articulate popular-democratic interpellations in the ideological discourses of antagonistic classes."[31] Laclau's discovery of the "autonomous," nonclass-specific domain of popular-democratic struggle allows us to probe the ideological dimension of the unity between Sandinistas and campesinos. Any study of the FSLN's success in transforming itself from a group of fewer than two hundred militants in 1977 to the undisputed leader of a popular revolution will have to analyze its ability to integrate popular-democratic elements into their revolutionary program. In part, the campesino movement facilitated this task by, independently from the rest of the opposition, emptying all popular elements from Somocismo.

Conclusion

More importantly, the ideological articulation between the Sandinistas and the campesinos—neither a fusion nor tactical demagoguery—expanded the social-political horizon of each force.[32] Just as the merging of proletarian and peasant forms of action spurred the development of an autonomous campesino movement during the early 1960s, so the use of Sandinista and campesino forms of struggle and consciousness enhanced the potency and effectiveness of the alliance and contributed to their collective victory over the Somoza regime.[33]

Nevertheless, class struggle waged by revolutionary workers and campesinos may even have contradicted the immediate goals of the national revolutionary movement. As we saw in Chinandega, at critical moments in the late 1970s, Sandinista-led workers and campesinos pursued their own struggles. The campesinos seized land belonging to non-Somocistas and anti-Somocistas, thereby undermining a main component of the Sandinista multiclass strategy. Similarly, revolutionary ISA workers combated their Sandinista managers. Many workers called for the nationalization of the sugar mill, despite Sandinista plans to the contrary. While not wishing to create problems for the vanguard, these workers and campesinos themselves, however, saw no contradiction between the needs of their own class and those of the revolution. The campesino movement, in particular, had previously developed practical and ideological habits that were integral to its class identity. The voluntary, conscious delegation of authority to Andrés Ruíz Escorcia in 1961 or to the FSLN in 1978 did not extinguish this identity.

A revolutionary vanguard, perhaps unconsciously, may undermine class autonomy. Indeed, since 1980, the Sandinistas' curtailment of strikes, factory occupations, and land invasions underscores the dilemma of a party that seeks to build a coalition for national liberation in a society of extremely limited resources, great poverty, and high levels of class tension.[34] Those tensions, however, as we have seen in the Chinandegan countryside, are neither recent nor easy to eradicate, even in the interests of defending the revolution.

The autonomous development of popular movements before 1979 involved a search for common ground with the authorities and the elite. As part of this process, workers and campesinos eventually put forth goals couched in terms of patriotism, anti-feudalism, and the right to private property, concepts the authorities would appreciate. In Tonalá, Rancherías, and San José, these terms had no fixed meaning. Rather than rhetoric, they became cognitive tools to interpret and change reality. In the early 1960s, the campesinos responded to the terrorist regime of Juan Angel López with democratic organizational and cultural forms symbolized by the phrase, "we lead as equals." The campesinos of the 1980s have not discarded such precious tools, forged through decades of resistance to the agrarian elite.

Since 1979 the Sandinistas have contributed to the development of relatively democratic politics and communication in places like San José, Tonalá, and Sirama. But the relationship between the vanguard and the campesinos still suffers from some misunderstanding. This problem has become especially acute since the FSLN must continually redefine such old concepts as "agrarian reform" and "trade union" and introduce new ones, such as "patriotic bourgeoisie." Such terms are particularly hard to understand when today's patriotic bourgeois may have been yesterday's rico or oligarch. Similarly, a worker in San Antonio has difficulty comprehending the rhetoric of a Sandinista union leader who vehemently denounces the Somoza-era union, despite the Sandinista union's structural likeness to the "yellow" one. To compound the problem of communication, in defense against the U.S.-financed Contra war, the FSLN has substituted (largely military) obligation for what the campesinos' forged with difficulty—a sense of voluntary responsibility and commitment.

Moreover, a failure to fully understand the evolving campesino notion of private property has occasionally led some FSLN militants to stumble over their own ideological rigidity while politically educating people who have risked their lives in the struggle for land and national liberation. Some local functionaries on state farms have, at times, grievously failed to appreciate the campesinos' past struggles to defend their right to cut palm leaves on hacienda land or to fish in an estuary. That educators need educating is unavoidable in any process of revolutionary change. However, the challenge for the FSLN is to recognize the limitations of its own forms of representation, while striving for mutual understanding with the people in the fields and the mills. The campesinos gained political strength as they fought for land and labor demands; so too political revolutionaries gain force and wisdom when they struggle for the rights of campesinos and workers *and* for national liberation.

In the Chinandegan countryside, the Sandinistas have maintained a high degree of support, despite the intense efforts of the United States to strangle the revolution. That solid base of support was quite visible in the 1984 elections, when they gave the FSLN more than 70 percent of their vote.[35] Those results were the fruit of an alliance created in the 1970s between an autonomous campesino movement and the FSLN. The Sandinistas guaranteed with their lives the land for which the people had long struggled. Moreover, they guaranteed the campesinos the right to their own democratic organization. In return, campesinos actively participated in the Sandinista revolution. Thus, today many of the agrarian rebels from the 1950s and 1960s continue to participate actively and even have leadership positions in the Unión de Agricultores y Ganaderos (UNAG). UNAG's deep roots in Chinandegan history, and its origins (as the Asociación de Trabajadores del Campo) in the revolutionary alliance of the 1970s, are the preconditions for its success as the most democratic and efficient of all Sandinista organizations. Campesino revolutionaries like Apolonio Carrasco, Mariano Escorcia, and Oscar Osejo represent the juncture between two historical movements and are thus in a privileged position to interpret the campesino world to the Sandinistas in Managua, while at the same time pushing forward their goal of campesino liberation in Chinandega.

On the same battlefield where the campesinos fought twenty-five years ago, recently they have faced an even more treacherous enemy—the counterrevolution organized by the United States. By driving them into an unpopular draft and into economic desperation, the Contra war has put severe strains on the peasant-Sandinista alliance. Yet despite the ravages of war and growing poverty, the *agraristas* remain confident, for collectively the campesinos have vanquished an era: *El Tiempo de los Ricos*.

Appendix 1

Chronology

1890: Ingenio San Antonio founded.

1893–1909: José Santos Zelaya president of Nicaragua.

1912: Liberal insurrection (San Blás Massacre).

1912–25: U.S. Marine-backed Conservative governments.

1922: Ernesto Pereira leads one of many Liberal insurrections.

1925: Conservative Emiliano Chamorro overthrows Liberal-Conservative coalition government during brief Marine absence.

1926–27: Liberal Constitutionalist revolution.

February 1927: Chinandega burns in battle.

May 1927: Peace Treaty of Tipitapa signed.

1927–33: Sandino battles U.S. military intervention.

1928: Liberal José María Moncada elected president.

1932: Liberal Juan Bautista Sacasa elected president.

1933: U.S. Marines withdraw and Sandino agrees to a truce.

February 1934: Anastasio Somoza García, chief of the National Guard, organized by the United States Marine Corps, plans and carries out the assassination of Sandino.

May 1936: Somoza engineers coup d'état against Sacasa.

July 1936: San Antonio strike.

January 1937: Somoza officially becomes president.

May–June 1944: Anti-Somoza student strikes and demonstrations.

July 1944: Partido Socialista Nicaragüense founded, gives conditional support to Somoza.

April 1945: Labor Code becomes law. Anti-union repression in San Antonio.

1946–48: San José del Obraje and Tonalá founded.

Appendix 1

February 1946: Labor organization CTN founded by leftist militants.

February 1947: Leonardo Argüello, backed by Somoza, wins fraudulent elections against Aguado.

May 1947: Argüello charts independent course and is overthrown by the end of the month. United States does not recognize the new government, which is dominated by Somoza.

1948: Antileftist and anti-opposition repression. United States recognizes regime.

1949: CGT, Somocista-dominated labor federation, founded.

1950: Emiliano Chamorro, Conservative leader, and Somoza sign pact guaranteeing minority representation in government.

1954: Armed movement to overthrow Somoza crushed. Sutiavas launch protest against local hacendado.

1956: Rigoberto López Perez assassinates Somoza in León, and massive repression follows.

1957-1963: Luís Somoza president.

1957: San José del Obraje organization founded.

1958: CGT convention held in Chinandega. Union ban ends. Regino Escobar outwits Campuzano in San José.

1959: Several insurrectionary movements against Somoza. National Guard kills students in León demonstration. Sutiava rebels act against local hacendados. San José movement quelled.

1960: Andrés Ruíz Escorcia (pro-Somoza) wins leadership of CGT in 36–35 vote against PSN candidate (Escorcia is accused of fraud). SCAAS wins major construction strike. Matagalpa general strike ends in partial victory. Storm disaster occurs in Chinandega.

1961: Somozas back Bay of Pigs adventure. Nicaragua participates in Alliance for Progress. FSLN founded. Escorcia becomes leader of Chinandegan campesino movement. Regino Escobar dies.

1962–64: Juan Angel López institutes reign of violent repression, with from two to three hundred victims, including Sandinista Pablo Espinoza.

1962: Tonalá strike and occupations. Corinto strike. Rancherías campesinos win partial victory.

1963: René Schick becomes president. Agrarian reform law passed. Chinandegan movement continues despite repression. National Guard crushes Corinto strike.

1964–1965: Juan Angel López tried and found guilty of the murder of four peasants in Chinandega. Strike occurs at San Antonio. Tonalá and Sutiava movements achieve partial victory. FSLN and PSN support coalition, Movilización Republicana, and gain influence in campesino movement, especially in Jinotega and Matagalpa.

1966: René Schick dies.

1967: Opposition leader Agüero leads mass demonstration on January 22 against regime of Tacho Somoza, which ends in National Guard violence. FSLN, with local peasant support, fights National Guard at Pancasán in Matagalpa.

1971: Somoza-Agüero pact.

1972: Earthquake in Managua.

1973: Construction workers lead strike wave. Sutiavan land occupations.

1974: Strikes occur at San Antonio and elsewhere. Moderate opposition unifies in UDEL. FSLN captures hostages at elite party and wins demands.

1974–77: State of siege and massive human rights violations by Somoza regime.

1977: Rancherías, San José, and Sirama campesinos stage protests and face mass arrests. FSLN attacks National Guard in San Carlos and Masaya.

1978: Pedro Joaquin Chamorro assassination followed by mass protest strike.

February–March 1978: Monimbó and Sutiava insurrections.

May–June 1978: Land occupations throughout Chinandega.

June 1978: Managua Cathedral occupied by Tonaleños.

August 1978: FSLN takes over National Palace while Congress is in session, wins prisoner release and other demands.

September 1978: Insurrection in Matagalpa, followed by others in nearly every major town or city, crushed by National Guard.

September and December 1978: San Antonio strikes.

March 1979: Three FSLN tendencies unify.

June 4, 1979: Insurrection and general strike begin.

July 19, 1979: Insurrection triumphs.

Appendix 2

Characters and Places

Aguilar, Manuel: Union leader in the Ingenio San Antonio, 1944–48.

Alvarado family: Owners of Campuzano, the largest hacienda in Chinandega.

Asociación de Trabajadores del Campo (ATC): Rural workers' union founded by FSLN militants in 1978.

Astacio Cabrera, Hugo: Anti-Somocista activist, PLI leader, and attorney for Campuzano.

Avilés, Mónico: Rancherías leader.

Benard family: Original owners of San Antonio and major figures in the Conservative party.

Campos, Manuel: El Realejo union leader.

Cándia, Ramón: Born in 1904 in northern Chinandega. In the 1930s, he came to the Campuzano region to work on haciendas. In 1957, he became a key leader of San José.

Carrasco family: Father, Abraham, and sons, Apolonio and Gerónimo, were leaders of the Rancherías movement.

Cordero, Joaquin: San Antonio strike leader in 1936.

Cofradía de Santa Ana: An indigenous religious fraternity dating from the seventeenth century. In the 1890s, Balladares as jefe político expropriated their land. In 1959, the campesinos adopted a cofradía identity as a means to struggle for the land.

Comite Organizador de la Confederación de Trabajadores Nicaragüenses (COCTN): Somocista union group, 1944–49.

Confederación de Trabajadores Nicaragüenses (CTN): Leftist-dominated union federation, 1946–47.

Confederación General de Trabajadores (CGT): Union federation founded in 1949. From 1958 to 1960, socialists and Somocistas participated. In 1962, socialists founded the Independent CGT.

Deshon, Edmundo (Mundo): Member of an important Liberal, oligarchic family, who since the 1920s had invested in sugar mills and cotton gins. Member of the Campuzano group.

Ejidos: Land donated by government to *municipalidades*, designated for rental to poorer campesinos. Nearly 10 percent of western Nicaraguan land was ejidal in the 1950s.

El Maneadero: Hacienda owned by the Zavala family.

El Paraíso: Hacienda owned by the Horvilleur family.

Escobar, Regino: Leader of San José and Chinandegan campesino movement, who died as a result of Guardia-inflicted injuries in 1961.

Escorcia, Mariano: Union leader in Tonalá, currently active in UNAG.

Frente Sandinista de Liberación Nacional (FSLN): Revolutionary group founded by Carlos Fonseca, Tomás Borge, and Silvio Mayorga in 1961.

Guerrero, Irma (La Irma): Somocista political leader and congressional deputy.

Guido, Pablo: Tonalá union activist.

La Chunga: Hacienda owned by the Montealegre family.

López, Juan Angel: The most infamous Guardia comandante in Chinandegan history. In 1964, because he had killed so many, the Guardia relieved him of his command, tried him, and then released him. He died a natural death in 1976.

Martínez, Leoncio: Tonalá union leader.

Mayorga, Ruperto: Leader of the Liberal party and the union in Tonalá.

Meza, Celina: San José leader.

Montealegre family: Politically influential and economically powerful Liberal family; owners of La Chunga.

Obraje: A colonial indigo plantation. Later it was an indigenous ranch, purchased in the 1870s by the Baca family.

Osejo, Oscar: Leader of the campesinos of Sirama (near Chichigalpa).

Papi, Francisco Argeñal (Pancho Papi): Somocista functionary in the Agriculture Department and congressional deputy.

Partido Liberal Independiente (PLI): Middle-class opposition party founded in 1944.

Partido Liberal Nacionalista (PLN): The Somocista party after 1936.

Partido Socialista Nicaragüense (PSN): Marxist, pro-Soviet party founded in 1944.

Pellas family: Founding owners of the Ingenio San Antonio.

Pereira, Ernesto: Liberal insurrectionary leader from 1920 to 1927; jefe político of Chinandega during the 1940s and 1950s.

Ramírez, Domingo: Obrerista leader since the 1920s and a journalistic supporter of the campesino movement.

Rancherías: Name of the community that developed on the southern boundary of Campuzano, after a successful campesino fight for the Nuevos Ejidos.

Reyes, Marcelino: Guardia doctor, who as jefe político, appropriated one thousand manzanas of ejidal land and subsequently entered the conflict between Campuzano and the campesino movement.

Rodríguez Somoza brothers: Francisco, cousin of Luís Somoza, was Guardia comandante of Chinandega during the rise of the campesino movement. Juan José, brother of Francisco, was León comandante during the Sutiava revolt of 1959 and, like his brother, a moderate sympathizer of the campesino movement.

Ruíz Escorcia, Andrés: Leader of the Chinandegan campesino movement; secretary general of the CGT from 1960 to 1964.

Sánchez, Éntimo: Leader of the fight for the Nuevos Ejidos and of the Rancherías community.

San José del Obraje: Name of the village founded through the sale of one thousand manzanas of the Obraje hacienda in 1948.

Suazo, Juan: Born in 1911. A small-scale peasant, he was a principal leader of the San José organization.

Sutiava: Indigenous barrio of the city of León.

Tonalá: Town founded in 1946 through the donation of land from the hacienda El Paraíso.

Zapata, Engracia: Leader of the Tonalá campesinos. During the 1970s, her sons became active in the campesino movement and the FSLN.

Notes

All of the interviews cited in the notes were conducted by the author between 1983 and 1989. Although often listed together for the sake of brevity, all interviews were individual. In addition, I interviewed all informants more than once.

Introduction

1. Gerald Sider, "The Ties That Bind: Culture and Agriculture, Property and Propriety in the Newfoundland Village Fishery," *Social History* 5, no. 1 (January 1980): 24.

2. Ibid., p. 26. Sider's theses on counterhegemony are developed somewhat in opposition to the history that he studied, for he elaborates his notion of those "ties that bind" out of their absence in the Newfoundland villages.

3. Eric Wolf has provided a useful definition of peasants: "Populations that are existentially involved in cultivation and make autonomous decisions regarding the processes of cultivation." See Wolf, *Peasant Wars of the Twentieth Century* (New York, 1969), p. xiv. Carlos Cabarrús in *Génesis de una revolución: analisis del surgimiento y desarrollo de la organización campesina en El Salvador* (Mexico City, 1983) makes an excellent case for using the analytical category "semiproletariat" for understanding the revolutionary process in that country. He defines the semiproletarian in the Salvadoran context as follows: "The peasant who has on the average one manzana (1.7 acres) of land and also has to sell his labor power. . . we can conclude that the semi-proletariat forms the most fertile terrain for political militancy." See Carlos Cabarrús, "El Salvador: De Movimiento Campesino a Revolución Popular," in *Movimientos Populares en Centroamerica*, ed. Daniel Camacho and Rafael Menjívar (San José, 1985), pp. 363–64. Since most of the Chinandegan villagers did not own or have access to the land by 1960, neither semiproletarian nor peasant is an appropriate term.

4. See in particular, Craig Calhoun, *The Question of Class Struggle: Social Foundations of Popular Radicalism During the Industrial Revolution* (Chicago, 1982), and "The Radicalism of Tradition: Community Strength or Venerable Disguise and Borrowed Language," *American Journal of Sociology* 88, no. 5 (1983): 886–914. For an excellent application of the community solidarity approach to the Salvadoran case, see Douglas Kincaid, "Peasants into Rebels: Community and Class in Rural El Salvador," *Comparative Studies in Society and History* 29, no. 3 (July 1987): 466–94.

5. Calhoun, "The Radicalism of Tradition," p. 897.

6. William Roseberry, "Images of the Peasant in the Consciousness of the Venezuelan Proletariat," in *Proletarians and Protest*, ed. Michael Hanagan and Charles Stephenson (Westport, Conn., 1986), p. 165. Roseberry writes: "A class culture or class discourse is never given; it must be constructed from the cultural raw material presented from history."

7. Carol Smith, "Culture and Community: The Language of Class in Guatemala," in *The Year Left*, ed. Mike Davis (London, 1987), 2: 197–217. She writes: "Guatemalan Indians have never formed a single class, if one uses objective, economic criteria to define class position. But they have always been treated as a single class by non-Indians and thus have always been a class in relational terms" (p. 208).

8. On the uses of oral testimony I found the following studies thought-provoking:

Peter Winn, "Oral History and the Factory Study: New Approaches to Labor History," *Latin American Research Review* 14, no. 2 (Summer 1979): 137–39; Luisa Passerini, "Work, Ideology and Consensus under Italian Fascism," *History Workshop Journal* 13 (November 1979): 82–108; and Lygia Sigaud, "A Idealização numa Area de Plantation," *Contrapunto* (Rio de Janeiro) 2, no. 2 (November 1977): 115–26.

9. Although there seems to have been little organized Sandinista activity in Chinandega, I nevertheless regret not being able to provide greater detail concerning the U.S. occupation specifically and the U.S. domination over Nicaraguan politics and economics generally. Among the scholarly studies that do emphasize the United States' impact on Nicaragua are: Richard Millet, *The Guardians of the Dynasty* (Maryknoll, N.Y., 1977); George Black, *The Triumph of the People* (London, 1981); Jaime Wheelock, *Imperialismo y Dictadura* (Mexico City, 1975); C. Quijano, *Ensayo sobre el imperialismo de los Estados Unidos* (Montevideo, Uruguay, 1970); Juan Luís Vásquez, "Luchas Políticas y Estado Oligárquico," in *Economía y Sociedad en la Construcción del Estado en Nicaragua*, ed. Alberto Lanuza (San José, 1983); and Amarú Barahona, "Intervención Extranjera y Dictadura," in *Economía y Sociedad en la Construcción del Estado en Nicaragua*, ed. Alberto Lanuza (San José, 1983).

10. E. G. Squier, *Nicaragua: Its People, Scenery, Monuments* (New York, 1860), p. 343.

11. Julián Guerrero, *Chinandega* (Managua, 1964), p. 80. Before the cotton boom, Chinandega's oranges were so widely known that a slogan in a Managua anti-interventionist demonstration in the early 1920s was *Arriba las naranjas de Chinandega!* (Long live the oranges of Chinandega!).

12. David Radell, *Historical Geography of Western Nicaragua: The Spheres of Influence of León, Granada, and Managua, 1519–1965* (Berkeley, Calif., 1969), p. 23.

13. Jaime Incer, *Nueva Geografía de Nicaragua* (Managua, 1970), pp. 432–64.

14. Vásquez in "Luchas Políticas" and Barahona in "Intervención Extranjera y Dictadura" present analyses of the class configuration of Nicaraguan society during this period.

15. Jaime Biderman, "The Development of Capitalism in Nicaragua," *Latin American Perspectives* 10, no. 1 (Winter 1983): 13; Gustavo Gutiérrez Mayorga, "Historia del Movimiento Obrero de Nicaragua (1900–1977)," in *Historia del Movimiento Obrero en América Latina*, vol. 2, ed. Pablo González Casanova (Mexico City, 1985), p. 198. These authors, despite their valuable work, tend to present a portrait of a traditional society. ISA, for example, could prosper because over 15 percent of the adult population—including artisans, petty merchants, farmers, professionals, and businessmen—had incomes sufficient to purchase their commodity. Second, no semi-servile bonds prevented ISA from obtaining seasonal labor.

16. Sidney Mintz, "The Rural Proletariat and the Problem of Rural Proletarian Consciousness," *Journal of Peasant Studies* 1, no. 3 (April 1974): 291–325, an article on the consciousness of sugar workers, particularly in relation to technological development, is especially useful.

17. For a more extensive historiographical discussion of Somoza and the labor movement, see Jeffrey Gould, "Amigos Peligrosos, Enemigos Mortales," *Revista de*

Historia (Costa Rica) 6–7, nos. 12–13 (June 1986): 19–66, and "For an Organized Nicaragua: Somoza and the Labour Movement (1944–1948)" *Journal of Latin American Studies* 19 (November 1987): 353–87. This discussion of Somocista populism follows the methodological advances of Daniel James, *Resistance and Integration: Peronism and the Argentine Working Class, 1946–1976* (Cambridge, 1988). Amalia Chamorro's, "Estado y hegemonia durante el somocismo," in *Economia y Sociedad*, ed. Lanuza, pp. 243–71, offers an excellent model for understanding Somocismo as a hegemonic force.

18. See Wolf, *Peasant Wars*; and James Scott, *The Moral Economy of the Peasant: Rebellion and Subsistence in South East Asia* (New Haven, Conn., 1976), and "Hegemony and the Peasantry," in *Politics and Society* 7, no. 3 (1977): 267–96. For a superb discussion of theories of agrarian revolt and revolution see Steven Stern's introduction to his edited volume *Resistance, Rebellion, and Consciousness in the Andean World* (Madison, Wis., 1987), pp. 3–28.

19. Peter Winn provides a brilliant model for a "bottom-up" approach to revolution, in *Weavers of Revolution: The Yarur Workers and Chile's Road to Socialism* (Oxford, 1986).

Chapter 1

1. On the concept of double consciousness, see Juan Martínez-Alier, "Notas Sobre el Franquismo," *Papers Revista de Sociologia* 8 (1978): 31–32.

2. W. Newell, U.S. Consular Report, Department of Commerce and Labor, July 15, 1892; ISA's company history, Nicaragua Sugar Estates Ltd., *El Ingenio San Antonio, 1890–1953* (Granada, 1953), p. 4.

3. Rodrigo Quesada M., "El Comercio entre Gran Bretaña y América Central (1851–1915), *Anuario de Estudios Centroamericanos* 11, no. 2 (1985): 90.

4. W. Newell, U.S. Consular Report, July 15, 1892.

5. Frutos M. Chamorro, *La Ruidosa Quiebra* (Granada, 1898), p. 11, mentions that in 1895, Zelaya momentarily gave a concession to Juan Callejas of Chinandega for the "free introduction of sugar," which would have financially destroyed San Antonio. On the problems of the San Antonio stockholders, the Cuadra family, see Diego Chamorro, *El Panterismo Nicaragüense* (Granada, 1898), p. 39; and the testimony of Senator Cuadra Pasos in *La Gaceta*, March 13, 1916.

6. Frutos M. Chamorro, *La Ruidosa Quiebra,* p. 40.

7. R. Day, U.S. Consular Report, U.S. State Department, no. 53 (July 30, 1897).

8. See *Estudio Comparativo de Partidos Políticos* (Managua, 1923), pp. 112–13.

9. *Bulletin of the American Republics* 20 (1905): 663; Toribio Tigerino, *El Tratado Chamorro-Bryan* (Managua, 1943), p. 19. Moreover, in 1905, Adolfo Benard, a major stockholder in ISA, supported Zelaya's reelection campaign. See *El Independiente* (León), January 1, 1905.

10. *Estudio Comparativo*, pp. 108–12; *Bulletin of the American Republics* 23 (1906): 171–72.

11. Nicaragua Sugar Estates Ltd., *Ingenio San Antonio*, p. 4; U.S. Consular Report, Department of Commerce and Labor, no. 258 (1902), p. 447; *Bulletin of the American*

Republics 27 (1908): 938. In order to arrive at the territorial expansion figure, I consulted the original land titles and deeds, thanks to the generous cooperation of Nicaragua Sugar Estates.

12. U.S. Consular Report, Department of Commerce and Labor, no. 326, p. 74; *Bulletin of the American Republics* 23 (1906): 172.

13. "Reminiscencias Históricas de Toribio Tigerino," *Revista Conservadora* 40 (January 1964): 6; José Joaquín Morales, *Memorias de lo Vivido y lo Visto* (Granada, 1961), p. 73. Nevertheless, these military measures seem quite exceptional. Laborers clearly resented state coercion. A report in the *Bulletin of the American Republics* 6 (1899): 1,421, stated: "The coffee crop of Nicaragua, which is now being gathered, is reported as yielding only about one-half the usual quantity of berries. The laborers are asking high wages and are indisposed to work."

14. On this rebate, see *Estudio Comparativo*, pp. 112–13.

15. Nicaragua Sugar Estates Ltd., *Ingenio San Antonio*, p. 4.

16. U.S. Department of State General Records, RG 59,817.00/2013, National Archives.

17. U.S. Department of State General Records, RG 59,817.00/2059, National Archives.

18. Interview with Alberto Cortés, Chichigalpa, Nicaragua, November 1983. Most of my informants, pensioned San Antonio workers, asked for anonymity. Respecting their wishes, I will cite "oral sources." All of the interviews cited in this book were conducted by me, for this chapter, in Chichigalpa between 1983 and 1985, except where otherwise noted.

19. *Escritura Social de Nicaragua Sugar States Ltd.* (Granada Nicaragua, 1935); Municipio de Chichigalpa, *Escritura de Terrenos Ejidales* (1895). See also Manuel Morales Cruz, "Informe sobre la situación de los Terreno, del ISA que anteriormente fueron Ejidales," a report probably prepared for the ISA in the 1960s, which shows that ISA acquired only 737 manzanas of ejidal land, though it does not discuss indigenous land.

20. Oficina Central del Censo, *Censo General de la República de Nicaragua de 1920* (Managua, 1920); Mariano Barreto, *Recuerdos de Chichigalpa, Corinto y Chinandega* (León, 1921).

21. Nicaragua Sugar Estates Ltd., *El Ingenio San Antonio*, p. 5; Harold Playter, *Nicaragua, A Commercial and Economic Survey* (Washington, D.C., 1927), p. 35.

22. *Libro de Cuentas del ISA,* 1910–18, an account book of the ISA, in the possession of an employee. The account book includes contracts with the colonos, as well as with wood and cane suppliers. The Liberal party affiliation was derived by comparing the names with other sources. One colono, Fornos, had been mayor of Chichigalpa under the Zelaya regime.

23. Arnoldo Silva León, *Cuba y el Mercado Internacional Azucarero* (Havana, 1975), pp. 19–20; *El Ingenio San Antonio*, p. 4.

24. *El Ingenio San Antonio*, pp. 4–6.

25. This data is from the personnel files of ISA in Chichigalpa. The Departamento de Recursos Humanos kindly let me consult the *fichas* (cards) of retired workers. These cards contained birthplace and literacy data.

26. *El Cronista* (León), August 6, 1925.

27. Oral Sources.

28. *El Cronista*, July 22, 1924; January 6, 1926. Chinandegan cotton growers paid field hands more than one dollar a day, when ISA was paying its field labor forty cents a day.

29. Field worker wages simply did not allow for the accumulation of savings necessary to buy land or to make significant farming improvements, however, the *plantel* was an excellent market for peasant goods. The market women (*vivanderas*) sold directly to the mill workers.

30. *Centro-America* 7, no. 4 (October–December 1915): 633. In 1916 the company built a playing field.

31. Interview with Hermogenes Solis, Chichigalpa, February 1986.

32. Oral Sources.

33. Milagros Palma, *Por los senderos míticos de Nicaragua* (Managua, 1984), pp. 124–31.

34. Michael Taussig, *The Devil and Commodity Fetishism in South America* (Chapel Hill, N.C., 1980), p. 110.

35. Ibid., p. 101.

36. Ministry of Labor and Agriculture, *Memorias del Ministerio de Agricultura y Trabajo, 1934–1935* (Managua, 1935), p. 35.

37. Although only oral evidence of field worker strikes have been uncovered, in 1923 management jailed twenty-three *fogoneros* (furnace operators) for staging a strike in protest against increased hours. See *El Centroamericano*, February 2, March 1, and March 23, 1923.

38. *Diario de Granada*, May 12, 1907.

39. *El Independiente* (León), August 19, 1919.

40. A Chinandegan peasant revolutionary of considerable local reknown, Francisco Sequeira, "Cabuya," also rejected the terms of the peace treaty.

41. *El Cronista*, August 1, 1924 and the *Actas de la Central de Obreros*, 1917–29, in the possession of Toribio Muñoz, Chinandega.

42. Report of August 25, 1926, U.S. Department of State General Records, RG 59,817.00/3769, National Archives.

43. Oral Sources; *La Información* (Chinandega), October 13, 1935.

44. *La Gaceta*, March 16 and 23, 1916; Martín Benard was ministro de hacienda under Emiliano Chamorro (1916–20). The Benards were the principal leaders of the Granada faction of the Conservative party, which sometimes allied with and at other times opposed the Emiliano Chamorro faction.

45. The international price in U.S. cents per pound in 1925 was 2.2; in 1926, 2.2; in 1927, 2.6. Silva León, *Cuba y el mercado*, p. 53; and Pedro Belli, "Prolégomeno para una historia económica de Nicaragua, 1905–1966," *Revista del Pensamiento Centroamericano* 30, no. 146 (January–March, 1975): 8.

46. Ministry of Labor and Agriculture, *Memorias del Ministerio de Agricultura y Trabajo*, p. 34.

47. Letter dated June 28, 1928 from Nicaragua Sugar Estates to the U.S. Embassy, U.S. Department of State General Records, RG 59,817.00/6135, National Archives.

48. Ministry of Labor and Agriculture, *Memorias del Ministerio de Agricultura y Trabajo*, p. 35.

49. *Diario de Occidente*, March 20, 1929.

50. Cited in Belli, "Prolégomeno," p. 6.

51. *Diario de Occidente*, March 8, 1929; Oral Sources. It should be stressed that the Benards did not support Chamorro's coup, nor did they wish to go to war once he was in power. Nevertheless, it is likely that they financially supported the government effort against the revolutionaries.

52. *Diario de Occidente*, May 23, 1929; *El Cronista*, January 8, 1931.

53. "Informe del Presidente de la Junta Directiva a la Junta de Accionistas" (report of the president of the San Antonio sugar mill to the stockholders), February 1934, February 1944, and February 1946; *Memorias del Ministerio de Hacienda y Crédito* (Managua, 1925–26); Playter, *Nicaragua*, p. 62; U.S. Department of Commerce, *Supplement to Commerce Reports*, no. 34a, September 14, 1917. For a general description of the type of mill ISA purchased in 1916, see George Rolph, *Something About Sugar* (San Francisco: 1917), pp. 22–33.

54. *Diario de Occidente*, March 21, 1929.

55. Ibid., March 8, 1929.

56. Interview with Martín Tercero, Chinandega, Nicaragua, November 1984. One Chinandegan former peon who became a popular liberal caudillo, Francisco Sequira, known as "Cabuya," refused to turn in his arms. He was killed by U.S. Marines. See Miguel Garquín, *La Muerte de Cabaya* (El Viejo, 1974).

57. January 28, 1928, U.S. Department of State General Records, RG 59,817.00/5045, National Archives.

58. In the two electoral districts combined, which include the mill workers' living quarters, the Liberals received 89 percent of the vote in the 1932 presidential election.

59. *América* (Chichigalpa), November 24, 1931; *Diario de Occidente*, November 24, 1931. Oral Sources.

60. November 28, 1931, U.S. Department of State General Records, RG 59,800B/810.5, National Archives.

61. *Diario de Occidente*, April 20, 1929.

62. *Información* (Chinandega), February 16, 1936; oral sources report that before the 1936 strike the field workers earned only 20 cents per tarea (task) and that they had to pay 10–15 cents a day for food in the cocinas.

63. Ministry of Labor and Agriculture, *Memorias del Ministerio de Agricultura y Trabajo*.

64. L. H. Leach, "Report on Economic Conditions in the Republic of Nicaragua, November, 1932," Department of Overseas Trade, London, 1933, p. 86; Belli, "Prológomeno," p. 6.

65. Ambassador Lane to the Secretary State, Telegram 17, February 18, 1936, *Confidential U.S. Diplomatic Post Records (1930–1945)*, University Publications microfilms. See also Onofre Guevara and Carlos Bermudez, *El Movimiento Obrero en Nicaragua* (Managua, 1985), pp. 111–15.

66. See *Información*, January–July 1936, for the transformation of the social democratic wing of the Liberal party in Chinandega. Interviews with Domingo Ramírez, editor of the newspaper and Chinandegan political leader, Chinandega, 1984–85.

67. All of the fifteen informants from this period remember details of Joaquín

Cordero's life. On smallpox, see *El Centroamericano*, August 28, 1931.

68. *La Nueva Prensa*, May 24, 1936 (union list); *La Nueva Prensa*, May 9, 1936 (Somoza support letter); Oral Sources.

69. "Informe del Presidente de la Junta Directiva," August 1936; *El Cronista*, July 7, 1936. ISA exported one-half of its production (5,000 tons) to Honduras and sold the remainder domestically at the artificially high price of 6 cents a pound, earning a net profit of over 3 cents per pound. Annual profits are documented in "Informe de la Junta," February 1936; Nicaragua Sugar Estates Ltd., *El Ingenio San Antonio*, p. 5.

70. "Informe del Presidente de la Junta Directiva," August 1936.

71. *El Cronista*, July 9, 1936.

72. *El Eco de Managua*, July 12, 1936; *La Noticia*, July 7, 1936; *El Cronista*, July 7, 1936; Oral Sources. The implied or real use of force in strikes has been a constant occurrence in Nicaraguan labor history. The union militants' blockage of the train and their march from colonia to colonia is reminiscent of the late nineteenth-century strikes in the United States. See David Montgomery, "Strikes in Nineteenth-Century America," *Social Science History* 4, no. 1 (February 1980): 95. It is impossible to determine whether field workers also shouted "viva Somoza," although it is safe to assume that Cordero and his followers did not.

73. "Informe del Presidente de la Junta," August 1936.

74. *El Cronista*, July 9, 1936.

75. *El Cronista*, July 21, 1936; *La Guardia Nacional*, July 1936; Oral Sources.

76. *La Guardia Nacional*, July 1936.

77. Gustavo Alemán Bolaños, "El Ingenio San Antonio: Vision de un periodista en 1937," published in *Nicaragua Agricola e Industrial*, furnished to the author by Nicaragua Sugar Estates Ltd., Managua. Alemán Bolaños had recently written *Sandino! Un estudio completo del heroe de las Segovias* (San Salvador, 1937).

78. Oral Sources.

79. Ibid.

Chapter 2

1. For more details about the 1937–44 period, see Jeffrey Gould, "Amigos Peligrosos, Enemigos Mortales: Somoza y el movimiento obrero, 1944–1946," *Revista de Historia* (Costa Rica) 6–7 (July 1985–June 1986): 12–13.

2. *Tribuna Obrera*, October 17, 1943; October 12, 1943, U.S. Department of State General Records, RG 59,817.00B/47, National Archives; see also Archivo Presidencial AGN (Archivo General de Nicaragua), Box 355. On February 4, 1947, Somoza said of Lombardo's visit, "Como fui informado [after his speech Lomobardo] continuó dando instrucciones a algunos líderes obreros de Nicaragua con quienes el sostuvo conferencias privadas durante su corta permanencia en el país." Somoza mentioned November 1943 as the date of the visit. Other sources suggest that the visit occurred in 1942.

3. See Jeffrey Gould, "For an Organized Nicaragua: Somoza and the Labor Movement," *Journal of Latin American Studies* 19, no. 2 (November 1987): 353–87.

4. U.S. Department of State General Records, RG 59,817.00B/51, National Archives.

5. U.S. Department of State General Records, RG 817.00B/51, National Archives; *La Nueva Prensa*, May 28, 1944.

6. On anti-Somoza student protests, see *La Flecha* and *La Nueva Prensa* June 26 through July 4, 1944. On PSN divisions with respect to the tactical alliance, see Gould, "For an Organized Nicaragua," pp. 363–64, n. 26.

7. Gould, "For an Organized Nicaragua," appendixes A and B; Ministry of Labor, *Memorias del Ministerio de Trabajo*, 1957–59, 1963–69, 1970. By 1948 union membership dropped to 2,500. See Ignacio A. Gutiérrez, "Sindicalismo" (Thesis, Universidad Nacional Autónoma de Nicaragua, León, 1949).

8. For examples of regime repression of Somocista unionism, see Gould "For an Organized Nicaragua," pp. 372–74.

9. Production data from ISA's company history, Nicaragua Sugar Estates Ltd., *El Ingenio San Antonio, 1890–1953* (Granada, 1953), p. 9. Data on profits come from, "Informe del Presidente de la Junta Directiva a la Junta de Accionistas" (Report of the president of the San Antonio sugar mill to the stockholders), February 1945.

10. In 1939 Somoza offered the company seven million córdobas ($1.4 million) to buy the sugar mill (U.S. Department of State General Records, RG 59,817.00:61351/5, National Archives). Other reports (January 1 and January 12, 1940) mention that the company gave Somoza a "gift" of forty shares and that it payed the dictator "extortion money" (U.S. Department of State General Records, RG 59,817.00:8762 and 817.00: 8753, National Archives).

11. *La Gaceta*, March 8, 1945; *La Flecha*, June 22, 1945; *El Eco de Managua*, June 17, 1945; "Informe del Presidente de la Junta," February 1947.

12. *La Flecha*, December 13 and 16, 1944. Interview with Manuel Aguilar, Isla de Ometepe, December 1983.

13. "Hoja Suelta," a leaflet prepared by ISA labor activists associated with COCTN, in the possession of Toribio Muñoz, Chinandega.

14. Although some informants claim that ISA ended the zafra one month early to damage the union, other sources suggest that the company took advantage of fortuitous circumstances. The rainy season of 1944 was very dry, and sugar plantations throughout the region were harmed (*Nueva Prensa*, January 5, 1945; and *El Cronista*, January 28, 1945). With the exception of 1939, the 55.56 inches of rain recorded in 1944 was the lowest level since 1923. When ISA announced the end of the zafra two weeks before its completion, the labor movement did not object or point to the existence of uncut cane (*La Flecha*, March 16, 1945). However, Juan Lorío and Armando Amador, PSN leaders, asserted that ISA destroyed 300 manzanas of cane in order to drive up the price of sugar and to repress the union (*La Unión Nacional en Nicaragua* [Guatemala, 1946], pp. 9 and 22).

15. *La Noticia*, April 5 and 10, 1945; *Novedades*, April 15, 1945; *La Flecha*, April 7–12, 1945; "Informe del Presidente de la Junta," August 1945.

16. These figures come from a study in the inactive personnel files of the Ingenio San Antonio. *La Flecha*, January 7, 1947 remarks that "over one thousand workers" had arrived in Chichigalpa looking to take part in the zafra. The earlier division based on the segregation of the Chichigalpinos no longer existed during the 1940s. Nevertheless, the segregation of factory and field workers did exist quite visibly. The PSN leader

Armando Amador noted that while factory workers lived in rooms of three by three meters near the mill, the field workers in the colonias lived in what they called "pig sties" and slept on boards (*Nueva Prensa*, June 26, 1945).

17. "Informe del Presidente de la Junta," February 1946.

18. U.S. Department of State General Records, RG 59,817.00/1–2846 and 1–3046, National Archives; *La Flecha*, January 24, 1946.

19. *La Flecha*, February 11, 1946; U.S. Department of State General Records, RG 59,817.00B/3–1046, National Archives.

20. *Nueva Prensa*, February 27, 1946.

21. The date of the Somoza-PSN negotiations is unclear. They started after the January 1946 opposition demonstration in which the PSN actively participated, and they ended before the May Day demonstration in which PSN-Somoza relations were already quite cold. The PSN speeches were antagonistic toward the regime. Amador stated: "The workers triumph when they avoid the Labor Ministry" (*Nueva Prensa*, March 3, 1946; *La Noticia*, May 3, 1946; U.S. Department of State General Records, RG 59,817.00/10–3–46, National Archives).

22. *El Liberal Nacionalista*, April 14, 1946; *La Flecha*, April 23, 1946.

23. *Nueva Prensa*, May 21, 1946.

24. *La Flecha*, May 28, 1946; *Nueva Prensa*, June 1 and 4, 1946. ISA also agreed to build a hospital and promised to build a union hall and eliminate gambling and liquor outlets (a remunerative business for the Guardia Nacional).

25. *Nueva Prensa*, June 4 and 7, 1946.

26. Ibid.; Oral Sources.

27. *Nueva Prensa*, June 7, 1946.

28. Ibid.; interview with Manuel Aguilar, Ometepe Island, December 1983.

29. *Nueva Prensa*, June 11, 1946.

30. Ibid., June 15, 1946; Oral sources.

31. Archivo Presidencial AGN, Box 332; Several informants identified the signers of the letter dated June 13, 1945. Amador escaped because Lt. Gabuardi "was drunk."

32. Rafael Jiménez recalled the conversation, and other militants recalled being told its contents. Unfortunately, when Knut Walter graciously pointed out the letter signed by the workers, it was impossible to reestablish contact with Aguilar.

33. Aside from the demonstration in Managua, the opposition staged a demonstration in Chinandega that attracted 7,000 people (quite impressive when the department's total population was only 68,000 in 1940). *Nueva Prensa*, February 5, 1946. The student movement was pushing the rest of the opposition to the left and actively sought alliances with the PSN.

34. Archivo Presidencial AGN, Box 319, telegram from Mayorga to Somoza, June 22, 1946.

35. *Nueva Prensa*, July 4, 1946; Oral sources.

36. "Código de Trabajo," in *La Gaceta*, February 2, 1945, p. 88. Also published by the government the same year as a pamphlet.

37. Seven informants remembered the phrase "Quien no está con 'el hombre,' lleva la causa perdida."

38. Oral sources; *Trabajo* (San José, Costa Rica), June 22, 1946, which reported on the CTN campaign against Céspedes. Archivo Presidencial AGN, Box 356, letter from Céspedes dated February 13, 1947 mentions his resignation in 1946. Inside the sugar mill, union anger was directed against Juan Silva, who was accused of establishing a racket whereby workers had to pay him in order to receive the newly awarded vacation pay from the company.

39. The CTN had some 15,000 dues-paying members and probably another 15,000 adherents. U.S. Department of State General Records, RG 59,817.00B 12–446 and 10–346, National Archives. On May Day 1946, the CTN in the capital area alone, mobilized between 25,000 and 30,000 workers. Since only 170,000 people voted in the February 1947 election, it is safe to assume that the leftist CTN had influence over 20 percent of the electorate. Thomas Leonard, in *The United States and Central America* (University, Ala., 1984), cites a State Department document that offered the exaggerated estimate of PSN electoral strength at 75,000 voters, or close to 45 percent of the electorate.

40. State Department observers reported on the election by studying the lines identified with each candidate. On that basis they concluded that anti-Somocista Aguado won by a 3:1 margin. In Chinandega, Aguado unofficially won 9,157 votes to the Somocista Argüello's 3,368 (U.S. Department of State General Records, RG 59,817.00/2–2647, National Archives).

41. From 1945 to 1946 sugar production increased from 167,000 to 267,000 quintals. Nicaragua Sugar Estates Ltd., *El Ingenio San Antonio*, p. 9.

42. *La Prensa*, March 4, 1947; *Diario Nicaragüense*, March 5, 1947. According to oral testimony, the canecutters suffered collectively the following year when the company adjusted the piece rates to the performance of the winner.

43. *La Prensa*, March 5, 1947. Unfortunately, it is quite difficult to guage the reaction of the 279 veteran workers. Presumably some were members of the union, but perhaps two hundred, or 15 percent of the labor force accepted, to varying degrees, ISA's "solution to the social question."

44. *La Prensa*, March 5, 1947; *La Flecha*, March 4 and 5, 1947.

45. *Nueva Prensa*, March 4, 1947; *La Flecha*, March 18, 1947; Oral sources. See "Labor Code," *Gaceta Nacional*, February 2, 1945, Title Vl, chap. 3, where planting and harvesting are defined as in the "collective interest." Labor opposed this clause, which did involve Somoza's betrayal of June 1944's promise to give rights to rural workers. Later amendments further obstructed labor organizing in the field, by requiring a 60 percent literacy rate in any peasant union.

46. *La Noticia*, March 20, 1947; *La Prensa*, March 23, 1947; *Nueva Prensa*, March 24, 1947; Oral sources.

47. *La Prensa*, March 23, 1947.

48. *La Noticia*, March 20, 1947. I still have some doubt about the degree to which the strike ever got off the ground. The repression came so rapidly and was so surgically precise that the informants' memories are contradictory. It is clear that the union was organizing a strike for that day; the Somocista unionists denounced the strike; the repression came the same day. Leytón published a report, dated March 24, 1947, that cites "un incidente contra la ley y la autoridad," but it is unclear whether he means a strike or his arrest.

49. Archivo Presidencial AGN, Box 342, letter from Rubén Leytón to Somoza García, October 25, 1947.

50. Ibid.

51. *La Flecha*, March 26, 1947. The unemployment during 1947, which may have affected up to 10,000 people in Managua, seems to be tied to the termination of war-related projects. Structural unemployment occurred in 1949. See Armando Amador, *La depresión en un sistema dictatorial* (Guatemala City, 1949), p. 3. Nevertheless, between 1945 and 1950, the industrial sector grew by 6.2 percent annually.

52. *La Nueva Prensa*, August 4, 1947; *Diario Nicaragüense*, April 10, 1947; *La Prensa*, March 29, 1947. The brewery workers seem to have won the strike.

53. Amador, *La depresión*, p. 16.

54. Ibid.

55. *Nueva Prensa*, May 17, 1947.

56. U.S. Department of State General Records, RG 59,817.00/5–2647, 5–2747, and 6–1247, National Archives.

57. U.S. Department of State General Records, RG 59,817.00/6–47, 6–947, 6–2547, 6–2647, and 7–147, National Archives. The embassy reported on July 1 that "practically all leaders of the Socialist Party and of university student groups are now under arrest, in hiding, or in asylum" (817.00/7–147).

58. *Nueva Prensa*, June 17, 1947, mentions Mayorga's firing along with what the company called other "vagos y agraristas."

59. Amador, *La depresión*, p. 18.

60. Archivo Presidencial AGN, Box 342, letter dated October 27, 1947 from Lieutenant Jorge Granera to Somoza G.

61. Ibid.

62. *La Flecha*, January 24, 1948; U.S. Department of State General Records, RG 59,817.00/00B 1–2048, National Archives. The State Department agreed with Amador's analysis of the January 1948 jailings that two factors influenced Somoza's repression—fear that the Socialists would join a revolutionary movement and a need to gain "international capital in anti-communism" since his regime was still not recognized by the United States.

63. *El Mundo*, December 5, 1948.

64. *El Mundo*, December 17, 1948; Oral sources.

65. *Nueva Prensa*, January 5, 1949.

66. Ibid.; *La Prensa*, January 5, 1949 and February 11, 1949; *La Noticia*, January 18, 1949. *El Mundo*, February 11, 1949; Oral testimony suggests an organized cane cutters strike did take place in response to the cut in piece rates, although the newspaper accounts are vague.

Chapter 3

1. Oficina Central del Censo, *Censo General de la República de Nicaragua de 1920* (Managua, 1920).

2. See Harold Playter, *Nicaragua, A Commercial and Economic Survey* (Washington, D.C., 1927), pp. 33–36; J. M. Caldera, *Guía Industrial de Nicaragua* (Managua, 1923), appendix. The employment estimate is based on the fact that these smaller sugar

mills employed approximately sixty seasonal workers in nonagricultural tasks. See *La Gaceta*, July 11, 1936. This estimate is shared by the following informants (interviewed in Chinandega, 1984–85) who worked in the mills at various times between 1920 and 1945: José Santos Granera, Eduardo Briceño, Alejandro Malta, Antonio Torres Hernandez, and Alberto Orozco.

3. *El Cronista* (León), October 21, 1934; *Nueva Democracia* (Chinandega), June 16, 1929; interview with Toribio Muñoz, Chinandega, 1985.

4. *El Cronista*, August 1, 1924; "Libro de Actas de la Central de Obreros" (minute book of the Workers Central), Chinandega, 1917–36, in the possession of Toribio Muñoz.

5. Domingo Ramírez, "Apuntes sobre el movimiento obrero chinandegano," unpublished manuscript. Ramírez published excerpts from this manuscript in *Voz de Occidente* (Chinandega), July 10, 1977.

6. *Nueva Democracia*, September 15, 1929; *El Cronista*, October 11, 1933.

7. The last two meanings could also have an ethnic referent, since the process of *mestizaje* of the native population continued until 1920 in Chinandega. As late as 1890 one of the two largest barrios was made up exclusively of Indians with their own lands. The 1920 census lists only fifty *cobrizos* (Indians) in Chinandega but over six thousand *negros* (blacks), 13 percent of the total population. Since there was no discernable Afro-Nicaraguan population in Chinandega, it is probably safe to assume that "negro" referred to Indians who had ceased to define themselves as such.

8. *Nueva Democracia* between May and November 1929 makes numerous references to the "Hero of the Segovias" and condemnations of the "Yanqui intervention." See in particular the issues of June 23 and October 20, 1929.

9. *Información* (Chinandega), August 11, October 18, and November 10, 1935; *El Cronista*, December 21, 1933; *Memorias de la Alcaldía de Chinandega* (Chinandega, 1935 and 1936); *El Democrático* (Chinandega), September 2, 9, and 30, 1934; interviews with Toribio Muñoz and D. Ramírez, Chinandega, 1985.

10. *Información*, December 29, 1935; January 19, May 24 and 31, June 7, 1936; interview with D. Ramírez. The Chinandegan group, while running a presidential candidate had no contact, for example, with the leftist Nicaraguan Workers' party (which only had bases in Managua and Masaya).

11. Somoza appointed Pereira senator two weeks after the coup, "a petición obrera." *Información*, June 28, 1936. Ramírez maintained a critical posture. Thus, one month after the coup he wrote, "When the politicians want to win an election they act like the best socialists in the world . . . later . . . they scream 'communist!' "

12. Domingo Ramírez, "Apuntes,"; interviews with D. Ramírez and Martín Tercero, the only non-PSN leader of the mechanics' union, Chinandega, 1985. Pereira also played the role of mediator between the Somocista and Socialist tendencies in January 1945.

13. For more on the Chinandegan labor movement from 1943 to 1945, see Jeffrey Gould, "To Lead as Equals" (Ph.D. diss., Yale University, 1988), chap. 3.

14. Manuel Santamaría was elected senator (alternate) in 1935 and had been a leader of the radical wing of the obreristas since 1929 (*Nueva Democracia*, June 30, 1929). A PSN militant stated to me in an interview that when Santamaría was a PSN leader in the

forties, he had commented that he considered himself a radical democrat.

15. Interviews with M. Ríos, E. Rivera, A. Malta, A. Hernández, J. Granera, E. Briceño, and J. Galeano, Chinandega, 1985.

16. The tanning industry grew by 8 percent annually between 1945 and 1950 (Economic Commission for Latin America, *Economic Survey of Latin America* [New York, 1967]). In 1946, Chinandegan tanneries produced 41 percent of the nation's leather, worth 313,000 córdobas (U.S. $62,000). Dirección General de Estadísticas y Censos (DGEC), *Anuario Estadístico, 1947* (Managua, 1948). On the tannery owners, see *Tribuna Obrera*, December 12, 1943 and March 5, 1944; *Nueva Democracia*, September 15, 1929; *Nueva Prensa*, May 19, 1946.

17. Interviews with M. Ríos, E. Rivera, A. Malta, A. Hernández, J. Granera, E. Briceño, and J. Galeano, Chinandega, 1985.

18. Leaflet addressed to "A los trabajadores en general," signed by the Comité Ejecutivo del Sindicato de Teneros (Ríos, Briceño, Rivera, Gustavo Martínez, and Armando Miranda.), in the possession of Toribio Muñoz.

19. Interviews with Alberto Orozco and E. Briceño, Chinandega, 1985–86.

20. *La Flecha*, February 11, 1945.

21. Interviews with E. Briceño, M. Ríos, and E. Rivera, Chinandega, 1985–86.

22. Ministry of Labor and Agriculture, *Memorias del Ministerio de Agricultura y Trabajo, 1945* (Managua, 1946); DGEC, *Censo General de la República de Nicaragua, 1950*, vol. 4 (Managua, 1952); oral sources.

23. Interviews conducted between 1984 and 1986 with the informants cited in note 2 above and with the Chinandegan labor activists, Concepcíon Delgado (masons' union), A. Malta (mechanics' union), T. Muñoz (shoemakers' union), José Zelaya (carpenters' union), and Tomás Valle (shoemakers' union) provided the basis for this analysis of workers' culture.

24. *Nueva Prensa*, May 16 and 19, 1946.

25. Archivo Presidencial, AGN (Archivo General de Nicaragua), Box 332, Letter from FOCCH leaders, Delgado, H. Gaitán, A. Orozco, and M. Tercero to A. Somoza G, June 1946. This letter denounces the visit of the Chinandegan Somocistas. Also Archivo Presidencial AGN, Box 332, Telegram from Somoza G. to Justo Sánchez (FOCCH), June 22, 1946, confirming meeting with FOCCH leaders.

26. *Nueva Prensa*, June 12 and 19, 1946.

27. *Nueva Prensa*, July 16, 1946; interview with A. H. Torres, Chinandega, 1985.

28. Interviews with A. H. Torres, A. Malta, and E. Briceño, Chinandega, 1985.

29. *La Noticia*, August 21, 1946; interviews with Martín Tercero (ex-president of the Casa Obrera) and Torres, Chinandega, 1985.

30. This theme will be further developed in chapters 4 and 7. See also Luis Cantarero, "The Economic Development of Nicaragua, 1920–1947" (Ph.D. diss., Iowa State University, 1948), pp. 63 and 210–12. Oficina Central del Censo, *Censo General de la República de Nicaragua de 1920* (Managua, 1920) shows 75 percent of the rural population as *jornaleros* (rural laborers). Nevertheless, since the census was taken in January many peasants would have been working in the cane harvest.

31. *La Noticia*, June 15, 1946; *La Flecha*, January 28, 1948.

32. DGEC, *Anuario Estadístico 1938 and 1947* (Managua, 1948).

33. DGEC, *Censo de la Población, 1950*, vol. 3: *Chinandega* (Managua, 1952).

34. *Nueva Prensa*, February 22, March 7 and 29, 1946.

35. *Nueva Prensa*, March 29, April 24, and November 7, 1946; interviews with the following rural organizers for the FOCCH: Juan Mendoza, C. Delgado, A. Malta, E. Briceño, M. Campos, J. S. Granera, and T. Valle, Chinandega, 1984–86; A. Orozco, El Viejo, 1985.

36. Interview with Alberto Orozco, El Viejo, 1985.

37. Estimate based on DGEC, *Censo de la Población, 1950*, vol. 3: *Chinandega*.

38. *La Flecha*, January 9, 1947; interviews with Mendoza and A. H. Torres (Chinandega, 1985).

39. *El Mundo*, January 26 and March 29, 1949. See chap. 4 for a discussion of the the rebirth of Chinandegan unionism in 1958.

40. With few exceptions the leftist informants used this phrase: "Estábamos principiando." The collective use of the words probably refers to an acknowledgement at the time that few of the organizers had any experience before 1944. However, the phrase is something of an apology for their collective errors and in particular for their relative passivity toward the Somoza regime. Yet it is also a profound lament for the movement they loved so dearly, which was quickly snuffed out by the Guardia.

41. U.S. Department of State General Records, RG 59,817.00/00B 1–1048, National Archives.

42. On rural organizing in the 1940s, see, for example, Clodomiro Moraes, "Peasant Leagues in Brazil" (pp. 453–502); and Petras and Zeitlin, "Agrarian Radicalism in Chile," (pp. 503–32) in *Agrarian Problems and Peasant Movements in Latin America*, ed. Rodolfo Stavenhagen (New York, 1970).

43. Victor Bulmer-Thomas (*The Political Economy of Central America Since 1920* [Cambridge, 1987], p. 134) suggests that the United States finally recognized Somoza, in April 1948, as part of a deal whereby Somoza withdrew the Guardia from Costa Rican soil, thus ensuring the victory of José Figueres's army over the leftist-supported Picado government.

Chapter 4

1. Dirección General de Estadísticas y Censos (DGEC), *Censo Agropecuario de Nicaragua* (Managua, 1952).

2. Interview with Ramón Cándia, San José del Obraje, 1984.

3. Interview with Ramón Cándia.

4. See DGEC, *Boletín de Estadística* 3, no. 8 (1960). Average corn yield per manzana in Chinandega was twelve quintals (twelve hundred pounds) per manzana. Interviews with Ramón Cándia, Juan Suazo, Pedro Suazo, and Armando González, all of whom agreed on approximate corn yield, San José del Obraje, Chinandega, February–March 1985.

5. In 1984, veteran San José campesino activists dictated a history of their land struggles. The original result of their efforts was barely legible or comprehensible. In soliciting their aid so that I might better understand the document, a new twenty-page document, called here "The History of Agrarian Conflict," was in effect created. I cite

this document as Juan Suazo, Ramón Cándia, and Pedro Suazo, "The History of Agrarian Conflict," unpublished manuscript. Many of my interviews, over the following year, had to do with clarifying aspects of the original text. When a statement is based on the text, but clarified in an interview, I will cite both.

6. *La Noticia* (Managua), January 1, 1958; Ubilla Baca was released in December 1958. He organized a guerrilla band and died fighting the Somoza regime, in 1959.

7. *El Centroamericano* (León), May 15, 1958.

8. The figures regarding place of origin of the 28 evicted were obtained from oral interviews and from documents in the possession of the San José community. The Suazos and Cándia also made occupational and geographical identifications of original participants whose names appear in "The History of Agrarian Conflict."

9. Tales of "kind-hearted ricos" from the days before "cotton fever" (as Juan Suazo called it) abound in all of my interviews with Chinandegan veterans of that era, with the exception of sugar mill workers.

10. DGEC, *Censo Nacional de 1950, Agropecuario* (Managua, 1952).

11. DGEC, *Censo Nacional de 1971, Agropecuario* (Managua, 1971).

12. Oficina Central del Censo, *Censo General de la República de Nicaragua de 1920* (Managua, 1920); DGEC, *Censo Nacional, Ocupaciones* (Managua, 1963).

13. *El Centroamericano*, May 7, 1958; *La Noticia*, August 4, 1959. Although I have been unable to identify the political affiliation of Manuel Antonio Baca in the 1890s, most Bacas in León and Chinandega belonged to an anti-Zelaya, regionally based faction of the Liberal party that staged an unsuccessful revolution in 1896. Dr. Timoteo Baca's political activities are much clearer. In 1926 and 1927 he was the principal U.S.-based agent/emissary of the Liberal Constitutionalist revolutionaries, and as such he was closely watched by the FBI. In 1964, Dr. Timoteo Baca (Manuel Antonio's son) was still an important figure in the official Liberal party. See Partido Liberal Nacionalista, *Homenaje a Crisanto Sacasa* (León, 1964).

14. Three documents support this affirmation: a letter found in the archives of the León Cathedral, from a priest, Macario Vargas, dated February 10, 1890, in which he refers to elite attempts to usurp the lands of the Indian Cofradía de Santa Ana; the transcript of an 1895 León court case, circulated by Andrés Ruíz Escorcia (hereafter A. Escorcia) of the Confederación General de Trabajadores and published in *Novedades*, July 28, 1959; and an unedited manuscript written in 1961 by an obscure tailor, Rafael Cantillano. Although many of his affirmations are not yet verified, I assume that Cantillano, the tailor, used primary sources.

15. Azucena Navas et al., *Algunos Elementos Para Un Analisis De Los Períodos Críticos Del Algodón En Nicaragua*, (León, 1983), pp. 4–5.

16. Interviews with the Suazos, Cándia, and Éntimo Sánchez, San José, 1984–86, Rancherías, 1985. Although Regino was no older than the other participants, he was always referred to as "Don Regino."

17. Interviews with Suazos and Cándia, San José, 1984–86.

18. *Diario Oficial*, March 23, 1916; Suazo, Cándia, and Suazo, "The History of Agrarian Conflict," p. 2.; *La Prensa*, March 13, 1961.

19. Interviews with Suazos and Cándia, San José, 1985.

20. The directorate identified from documents in the possession of Juan Suazo.

21. Interviews with Juan Suazo, San José, 1985. Don Juan was clearly the most lucid informant about the San José struggle. He generously allowed me to interview him eighteen times between December 1984 and July 1988.

22. Interview with Juan Suazo, San José, 1985.

23. Information obtained in the Property Register in Managua.

24. Interview with Juan Suazo, San José, 1985.

25. Ibid. The directiva accepted Regino's view up to a certain point. My informants' consistent use of *conquistar* (conquer) to describe the recruitment process is indicative of the type of relation established between the organizer and those he recruited. In Nicaraguan usage, *conquistar* also describes a man's seduction of a woman.

26. Interviews with Armando González Suazo, Cándia, and Suazo, San José del Obraje, February 1985; Suazo, Cándia, and Suazo, "The History of Agrarian Conflict," p. 2. "Ya estorbaban," stated by Ramón Cándia.

27. *Novedades*, June 7, 1958. In 1958, the government inaugurated the town, complete with a church donated by Dr. Baca. Reyes lobbied to name the town Villa Salvadorita, in honor of the widow of the recently slain dictator Anastasio Somoza García.

28. Suazo, Cándia, and Suazo, "The History of Agrarian Conflict," p. 2; *El Centroamericano*, May 7, 1958; interview with Ramón Cándia, December 1984.

29. Suazo, Cándia, and Suazo, "The History of Agrarian Conflict," p. 2.

30. Ibid., p. 3.

31. *El Centroamericano* (León), May 7, 15, 1958; interviews with the Suazos and R. Cándia, San José, 1985. The rebuilding of the boundary markers occasionally involved "planting" wooden posts which then would grow into trees.

32. Suazo, Cándia, and Suazo, "The History of Agrarian Conflict," p. 4.

33. Interview with Ramón Cándia, San José, February 1985.

34. *Novedades*, June 14, 1946; *La Flecha*, June 14, 1956. ISA's company history, Nicaragua Sugar Estates Ltd., *El Ingenio San Antonio, 1890–1953* (Granada, 1953); I examine the ingenio's expansion in "To Lead As Equals" (Ph.D. diss., Yale University, 1988), pp. 116–23; *La Flecha*, June 13, 1956.

35. On Sutiava, see Jeffrey Gould, "La Raza Rebelde: Ethnicity and Class in Sutiava, 1920–1964" (paper delivered at the American Historical Association meetings, Cincinnati, Ohio, December 1988). Interview with Tomás Pérez, León, October 1983; *Novedades*, March 21–28, 1958; *La Prensa*, March 22–29, 1958; *La Hora*, March 26, 1958.

36. *El Gran Diario*, March 25, 1958; *La Prensa*, March 25, 1958.

37. Victor Bulmer-Thomas, *The Political Economy of Central America Since 1920* (Cambridge, 1989), p. 169.

38. *La Prensa*, April 12, 1958.

39. *Novedades*, April 19, 1958; *La Prensa*, April 19, 1958.

40. Interviews with Antonio Torres Hernández, Alejandro Malta, Jacinto Galeano, Alberto Orozco, and Manuel Antonio Gutiérrez, Chinandega, 1983–86; *La Prensa*, March 25, 1958.

41. *La Prensa*, March 25, 1958; *Novedades*, March 25, 1958.

42. *La Noticia*, April 27, 1958.

43. *La Prensa*, April 2 and 17, 1958; interviews with Eduardo Guardado, Chinandega, 1985, Éntimo Sánchez, Rancherías, 1985, Juan Suazo, and Ramón Cándia, San José, 1985. *La Hora*, April 19, 1958.

44. Azucena Navas et al., *Dos etapas* (León, 1983), p. 13; also see Robert Williams, *Export Agriculture and the Crisis in Agriculture* (Chapel Hill, N.C., 1986), pp. 13–73; Pedro Belli, "Prolégomeno para una historia económica de Nicaragua, 1905–1966," *Revista del Pensamiento Centroamericano* 30, no. 146 (January–March, 1975): 2–30.

45. Azucena Navas et al., *Dos etapas* (León, 1983), p. 13; also see Robert Williams, *Export Agriculture and the Crisis in Agriculture* (Chapel Hill, N.C., 1986), pp. 13–73; Pedro Belli, "Prolégomeno para una historia económica de nicaragua, 1905–1966," *Revista del Pensamiento Centroamericano* 30, no. 146 (January–March, 1975): 2–30.

46. Navas et al., *Dos etapas*, p. 2.

47. International Bank for Reconstruction and Development (IBRD), *Current Economic Position and Prospects of Nicaragua* (Washington, D.C., August 14, 1962), p. 2; Navas et al., *Dos etapas*, p. 4.

48. International Bank for Reconstruction and Development (IBRD), *Current Economic Position and Prospects of Nicaragua* (Washington, D.C., August 14, 1962), p. 2; Navas et al., *Dos etapas*, p. 4; Williams, "Export Agriculture," pp. 197–98. The decline in cotton acreage also includes that large area devastated by the eruption of the Cerro Negro volcano in 1958.

49. Navas et al., *Dos etapas*, p. 5; *La Flecha*, September 24, 1958; *Novedades*, March 8, 1958. DGEC, *Boletín de Estadísticas* 3, no. 8 (Managua, 1960). Textile production, for example, dropped from 7.2 million yards in 1955 to 6.2 million yards in 1957. Also see IBRD, *Current Economic Position and Prospects of Nicaragua*, p. 3.

50. During the growing year 1958–59, the average yield in Chinandega was 11.25 quintals (1,125 pounds) per manzana. No other department in Nicaragua averaged more than 9.9 (DGEC, *Boletín de Estadísticas* 3, no. 8); interviews with the Suazos and Cándia.

51. *El Centroamericano*, May 7, 1958.

52. Ibid., May 15, 1958.

53. *Registro de Propiedad* (Managua), no. 554, tomo 7, folio 20 and 21, and tomo 147, folio 47. In 1921, in exchange for banana lands on the Honduran coast, Samuel Zemurray sold Campuzano to General Alvarado for $33,000 (in addition to the Honduran plantations). For a discussion of the deed, see Jeffrey Gould, "To Lead as Equals" (Ph.D diss., Yale University, 1988), p. 277.

54. Julio Ycaza Tigerino, *Discursos Parlamentarios* (Mexico City, 1975), pp. 76–94; Doña Tesla must have been a trifle nervous about her own lawyer, Meza y Salorio, for he was Alfonso Juarez's father-in-law. Later, in 1958, she would fire Meza.

55. *El Centroamericano*, May 15, 1958; *La Noticia*, September 27, 1959.

56. *Novedades*, August 16, 1958; *La Noticia*, September 9, 1958.

57. *Novedades*, August 16, 1958; *Gran Diario*, October 22, 1958; *El Centroamericano*, October 17, 1958.

58. *La Noticia*, April 16, September 13, and October 1, 1958.

59. Suazo, Cándia, and Suazo, "The History of Agrarian Conflict," p. 4.

60. Interview with Juan Suazo, June 1985. An article recounting Astacio Cabrera's

prison experience appeared in *El Nuevo Diario*, September 21, 1986.

61. In "The History of Agrarian Conflict" the first sentence of the quote is attributed to Colonel Rodríguez. After many interviews and collective discussions, the Suazos and Ramón Cándia agree on Escobar's words.

62. An earlier draft of "The History of Agrarian Conflict," with more input from Cándia, contains this quote. It was subsequently substantiated by the other key witnesses.

63. Interviews with the Suazos and Ramón Cándia.

64. Interviews with Suazo, Cándia, and Suazo; Suazo, Cándia, and Suazo, "The History of Agrarian Conflict," p. 5.

65. Interviews with the Suazos, Cándia, Eduardo Guardado, and Éntimo Sánchez.

66. Criminal Docket in Corte de Apelaciones, León, "Tesla de Alvarado v. Regino Escobar y 64 mas, October 24, 1958," *Amparo de Posesión*, Legajo, Folio 69.

67. Ibid., December 20, 1958, annotation "salida." Suazo, Cándia, and Suazo, "The History of Agrarian Conflict," p. 6.

68. Interview with Hugo Astacio Cabrera, Chinandega, September 1985. Astacio's memory about his activities as a legal counsel to Deshon is quite vague.

69. Suazo, Cándia, and Suazo, "The History of Agrarian Conflict," p. 6; interviews with Ramón Cándia, the Suazos, and Astacio Cabrera; *El Gran Diario*, June 3, 1958 cites a new five córdoba fee to use the fishing grounds.

70. Suazo, Cándia, and Suazo, "The History of Agrarian Conflict," p. 6; interviews with Ramón Cándia, the Suazos, and Astacio Cabrera.

71. Suazo, Cándia, and Suazo, "The History of Agrarian Conflict," p. 6; interviews with Ramón Cándia, the Suazos, and Astacio Cabrera.

72. Suazo, Cándia, and Suazo, "The History of Agrarian Conflict," p. 6; interviews with Tonaleños Ruperto Mayorga, Engracia Zapata, and Mariano Escorcia, 1985.

73. Suazo, Cándia, and Suazo, "The History of Agrarian Conflict," p. 6; interviews with Cándia and J. Suazo. Eduardo Guardado, a Chinandegan jeweler, who served as an intermediary between the CGT and the campesino movement from 1961 to 1964, in several interviews in 1985 argued that Regino was merely trying to avoid payment of Buitrago's fees.

74. *El Centroamericano*, February 9, 1956 for Callejas's arrest. He publicly attacked Buitrago on July 28, 1959. A. Escorcia would later accuse Buitrago of swindling San José funds (letter in possession of author). The Suazos and Cándia deny they ever signed this letter.

75. The Suazos, Cándia, and González identified the group from a community census in the possession of the group, drawn up by the CGT, in 1961.

76. *La Noticia*, April 5, 1959; *El Centroamericano*, April 5, 1959.

77. *La Prensa*, May 9, 1959; *Novedades*, May 7, 1959; interviews with Tomas Perez, León, November 1983; Gerónimo Morales, León-Sutiava, October 1983. See also Gould, "La Raza Rebelde."

78. *La Prensa*, May 9, 1959; *El Gran Diario*, May 9, 1959.

79. *La Prensa*, May 19, 1959; *La Noticia*, May 19, 1959.

80. *La Noticia*, May 19–22, 1959; *La Prensa*, May 19–20, 1959.

81. *Novedades*, May 30, 1959; *La Noticia*, May 29, 1959; *La Prensa*, May 30, 1959.

82. *Novedades*, May 21–23, 1959; *La Noticia*, May 23, 1959; Suazo, Cándia, and Suazo, "The History of Agrarian Conflict," p. 12; interviews with San José informants.

83. *La Prensa*, May 20, 1959.

84. Callejas's articles appear in *La Noticia*, May 23, 24, and 26, 1959. There are two possible explanations for Callejas's aid to the campesinos. He may have become Deshon's paid agent several months later. In that case, his earlier attempt at dividing the organization was actually gratuitous labor. The more sinister possibility is that he was already an agent for Deshon and Campuzano when the campesinos were jailed and that he attacked Campuzano and defended the San José campesinos in order to more effectively infiltrate the movement. Suazo, Cándia, and Suazo, "The History of Agrarian Conflict," p. 13.

85. *Novedades*, December 31, 1958; *La Prensa*, January 14, 1959.

86. Juan Martínez-Alier, *Los Huachilleros de Perú* (Lima, 1973); Eric Hobsbawm, "Peasants and Politics," *Journal of Peasant Studies* 6, no. 1 (October 1973): 3–22.

87. Interviews with Suazos, Cándia, Tomás Pérez, and Gerónimo Morales; 1895 León Court Transcript. The best existing study on Sutiava can be found in Richard N. Adams, *Cultural Surveys of Panama, Nicaragua, Guatemala, El Salvador, and Honduras* (Detroit, 1976), pp. 238–55.

88. Interview with Marcos Amaya, Sutiava, 1988.

89. See Adams, *Cultural Surveys*, pp. 238–55.

90. *La Prensa*, May 12, 1959. DGEC, *Chinandega* (Managua, 1964).

91. Interview with Juan Suazo, June 1985; *El Centroamericano*, July 19, 1959; *La Noticia*, July 24–28, 1959.

92. Suazo, Cándia, and Suazo, "The History of Agrarian Conflict," pp. 15–16. Interview with Juan Suazo, June 1985, October–December 1985. *La Noticia*, July 28, 1959. Fredi Callejas told a radically different tale. He claimed that Buitrago tried to get the campesinos to plead guilty to lesser charges. Callejas, in this version, valiantly persuaded Regino to hold out. In light of all we know about Fredi and about Juan Suazo, Fredi's story seems pathologically but purposefully fanciful.

Chapter 5

1. Michael Jimenez, in a highly perceptive commentary (for which I am very appreciative) on a preliminary version of this material, used this phrase, "learning curve of experience." [Latin American Labor History Conference. New Haven, April 1986]; *La Noticia*, September 22, 1959; *Novedades*, September 22, 1959.

2. Juan Suazo, Ramón Cándia, and Pedro Suazo, "The History of Agrarian Conflict," unpublished manuscript, p. 18; interviews with Cándia and the Suazos. The written version suggested unity at the time of A. Escorcia's arrival.

3. *La Noticia*, September 22, 1959; *Novedades*, September 27, 1959.

4. *La Noticia*, September 27, 1959; *Novedades*, September 27, 1959.

5. *La Noticia*, September 27, 1959.

6. For a discussion of the "Prussian road" to agrarian capitalism, see the classic analysis of Barrington Moore, *The Social Origins of Democracy and Dictatorship* (Boston, 1966); Theda Skocpol, *States and Social Revolution* (Cambridge, 1979),

pp. 106–10; Alain de Janvry, *The Agrarian Question and Reformism in Latin America* (Baltimore, 1981), pp. 95–136.

7. Numerous references to Reyes's activities as a renter of ejidal lands to campesinos were made in public and private reports of the CGT during the months of July and December 1961 (communiques in possession of A. Escorcia, Managua). According to interviews with Éntimo Sánchez, Gerónimo Carrasco, Rancherías, 1984–85; Mónico Avilés, Puente Real, Chinandega, 1986; and Eduardo Guardado, Chinandega, 1984–85, Reyes's rents were at least twice as high (300 córdobas a month) as those of peasants of middle-sized farms in the Grecia area.

8. *Novedades*, February 24, 1960.

9. On Guerreros's role in the ejidal conflict, the CGT reports of 1961 refer amply to her relation to Reyes. Also *La Prensa*, July 8, 1962. The informants cited in note seven all claim that indeed Irma Guerrero, who several years later would become the "dictator" of Chinandega, was the mistress of Dr. Reyes.

10. The Deshons were intermarried with the Callejas family, the preeminent Liberal oligarchical family. In the late 1950s a Callejas was mayor of Chinandega and in the late 1960s a Callejas Deshon was vice president of Nicaragua. The patriarch of the Alvarado family had been a Central American Liberal revolutionary hero and had been involved in a revolution in Honduras in the early twenties (he escaped to Chinandega) and then again as a fighter on the side of the democratic forces in Salvador and Guatemala in the 1940s. That political prestige enhanced the national political clout of his son Virgilio.

11. *La Prensa*, September 12, 1961.

12. Interviews with the Suazos, Ramón Cándia, San José, 1985; and Mónico Avilés, Puente Real, 1986. On the expropriation of the Cofradía, see Jeffrey Gould, "To Lead as Equals" (Ph.D diss., Yale University, 1988), p. 318.

13. *El Centroamericano*, December 3, 1959; *Novedades*, January 7, 1960; *La Noticia*, January 6 and December 30, 1960.

14. The church as an institution did not seem to play a major role in their lives. Certain beliefs had a religious aspect, for example a belief in the nearby presence of evil-spirited dwarfs (*duendes*). The communal land had been called San José del Duende. The account of San Martin is based on oral sources, in particular, Juan Suazo, San José, 1986, 1988.

15. *Impacto*, July 5 and 27, 1960.

16. See, for example, Carlos Vilas, *The Sandinista Revolution* (New York, 1986), p. 63. Though Vilas's analysis of rural class structure is fine, his use of the term "itinerant proletariat" does not allow for the relatively stable proletariats of San José and Tonalá.

17. *La Prensa*, July 21, 1961; *La Noticia*, July 20, 1961.

18. Interviews with Juan Suazo, San José, 1985; Éntimo Sánchez, Rancherías, 1985; and Felix Cándia, San José, 1985.

19. See Unión Panamericana, *América en Cifras 1960*, no. 6 (Washington D.C., 1960), pp. 10–22, and *América en Cifras 1963*, no. 5 (Washington D.C., 1965), pp. 90, 111; U.S. Department of Labor, *Labor Digest*, no. 53 (Washington D.C., 1964); and "Estadística Industrial, 1961" (Managua, 1962). The August 18, 1961 issue of the

progovernment newspaper *Novedades* states that field laborers in the area were paid three to five córdobas per day.

20. Interviews conducted in 1983–85 with Éntimo Sánchez, Gerónimo Carrasco, Rancherías; Oscar Osejo, El Viejo; and Felix Cándia, San José.

21. This illegal form of delaying payments was denounced consistently by the CGT (documents in the possession of A. Escorcia). Some of the communiques were synthesized in *La Prensa*, August 3, 1961. Also see *Novedades*, August 18, 1961.

22. *La Noticia*, October 29 and 30, 1960; *La Prensa*, October 30, 1960.

23. *La Prensa*, February 8 and 14, 1961. Interviews with Pedro Suazo, Ramón Cándia, Gerónimo Carrasco, Éntimo Sánchez, and E. Guardado.

24. Interviews with Pedro Suazo, Ramón Cándia, Gerónimo Carrasco, Éntimo Sánchez, and E. Guardado. *La Prensa*, February 10, 1961.

25. *La Prensa*, February 10 and 14, 1961.

26. *La Prensa*, February 8 and 14, 1961.

27. *La Prensa*, February 15, 1961.

28. *La Prensa*, February 14, 1961.

29. Ibid.

30. *La Prensa*, February 14–15 and 21 and March 5, 1961. Narrative also based on interviews with the participants: the Suazos, the Cándias, Guardado, Avilés, Sánchez, and Carrasco and their comments on "The History of an Agrarian Conflict," p. 22

31. Interviews with the Suazos, the Cándias, Guardado, Avilés, Sánchez, and Carrasco.

32. Ibid.; *La Prensa*, February 10, 1961.

33. Many studies of peasant mobilization suggest, in contrast to the San José experience, that if organization is not externally induced, peasant actions are usually spontaneous. Similarly, many scholars emphasize the material self-interest involved in agrarian movements. For two important examples from different perspectives, see Eric Hobsbawm, "Peasants and Politics," *Journal of Peasant Studies* 6, no. 1 (October 1973): 3–22; and Henry Landsberger and Cynthia Hewitt, "Ten Sources of Weakness and Cleavage in Latin American Peasant Movements," in *Agrarian Problems and Peasant Movements in Latin America*, ed. Rodolfo Stavenhagen (New York, 1970).

34. *Impacto*, September 22 and 28, 1960; *La Noticia*, September 17, 1960. Interviews with Alejandro Malta and Eduardo Briceño, Chinandega, 1985.

35. *La Prensa*, March 25, 1958.

36. See *Hispanic American Report* 14 (July 1961): 400. See chapter 8 for a discussion of Somoza's relations with the labor movement.

37. Interviews with A. Escorcia, Eduardo Guardado (Escorcia's liaison in Chinandega), and Juan Suazo.

38. Ibid.

39. *La Prensa*, March 5, 1961.

40. *La Prensa*, March 6, 1961.

41. *La Noticia*, March 7, 1961; interview with A. Escorcia.

42. *La Prensa*, September 3, 1961.

43. *La Prensa*, March 18, 1961. The commission claimed that the campesinos had a right through *prescripción extraordinaria*. Although the commission had no legal

authority, its actions and findings were politically significant. The group of professionals belonged (along with A. Escorcia) to an embryonic political party that would later in the year emerge as the Partido Acción Revolucionaria (PAR), a short-lived moderate leftist group. See Gould, "To Lead as Equals," p. 322.

44. *La Prensa*, April 24, 1961; interview with A. Escorcia.

45. Telegram from A. Escorcia to Juan Suazo, in the possession of A. Escorcia. On Regino Escobar's suffering at the hands of the National Guard, see *Impacto*, June 29, 1960, and Suazo, Cándia, and Suazo, "The History of Agrarian Conflict." On the links between his death and the beatings, see chapter 6. All informants believed that Regino's death in August 1961 was caused by the Guardia.

46. *Novedades*, April 30 and May 3, 1961; *La Noticia*, May 3, 1961; *La Prensa*, May 3, 1961; interviews with Juan Suazo, Ramón Cándia, Mónico Avilés, Éntimo Sánchez, and Gerónimo Carrasco.

47. *Novedades*, April 30 and May 3, 1961; *La Noticia*, May 3, 1961; *La Prensa*, May 3, 1961; interviews with Juan Suazo, Ramón Cándia, Mónico Avilés, Éntimo Sánchez, and Gerónimo Carrasco.

48. *Hispanic American Report* 14 (July 1961): 400; interview with A. Escorcia.

49. Data on Nuevos Ejidos groups comes from a census drawn up by the CGT, which was then analyzed separately by various informants including Éntimo Sánchez, Gerónimo Carrasco, Eduardo Guardado, and Mónico Avilés.

50. On Somoza's agrarian reform proposal in 1961 (modified in a conservative direction before its enactment in 1963), see Moises Poblete Troncoso, *La Reforma Agraria en America Latina* (Santiago, 1961), pp. 160–62; on the Alliance for Progress, see de Janvry, *The Agrarian Question*, and Ernest Feder, "Counterreform," in *Agrarian Problems and Peasant Movements in Latin America*, ed. Rodolfo Stavenhagen (New York, 1970), pp. 173–224.

51. On Reyes's court victories, see *Novedades*, February 24, 1960; *La Prensa*, March 15, 1961; *El Centroamericano*, March 14, 1961. On the ejidal grant, see *La Gaceta*, January 28, 1916; on the dispute with Campuzano, see *La Gaceta*, March 8, 1918, and *La Verdad* (Chinandega), February 3, 1918. By 1918, the municipality had claimed only 1,000 hectares and later a total of 2,000 manzanas.

52. This affirmation is based on interviews with representatives of both groups.

53. This affirmation is based on interviews with representatives of both groups.

54. *La Noticia*, May 11, 1961; *La Prensa*, May 16, 1961.

55. *La Prensa*, May 13, 1961; *El Centroamericano*, May 11–12 and 14, 1961; interview with Sutiava leader, T. Perez.

56. Despite the repudiation of campesino activists in Sutiava and Chinandega, Argeñal would continue to define himself as a campesino "leader" or "protector." In the 1970s he served as congressional deputy, and today he resides in Miami, actively supporting the "democratic resistance."

57. *La Prensa*, June 8, 1961.

58. Ibid.; interviews with Éntimo Sánchez and Mónico Avilés.

59. *La Prensa*, June 8, 1961.

60. Ibid.

Chapter 6

1. See E. P. Thompson, "Eighteenth-Century English Society: Class Struggle without Class?" *Social History* 4, no. 2 (May 1978): 133–65.

2. Before 1930 a peón would have had to enlist in the army of his patron's party. After the last Liberal-Conservative civil war, in 1927, the peón also had to vote for or attend rallies in support of the hacendado's political party. In return, the patrón owed the campesino the means to subsistence—access to hacienda land for planting, hunting, fishing, and wood gathering.

3. Jaime Biderman, "Class Structure, the State and Capitalist Development in Nicaraguan Agriculture" (Ph.D diss., University of California, Berkeley, 1982), p. 93.

4. Ibid., p. 94.

5. William Roseberry, "Images of the Peasant in the Consciousness of the Venezuelan Proletariat," in *Proletarians and Protest*, ed. Michael Hanagan and Charles Stephenson (Westport, Conn., 1986), which is also the source of the epigraph to this chapter, and "Domestic Modes, Domesticated Models," *Journal of Historical Sociology* 1, no. 4 (December 1988): 423–30. Lowell Gudmundson, *Costa Rica before Coffee: Society and Economy on the Eve of the Export Boom* (Baton Rouge, La., 1986).

6. See among Eric Wolf's many stimulating works, *Peasant Wars of the Twentieth Century* (New York, 1969). James Scott's theoretical contributions to the study of peasant revolt are found in *The Moral Economy of the Peasant: Rebellion and Subsistence in South East Asia* (New Haven, Conn., 1976) and "Hegemony and the Peasantry," *Politics and Society* 7, no. 3 (1977): 267–96.

7. E. P. Thompson, in "Eighteenth-Century English Society," states: "Hence the contest for symbolic authority may be seen, not as a way of acting out ulterior 'real' contests, but as a real contest in its own right" (p. 159). Thompson argues that the symbolic contest in England was so important "owing to the weakness of other organs of control: the authority of the Church is departing, and the authority of the schools and mass media had not arrived" (p. 158). In Chinandega, church and education were not influential and radio had just arrived in the villages.

8. Raymond Williams, *Marxism and Literature* (Oxford, 1977), p. 122. Also see Paul Willis and Phillip Corrigan, "Orders of Experience: Working Class Social Forms," *Social Text* 7 (Spring and Summer 1983): 85–103; and Juan Martínez-Alier, *Los Huachilleros en Perú* (Lima, 1973), pp. 75–79.

9. *La Noticia*, June 27, 1961

10. *La Prensa*, July 5, 1961; *Novedades*, July 6, 1961.

11. *La Prensa*, July 21, 1961; *El Centroamericano*, July 20, 1961; interview with Éntimo Sánchez, Rancherías, January 1985; interview with Mónico Avilés, Puente Real, Chinandega, November 1985.

12. *Novedades*, July 20, 1961; *La Prensa*, July 26, 1961.

13. *Novedades*, July 22, 1961.

14. "Communique of the CGT," August 21, 1961, in the possession of A. Escorcia, Managua.

15. Telegram from Edmundo Deshon to A. Escorcia, August 29, 1961, in possession of A. Escorcia.

16. Descriptive account (unpublished) in the possession of A. Escorcia; *La Prensa*, September 5, 1961; interviews with E. Sánchez and M. Avilés.

17. *Novedades*, September 6, 1961; *La Prensa*, September 6, 1961; interviews with Sánchez and Avilés.

18. *Novedades*, September 6, 1961; *La Prensa*, September 6, 1961; interviews with Sánchez and Avilés.

19. *Novedades*, September 6, 1961; *La Prensa*, September 6, 1961; interviews with Sánchez and Avilés.

20. Interview with A. Escorcia, Managua, June 1985; *La Prensa*, September 10, 1961; *La Noticia*, September 9, 1961; CGT communique, September 9, 1961, in possession of A. Escorcia.

21. *La Prensa*, September 8 and 9, 1961; interview with A. Escorcia, Managua, 1985.

22. *La Prensa*, September 10, 1961.

23. Interview with A. Escorcia; *La Noticia*, September 9, 1961; *La Prensa*, September 10, 1961

24. CGT document in possession of A. Escorcia.

25. See James Scott, "How Traditional Rural Patrons Lose Their Legitimacy," in *Friends, Followers and Factions*, ed. Steffen Schmidt et al. (Berkeley, Calif., 1977), p. 447. He argues that "fundamental social right" to subsistence served as the legitimizing cornerstone of patron-client relations. Scott's theoretical construct was itself influenced by E. P. Thompson, who in the "Moral Economy of the English Crowd" (*Past and Present*, no. 50 [February 1971]: 76–136), defined the "moral economy" of the eighteenth-century English poor as "a popular consensus as to what were legitimate and illegitimate practices in marketing, milling, baking, etc. This in turn, was grounded upon a consistent traditional view of social norms and obligations, of the proper economic function of several parties within the community" (p. 79). See Roseberry's perceptive critique of the use of moral economy to analyze contemporary cultures in "Images of the Peasant."

26. My analysis of traditional Chinandegan cultural forms is based on interviews with thirty informants (aged sixty or over) during the period October 1984–February 1986.

27. CGT Communique, August 21, 1961.

28. For the San José view of the ejidal conflict in August 1961, see Jeffrey Gould, "To Lead as Equals" (Ph.D. diss., Yale University, 1988).

29. "Chinandegan campesinos" refers here to those other than the San José campesinos. On gifts, Pierre Bourdieu writes: "Giving is also a way of possessing (a gift which is not matched by a counter-gift creates a lasting bond, restricting the debtor's freedom and forcing him to adopt a peaceful, cooperative, prudent attitude)." Pierre Bourdieu, *Outline of a Theory of Practice* (New York, 1977), p. 195.

30. The proximity of symbolic and violent forms of struggle relates to Bourdieu's analysis of "symbolic violence," or domination. He writes in *Outline* (p. 191) that in precapitalist economies there is "a great need for symbolic violence" because "it cannot count on the implacable, hidden violence of objective mechanisms, it resorts simultaneously to forms of domination which may strike the modern observer as more brutal

. . . more barbarous, or at the same time, as gentler, more humane, more respectful of persons." For a good history of the National Guard, see Richard Millet, *The Guardians of the Dynasty* (Maryknoll, N.Y., 1977).

31. René Herrera Zúñiga, "Nicaragua: El Desarrollo Capitalista y la Crisis de la Dominación Burguesa," *Foro Internacional* 20, no. 4 (April 1980): 627. For an excellent analysis of the Somocista state, see Carlos Vilas, *The Sandinista Revolution* (New York, 1986), pp. 98–101.

32. *La Prensa*, September 13, 1961.

33. *La Prensa*, September 19, 1961.

Chapter 7

1. Interview with Mariano Escorcia, Tonalá, July 4, 1985; Dirección General de Estadísticas y Censos (DGEC), *Censo de la Población*, vol. 4 (Managua, 1952).

2. Ira Katznelson, *City Trenches* (New York, 1981), pp. 25–45.

3. Herbert Gutman, *Work, Culture, and Society in Industrializing America* (New York, 1976), pp. 3–78.

4. Registro de Propiedad (Managua), no. 554, tomo 203, folios 93 and 94; and tomo 107, folios 112 and 113. Also see Heriberto Carillo, "Origen de la Comundidad Indígena de El Viejo," Supplemento Dedicado al Virgen del Hato *Alerta* (1977): 7–10, esp. 9.

5. Alfonso Valle, *Interpretación de Nombres Geográficos Indígenas de Nicaragua* (Managua, 1944), p. 162.

6. Interviews with Pablo Guido, Domingo Castillo, Ramón Cándia, Juan Suazo, and Ruperto Mayorga, 1985–86.

7. *Memorias de la Recaudador General de Aduanas, 1938* (Managua, 1939); DGEC, *Anuario de Estadísticas de 1938* (Managua, 1939).

8. *Memoria de la Recaudador General, 1939* (Managua, 1940).

9. See John Coatsworth, "Railroads, Landholding, and Agrarian Protest in the Early Porfiriato," *Hispanic American Historical Review* 54 (February 1974): 48–71. While Coatsworth discusses the far more dramatic impact of the modernization of Mexican transportation, his insights certainly have relevance in the Chinandegan case, with respect to the eventual consequences of the Puerto Morazán line, but also with respect to the promise of the highway to Somotillo (completed in 1962), which undoubtedly had an important impact on the development of the agrarian conflicts, especially those over the Nuevos Ejidos.

10. *Registro de Propiedades* (Managua), no. 554, tomo 147, folios 20, 47, and 48. The 1903 land deed to Campuzano includes the area that later formed El Paraíso. In 1920, the sale from Samuel Zemurray "Sam, the banana man" to the Honduran, liberal general, Ernesto Alvarado, cites Campuzano's western border with El Paraíso, then owned by the López family.

11. November 10, 1943, U.S. Department of State General Records, RG 59,817. 861.31, National Archives. *La Noticia*, June 15, 1946.

12. See n. 6 above. Also see José M. Zelaya, "Agriculture in Nicaragua," Pan American Union (Washington, D.C., 1945), pp. 24–25.

13. Pablo Guido, 1984; Mayorga, 1985.

14. DGEC, *Censo General de la República de Nicaragua, 1950*, vol. 4 (Managua, 1952), p. 304.; A document found in the municipalities collection of the Nicaraguan Archivo Nacional, dated July 26, 1951, confirms that Somoza gave a "titulo provisional al pueblo como un obsequio" (a gift of provisional deed to the people); Julián Guerrero and Lola Soriano, *Chinandega* (Managua, 1964), p. 198.

15. Various informants used this phrase to describe their village.

16. The 1950 estimate is based on the number of rural "Por Cuenta Propia" (neither employers nor employees) in the municipality of Puerto Morazán in the 1950 census.

17. The 1960 estimate is based on the number of "Por Cuenta Propia" in the municipality of Puerto Morazán in the 1963 census.

18. Descriptions of sales "al futuro" to "acaparadores" were offered by most informants as the standard selling practice for tenants and smallholders. Also see International Bank for Reconstruction and Development (IBRD), *The Economic Development of Nicaragua* (Baltimore, Md., 1953), p. 313; Jaime Biderman, "Class Structure, the State and Capitalist Development in Nicaraguan Agriculture" (Ph.D. diss., University of California, Berkeley, 1982), p. 100.

19. Interview with Engracia Zapata, Corinto, 1985.

20. Interview with Mariano Escorcia, El Viejo, 1985.

21. Guerrero and Soriano, *Chinandega*, p. 198; interviews with Ruperto Mayorga, Chinandega, 1984–85.

22. Dirección General de Estadísticas y Censos, *Boletín de Estadísticas* 3, no. 2 (1956): 30; José Tigerino Medrano, *Breves Apuntes Sobre la Mano de Obra en el campo* (Managua, 1962), pp. 21–27.

23. Interview with Pablo Guido, Tonalá, 1984.

24. Interview with Pablo Guido.

25. Estimate of profits based on Azucena Navas et al., *Algunos Elementos Para Un Analisis De Los Períodos Críticos Del Algodón En Nicaragua*, (León, 1983). Pedro Belli, "Prolégomeno para una historia económica de Nicaragua, 1905–1966," *Revista del Pensamiento Centroamericano* 30, no. 146 (January–March, 1975): 29; Robert Williams, *Export Agriculture and the Crisis in Agriculture* (Chapel Hill, N.C., 1986), pp. 28–34; Biderman, "Class Structure," p. 179.

26. Williams, *Export Agriculture*, pp. 48–51; Biderman, "Class Structure," p. 105; Orlando Nunez, *El Somocismo y el Modelo Capitalista Agro-Exportador* (León, 1980), pp. 101–5; interviews with Pablo Guido, Domingo Castillo, Mariano Escorcia, 1984–85; and Engracia Zapata, Corinto, 1985.

27. International Bank for Reconstruction and Development (IBRD), *Current Economic Position and Prospects of Nicaragua* (Washington D.C., February 11, 1955), p. 7; *La Prensa*, March 7, 1959; *El Centroamericano*, January 31, 1959.

28. The occupational statistics come from DGEC, *Censos Nacionales* for 1950 and 1963 and refer to the municipality of Morazán. The laborer percentage for the town of Tonalá probably declined slightly during the period.

29. Estimate based on number of rural, eonomically active residents in category of "Por cuenta propia" in the municipality of Puerto Morazán, in the 1963 census. The village of Tonalá included one-half of the municipality's population.

30. Jaime Biderman, "The Development of Capitalism in Nicaragua," *Latin American Perspectives* 10, no. 36 (Winter 1983): 7–32. Biderman argues, following Alain de Janvry, that "functional dualism" was an important part of Nicaragua's development. In general terms, the Chinandegan case shows few people who fit into the model, such as the smallholders of Tonalá.

31. Such elite accusations against campesinos were not new. What was different in 1961 was the intensity of the antagonism and the violent threats of the hacendados.

32. DGEC, *Censos Nacionales de 1963* (Managua, 1967); interview with Engracia Zapata, Corinto, 1985.

33. Interview with Mariano Escorcia, El Viejo, 1985.

34. Tonaleños complained about having to obtain commodities at RATAS, or hacienda stores, where the prices were marked up by 300 to 400 percent. The testimony is unclear as to the mechanism whereby the hacendados would coerce them to buy on the haciendas since they did not live there. In a few cases the hacendados still payed in scrip, "vales" as late as 1960, and thus could coerce worker consumption.

35. Communique of the CGT dated August 3, 1961, in the possession of A. Escorcia; *La Prensa*, August 29, 1961.

36. CGT communique, July 31, 1961, in the possession of A. Escorcia; the Tonalá union claimed that the hacendados built a private road to Chinandega.

37. *Novedades*, August 18, 1961; *La Prensa*, August 23, 1961.

38. Archivo Municipal AGN (Archivo General de Nicaragua), document dated July 26, 1951; CGT communique, July 31, 1961; interviews with A. Escorcia, Managua, 1985, and Ruperto Mayorga, Chinandega, 1985.

39. *La Prensa*, August 1, 1961; CGT communique, July 31, 1961.

40. Interviews with Leoncio Martínez, Corinto, 1985–86, and with A. Escorcia, Managua; and Engracia Zapata, Corinto, 1985.

41. CGT communique, August 10, 1961.

42. *La Prensa*, September 15, 21, and 23, 1961.

43. Interview with Ruperto Mayorga, Chinandega, 1985.

44. CGT communique, October 3, 1961; also see *La Prensa*, October 9, 1961.

45. CGT communique, October 3, 1961; also see *La Prensa*, October 9, 1961. interviews with Mariano Escorcia, Domingo Castillo, Eduardo Guardado, Engracia Zapata, and Pablo Guido, 1984–86.

46. Interview with Mariano Escorcia, El Viejo, 1985.

47. CGT communique, October 25, 1961, in the possession of A. Escorcia; interviews with Mariano Escorcia, El Viejo, 1985; and Ruperto Mayorga, Chinandega, 1985.

48. Interview with Mariano Escorcia, El Viejo, 1985.

49. Interviews with Leoncio Martínez, Corinto; Domingo Castillo, Tonalá; and Engracia Zapata, El Viejo, 1984–86.

50. Interview with Mariano Escorcia, El Viejo, 1985.

51. Document found in the possession of the San José community, entitled, "Decreto Oficial por la Espoza del Presidente general José Santos Zelaya," March 28, 1911. I have been unable to verify the authenticity of the document.

52. Untitled document written by Cantillano in 1961 at the behest of the Tonalá

union. Many witnesses claim that Cantillano possessed a large trunk that contained hundreds of papers from the Zelaya era (they were burned accidentally during the 1978 insurrection). Since I have been able to verify many of the facts in Cantillano's four-page manuscript, I assume that he used authentic documents as well as oral tradition passed on to him by his uncle who worked in some administrative capacity for Zelaya.

53. Before 1946, the Tonalá area belonged to the municipality of El Viejo. Liberals rolled up ten to one majorities over the Conservatives in El Viejo in the elections of 1924, 1928, and 1932. See Consejo Nacionale Elecciones, *Informe Sobre las elecciones de 1924 y 1928* (Managua, 1929). Liberal party sources show over 90 percent of Tonalá adult inhabitants enrolled in the party in 1962. For the department as a whole, 60 percent were registered Liberals. José Zepeda Alaníz, "Resúmen Comparativo de las Inscripciones," January 19, 1962.

54. Centro de Investigaciones de la Reforma Agraria (CIERA), *Por Eso Defendemos Las Tierras: Historia Agraria de las Segovias Occidentales* (Managua, 1984), pp. 101–15; Gustavo Niederlin, *The State of Nicaragua* (Philadelphia, 1898); Valeria Blais, *Nicaragua, Condizioni Naturali ed Economiche* (Rome, 1925), p. 58; Also see the "Ley Agraria" of 1903 reprinted in *Guía de Nicaragua* (Managua, 1906), pp. 22–48.

55. Interview with Pablo Guido. Other informants including Ramón Cándia, Leoncio Martínez, Eduardo Guardado, Domingo Castillo, and Éntimo Sánchez on different occasions made similar statements.

56. On the concept of common ground, see Juan Martínez-Alier, *Hacienda, Plantations and Collective Farms* (London, 1977).

57. Article 57, in *Constitution of the Republic of Nicaragua, 1950* (Washington D.C., 1954), pp. 10–11; Article 71 called for land reform: "The State shall encourage the proper division of uncultivated large landholdings [latifundios] and will favor the preservation of medium and small rural holdings."

58. See Moisés Poblete Troncoso, *La Reforma Agraria en América Latina* (Santiago, 1961), pp. 168–70. Luis Somoza sent an agrarian reform bill to the Congress in August 1961, five months after Kennedy unfolded the Alliance for Progress plan. The bill only became law in April 1963. The unusually long delay between its introduction and its approval reflected the opposition of agrarian interests inside and outside of the regime. The law was much more generous to landlords than was the original bill.

59. See Alain de Janvry, *The Agrarian Question and Reformism in Latin America* (Baltimore, 1981), pp. 264–68; Silvia Terán, "Formas de Conciencia Social de los Trabajadores del Campo," *Cuadernos Agrarios* 1, no. 4 (October–December 1976): 20–36.

60. Interview with Pablo Guido, Tonalá, 1985.

61. See Martínez-Alier, *Haciendas, Plantations, and Collective Farms*, p. 137; Luisa Paré, *El Proletariado Agrícola en México* (Mexico City, 1977), p. 165.

62. Interviews with Mariano Escorcia, Leoncio Martínez, Ruperto Mayorga, Engracia Zapata, and Pablo Guido, 1984–86.

63. *La Prensa*, July 5, 1961; *Navedados*, July 6, 1961.

64. "Ley Agraria" of 1903, in *Guía de Nicaragua* (Managua, 1906). The 1917 agrarian law, still in effect in 1962, did not alter the 1903 law substantially. Interviews

with Mariano Escorcia, A. Escorcia, Leoncio Martínez, and Engracia Zapata.

65. *La Noticia*, January 6, 1962; *La Prensa*, January 4, 1962. Mariano Escorcia, however, remembers how mortified he was when, upon leaving prison several days later, he learned from his fellow campesinos that Radio Havana had broadcast his name as a peasant leader. Personal contact between the Left and the Tonalá, Nuevos Ejidos, and San José groups was extremely limited before 1963. Although FSLN pioneer Germán Pomares was from El Viejo, he left the area to fight in the central highlands and thus had no contact with the Tonalá movement in 1962, according to union informants.

66. Interview with M. Escorcia, El Viejo, 1989.

67. Interview with M. Escorcia, El Viejo, 1985.

68. Interview with Pablo Guido, Tonalá, 1984.

69. Interview with Pablo Guido, Tonalá, 1985.

70. Interview with Leoncio Martínez, Corinto, 1986.

71. *La Prensa*, January 5, 1962. M. Escorcia does not recall citing the donation.

72. *La Prensa*, January 5, 1962. "Our only leader is our necessity" does not appear in the article but was recalled by M. Escorcia.

73. Interviews with Guido, Martínez, E. Zapata, and Mariano Escorcia. Each of the statements in the narrative was corroborated by at least three informants.

74. William Roseberry, "Images of the Peasant in the Consciousness of the Venezuelan Proletariat," in *Proletarians and Protest*, ed. Michael Hanagan and Charles Stephenson (Westport, Conn., 1986), pp. 149–69.

Chapter 8

1. Jaime Wheelock, *Imperialismo y Dictadura*, rev. ed. (Havana, 1980), pp. 141–89.

2. Harry W. Strachan, *Family and Other Business Groups in Economic Development: The Case of Nicaragua* (New York, 1976), pp. 9–14.

3. Victor Bulmer-Thomas, *The Political Economy of Central America* (Cambridge, 1987), pp. 190–99.

4. Dirección General de Estadísticas y Censos, (DGEC) *Boletín de Estadístico* 3, no. 2 (1956). Consumer prices went down 10 percent following this study. The minimum wage was set in June 1963 at 8.4 córdobas for urban workers and 7.6 córdobas for rural workers. Also see Jeffrey Gould, "To Lead as Equals" (Ph.D diss., Yale University, 1988), p. 418.

5. *Orientación Popular*, July 3, 1960, quoted in Gustavo Gutiérrez Mayorga, "El reformismo artesanal en el movimiento obrero nicaragüense," *Revista de Pensamiento Centroamericano*, no. 159 (April–June 1978): 2–21; Juan Lorío, *Nuestra Cuestión Sindical* (Managua, 1961), p. 16.

6. *Impacto*, June 21, 1960; *La Noticia*, June 24 and September 7, 1960.

7. *La Noticia*, July 7, 1960.

8. *La Noticia*, July 9–10, 1960; *Impacto*, July 7, 1960; Lorío, *Nuestra Cuestión Sindical*.

9. Ministry of Labor, *Memorias del Ministerio de Trabajo, 1952–57* (Managua, 1958) and *Memorias del Ministerio de Trabajo, 1957–62* (Managua, 1963). A revision

of periodical sources subtantiates this claim. See also Gutiérrez, "El reformismo artesanal."

10. Lorío, *Nuestra Cuestión Sindical*, p. 23.

11. *La Noticia*, June 24 and October 20, 1960.

12. *La Prensa*, October 19, 21, 23–24, 1960; interview with Tomás Pravia, Matagalpa, 1989.

13. The Managua shoeworkers also went on a strike, which ended with the storm. *La Noticia*, June 24, 1960; *Impacto*, June 14, 16, 21, 27; August 24; and September 29, 1960; Lorío, *Nuestra Cuestión Sindical*, pp. 34–38. *La Noticia*, October 29–30, 1960; citation from Lorío, *Nuestra Cuestión Sindical*, p. 37.

14. *Hispanic American Report* 14 (January 1961): 781. The one exception to urban labor passivity under the state of siege was a PSN-led printers' strike in March 1961. Ten shops, with 140 printers, joined the strike, but it failed because of lack of support from the CGT and perhaps also red-baiting in the press. See A. Escorcia, *Informe del Comité Ejecutivo al VIII Congreso del CGT "Regino Escobar"* (Managua, 1964), p. 9. *La Noticia*, March 3, 1961; *La Prensa*, March 7, 1961.

15. *La Noticia*, May 3, 1961; *Novedades*, May 3, 1961; *La Prensa*, May 3, 1961.

16. *Hispanic American Report* 14 (July 1961): 400.

17. See Table 2. Also see John Ryan et al., *Area Handbook for Nicaragua* (Washington, D.C., 1970), p. 267; U.S. Department of Labor, *Labor Law and Practice in Nicaragua* (Washington, D.C., 1964), pp. 39–40.

18. Lorío, *Nuestra Cuestión Sindical*, p. 10.

19. Ibid., p. 33.

20. See "Libro de Actas del Sindicato Campesino de Realejo" (minute book of the campesino union), El Realejo, September 1961–March 1962. The Somocistas began an unsuccessful organizing drive on the Posoltega banana plantation in August 1961 (*Novedades*, August 26, 1961; *La Prensa* August 9, 1961) followed by a PSN organizational drive on the same plantations; interviews with Alberto Orozco, Angel Zelaya, and Manuel Antonio Gutiérrez.

21. Hugh Thomas, *The Cuban Revolution* (New York, 1977), p. 533.

22. Shepard Forman, "The Significance of Participation," in *Political Participation in Latin America*, ed. John Booth and Mitchell Seligson (New York, 1979), pp. 41–42.

23. The task of camouflaging the class interests of Somocistas would become increasingly difficult when the protest movement expanded throughout the region.

24. Cesar Barahona, *La Noticia*, January 23, 1962.

25. Speech reproduced in *La Vanguardia*, June 1962.

26. DGEC *Censos Nacionales*, vol. 5, 1963 (Managua, 1967) lists 18,195 office workers and 12,143 professionals as well as 1,200 higher-level managers. This salaried middle class represented about 5 percent of the nation's economically active population (EAP) but some 20 percent of the urban EAP. While it is more difficult to measure the growth of the self-employed professionals, there is no doubt that the Reyes group was a typical expression of urban middle-class involvement in agriculture. On middle-class professional cotton growers, see Robert Williams, *Export Agriculture and the Crisis in Agriculture* (Chapel Hill, N.C., 1986), pp. 22–35

27. On Astacio Cabrera's jail sentence, see *El Nuévo Diario*, September 21, 1986.

For an intelligent example of the progressive wing of the PLI's position on agrarian reform, see Adan Selva, *En Defensa del Pueblo: Contra la Dinastía* (Managua, 1961).

28. Ignacio Briones Torres, "Angustia y Esperanza en Nicaragua," *Combate* 3, no. 17 (1961): 44–50. It is worth noting that the Sandinistas and the left-wing alliance group known as Movilización Republicana had close connections to the PSN.

29. There are some important exceptions. The Partido Acción Revolucionaria (PAR), a small group of social democratic professionals in Managua, through their ties to A. Escorcia attempted to aid the campesinos. Some of the Chinandegan militants attended seminars of the PAR during the reign of Juan Angel López (1962–64). Similarly, the Movilización Republicana, with ties to the PSN and to the pro-Cuban student movement, allowed the FSLN to work through its party structure from 1963 to 1966. The FSLN made important contacts with workers in Corinto and El Viejo, usually working through contacts with the PSN youth wing.

30. *Novedades*, April 25–26, 1957; *El Gran Diario*, October 29, 1958.

31. DGEC *Censos Nacionales*, vol. 5, 1963 (Managua, 1967).

32. *Impacto*, May 7, 1960; Ryan et al., *Area Handbook for Nicaragua*, p. 291.

33. See Gould, "To Lead as Equals," pp. 444–46; *Gran Diario*, October 16, 1958.

34. A. Escorcia, *Informe Presentado por el Comité Ejecutivo de la CGT al VIII Congreso "Regino Escobar"* (Managua, 1964).

35. Telegram from Roberto Zepeda to A. Escorcia, June 19, 1961, in the possession of A. Escorcia, Managua; *La Prensa* August 30, 1961; A. Escorcia, *Informe Presentado*, pp. 2–6.

36. *Novedades*, February 23–24, 1962; *La Prensa*, February 24, 1962.

37. *Novedades*, February 28, 1962; *La Prensa*, February 25, 1962; *La Noticia*, March 1, 1962; A. Escorcia, *Informe Presentado*, pp. 2–3.

38. *La Noticia*, March 1, 1962.

39. *Novedades*, June 18, 1961; *Flecha*, September 24, 1961; Jaime Biderman, "Class Structure, the State and Capitalist Development in Nicaraguan Agriculture" (Ph.D. diss., University of California, Berkeley, 1982), p. 179; interviews with Mariano Escorcia, El Viejo; E. Zapata, Corinto; and Pablo Guido, Tonalá, 1984–86.

40. Interview with M. Escorcia, El Viejo, 1985.

41. Interview with M. Escorcia; also see *La Prensa*, February 28, 1962; *El Centroamericano*, March 1, 1962; *La Noticia*, March 1, 1962; *Hispanic American Report* 15 (April 1962).

42. *La Prensa*, February 29, 1962.

43. *El Centroamericano*, March 6, 1962; *La Noticia*, February 22, 1962.

44. *Novedades*, February 28, 1962; "Libro de Actas del Sindicato Campesino de Realejo," March 22, 1962.

45. Interviews with Manuel Campos, El Realejo, 1985. Campos's story was substantiated by long-term friends José Chevez and José Madríz, El Realejo, 1985.

46. Archivo Presidencial AGN (Archivo General de Nicaragua), Box 69, Letter from Campos to "Sr. Ministro de Cultos, December 9, 1950; and letter freeing Campos, from Minister Salmeron (Gobernación) to the mayor of El Realejo, December 14, 1950.

47. "Libro de Actas del Sindicato Campesino de Realejo," September 14, 1961.

48. *El Realejo*, March 4, 1962; interviews with Campos and Madriz, El Realejo, 1985–86.

49. *El Realejo*, March 4, 1962; interviews with Campos and Madriz, El Realejo, 1985–86; *El Centroamericano*, March 6, 1962.

50. Sidney Mintz ("Rural Proletarians and the Problem of Rural Proletarian Consciousness," *Journal of Peasant Studies* 1, no. 3 [1974]: 310) defines "individualization" as a key component of class consciousness: "The objectification of labor and the alienation of the laborer enables the individual to objectify himself as regards traditional social forms." The Chinandegan workers appear to have engaged in this type of self-objectification. But they have done so, at least in part, collectively. Mintz's astute analysis does seem particularly relevant to the problems of individual responsibility and authoritarianism in collective action.

51. "Libro de Actas del Sindicato Campesino de Realejo," March 4, 1962: "Acordamos Participar de la Huelga de Corinto."

52. Ibid., February 22, 1962: "Representamos a la Huelga de Corinto."

53. Florencia Mallon, "Peasants and Rural Laborers in Pernambuco," *Latin American Perspectives* 4 (Fall 1978): 68.

54. For an interesting argument about the importance of semiproletarians—peasant laborers—in the Salvadoran revolutionary movement, see Carlos Cabarrús, *Génesis de una revolución: analisis del surgimiento y desarrollo de la organización campesina en El Salvador* (Mexico City, 1983), pp. 363–65.

55. *La Noticia*, March 2, 1962.

56. Ibid., March 16, 1962.

57. A. Escorcia, *Informe Presentado*, p. 3; *La Noticia*, March 3 and 8, 1962.

58. *La Noticia*, March 1, 1962; "Libro de Actas del Sindicato Campesino de Realejo," March 4, 1962.

59. *La Noticia*, March 15 and February 20, 1962; interviews with Mónico Avilés, Puente Real; Éntimo Sánchez, Rancherías; and Eduardo Guardado, Chinandega.

60. *Novedades*, February 21, 1962; *La Prensa*, February 23, 1962. Interviews with Mariano Escorcia, El Viejo, 1985–86; Leoncio Martínez, Corinto, 1986; Pablo Guido, and Domingo Castillo, Tonalá, 1984–86.

61. Interview with A. Escorcia, Managua, November 2, 1985. Escorcia's version is substantiated by interviews with his intermediary in Chinandega, Eduardo Guardado. Also see *La Prensa*, March 23, 1962, which refers to the conversation between Somoza and Escorcia.

Chapter 9

1. On the recruitment of Ramírez, see *La Prensa*, February 23, 1962; *La Noticia*, February 28, 1962. Many inhabitants of Puerto Morazán moved to the hacienda Palacios following the destruction of the railroad in 1960. Ramírez aided in their struggle for land by writing newspaper articles and pressuring the regime. See *La Prensa*, October 5, 1961; and Domingo Ramírez, "Apuntes Históricos del Movimiento Obrero en Chinandega" (unpublished manuscript). On January 23, 1961, Ramírez presented the case of the Morazán campesinos to President Luis Somoza at a rally

attended by some 5,000 campesinos (*Novedades*, January 25, 1962).

2. Account published in *La Noticia*, March 28, 1962. Mariano Escorcia, Leoncio Martínez, Pablo Guido, Domingo Castillo, and Engracia Zapata substantiated Ramírez's account.

3. *La Noticia*, March 28, 1962; Ramírez in the article and in person confirmed this account.

4. *La Noticia*, March 15, 1962.

5. *La Noticia*, March 18, 1962.

6. *La Prensa*, November 9, 1961.

7. All campesino informants considered those members of the Reyes group as "campesinos ricos." Also see *Novedades*, April 3, 1963.

8. Interviews with A. Escorcia and Eduardo Guardado. *Novedades*, February 22, 1962; *El Centroamericano*, April 7, 1961.

9. *La Prensa*, April 4, 1963.

10. *Novedades*, March 22, 1962; Ramírez, "Apuntes Históricos"; *El Centroamericano*, April 7, 1961.

11. The name perhaps reflected a measure of popular defiance by turning an elite epithet into an expression of pride. From this point on the Nuevos Ejidos group will be called Rancherías. See A. Escorcia, *Informe Presentado por el Comité Ejecutivo de la CGT al VIII Congreso "Regino Escobar*, (Managua, 1964), p. 21. Interviews with E. Sánchez, E. Guardado, and M. Avilés.

12. *Novedades*, April 9, 1962; *La Nación*, April 27, 1962. Interviews with E. Sánchez, Gerónimo Carrasco (Rancherías), and Mónico Avilés, Puente Real, 1985.

13. Interviews with Juan Suazo, Pedro Suazo, Ramón and Felix Cándia, San José, 1984–86; Éntimo Sánchez, Rancherías, 1985; and Mónico Avilés, Puente Real, 1986.

14. *La Noticia*, April 14, 1962; Juan Suazo, Ramón Cándia, and Pedro Suazo, "The History of Agrarian Conflict," unpublished manuscript. Also see Jeffrey Gould, "To Lead as Equals" (Ph.D diss., Yale University, 1988), pp. 484–86.

15. Although Somoza had ceded the hacienda Palacios to the Morazán inhabitants, their leader was arrested again in April 1962. See *La Noticia*, April 14, 1962. Cañanlipe, located about twenty-five kilometers northeast of San José, was the scene of a conflict between campesinos and latifundistas including the Montealegres. In April 1962, campesinos were arrested for protesting high land rents and the fencing of public lands. *La Noticia*, April 28, 1962; *La Prensa*, April 25, 1962.

16. Interview with Ramón Cándia, San José, 1985.

17. Interviews with Juan Suazo, Pedro Suazo, Ramón and Felix Cándia, Éntimo Sánchez, and Mónico Avilés.

18. Eliseo Velásquez, for example, an obrerista of the thirties, as mayor of Chinandega gave the ejidal land to Reyes. Three other obrerista leaders had become hard-line anticommunist supporters of Juan Angel López. *La Noticia*, February 7, 1964.

19. On Irma's cultivation of peasant support, see *La Noticia* April 11, 1964 and *La Prensa*, June 17, 1964. On her anticampesino activities, see *La Prensa*, June 6, 1962.

20. See Archivo Presidencial AGN (Archivo General de Nicaragua), Box 81. "Letter from Ricardo Alvarado to A. Somoza," 1967. Alvarado discusses the Chinandegan struggle between Irma Guerrero and Vice President Callejas Deshon. He also accuses

Guerrero of being the "intellectual leader of a mafia" and of being a "terrateniente por todo parte." The Montealegres, with two cabinet ministries, were close allies of the opposing Deshon-Callejas faction.

21. On Zelaya's appointment, see *La Prensa*, April 17, 1961; on his well-known alliance with Irma Guerrero, see Archivo Presidencial AGN, Box 81, "Letter from Ricardo Alvarado to A. Somoza," 1967.

22. Thus, for example, in December 1963, President Schick, who succeeded Somoza in May 1963, sent the Chinandegan jefe político orders to stop charging a personal tax on mangrove bark (Archivo Municipal AGN, Box 77, December 20, 1963). Schick's telegram to Nororí stated: "No puede cobrar por mangle."

23. For government employment, see U.S. Department of Labor, *Labor Law and Practice in Nicaragua* (Washington D.C., 1964).

24. Interview with A. Escorcia, Managua, 1985.

25. Interview with Juan Suazo, San José, 1986.

26. Ibid. This statement came after a year of interviews and was extremely painful for Don Juan. I am very grateful for his candor.

27. Interview with Mónico Avilés, Puente Real, Chinandega, 1985.

28. Handwritten letter to A. Escorcia dated November 1963 from Tonalá campesina (probably Cristina Hernández).

29. Interview with Éntimo Sánchez, Rancherías, 1984.

30. Interview with Mónico Avilés, Puente Real, February 1986. On A. Escorcia and political language, see interviews with the Suazos, Éntimo Sánchez, Mónico Avilés, Gerónimo Currasco, Mariano Escorcia, and E. Guardado.

31. Typed letter to President Luis Somoza signed by San José leaders, in possession of A. Escorcia, Managua.

32. *La Noticia*, January 19, 1962.

33. Another letter signed by the San José leadership makes the same charges and adds, "desmentimos de una vez por todas el decir calumnioso contra el Secretario General de la C.G.T. Sr. Andrés Ruíz Escorcia" (Once and for all we reject the calumny against Escorcia). A. Escorcia possesses several other documents that neither the Suazos nor Cándia remember signing.

34. A. Escorcia sincerely believed in the goals of the campesino movement and indeed suffered arrests and death threats. Nonetheless, the way he narrates his own role in the movement suggests that he believed or wished to believe that the campesinos could only act under his leadership.

35. Interviews with E. Sánchez, M. Avilés, J. Suazo, and G. Carrasco.

36. Interview with Juan Suazo, San José, 1980. Somoza quotation cited in interview with Domingo Sánchez, Managua, 1989.

37. Interview with Éntimo Sánchez, Rancherías, 1984; *La Noticia*, April 25, 1962; *El Centroamericano*, April 25, 1962.

38. *La Noticia*, April 25, 1962; *El Centroamericano*, April 25, 1962. The highway also drove up land values and increased the resolve of the Reyes group to hold on to the land.

39. *La Noticia*, April 25, 1962; *El Centroamericano*, April 25, 1962; A. Escorcia, *Informe Presentado*, p. 21; *La Prensa*, April 25, 1962.

40. *La Noticia*, May 3, 1962; *La Prensa*, May 3–4, 1962.

41. *El Centroamericano*, May 19, 1962; "Libro de Actas del Sindicato Campesino de Realejo" (minute book of the campesino union), El Realejo, June 2, 1962.

42. *El Centroamericano*, May 19, 1962; "Libro de Actas del Sindicato Campesino de Realejo" (minute book of the campesino union), El Realejo, June 2, 1962; interview with Alberto Orozco, El Viejo, 1984. Following this incident Clemente Guido apparently joined the FSLN in the central highlands.

43. David Radell, *Historical Geography of Western Nicaragua* (Berkeley, Calif., 1969), p. 252; *La Prensa*, June 2, 1962 and May 24, 1962; *Hispanic American Report* 15 (August 1962): 505.

44. See map in Radell, *Historical Geography*, p. 251. *La Prensa*, June 3 and 8, 1962.

45. *La Prensa*, June 6, 1962; interviews with Alberto Orozco and Manuel Antonio Gutiérrez, the secretary general of the Chinandegan Workers' Federation in 1962.

46. Following his presidential term, Luis Somoza became an active leader in the stockbreeders' association and its representative on the Instituto Agrario Nicaragüense. INFONAC was clearly annoyed with the plantation owners Baquillard and Mántica (*La Prensa*, May 24, 1962).

47. *Hispanic American Report* 15 (July 1962): 408.

48. *La Prensa*, May 4, 1962; The "cemetery of failed ideology" quotation was attributed to Roberto González, a Somocista labor leader since the 1940s.

49. *La Noticia*, May 18–19, 1962; *La Prensa*, May 18, 1962; interviews with D. Ramírez, E. Sánchez, and M. Avilés.

50. *La Prensa*, May 26–27, 1962.

51. *La Prensa*, June 2–3, 7, and 9, 1962; interview with Alberto Orozco. The union did not recover from the blow.

52. *La Noticia*, June 1 and 9, 1962.

53. *La Noticia*, June 9, 12–13, 1962; *El Centroamericano*, June 13, 1962; interviews with M. Avilés, A. Escorcia, and E. Sánchez.

54. *La Noticia*, June 14, 1962.

55. Ibid.; *Novedades*, June 15, 1962.

56. *Novedades*, June 15, 1962. All reports list two separate arrests of 32 and 87 campesinos. *Novedades* claims that all 117 (instead of 119) were released, but *La Noticia* claims that only 87 were released.

57. Convenio signed by A. Escorcia and Argeñal Papi before Comandante Rodríguez Somoza, June 13, 1962. Reproduced in *La Noticia*, June 17, 1962.

58. Ibid.

59. On Astacio's honors, see *La Noticia*, June 12, 1962. Astacio apparently did act as the lawyer of the Rancherías campesinos in June 1962.

60. Interview with Éntimo Sánchez.

Chapter 10

1. Interviews with Entimo Sánchez, Rancherías, 1985; Eduardo Guardado, Chinandega, 1985; Gerónimo Carrasco, Rancherías, 1984; and Monico Avilés, Puente Real, 1986.

2. *Orientación Popular*, September 21, 1963; *La Prensa*, January 29, 1964; *La Noticia*, January 29 and 31, 1964.

3. Norma Stoltz Chinchilla, "Women in the Revolutionary Movements," in *Revolution in Central America*, ed. Stanford Central American Network (Boulder, Colo., 1983), p. 427; Aida Redondo Lobo, "La mujer en la construcción de la nueva sociedad," in Richard Harris and Carlos Vilas, eds., *La Revolución en Nicaragua* (Mexico City, 1985), p. 244.

4. I arrived at these figures through a comparison of the categories "jefes de familias—mujeres" in the 1950 and 1963 censuses.

5. My study of Chichigalpan birth certificates demonstrates that the number of illegitimate births rose from 60 percent of the total number of births in 1903 to 77.5 percent in 1919. However, we cannot equate the census category of illegitimacy with female heads of families; it referred solely to the mother's marital status. Assuming "free union" status when an unrelated male registered the illegitimate birth, these figures suggest that the percentage of female heads of households probably increased from approximately 25–30 percent to perhaps 40 percent during the first two decades of the century.

6. Similarly, in two of the three departments where jornaleros formed less than 50 percent of the labor force, the illegitimacy rate was under 35 percent. Moreover, those departments with high jornalero populations and low illegitimacy rates were in the relatively more "backward" central highlands—Estelí, Chontales, and Matagalpa. Similarly Masaya, with a lower jornalero population and high illegitimacy, is a predominantly urban-based department.

7. Oficina Central del Censo, *Censo General de la República De Nicaragua de 1920* (Managua, 1920). The census was taken in January, during the sugar and coffee harvests. Apparently very few Chinandegans migrated to the coffee zones. Since the sugar plantations were quite close to the urban core, it is somewhat doubtful that the harvest would have affected the census results with regard to gender (it would, however, have tended to lump all seasonal laborers into the jornalero categrory). The 1950 census taken during the dead season shows a notable increase in the sex ratio.

8. Dirección General de Estadísticas y Censos (DGEC), *Censo de la República de Nicaragua, 1950* (Managua, 1952). Even if we take into account the differential between the number of widowers and widows, women still represented 59 percent of the urban population.

9. Ministry of Development, "Informe del Jefe Político Tigerino," *Memorias del Ministerio del Fomento* (Managua, 1916).

10. These figures are based on an examination of tax rolls in the *Libro del Alcalde* (Chinandega, 1928 and 1932). Florencia Mallon in "Gender and Class in the Transition to Capitalism" (*Latin American Perspectives* 13, no. 1 [Winter 1986]: 154) argues that in Peru men dominated interprovincial and international commerce, while women dominated other spheres. Chinandegan women seem to have made a bit more progress in the realm of nonlocal commerce.

11. *El Centroamericano*, November 4, 1920.

12. Ibid., September 7, 1922.

13. DGEC, *Censo de la República, 1950*, vol. 3 (Managua, 1952).

14. DGEC, *Censo de la República, 1963* (Managua, 1967).

15. *La Prensa*, June 7, 1956; *Novedades*, April 28, 1960; *Impacto*, June 6, 1960.

16. The 1950 census shows 888 female domestic servants in Chinandega (total departmental population was 81,000).

17. Anna Rubbo and Michael Taussig, "Up Off Their Knees: Servanthood in Southwest Colombia," *Latin American Perspectives* 10, no. 39 (Fall 1983): 19.

18. See Elsa Chaney and Mary Garcia Castro, eds., *Muchachas No More: Household Workers in Latin America and the Caribbean* (Philadelphia, 1989); Grace Esther Young, "The Myth of Being Like a Daughter," *Latin American Perspectives* 14, no. 54 (Summer 1987): 365–80; Ximena Bunster and Elsa Chaney, *Sellers and Servants: Working Women in Lima Peru* (New York, 1985). All of these works document in different ways challenges to paternalistic ideology of household workers.

19. Oral testimony suggests that often ten servants worked in the homes of the wealthiest families of the elite. For a historical perspective on the colonial roots of the "big house" phenomenon, see Bunster and Chaney, *Sellers and Servants*, pp. 25–30.

20. Interview with Uriel Somarriba, Chichigalpa, 1983.

21. Michael Jiménez, "Incautious Women and Their Bastard Children: Patriarchy in Crisis and the Roots of Rural Rebellion in Central Colombia, 1900–1930" (Paper delivered at the Latin American Labor History Conference, New Haven, Connecticut, 1987), pp. 31–32. Jiménez has published a revised version of this paper, entitled "Gender, Class, and the Roots of Peasant Rebellion in Central Columbia, 1900–1930," in *Everyday Forms of Peasant Resistance*, ed. Forrest Colburn (Armonk, N.Y., 1989).

22. Interviews with Chinandegan workers. The department of Chinandega, with a population in 1963 of 128,000, had over five hundred houses of prostitution. See, for example, *La Flecha*, September 25, 1958.

23. *La Flecha*, September 25, 1958.

24. Jeffrey Gould, "La Raza Rebelde: Ethnicity and Class in Sutiava, 1920–1960" (paper delivered at the American Historical Association meetings, Cincinnati, Ohio, December 1988).

25. Cándida Pastrán had worked as the director of the new elementary school founded in 1959. She energetically had defended her husband and other arrested campesino rebels. See *La Noticia*, May 23, 1959. According to the Cándias and the Suazos, Regino's widow's betrayal after Regino's death was so complete that after the revolution of 1979 she publicly condemned the San José organization for taking over Deshon's lands.

26. Interview with Hugo Astacio Cabrera, Chinandega, 1985.

27. On the concept of "masculinization," see Deborah Levinson, "Gender and Class in the Guatemalan Labor Movement" (paper delivered at the Fourth Annual Conference on Latin American Labor History, Yale University, April 1987).

28. *La Prensa*, September 22, 1956.

29. Interview with Engracia Zapata, Corinto, 1986.

30. Women represented about 15 percent of the militants in the San José organization in 1958 and 30 percent of the organization in 1962. In Tonalá, women represented at least 30 percent of the militants in 1961 and increased subsequently. More Tonaleñas worked in cotton when the union began. Already in 1952, fifteen thousand Nicaraguan

women worked in the cotton harvest which then employed some fifty thousand workers. (U.S. Department of State General Records, RG 59,817.00/12–2452, National Archives).

31. The Sutiavas participated primarily as auxiliaries in a movement dominated by men. In this sense the women's organization resembled the housewives committees that emerged in Bolivia during the early 1960s. Gloria Ardaya Salinas ("The Barzolas and the Housewives Committees," in *Women and Change in Latin America*, ed. June Nash and Helen I. Safa [South Hadley, Mass., 1986], pp. 326–43) strongly criticized such auxiliary groups.

32. *El Gran Diario*, March 28, 1958; Ernestina Roque belongs to one of the principal lineages in Sutiava and one that played vital roles in protest movements in the twenties and fifties.

33. June Nash, "Resistance as Protest: Women in the Struggle of Bolivian Tin Miners," in *Women Cross-Culturally: Change and Challenge*, ed. Ruby Rohrich-Leavitt (The Hague, 1973), pp. 261–71.

34. Temma Kaplan, "Female Consciousness and Collective Action: The Case of Barcelona, 1910–1918," *Signs: Journal of Women in Culture and Society* 7, no. 3 (Spring 1982): 545.

35. Ibid., p. 564.

36. Ibid., p. 565.

37. Letter to A. Escorcia from Tonaleño campesina militant, November 1963, in the possession of A. Escorcia, Managua.

38. *La Noticia*, November 8, 1963; interviews with Felipe Marcia, Ton Valle, El Viejo, 1985; E. Zapata; and L. Martínez; On "El Hato," see *La Noticia*, June 20 and 30, 1962.

39. Letter from San José campesinos addressed to Luis Somoza, April 1963, in the possession of A. Escorcia. While some informants attribute this letter and the following one to Celina Meza, other evidence suggests that the author was Victoria Munguía.

40. See, for example, A. Escorcia's letter to *La Prensa*, December 27, 1961 and CGT communiques from June–September 1961.

41. *La Prensa*, March 3, 1963.

42. Callejas wrote the articles for *La Noticia*, April 16 and 23, 1963. On the Guardia's subsequent actions, see Pedro Suazo's denunciations in *La Prensa*, April 19–20, 1963; interview with Pedro Suazo, San José del Obraje, 1983.

43. Letter to A. Escorcia from San José female militant, April 1963, in possession of A. Escorcia.

Chapter 11

1. See Robert Williams, *Export Agriculture and the Crisis in Central America* (Chapel Hill, N.C., 1986); and Victor Bulmer-Thomas *The Political Economy of Central America* (Cambridge, 1987).

2. See U.S. Department of Labor, *Labor Law and Practice* (Washington D.C., 1964), pp. 33–49; the reforms included penalties for late payments, broadened social security, and labor code protection for government employees.

3. *La Prensa*, June 12, 1963 to June 28, 1964. Mechanization, stalled by the 1962 strike, proceeded rapidly in 1963 and threatened unemployment. The FSLN participated in the Corinto unions, signifying an important step in overcoming political cultural divisions (*La Prensa*, June 14, 1963).

4. *Novedades*, December 4, 1963. On the repression of López against the leftists, see *Orientación Popular*, July 21 and September 21, 1963.

5. "Informe del Presidente de la Junta Directiva a la Junta de Accionistas" (report of the president of the San Antonio sugar mill to the stockholders), February 1965; *La Prensa*, December 15, 1964; *La Noticia*, December 15, 1964.

6. *La Noticia*, December 15–16, 1964. The workers were aware that the world sugar price had increased by some 500 percent since the Cuban Revolution. Interviews with Alfonso Cerda and Esteban Cano, Chichigalpa, 1983.

7. *La Prensa*, December 15–16, 1964. According to this account, ISA suffered losses of three million dollars during the strike. However, that figure was vastly inflated by the company or the newspaper for its propagandistic value, since ISA produced only some twelve million dollars worth of sugar during the four-month zafra. See *La Prensa*, December 17, 1964.

8. Soon Managua textile and construction workers engaged in four major strikes. See *La Prensa*, issues throughout September 1965. Before these strikes, during the first two years of the Schick administration (1963–65), there were twenty-two strikes. In Chinandega, there were strikes at ISA, Corinto, banana planatations, the cotton gin of La Virgen, and bakeries Novedades, June 26, 1965.

9. The martyred FSLN leader Carlos Fonseca wrote of the 1963–65 period, "The first defeat [Bocay 1963] led to a position marked with a reformist streak." Fonseca, "Zero Hour," in *Nicaragua: the Unfinished Revolution*, ed. Peter Rosset and John Vandermeer (New York, 1986), pp. 174–75.

10. Interview with Leoncio Martínez, Corinto, 1985.

11. Rodolfo Mejía Ubilla, "Problemática de la Reforma Agraria," *Revista Conservadora del Pensamiento Centroamericano* 10, no. 59 (August 1965): 34.

12. *La Gaceta*, February 9, 1963.

13. Cristóbal Rugama, *La Reforma Agraria de Nicaragua* (Managua, 1976), pp. 8–11. After one year of operation, IAN faced a backlog of ten thousand land disputes. *La Prensa*, August 6, 1965.

14. Rodolfo Mejía Ubilla, "Problemática de la Reforma Agraria," *Revista Conservadora del Pensamiento Centroamericano* 10, no. 59 (August 1965): 34.

15. Rugama, *La Reforma*, p. 8. Although many of the 16,500 "titled" peasants had settled in the frontier departments of Jinotega, Matagalpa, Boaco, Chontales, and San Juan before the institute started functioning in July 1964, the promise of an IAN title stimulated many other families to migrate.

16. On the Alliance for Progress, see Alain de Janvry, *The Agrarian Question and Reformism in Latin America* (Baltimore, Md., 1981); Rodolfo Stavenhagen, ed., *Agrarian Problems and Peasant Movements in Latin America* (New York, 1970); Poblete Troncoso, *La Reforma Agraria en America Latina* (Santiago, 1961).

17. *La Gaceta*, February 9, 1963, p. 886.

18. Estimate based on *Censo Agropecuario*, 1952 (Managua, 1952).

19. Mejía Ubilla, "Problemática de la Reforma Agraria," p. 34.

20. Luis Somoza, "Origen, Aplicación y Problemas de la Ley de Reforma Agraria," *Revista Conservadora* 10, no. 59 (August 1965): 76.

21. *La Noticia*, January 22, 1965.

22. U.S. Department of State General Records, RG 59,717/1–30–52, National Archives. The report states that of the 3,500 Guardia in 1952, "700 were off picking cotton or coffee." It is a well known fact that the Somoza's used Guardia labor in their sugar plantation Montelimar.

23. John Ryan et al, *Area Handbook for Nicaragua* (Washington D.C., 1970), p. 235.

24. Mejía Ubilla, "Problemática de la Reforma Agraria," p. 37.

25. *La Prensa*, October 6, 1964.

26. Telegram from A. Terán to Ministro de Gobernación, November 24, 1950, Archivo Presidencial AGN (Archivo General de Nicaragua), Box 69.

27. R. Deshon to Ministro de Gobernación, April 12, 1964, Archivo Presidencial AGN, Box 92.

28. Guerrero y Solariano, *Monografía de Chinandega* (Managua, 1964), p. 130; *La Noticia*, January 15, 1965.

29. Williams, *Export Agriculture*, p. 204.

30. *La Prensa*, May 16 and 23, 1964.

31. *La Prensa*, June 17, 1964; *La Noticia*, June 18, 1964.

32. On several occasions from 1963 to 1965, hacendados claimed they had spotted guerrilla bands on Cosigüina or near Tonalá. See *La Prensa*, August 8, 1962 and June 27, 1963; *La Noticia*, June 18, 1964.

33. Mejía Ubilla, "Problemática de la Reforma Agraria," p. 31.

34. *La Noticia*, August 25, 1964; interviews with Mariano Escorcia, Leoncio Martínez, and Engracia Zapata. See Jeffrey Gould, "To Lead as Equals" (Ph.D diss., Yale University, 1988), pp. 563–75.

35. *La Prensa*, June 20, 1964.

36. *La Noticia*, June 23 and 29, 1964.

37. Interviews with Martínez, M. Escorcia, and Zapata. The Tonaleños in particular cited articles 19, 21, and 26 of the agrarian reform law.

38. *La Noticia*, July 24–25, 1964; interviews with Ruperto Mayorga, L. Martínez, M. Escorcia, and Pablo Guido.

39. *La Prensa*, July 24, 1964.

40. Gustavo Sandoval, the Chinandegan police chief and a lower echelon obrerista, felt strange accompanying this Guardia patrol, prepared for war. Interview with Sandoval, Chinandega, 1985; *La Noticia*, August 14 and 22, 1964.

41. *La Prensa*, July 19 and 30, 1964; *La Noticia*, August 5 and 18, 1964. The cotton growers hoped that the harvesters would solve a constant labor shortage, which allowed workers to quit on the slightest provocation and find work elsewhere. On one hacienda that employed three thousand workers, only 25 percent stayed throughout the harvest. *La Prensa*, April 4, 1965.

42. *La Prensa*, August 18, 1964; interviews with Manuel Antonio Gutiérrez, Jacinto Galeano, Alejandro Malta, and Alberto Orozco suggest over one thousand campesinos attended.

43. *La Noticia*, August 13, 1964.

44. *La Noticia*, August 25 and October 9, 1964; *La Prensa*, September 22, 1964. The union militants were released from prison after a few days in some cases, weeks in others. Interviews with M. Escorcia, L. Martínez, D. Castillo, P. Guido, and E. Zapata.

45. *La Noticia*, August 25 and October 9, 1964; *La Prensa*, September 22, 1964. Interviews with M. Escorcia, L. Martínez, D. Castillo, P. Guido, and E. Zapata. *La Noticia*, October 20, 1964; *La Prensa*, October 25, 1964.

46. Quoted in *La Noticia*, October 20, 1964.

47. Interviews with M. Escorcia, L. Martínez, and E. Zapata.

48. Letter from R. Mayorga to A. Escorcia, November 1964, in the possession of A. Escorcia, Managua.

49. Ibid.; interview with Ruperto Mayorga, Chinandega, 1985.

50. Interview with Engracia Zapata, Corinto 1985.

51. *La Prensa*, July 20, 1977. In 1977, Engracia's group invaded San Miguelito. Immediately following arrests by the Guardia, Ruperto's group invaded the same lands.

52. Interview with Ruperto Mayorga, Chinandega, 1983..

53. *La Prensa*, December 7, 1971.

54. Interview with Engracia Zapata and Felipe Marcia. For example, in 1964 Guerrero helped move the seat of the municipality from Puerto Morazán to Tonalá (*La Prensa*, June 1, 1978).

55. Interview with Engracia Zapata.

56. Interviews with M. Escorcia, L. Martínez, P. Guido, and A. Escorcia. Escorcia claimed that Cervantes had put a contract out on him during this period (*La Noticia*, November 26, 1964). The government gave E. Cervantes administrative control over all aspects of the colony's economic and social life. Thus when Mariano and Leoncio began to organize a production cooperative, Cervantes apparently vetoed the proposal. D. Castillo, however, does not recall the veto. M. Escorcia and L. Martínez were persecuted in 1966. See *La Prensa*, March 17, 1966; interview with M. Escorcia, El Viejo, July 1989.

57. Interview with Pablo Guido, Tonalá, 1985.

58. Quoted in Rugama, *La Reforma*, p. 18.

59. Interview with Pablo Guido, Tonalá, 1984; statistics on land and occupations from interviews with D. Castillo and M. Escorcia.

60. Alain de Janvry in *The Agrarian Question* writes, "By giving land to peasants, the reform sector creates a conservative agrarian petty bourgeoisie and thus reduces the threat of social instability in the countryside" (p. 218).

61. See *La Noticia*, July 6, 1964; *La Prensa*, January 9, 1965; Mejia Ubilla, "Problemática de la Reforma Agraria."

62. *La Noticia*, July 20, 1962; *La Prensa*, March 31, 1963 and January 6, 1965. Apparently, some of these families illegally rented their land out to others.

63. Interview with Entimo Sánchez, Rancherías, 1985.

64. Letter from Abraham Carrasco to A. Escorcia, June 22, 1963, in the possession of Escorcia.

65. *La Prensa*, March 29, 1963.

66. *Novedades*, April 3, 1963; interview with Apolonio Carrasco.

67. Through 1979, campesinos from Rancherías, San José, and Tonalá maintained semiclandestine contacts. Interviews with the Carrascos, the Suazos, M. Escorcia, Martínez, Avilés, and Escorcia.

68. Telegram from Police Director Carlos Chávez to Ministro de Gobernación, June 4, 1968, Archivo Presidencial AGN, Box 92 refers to conflicts in Rancherías in 1965 and 1968. Also letter from A. Carrasco to A. Escorcia, in the possession of the latter, refers to violent conflict with neighboring terratenientes on May 6, 1965. In 1968 and 1972, Rancherías struggled with Campuzano over fishing and hunting rights on the island of Moyotepe. (Letter from Vice-Minister of Gobernación to Nororí, November 19, 1968, Archivo Presidencial AGN, Box 92). Rancherías campesinos, as in Tonalá, engaged in strike activity on the cotton plantations. See *Novedades*, January 10 and 12, 1963.)

69. Interview with Marcos Amaya, León, March 1988. For other sources and a more extensive analysis, see Jeffrey Gould, "La Raza Rebelde de Sutiava: Class and Ethnicity in Sutiava, Nicaragua 1920–1964" (paper presented at the American Historical Association meetings, Cincinnatti, Ohio, December 1988).

70. *La Prensa*, May 13, 1961.

71. *Novedades*, April 19, 1963.

72. *El Centroamericano*, April 5, 1962. Interviews with Estéban Bárcenas, T. Perez, and Gerónimo Morales, March–July 1988.

73. Mejia Ubilla, "Problemática de la Reforma Agraria," p. 47; *La Noticia*, October 5, 1964.

74. *La Prensa*, October 6, 1964.

75. *La Prensa*, July 6, 1964. On jurisdictional dispute, see *Novedades*, June 21, 1965.

76. *La Noticia*, March 23, 1965. Interviews with T. Perez, Esteban Barcenas, and Ramón Martínez, León, March and July 1988.

77. Interviews with Tomás Perez, León, 1983 and 1988.

78. On the founding of the FSLN cell in Sutiava, see Pilar Arias, *Nicaragua: Revolución, Relatos de los Combatientes* (Mexico City, 1980), pp. 70–79. Bayardo Arce noted that Sutiava, at the time, was still Somocista and that the Congressman Francisco Argeñal Papi "se ganaba a la gente por medio de paternalismo." Also, see Omar Cabezas, *La Revolución es algo mas grande que una vasta estepa verde* (Managua, 1983), p. 52.

79. *La Prensa*, September 10 and 12, 1973; interviews with T. Pérez and Chilo Flores, León, 1988.

80. *La Prensa*, September 15, 1973; *Novedades*, September 18, 1973.

81. *La Prensa*, September 19, 1973; interviews with Flores and T. Pérez.

82. *La Prensa*, September 19, 1973; interviews with Flores and T. Pérez.

Chapter 12

1. George Black (*The Triumph of the People* [London, 1981] p. 44) estimates two hundred to six hundred deaths. Other estimates were substantially lower.

2. Sergio Ramírez, *Las Armas del Futuro* (Managua, 1987), p. 170.

3. *La Prensa*, June 11, 1978.

4. *La Prensa*, January 9 and 18, 1974. Also see Gustavo Gutiérrez Mayorga, "Historia del Movimiento Obrero de Nicaragua (1900–1977)," in *Historia del Movimiento Obrero en América Latina*, vol. 2, ed. Pablo González Casanova (Mexico City, 1985), p. 238. On inflation, see table in Carlos Vilas, *The Sandinista Revolution* (New York, 1986), p. 96. See also Jaime Wheelock, *Imperialismo y Dictadura*, rev. ed. (Havana, 1980), p. 104. Using *La Prensa*, Wheelock counted 237 labor conflicts in 1972.

5. *La Prensa*, January 9 and 18, 1974.

6. Ibid.; *El Centroamericano*, February 15, 1974.

7. Rosa Pochet and Abelino Martínez, *Nicaragua, Iglesia: Manipulación o Profecía* (San José, 1987), p. 13.

8. Ibid., p. 15.

9. On the effects of the Medellín conference, see Michael Jiménez, "Toward a Social History of Radical Christianity in Latin America," *International Labor and Working-Class History* 34 (Fall 1988): 3–21; Tommi Sue Montgomery, "Liberation and Revolution: Christianity as a Subversive Activity," in *Trouble in our Backyard: Central America in the Eighties*, ed. Martin Diskin (New York, 1983), pp. 75–100. Michael Dodson, "Nicaragua: The Struggle for the Church," in *Religion and Political Conflict in Latin America*, ed. Daniel Levine (Chapel Hill, N.C., 1986), pp. 79–105.

10. Tommi Sue Montgomery, "Liberation and Revolution," pp. 82–83.

11. Jorge Cáceres et al., *Iglesia, Política y Profecia: Juan Pablo Segundo en Centroamérica* (San José, 1983), p. 89.

12. Ibid., p. 93.

13. L. Samandú and R. Jansen, "Nicaragua: Dictadura Somocista, Movimiento Popular e Iglesia 1968–1979," *Estudios Sociales Centroamericanos* 33 (September 1982): 189–219. Also see Luis Serra, "Ideología, religion y lucha de clases," in *La Revolución en Nicaragua*, ed. Richard Harris and Carlos Vilas (Mexico City, 1985), pp. 258–86; Michael Dodson and Tommie Sue Montgomery, "The Churches in the Nicaraguan Revolution," in *Nicaragua in Revolution*, ed. Thomas Walker (New York, 1982), pp. 161–80.

14. Teofilo Cabestrero, *Revolucionarios por el Evangelio Testimonios de 15 Cristianos en el Gobierno Revolucionario de Nicaragua* (Bilbao, 1983), p. 153.

15. Interview with Carlos Centeno, León, February 1986. Also see *Memorias de la Asociación de Trabajadores del campo* (Managua, 1980).

16. Interview with Carlos Centeno, León, 1986.

17. Interview with Salvador Ramírez, León, February 1986.

18. Interviews with FSLN militants C. Centeno and S. Ramírez. Humberto Ortega refers to the rural participation in Departmento de Ciencias Sociales (Sección de Historia), National Autonomous University of Nicaragua, *Apuntes de Historia de Nicaragua*, vol. 2 (Managua, 1980), p. 319. Rural participation in urban insurrections was atypical in 1978.

19. Luis Serra, "Ideología, religión, y lucha de clases"; interview with Domingo Castillo, El Viejo, 1988.

20. Cabestrero, *Revolucionarios por el Evangelio*, p. 130. Interviews with Apolonio and Gerónimo Carrasco, Éntimo Sánchez, and Julio Argeñal Chinandega, 1984–86. Apolonio Carrasco in an interview in *Barricuda*, July 4, 1989, refers to Padre Lovo's arrival in 1974.

21. Cabestrero, *Revolucionarios por el Evangelio*, p. 134.

22. Pochet and Martínez, *Nicaragua: Iglesia*, p. 140.

23. Centro de Estudios y Publicaciones, *Nicaragua A Un Año de la Victoria* (Lima, 1980), pp. 160–66.

24. Karl Marx, *The Eighteenth Brumaire of Luis Bonaparte* (New York, 1963), p. 15. Marx's *The German Ideology* (New York, 1978), p. 53, is the source of the epigraph to this chapter.

25. Letter from Juan Francisco Rostrán and Nicolás Sánchez to IAN, February 9, 1977; "Informe del Instituto Agrario Nicaragüense al Congreso," June 9, 1978, both in the possession of A. Escorcia. *Voz de Occidente*, July 31, 1977, claims that the majority of colonos were renting their land to others, many because they could not afford to work it. *La Prensa*, June 12, 1978 discusses corruption in the Chinandegan colonias.

26. This estimate was made on the basis of a comparison between the arrest list published in *La Prensa*, June 1978, and the census taken by the San José del Obraje organization in 1961.

27. Interviews with Félix Cándia, Pedro Suazo, the Carrascos, and Éntimo Sánchez.

28. Ibid.; *La Prensa*, July 3 and 6, 1977; "Informe del IAN al Congreso."

29. Interview with A. Escorcia, Managua, 1985. Escorcia felt that he was paying off a debt to the campesino cause.

30. Unpublished manuscript signed by Félix Cándia, Alonso Betanco, and other young San José militants, 1979, located in San José del Obraje.

31. *La Prensa*, July 3, 1977. The article neglected three other Campesino invasions of ejidatario-possessed land. It is worth noting that Venerio was a prominent anti-Somocista.

32. Agreement entitled, "Compromiso," imposed by the National Guard, obligating San José campesinos to respect Deshon's property, Chinendaga, signed June 28, 1977.

33. "Actas y Acuerdos del Sindicato del ISA," 1966–74. International Finance Corporation, "Project Appraisal Report—Propiedades Azucareras de Nicaragua Limitada," March 1, 1976, p. 3.

34. Cristian Sepúlveda, "Capitalismo Agroexportador, Estado y Rentabilidad: El Circuito Cafetalero y Azucarero en Nicaragua," *Estudios Sociales Centroamericanos* 13, no. 38 (May–August, 1984): 61.

35. International Finance Corporation, "Project Appraisal Report—Propiedades Azucareras de Nicaragua Limitada," March 1, 1976, p. 3.

36. "Informe del Presidente de la Junta Directiva a la Junta de Accionistas" (report of the president of the San Antonio sugar mill to the stockholders), August 1974.

37. "Informe del Presidente de la Junta," August 1974; interviews with Ramón Martínez, Lorenzo Roque, Alfonso Cerda, and Heromógenes Solís, Chichigalpa, 1983–85.

38. *La Prensa*, January 21, 1974.

39. Interviews with Ismael Gaitan, A. Cerda, and H. Solís.

40. Organization of American States, *Report on the Situation of Human Rights in Nicaragua* (Washington, D.C., 1978).

41. "Informe del Presidente de la Junda," February 1978.

42. See Sepúlveda, "Capitalismo Agroexportador," pp. 63–64.

43. Eduardo Baumeister, "Estructuras Productivas y Reforma Agraria," in *La Revolución en Nicaragua*, ed. Richard Harris and Carlos Vilas (Mexico City, 1985), pp. 51–80.

44. "Informe del Presidente de la Junta," February 1978.

45. In 1975 a group within the FSLN split off and formed the "Proletarian Tendency," which gave priority to the organization of the urban and rural proletariat. The remaining group of the FSLN became known by their strategy as the Prolonged People's War (GPP). They argued for a modified Maoist strategy of developing political, military bases among the peasantry in the central highlands. In 1977, Sandinistas formed another group known as the "Tercerista" faction, which argued for alliances with the bourgeoisie and for the initiation of actions leading to an insurrection. The factions reunified in January 1979. See Equipo Interdisciplinario Latinoamericano, *Teoría y Práctica Revolucionarias en Nicaragua* (Managua, 1983), pp. 109–14. For a fascinating look at the divisions, see the intersting work of Omar Cabezas, *Una Carta de Amor para Hombres* (Managua, 1989). Cabezas emphasizes the lack of importance to most Sandinistas outside of the highest echelons of the factional splits.

46. Interview with Lorenzo Roque, Chichigalpa, 1983.

47. Interviews with Uriel Somarriba, Adolfo Galeano, Marcos Jirón, Ismael Gaitán, and Ramón Martínez. "Libro de Actas del Sindicato del ISA," September 1978.

48. Interviews with Uriel Somarriba, Adolfo Galeano, Marcos Jirón, Tomás, Ismael Gaitán, and Ramón Martínez. "Libro de Actas del Sindicato del ISA," September 1978.

49. James Dunkerley, *Power in the Isthmus: A Political History of Modern Central America* (London, 1988), p. 248. Also see Equipo Interdisciplinario Latinoamericano, *Teoría y Práctica*, pp. 136–40.

50. *La Prensa*, September 4, 1978. The pro-Sandinista Movimiento Pueblo Unido also played a vital organizational role in the ISA mass movement in late 1978 to 1979.

51. *La Prensa*, September 8, 1978.

52. "Informe del Presidente de la Junta," February 1979.

53. Ibid., February 1979.

54. Interviews with ISA workers. *El Centroamericano*, December 5, 1978; *La Prensa*, December 2 and 5, 1978.

55. "Informe del Presidente del ISA," February 1979.

56. Interview with Ramón Martínez (president of union); "Libro de Actas del Sindicato del ISA," December 1978; interview with Francisco Cano, Managua, 1986.

57. This account is based on interviews with F. Cano, L. Roque, and I. Gaitán, Chichigalpa, 1983–86. I attempted unsuccessfully to interview Manuel Coronel Kautz, who currently has an important position in the the Ministry of Agriculture.

58. *La Prensa*, December 5, 1978.

59. "Informe del Presidente de la Junta," February 1979; interview with L. Roque.

60. Interviews with F. Cano, L. Roque, and I. Gaitán, Chichigalpa, 1983–86.

61. Oscar Osejo's statement, "Declaración Testifical," to the ISA, INRA, León,

February 7, 1980; interviews with Oscar Osejo; *La Prensa*, June 16, 1978.

62. Oscar Osejo's statement, "Declaración Testifical," to the ISA, INRA, León, February 7, 1980; interviews with Oscar Osejo; *La Prensa*, June 16, 1978.

63. Ibid.

64. Vilas, *The Sandinista Revolution*, p. 117.

65. *La Prensa*, May 10, 1978; interview with Juan Alberto Zapata and Felipe Marcia, Corinto, 1985.

66. Interview with Juan Alberto Zapata, Corinto, 1985; *La Prensa*, May 18, 1978; "Libro de Actas Sindicato Campesino de Tonalá" (minute book of the campesino union), Tonalá, June 1978, in the possession of Felipe Marcia, Ton Valle, Chinandega.

67. *La Prensa*, May 18, 1978. See also Black, *The Triumph of the People*, p. 123. The remainder of the quote is remarkably similar to the union statement of 1961.

68. *La Prensa*, June 3, 6, and 16, 1978. Interviews with Oscar Osejo and Felipe Marcia.

69. Unpublished manuscript signed by Félix Cándia, Alonso Betanco, and other young San José militants, 1979, located in San José del Obrajo.

70. Venerio, a Conservative, was a strong opponent of the regime since the early 1960s; interviews with Oscar Osejo, A. Galeano, and E. Fornos.

71. Lucrecia Lozano, *De Sandino al Triunfo de la Revolución* (Mexico City, 1985), p. 262.

72. Interviews with O. Osejo, F. Cano, and I. Gaitán; Lozano, *De Sandino al Triunfo*, p. 268.

73. Interviews with Juan and Pedro Suazo and Ramón and Félix Cándia.

74. Ibid.

75. Ibid.

Conclusion

1. Laura Enriquez, "Half a Decade of Sandinista Policy-Making," *Latin American Research Review* 22, no. 3 (1987): 209–22, contains an excellent review of recent studies on the Sandinista revolution. Also see Carlos Vilas, "Popular Insurgency and Social Revolution in Central America," *Latin American Perspectives* 15, no. 56 (Winter 1988): 55–77.

2. Carlos Vilas, *The Sandinista Revolution* (New York, 1986), p. 86.

3. Daniel James (*Resistance and Integration: Peronism and the Argentine Working Class, 1946–1976* [Cambridge, 1988]) has virtually overturned the corporatist paradigm by demonstrating how Peronist workers used their own cultural resources to transform populist discourse into a language of autonomous class struggle. His work has strongly influenced this study. Ernesto Laclau's theory of populism (in *Politics and Ideology in Marxist Theory* [London, 1982], pp. 143–98) has inspired Vilas's work, as well as my own. Vilas's notion of the "popular" and my own use of the term Somocista populism derive directly from Laclau's analysis. Nonetheless, Laclau's description of the Somocista state as a "bureaucratic excrescence imposed by force upon the rest of society" suggests that he would not approve of my use of his theoretical concepts. Nonetheless, I hope to have demonstrated that from 1936 to 1966 the Somoza regimes,

in Laclau's terms, attempted "to develop the potential antagonism of popular interpellations" against the landed oligarchy, while struggling to keep that antagonism within rigid limits that would not threaten the emerging Somocista faction of the bourgeoisie. The fact that the Somozas did not succeed and that after 1966 their regime began to resemble a "bureaucratic excrescence" should not invalidate this analysis.

4. For particularly good studies, see Vilas, *The Sandinista Revolution*, pp. 127–75; John Booth, *The End and the Beginning* (Boulder, Colo., 1985); Eduardo Baumeister, "Estructuras Productivas y Reforma Agraria," in *La Revolución en Nicaragua*, ed. Richard Harris and Carlos Vilas (Mexico City, 1985), pp. 51–80; and James Dunkerley, *Power in the Isthmus: A Political History of Modern Central America* (London, 1988).

5. Vilas, *The Sandinista Revolution*, p. 125.

6. Ibid., p. 48.

7. For an excellent introduction to that Sandinista subculture, see Instituto de Estudios del Sandinismo, ed., *Ahora Se Que Sandino Manda* (Managua, 1986).

8. Vilas, *The Sandinista Revolution*, p. 120.

9. Vilas, "Popular Insurgency," p. 71.

10. Carol Smith, "The Petty Bourgeoisie as a 'Fundamental' Revolutionary Class in Nicaragua," *Labour, Capital and Society* 19, no. 1 (April 1986): 29. Smith makes the bold and fascinating argument that "the petty bourgeoisie is freer of . . . the fetishized relations through property than is the proletariat of the periphery—or even of the core capitalist formations" (p. 28).

11. Vilas, *The Sandinista Revolution*, p. 117. Vilas shows that in Chinandega 39 percent of the Sandinista fighters were workers, field workers, and peasants. For Matagalpa, the figure was 30 percent, and Leon, 26 percent. The national average was 19.5 percent.

12. Oscar Osejo's statement, "Declaración Testifical," to the ISA, INRA, León, February 7, 1980.

13. Dunkerley, *Power in the Isthmus*, p. 246.

14. Tommi Sue Montgomery, "Cross and Rifle: Revolution and the Church in El Salvador and Nicaragua," *Journal of International Affairs* 36 (Fall–Winter 1982–83): 209. Here, Montgomery follows George Black's analysis in *The Triumph of the People* (London, 1981).

15. Baumeister's work on the structural roots of the rural alliance is particularly good; see "Estructuras Productivas y Reforma Agraria," pp. 51–80.

16. Carol Smith, "Culture and Community: The Language of Class in Guatemala," in *The Year Left*, ed. Mike Davis (London, 1987), 2:202.

17. See, for example, Vilas, *The Sandinista Revolution*; Booth, *The End and the Beginning*; Baumeister, "Estructuras Productivas y Reforma Agraria"; and Dunkerley, *Power in the Isthmus*.

18. Gerald Sider, "The Ties That Bind: Culture and Agriculture, Property and Propriety in the Newfoundland Village Fishery," *Social History* 5, no. 1 (January 1980): 1–39.

19. See, for example, Henry Landsberger, *Latin American Peasant Movements* (London, 1969); and Eric Hobsbawm, "Peasants and Politics," *Journal of Peasant Studies* (October 1973): 3–22. On the semiproletarian status of Nicaraguan peasants,

see Jaime Biderman, "Class Structure, the State and Capitalist Development in Nicaraguan Agriculture" (Ph.D. diss., University of California, Berkeley, 1982).

20. For a stimulating comparison, see Juan Martínez-Alier, *Plantations, Haciendas and Collective Farms* (London, 1977).

21. Theda Skocpol, "What Makes Peasants Revolutionary?" in *Power and Protest in the Countryside*, ed. Robert Weller and Scott Gugenheim (Durham, N.C., 1982), pp. 157–79.

22. Florencia Mallon's recent work, "Peasants and State Formation in Nineteenth-Century Mexico: Morelos, 1848–1858," *Political Power and Social Theory* 7 (1988): 1–54, should force us to rethink the "autonomous village" style of revolution as well. Mallon writes: "The image of the peasant soldier cultivating and defending the land with a gun on his back, the attempt to wring from a recalcitrant and fearful national government some real concessions on access to land and to local democracy . . . these things that gave Zapatismo its particular drama and flavor burst onto the historical stage in the Morelos of the 1850s" (p. 44). It was not, then, some isolated autonomous community suddenly violated by capitalism that rose up in 1910. On the contrary, Mallon suggests that Morelos's capacity to sustain a revolutionary movement derived from its extraordinary history not of isolation but of involvement in social and political struggles. Nevertheless, it is this rich history of communal struggle against elites that distinguishes Morelos from Chinandega before 1950 (and from other precipitate communities).

23. William Roseberry, "Images of the Peasant in the Consciousness of the Venezuelan Proletariat," in *Proletarians and Protest*, ed. Michael Hanagan and Charles Stephenson (Westport, Conn., 1986), pp. 149–69.

24. William Roseberry, "Domestic Modes, Domesticated Models," *Journal of Historical Sociology* 6, no. 4 (December 1988): 23–30.

25. Ibid.

26. Craig Calhoun, *The Question of Class Struggle: Social Foundations of Popular Radicalism during the Industrial Revolution* (Chicago, 1982), and "The Radicalism of Tradition: Community Strength or Venerable Disguise and Borrowed Language," *American Journal of Sociology* 88, no. 5 (1983): 886–914; Douglas Kincaid, "Peasants into Rebels: Community and Class in Rural El Salvador," *Comparative Studies in Society and History* 29, no. 3 (July 1987): 466–94. Kincaid's analysis of the 1932 uprising is superb.

27. Kincaid, "Peasants into Rebels," p. 491.

28. Calhoun, "The Radicalism of Tradition," p. 898.

29. See Vladimir I. Lenin, *What is to be done?* (Peking, 1967), and *State and Revolution* (Peking, 1967). Vilas reformulates the issue of representation in *The Sandinista Revolution*, pp. 37–45.

30. Laclau, *Politics and Ideology*, pp. 100–108.

31. Ibid., p. 108.

32. Although I have borrowed from Laclau, my formulations do not necessarily follow his theoretical work. One discrepancy is rooted in his concept of class. By analyzing the indeterminacy of the articulations between a worker's role in production, consumption, family, and politics, Laclau arrives at the conclusion that the concept of

"class struggle is . . . totally insufficient as a way of accounting for contemporary social conflicts" (Laclau, "New Social Movements and the Plurality of the Social," in *New Social Movements in Latin America*, ed. David Slater [Dordrecht, 1985], p. 29). In this study, I have used a concept of class (borrowed in part from Carol Smith) that stretches the limits of an economic definition, which Laclau employs. I have employed the term "campesino class" because the emergence of the movement involved forging a specific collective identity in antagonistic relation to the agrarian elite. Only with great difficulty could we call this identity "popular" or equate it with other autonomous social movements that have no class referents. The key to the formation of their class identity was the campesinos' capacity, predicated on the close proximity between work and community, to assimilate a multiplicity of identities—work (including peasant, wage laborer, and tenant), kinship, and communal. Here again, it seems that Laclau's insights are particularly relevant. Whether or not we call the reconstitution of these Chinandegan (working) communities a class movement, we can recognize the importance of the articulation of the different identities within them. Similarly, whether or not we see the FSLN as the class pole of a popular alliance, or we see the campesino movement as a class movement, in the end, thanks again to Laclau, we realize the decisive importance of the ideological link between them.

33. James Scott ("Revolution in the Revolution: Peasants and Commisars," *Theory and Society* 7 [1979]: 97–134) makes an excellent argument, rooted in a strikingly different historical context, which nonetheless parallels my own.

34. For a good discussion of the Sandinista policy towards the popular movements, see Marvin Ortega "La participación obrera en la gestión de las empresas del APP," in *La Revolución en Nicaragua*, ed. Richard Harris and Carlos Vilas (Mexico City, 1985), pp. 228–38; Vilas, *The Sandinista Revolution*, pp. 175–212; George Black, *The Triumph of the People* (London, 1981). On the strike in San Antonio, see *Barricada*, February 1, 1980.

35. See Instituto Histórico Centroamericano, *Envío* 4, no. 46 (1985) pp. 1–29. Preliminary electoral results indicate that the FSLN won the 1990 elections in rural El Viejo (Tonalá) and Sutiava and lost in San José and Rancherías.

Bibliographical Essay

As I mentioned in the introduction, the sources for historical research in Nicaragua are both scanty and scattered. The National Archive in Managua was small when I performed my research, but the dedicated staff was beginning to organize its collection. The paucity of both unpublished and published primary sources, and the lack of solid secondary sources led me to rely to a large extent on interviews with participants in the events that I studied. Since I discussed the oral testimony in the introduction, in this brief note I will focus on the primary sources that I used in preparing this book.

Unpublished Sources

There are two useful, if incomplete, sources in the National Archives of Nicaragua, in Managua. The presidential correspondence file covers the years 1934–48. This includes Somoza's correspondence as well as other documents, which one presumes his staff felt were important for him to consult. The Municipal Archive, although very disorganized at the time of my research, was extremely informative on local conditions in Chinandega. This file includes correspondence and reports from the jefe políticos to the Minister of Gobernación.

The U.S. Department of State General Records, available in microfilm from 1906 to 1954, were an invaluable source on economic and political events. During the New Deal years, in particular, the State Department employed competent observers in Nicaragua.

The Nicaragua Sugar Estates in San Antonio kindly let me examine their biannual company reports (1934–1979) and their noncurrent personnel files. I was also fortunate enough to gain access to other private, unpublished documents, in particular those of Andrés Ruíz Escorcia. His ample if disorganized files contain material ranging from official General Workers' Confederation (CGT) documents to the letters I discuss in chapters 9 and 10. Similarly, the campesinos of San José kept many documents, including those drawn up by the community and those written or saved by the late tailor from Tonalá, Rafael Cantillano. On the negative side, among the misfortunes caused by Somoza's repression of the labor movement in 1948 was the loss of most of the important union documents of that era. Fortunately, two Chinandegan obreristas, Domingo Ramírez and Tobias Muñoz, kept materials concerning primarily their own labor activities from 1920 to 1948. Ramírez's unpublished "Apuntes Sobre el Movimiento Obrero en Chinandega" is a largely personal and potentially fascinating account of his activities; unfortunately it is marred by his attempt to make it an objective historical study.

I also consulted extensively the microfilmed archives of the Registro de Propiedad in Managua. Unfortunately I was unable to locate some key pieces of the property puzzle in and around Campuzano because some of the original deeds date from the last century, before Zelaya organized the registry. I also consulted, with less fortune, the judicial archives of the Corte de Apelación del Occidente. The records of the unions in Realejo (1960s), Chichigalpa (1960s), the Ingenio San Antonio (1960–1979), and Tonalá (1970s) were, in contrast, quite helpful.

Published Primary Sources

The most useful published sources were newspapers, which I relied upon heavily to substantiate other sources as well as to fill in chronological gaps. In Nicaragua and in the Library of Congress I consulted at least one and often five newspapers annually from 1920 to 1979. Until 1950 the most informative newspapers were *La Noticia, La Flecha, El Cronista,* and *La Nueva Prensa,* as well as specifically labor papers, such as *Voz Obrera* and *Unidad.* Thanks to Domingo Ramírez I was able to study two Chinandegan papers that he edited from 1929 to 1938, *La Información* and *La Nueva Democracia.* For the study of the campesino movement, *La Noticia, La Prensa,* and to a lesser extent *Novedades* were key sources. Ramírez was the Chinandegan correspondent for *La Noticia* during the early 1960s. *La Gaceta,* the official government publication, was also a very useful primary reference source on congressional debates and particular laws.

The *Memorias del Ministerio de Fomento* and the *Memorias del Ministerio de Gobernación* were important sources on local government affairs. However, I could locate them only for a few years. The series of the *Memorias del Ministerio de Trabajo* is complete but of minimal importance for this work. The national censuses of 1920, 1950, and 1963 were, of course, an invaluable aid. The latter two in particular were conducted under international supervision and are quite reliable.

The United States Commerce (Washington, D.C.) published consular reports that contain important economic information. I consulted those published reports from 1900 to 1950. Similarly, *The Bulletin of the American Republics* (Washington, D.C.) had much useful economic information from the 1890s until 1910. The British Department of Overseas Trade published economic analyses entitled *Report on the Economic Conditions in the Republics of Guatemala, Honduras, and Nicaragua.* I obtained reports for 1921, 1922, and 1932 (all published the year after the year covered, in London).

The following travelers' accounts and guides were of use in understanding the economic and social background of Nicaragua from 1890 to 1920: Desirée Pector, *Etude Economique sur la Republique de Nicaragua* (Neuchâtel, 1893); Gustav Niederlin, *The State of Nicaragua* (Philadelphia, 1898); *Guía de Nicaragua* (Managua, 1906); Crisanto Medina, *Le Nicaragua en 1900* (Paris, 1900); M. Perigny, *Les Cinq Republique du l'Amerique Central* (Paris, 1911); and Valeria Blais, *Nicaragua, Condizioni Naturali ed Economiche* (Rome, 1925). A useful geographical study of Nicaragua is contained in Felipe Nerl Fernandez, *Geografía de America Central* (Guatemala City, 1926). W. W. Cumberland's *Nicaragua: An Economic and Financial Survey* (Washington, D.C., 1928), while often cited in secondary sources, has little material on Chinandega.

The memoirs I consulted were such highly charged partisan accounts of Liberal-Conservative strife that they are virtually indistinguishable from the straightforward political writing of the epoch, which also resembles memoirs: Frutos Chamorro's *La Ruidosa Quiebra* (Granada, 1898) is a bristling attack on the Zelaya regime from the point of view of the Conservative oligarchy; Diego Chamorro's *El Panterismo Nicaragüense* (Granada, 1898) is written from the same point of view; Zelaya's defense of his regime is contained in *La Revolución de Nicaragua y Los Estados Unidos* (Madrid, 1910; attributed to Ruben Dario). The Liberal attack on Conservative-United States rule can be read in the Comite pro-Nicaragua's *Nicaragua Intervenida* (Guatemala City, 1923). *Estudio Comparativo de Dos Partidos Politicos de Nicaragua* (Managua, 1923; attributed to Diego Chamorro) is a defense of the Conservative regime.

Until Armando Amador's study/memoir is published, we will have no good firsthand account of the 1940s labor movement. Nonetheless, a study by two participants in the movement, Onofre Guevara and Carlos Perez Bermudez, *El Movimiento Obrero en Nicaragua* (Managua, 1985), was quite useful for my work, although I disagreed with their analyses.

Gustavo Aleman's *Un Lombrasiano* (Mexico City, 1944) is a well-written, personal attack on Somoza García. William Krehm's *Democracias y Tiranias en el Caribe* (Havana, 1960) contains a fascinating journalistic account of the Somoza regime in the 1940s. The best memoir/study of the student opposition to Somoza is Miguel Jesus Blandon's *Entre Sandino y Fonseca Amador* (Managua, 1980). Rafael Cordoba Rivas's *Contribución a la Revolución* (Managua, 1984) also contains personal reflections on student Sandinismo in the 1940s. The writings of Adan Selva, including *Lodo y Ceniza* (Managua, 1960), provide the best accounts of the opposition movement during the late 1950s and early 1960s.

There has been precious little written on life in the Chinandegan countryside. Three novelistic memoirs aided me a great deal: Alejandro Astacio, *Las Dos Furias* (Madrid, 1959), an epic account of the peasant Liberal revolutionary leader "Cabulla"; José Roman, *Cosmapa* (Managua, 1942), the story of a failed attempt to develop a banana plantation near Chichigalpa, written by the author of one of the finest portraits of Sandino, *Maldito Pais* (Managua, 1979); Otto Schmidt, *Hijos del Campo* (Chinandega, 1964), a somewhat romanticized folkloric novel that nonetheless sheds light on the decay of paternalism in the Chinandegan countryside.

Secondary Sources

Over the past few years many books and articles have been written about Nicaragua. Most of these studies have sections devoted to history, but their primary focus is on the contemporary situation. Those studies that I found useful in the preparation of this book are as follows. Carlos Vilas's *The Sandinista Revolution* (New York, 1986) probably represents the best scholarship on contemporary Nicaragua and contains an excellent discussion of the 1950–79 period. Jaime Wheelock's *Imperialismo y Dictadura* (Mexico City, 1975) presents an excellent analysis of the Somoza regime and agro-export bourgeoisie. John Booth's *The End and the Beginning: The Nicaraguan Revolution* (Boulder, Colo., 1985) gives a substantial treatment of the role of the elites in the breakdown of the Somoza regime. Eduardo Baumeister's various articles, including "Estructuras Productivas y Reforma Agraria en Nicaragua" (in *La Revolución en Nicaragua*, ed. Carlos

Vilas and Richard Harris [Mexico City, 1985], pp. 51–80), provide a sophisticated treatment of the agrarian class structure before 1979 and its bearing on the current revolutionary process. Of equal value to my study was Orlando Nunez's *El Somocismo y el Modelo Agro-exportador* (Managua, 1980), especially his analysis of the cotton industry.

Economia y Sociedad en la Construcción del Estado en Nicaragua (San José, 1983) is a compilation of essays, written by Alberto Lanuza, Juan Luis Vasquez, Amaru Barahona, and Amalia Chamorro, that analyze Nicaraguan history from 1821 to 1979. Although often more theoretical than factual, collectively these essays provide an excellent historical introduction. Marcos Antonio Valle's *La Dictadura Somocista* (Managua, 1980) is an intelligent global analysis of the period 1912–47. Gustavo Gutierrez Mayorga's "Historia del Movimiento en Nicaragua" (in *Historia del Movimiento Obrero en America Latina*, vol. 2, ed. Pablo Gonzalez Casanova [Mexico City, 1985], pp. 196–252), contains a useful overview of the labor movement.

Several scholars based in the United States have made important contributions to Nicaraguan historiography. In particular, Jaime Biderman's "Class Structure, the State, and Capitalist Development in Nicaraguan Agriculture," Ph.D. diss., University of California at Berkeley, 1982, provides an excellent background in economic history. Richard Millet's *The Guardians of the Dynasty* is a serious, finely researched institutional history of the National Guard. Charles Stansifer's "José Santos Zelaya: A New Look at Nicaragua's 'Liberal Dictator,'" *Revista Interamericana* 7 (1977), is an important study based on extensive archival research, the first revisionist account of the Zelaya regime.

Several studies helped me to bring the Chinandegan popular movements into theoretical focus. James Scott's "Hegemony and the Peasantry" (*Politics and Society* 7, no. 3 [1977]: 262–96) helped me to think about the problems of constructing hegemony and counterhegemony in Chinandega. I would like to add that following the completion of my dissertation, on which this book is based, a student of Professor Scott's read my conclusion and then showed me Scott's "Revolution in the Revolution: Peasants and Commissars" (*Theory and Society* 7, nos. 1–2 [January–March, 1979]: 97–134). Upon reading it I was somewhat taken aback, for I realized that although our conclusions were derived from studies of very different types of agrarian societies, they were, nonetheless, remarkably similar. What I have lost in terms of originality, however, I have certainly gained by such good company. William Roseberry's "Images of the Peasant in the Consciousness of the Venezuelan Proletariat" (in *Proletarians and Protest*, ed. Michael Hanagan and Charles Stephenson [Westport, Conn., 1986], pp. 149–69), to a certain extent a critique of Scott's work, aided me enormously in thinking through the problem of how a class discourse is created. Similarly, Daniel James's *Resistance and Integration: Peronism and the Argentine Working Class, 1946–1976* (Cambridge, 1988) gave me insights into populism and working-class culture that clearly inspired much of my research. Finally, Sidney Mintz's work was extremely helpful in attempting to analyze a sugar mill and its workers. See in particular, *Caribbean Transformations* (Chicago, 1974), and *Worker in the Cane* (New York, 1974).

Index

Acevedo, Alejandro, 169–70

Acosta, Alcídes, 95, 108

Agrarian reform: Somocista program of, 247–52; campesino interpretation of, 252–53, 278; results of in Tonalá, 254–57; splits campesinos, 257–61; results of in Rancherías, 261–64; Sutiavan response to, 264–69. *See also* Instituto Agrario Nicaragüense

Agrarian Reform Act, 253, 254; Alliance for Progress impetus for, 247–48; substance of, 248–49; inspires demands for immediate land reform, 255

Agricultural machinery workers. *See* Repair Maintenance and Agricultural Machinery workers' union.

Agro-export bourgeoisie. *See* Reyes group

Agro-export economy: boom of, 10, 85; expansion of, 97, 115, 251; crisis of, 98; and industrialization, 182–83, 212–13; Corinto dockworkers' position within, 193; Chinandega as center of, 205; and breakup of peasant families, 226–27, 228; and land redistribution, 247

Aguacatillo, 77

Aguado, Enoc, 58

Agüero, Fernando, 190, 271

Aguilar, Manuel, 55–57, 60, 62–64, 75

Alemán Bolaños, Gustavo, 43

Alliance for Progress: and agrarian reform, 128, 175, 245, 247, 248

Alvarado, General (Campuzano owner), 4, 162

Alvarado, Tesla de, 94, 112, 114, 116, 117, 141–42, 162, 208, 212, 237; speech to campesinos, 85, 87, 95; evicts peasants from Las Cuchillas, 88; as personification of oligarchy, 99; claim of to Las Cuchillas, 100; meets with Escobar and Buitrago, 101–4; land donation of, 136–37, 144, 177, 179; self-identification with campesinos, 145

Alvarado, Virgilio, 162; threatens Timoteo Baca, 94; expresses solidarity with oligarchy, 116–17; offers uncultivated land to Tonaleño community, 163–64; describes Tonalá invasion, 178

Alvarado family, 94, 95, 172, 176; considers ejidal land as part of Campuzano, 91; and Liberal party, 116, 131

Amador, Armando, 54, 59, 61

Andrade, Padre, 118–19

Anti-Communism: as Somocista tool against enemies, 74, 107; and opposition to Somoza, 187–88; aimed at Cuba, 190; and schism in Rancherías, 262

Anti-Somocista opposition, 182, 220; hostility toward campesinos, 88; involvement of BANAMERICA group with, 184; rise of, 187–88; failure of workers and peasants to participate in, 191–92; and barrier to popular movement, 221, 225–26, 293–94; bridges gap to campesinos, 270–72; as conduit to support for Sandinistas, 283. *See also* Conservative party; Partido Liberal Independiente; Sandinistas

Argüello, Fanor, 254, 288

Argüello, Leonardo, 53, 58, 61, 81

Argüello family, 96, 258, 290

Arrimados (free squatters), 119–20

Article 204 (Nicaraguan labor code), 57, 75. *See also* Labor code

Artisans: organize anti-Conservative resistance, 32–33; economic differentiation with ideological unification among, 66–68; become union militants, 166, 171–72; social pride of, 189; in Sutiava, 265. *See also* Obrerismo

Asociación de Trabajadores del Campo (ATC), 274, 275, 288–89, 305

Astacio Cabrera, Hugo, 122, 167, 179; reputation, 102; orders arrest of San José community, 104–5; coerces signed statement from campesinos, 111–12; attempts to discredit San José movement, 114, 117–18; attacks Reyes as oppressor of campesinos, 144–45; collaboration with Guardia, 191; as "defender of the campesinos," 224; gloats over Deshon-Pastrán affair, 232; endorses distribution of latifundios, 248, 252

Astacio Cabrera family, 239

Avilés, Mónico, 214–15

Baca, Arturo, 173

Baca, Bob, 279

Baca, Manuel Antonio, 93, 189; land donation by, 90, 114, 117, 143, 173

Baca, Timoteo, 93, 94–95, 99, 122

Bakers' union, 219

Balladares, Manuel, 114, 118

Banana workers, 182, 193, 198, 219–20

Banco de America (BANAMERICA), 183, 184, 271, 281

Banco Nacional, 261, 266

IAFX7290 12/03/90 h

HD1531
N5G68
1990